AMISTAD'S ORPHANS

AMISTAD'S ORPHANS

An Atlantic Story of Children, Slavery, and Smuggling

Benjamin N. Lawrance

Yale

UNIVERSITY

PRESS

New Haven & London

Yale University Press books may be purchased in quantity for educational, business, or promotional use. For information, please e-mail sales.press@yale.edu (U.S. office) or sales@yaleup.co.uk (U.K. office).

Set in Electra type by Newgen North America.
Printed in the United States of America.

Library of Congress Cataloging-in-Publication Data
Lawrance, Benjamin Nicholas.
Amistad's orphans : an Atlantic story of children, slavery, and smuggling / Benjamin N. Lawrance
pages   cm
ISBN 978-0-300-19845-4 (hardback : alk. paper)
1. Amistad (Schooner)   2. Child slaves—History—19th century.
3. Children—Africa—History—19th century.   4. Orphans—Africa—History—19th century.   5. Slave trade—Africa—History—19th century.
6. Slave trade—America—History—19th century.   7. Human smuggling—Africa—History—19th century.   8. Human smuggling—America—History—19th century.   I. Title.
E447.L39 2015
326.0973'09034—dc23   2014010385

A catalogue record for this book is available from the British Library.

This paper meets the requirements of ANSI/NISO Z39.48–1992 (Permanence of Paper).
10 9 8 7 6 5 4 3 2 1

This book is dedicated to Wilson de Lima Silva, without whose love, support, and encouragement it would never have been.

The voice of wailing which comes to us from across the Atlantic, from the mourning relations of the deceased companions; or which moans in the night winds and in the surges of the deep that pass over their graves or watery beds, tells us in truer language, than can the survivors of the Amistad, what slavery is in its origin and progress.

—Extract of a speech delivered by the Reverend James W. C. Pennington to Mr. Henry and Mrs. Tamar Clark Wilson, Zion's Chapel, New York, N.Y., November 19, 1841, on the eve of their departure for Freetown, Sierra Leone, printed in the *Union Missionary Herald* 1, no. 2 (February 1842): 68

CONTENTS

Acknowledgments

This book began with a fellowship at the Gilder Lehrman Center for the Study of Slavery, Resistance, and Abolition at Yale University. Although my fellowship was not awarded based on this particular project—but rather for one about contemporary child trafficking in West Africa (that book is still in development)—when I arrived in New Haven, several colleagues, notably Bob Harms, alerted me to the child testimonies from which this book evolved. I would like to express my admiration and appreciation to David Blight, Dana Schaffer, Melissa McGrath, and Tom Thurston, who have worked together to make the GLC a superb research center; to its faculty and staff I owe a tremendous debt of gratitude.

Support for this book came in the form of a faculty fellowship from the National Endowment for the Humanities and the College of Liberal Arts at the Rochester Institute of Technology. I also benefited from the award of a University of California President's Faculty Research Fellowship and a residential fellowship at the W. E. B. Du Bois Institute for African and African American Research at Harvard University. The Conable Endowment for International Studies and its donors, especially the Starr Foundation, supported research travel.

A great number of research centers, universities, institutions, archives, and libraries were consulted over the course of several years. I would like to acknowledge the research support of: in the United States, the National Archives and Records Administration, Waltham, Massachusetts; the Amistad Research Center, Tulane University, New Orleans, Louisiana; Special Collections, Feinberg Library, State University of New York at Plattsburgh, New York; Yale University and Library Manuscripts Collection, New Haven, Connecticut; the Beinecke

Rare Books Library, Yale University, New Haven, Connecticut; Yale Divinity School Library, Yale University, New Haven, Connecticut; Foreign Missionary Society Collection, in the United Methodist Church Archives, Drew University, Madison, New Jersey; Bethel College Library, Bethel College, Mishawaka, Indiana; the Manuscripts Division, Library of Congress, Washington, D.C.; the History and Genealogy Unit, Connecticut State Library, Hartford, Connecticut; the New York Historical Society, New York, New York; New York Historical Society Library, New York, New York; the Mystic Seaport Museum, Mystic, Connecticut; the Library Manuscript Collection of Duke University, Durham, North Carolina; the Amistad Collection, Connecticut Historical Society, Hartford, Connecticut; the Chicago Historical Society, Chicago, Illinois; in the United Kingdom, the Bodleian Library of Commonwealth and African Studies at Rhodes House, Oxford University, Oxford; the United Kingdom Hydrographic Office, Taunton; the British National Archives, Kew, London; the British Library; the Caird Library, National Maritime Museum, Greenwich; the Cadbury Collection, the University of Birmingham Library, Birmingham; the Archives and Special Collections Library, School of Oriental and African Studies, London; the Brighton History Centre, Brighton Museum and Art Gallery, Brighton; the British and Foreign Bible Society Archives, Cambridge University, Cambridge; the Royal Pavilion and Museums, Brighton and Hove, Brighton; the National Portrait Gallery, London; and additionally, the National Archives of Canada, Ottawa, Canada; the Archivo Nacional de la República de Cuba, Havana, Cuba; Archivo Histórico Provincial de Camagüey and the Archivo Histórico Provincial Matanzas in Cuba; and the Sierra Leone National Archives.

An extraordinary community of scholars, students, archivists, cartographers, librarians, photographers, colleagues, and friends made this book possible. I would like to thank the following people who helped in many ways, from the very large to the very small, over the years: Roseanne Adderley, Jean Allman, Richard Anderson, Ruby Andrew, Alexandra Ault, Barbara Austen, Sandra Barnes, María del Carmen Barcia Zequeira, Gill Berchowitz, Laird Bergad, Kevin Blowers, Frances Bristol, James Campbell, Mariana Candido, Bidemi Carrol, Bimbola Carrol, Jorge Luis Chinea, Emma Christopher, Lucas Church, Julie Cochrane, Sara Cohen, Kevin Crawford, Carolyn de la Peña, Joan Duffy, Janice Ellen, Omnia El Shakry, David Eltis, Tim Erdel, Jorge Felipe, Mariane Ferme, Silvia Forni, Karen Fung, Orlando Felix Garcia Martínez, Abosede George, Anne George (for photographic assistance), Kurt Graham, Beverley Green, Sandra Greene, Charles Grench, Beverly Grier, Jennifer Hadley, Guy Hannaford, Clare Hasler, Christopher Harter, Ellen Hartigan-O'Connor, David Hill, Allen Howard, Mariel Iglesias Utset, Adam Jones, Debra Kimok, Bruce Kirby, Jacqueline Knörr, Jim Lance, Ellen Lawson, Henry Lovejoy, Paul Lovejoy, Katherine Luongo, Melissa Manson, Lucy McCann, Kristen McDonald, Matthew Millard, Joseph Miller, Philip Misevich, Ugo Nwokeji, Jim Oakes, Paul O'Pecko, Joe Opala, Emily Osborn, Monica Peters, Don Pirius, Susannah Rayner, Marcus Rediker, Richard L. Roberts, Jaime Rodrigues, Rachel Rowe, Padraic Scanlan, Philip Schwartzburg, Suzanne Schwarz, Rebecca Scott, Jeannie Sherman, Brian Shaw, Trudy Southern, Matthew Stackpole, Jim Sweet, Meredith Terretta, Fredrik Thomasson, Ann Totterdell, Konrad Tuchscherer (for bringing the cover photograph to my attention), Alie Mohamed Turay (for super research assistance), Dmitri van den Bersselaar, Jelmer Vos, Jeff Ward, Alison Welsby, Nathaniel Wiltzen, and Lewis Wyman. I cannot thank Marcus Rediker, Joseph Yannielli, and Michael Zeuske enough for everything they shared, consulted on, commented on, and ultimately improved. Walter Hawthorne needs special attention. Walter read everything, and words fail me when I try to describe his generosity of intellect and spirit.

Many dear friends offered support along the way. I have the most profound admiration for those who stood by me as I pushed ahead in the face of not insignificant professional difficulties. I would like to thank the following, who offered support and counsel at different moments: Neil Abernethy, Moradewun Adejunmobi, Emmanuel Akyeampong, Ned Alpers, Brad Anderson, Bruce Anderson, Ruby Andrew, Andrew Apter, Gareth Austin, Aaron Belkin, Sara Berry, Peter Bloom, Monique Borgerhoff-Mulder, Liz Borgwardt, Joan Cadden, Tim Caro, Bill Casey, Kate Collier, Cecilia Colombi, Emilio Contreras, Marisol de la Cadena, Sergio de la Mora, Carolyn de la Peña, Adela de la Torre, Don Donham, Andreas Eckert, Omnia El Shakry, Toyin Falola, Paula Findlen, Estelle Friedman, Abosede George, Noah Gwynn, Rick Halpern, Katie Harris, Iñes Hernadez-Avila, Dorothy Hodgson, Hillary Jones, Suad Joseph, Caren Kaplan, Nick Kelly, Mara Kolesas, Cathy Kudlick, Matthew Lawrence, Tom McCaskie, Stephan Miescher, Bettina Ng'weno, Emily Osborn, Tim Patten, Mark Phillips, Jeremy Rich, Simon Sadler, Lynn Schler, Dan Siegel, Julia Simon, Tom Spear, Eric Smoodin, Eteica Spencer, Scott Simon, Daniel Stolzenberg, Charles Turner, and Curt Zimansky. If I have omitted anyone from this list, I beg his or her forgiveness.

My colleagues and friends in Rochester have been so welcoming. I have found a new home and scholarly community in the Department of Sociology and Anthropology and the Program in International Studies. I am grateful for the friendship and collegiality of Barbara Bangs, Tom di Piero, Babak Elahi, Bob Foster, Nancy Foster Fried, David Hill, Joe Hale, Ann Howard, Christine

Kray, Nigel Maister, John Michael, Richard Newman, John Osburg and Jiao Qian, Joanne Stankiewicz, Debbie Steene, Liz Thornberry, Sharon Willis, Robert Ulin, Sara Varhus, Jamie Winebrake, and many others. I would also like to thank my remarkable personal assistant Cassandra Shellman. It is an extraordinary luxury to have such support.

The team at Yale University Press has been marvelous from the outset. I would like to express my deepest gratitude to Pamela Chambers, Laura Davulis, Ash Lago, Danielle D'Orlando, Christopher Rogers, Phillip King, Eliza Childs, and all the unnamed individuals who helped this book see the light of day. Margaret Puskar-Pasewicz provided superb editing and indexing services.

A special debt of gratitude is reserved for my mentor and friend Richard Roberts and his wife Amy. Both consoled me during some of my darkest days. The three of us shared meals and many drinks. Richard has guided, advised, coauthored, read, and reread. He rallied his troops when the going got tough, and was always a voice of reason and sanguinity. Together we have written two books and a third is on the way. His irreverence and integrity kept me in line as I flirted with insanity. He is a stalwart, a standup guy, a true mensch.

The last words I reserve for my family. My parents, Bob and Pam, witnessed this project from its inception. Their support and love is boundless. My brother Oliver, and my sister Sacha, my sister-in-law Jules, and my niece and nephews have been the source of encouragement and humor. But the most profound love and support have come from my husband, Wilson. When we met, I was in my darkest place; he drew me out and gave me the confidence to persist, improve, and succeed. As the book took shape, and our relationship deepened, it became my turn to support him through his most difficult life experience. That shared knowledge crystalized for me what is important—love and humanity—and what is not—pretty much everything else.

ILLUSTRATIONS

INTRODUCTION:
THE ORPHANS OF *LA AMISTAD*

In March 1917, Alexander Woods Banfield, a Canadian-British missionary, amateur linguist, and photographer, was traveling through southeastern Sierra Leone, inspecting mission stations for the British and Foreign Bible Society. Although he was headquartered in Lagos, Nigeria, his purpose was to evaluate the current status of proselytization efforts in the region and explore possibilities for new projects. Banfield toured various towns, villages, and abandoned sites. In the afternoon of March 16, he visited an old mission compound at Kaw-Mendi and the adjacent town. In a letter to his superior, he described how "the Mission premises" occupied "a large tract of land" of approximately "one mile long by half mile wide," and the town was "laid out in streets and lots." The mission was apparently in dire financial straits, as it was selling parcels of land "very cheaply."[1]

In his letter Banfield explained that the "American (Mendi) Mission" started more than seventy years earlier "when the last ship load of slaves was sent back from America" under the charge of a certain Mr. Raymond. He then relayed brief details of a remarkable encounter. "While here I met an old man that came back with Mr. Raymond. . . . He remembers a great deal of what he saw in America. He says that men talked for five years" about "what they were to do with these black slaves, and in the sixth year 'God cut the palaver' and they were sent back to Africa. This man must be 100 years old; he is still quite active." The "old man" Banfield referred to was none other than Ka'le, the sole living survivor of the Cuban slave ship *La Amistad*, who had been memorialized for posterity in William H. Townsend's 1840 etching "Little Kalé" (figure I.1). In 1917, "Pa Raymond," as he was then known, must have been at least eighty-five years old. His age and extraordinary personal history meant that his community

1

Fig. I.1. "Little Kalé," pencil sketch on paper by William H. Townsend, c. 1840
(Beinecke Rare Book and Manuscript Library, Yale University)

distinguished him with the honorific title "Pa," reserved for village elders. Although Banfield appears to have confused a few aspects—or possibly he relayed a few jumbled details from an aging mind—there can be no mistaking that he had just encountered Ka'le, a.k.a. George Lewis, a.k.a. Carly, Kali, or Kalee.[2]

Ka'le was one of an unknown number of children who endured a perilous journey in an illicit slave ship from the mangroves of the Galinhas coast, southeast of the British colony of Freetown, Sierra Leone, to the Spanish colony of Cuba in 1839. After being locked inside a rudimentary portside jail in Havana, Ka'le was sold to a provincial merchant and slave trader and put aboard *La Amistad* with fifty-two other recently arrived Africans. Once at sea, the adult Africans seized the ship from the Spanish-Cuban crew. After a futile attempt to return to Sierra Leone, the Africans and their vessel were captured by U.S. authorities and imprisoned in Connecticut in August 1839. John Warner Barber, a witness to the trials of the survivors, translated Ka'le's name as "bone" and described him as "a small boy, with a large head, flat and broad nose, stout built," and "about four feet, three inches tall." The trial in which they were embroiled rose to the highest level, reaching the U.S. Supreme Court in 1841. After returning to Sierra Leone in 1842 with thirty-four other survivors, Ka'le lived the remainder of his long life as an integral member of the tightknit Kaw-Mendi mission community. He lived through the turbulent times preceding the British annexation of the region in the 1880s and 1890s and witnessed the maturation of imperial rule over the British colony of Sierra Leone.[3]

The most remarkable element of Banfield's narration of the encounter concerns Ka'le's interpretation of the multiple trials' conclusion. Ka'le drew on the long Luso-African influence on coastal languages and the rich metaphor of Mende customary law and dispute resolution. His explanation that "God cut the palaver" (from *palavra*, Portuguese for word, speech, or talk) suggests that the Supreme Court's resolution of what historian Marcus Rediker might call "cultural business" was reached through discussion and was divinely ordained. Linguist Moradewun Adejunmobi explains that the term "palaver" has a long history in the African continent and was likely introduced to West Africa by Portuguese traders present in certain regions from the fifteenth century. Many local nineteenth-century palavers concerned "the traffic in slaves" among Spanish-Cubans, Americans, and local African chiefs. Indeed, in this light, the identification of the entire episode by the local idiom of "palaver" may signify an implicit awareness on the part of Ka'le of the international dimensions of the struggle.[4]

Also surely of interest is Ka'le's expansive chronology. There are many possible explanations for why older informants may, at times, extend the temporality of particular events. Ka'le accorded the momentous proceedings surrounding *La Amistad* six years of his life, whereas the trials lasted approximately twenty months and his entire sojourn in the United States only twenty-seven months in total. And so it was perhaps no small matter in this calculation that his personal experience of enslavement, from his initial kidnapping in his natal village to his liberation in 1841, lasted at least five or six years. Notwithstanding his unconventional journey through slavery and liberty, in the United States Ka'le was released from prison into the custody of a New Haven family relatively early in the proceedings. Together with three girls, also from *La Amistad*, he learned to read and write English, and he possibly converted to Christianity prior to or upon his return to Sierra Leone.[5]

That Ka'le's later years have received so little attention is perhaps because African assistants in missions rarely leave traces in archival records. We can only speculate about how many others, besides Banfield, met Ka'le with an equal

ignorance of his extraordinary life. Banfield appeared to have scant knowledge
of how, why, and under precisely what circumstances the former "slaves were
landed" in Sierra Leone, but he asserted, probably correctly, that "most" of the
Amistad survivors "were from this part of the country." If Banfield had heard of
the Amistad story, he did not let on. He seems to have undertaken no further
effort to uncover additional details; the experience of a child kidnapped from
his home and sold across the ocean was perhaps unremarkable. Fortunately for
us Banfield stumbled into the discrete world of the adult Ka'le in his twilight
years. And from his tantalizingly brief letter, we garner a uniquely personal
perspective on one of the most celebrated liberation struggles of the Atlantic
slave trade.

As I read this brief account, what puzzled me was Banfield's perceived lack
of curiosity about Ka'le's astonishing life story, and, more generally, his blasé
reportage about the presence of children in the Atlantic slave trade. There may
be several explanations for this. As a child, Banfield was very likely exposed to
bedtime stories from travelers and adventures like David Livingstone, Henry
Morton Stanley, Pierre de Brazzà, and Paul Belloni du Chaillu. Unsavory tales
from the "dark continent" and long-distance travel were nineteenth-century
staples and certainly no cause for alarm. As a missionary working in West Africa
Banfield had doubtless seen many former child slaves "rescued," "redeemed,"
and liberated expressly to be educated in mission schools. Recruiting former
child slaves to fill the pews of mission schools was part and parcel of colonialism. So perhaps an account of child slavery was commonplace. And he had also
witnessed firsthand attempts by European countries to extend abolition into
the continent and eradicate domestic slavery throughout their empires during
the formative decades of the colonial encounter. From the perspective of a participant engaged in the European civilizing mission, narratives of slavery and
liberation were perhaps standard fare.

Banfield's lack of interest, in 1917, is echoed today in academic scholarship in
several troublesome ways. For too long child slave lives have been considered
inaccessible to the historian, their experiences silenced by the past and un-
recoverable. When child slaves do emerge from archives or from oral testimonies, they are habitually the recipients of benevolence, charity, and sentimental-
ity. African children have been viewed as marginal to African slavery specifically
and in slave trades generally. They have often been described as peripheral to
kinship networks, undesirable to African slave traders, and most susceptible to
the forms of dependency that characterize African slave systems. African children have been portrayed as an insignificant component of the larger Atlantic
trade and as expendable space-fillers or an afterthought in slave ships.[6]

But perhaps most troubling is that the nineteenth century is routinely cast as the endgame in the long history of the trans-Atlantic trade. Far too many view the nineteenth century primarily as an age of abolition and the dramatic closing act of one of history's most shameful episodes. As such, the moral supremacy of abolition eclipses the lived experiences marking the expansion of slavery in continental Africa and new forms of labor coercion globally. Regardless of the contingencies and ideologies undergirding abolitionism—be they economic determinism, bourgeois humanitarianism, evangelical activism, or even a new morality born of political dislocation and military defeat—the effect is the same, the erasing of the history of the slavery's reinvention and reinvigoration. A social historical narrative, grounded in real economic shifts in Africa, gives way to a political narrative anchored by spectacular achievements in European parliaments. And its key personages are celebrated as emblematic of the evolution of humanitarian ideologies, their actions the logical extension of enlightenment ideas into neglected territories and benighted empires.[7]

This book follows the lives of six remarkable African children in an attempt to correct some of these persistent misconceptions. Building on recent advances in scholarship that demonstrate that the lived experiences of slave children are indeed recoverable, *Amistad's Orphans* argues that the role of African child slaves in the illegal slave trade has been significantly underestimated and their experiences misunderstood. Not only were children a critical constituency of nineteenth-century Atlantic slave-trading networks, but a reappraisal of their participation also compels us to recognize that the inception of abolitionism in the Atlantic marked the beginning of an age of child enslavement. I follow the lives of six African children to illustrate the broader experience of African child enslavement and mobility during the early to mid–nineteenth century. These six lives, although single threads, can be woven into a fabric for revisiting the African child slave experience and reevaluating the centrality of child mobility to the massive illegal trafficking enterprise undergirding the nineteenth-century trans-Atlantic trade.[8]

The six lives at the heart of this book constitute an imagined Atlantic family born of fictional kinship, molded by shared traumas, and united by a common goal of survival. *Amistad's Orphans* brings six child lives—three boys and three girls—into conversation for the first time since 1839, in an effort to recast thinking about children's experiences of slavery and forced migration. These children shared a connection, not the least of which was childhood, and, in ways we can barely discern, their common experiences enabled them to form what Paul Lovejoy might call "allegiances." The idea of a "slave ship family" first emerged from Philip Curtin's concept of "shipmate bonding." Other historians, such as Sidney Mintz and Richard Price, built on this concept by focusing on forms of social "attachment." Similarly, Walter Hawthorne's more recent exploration of the *mentalité* of the survivors of the slave vessel *Emilia* revisited "shreds of evidence" that pointed to the enduring strength of shipmate bonds. The virtual slave ship family that emerged from the harrowing experiences of transportation, capture, and disembarkation in Rio de Janeiro made possible the very physical and emotional survival of a small group that ultimately returned to West Africa. Building on this analytical framework, I advance six interdependent arguments to make sense of the shared experience of a family of children: namely, slave traders targeted children as prohibitions increased; ethnicity and identity had little meaning to child slaves; children's paths to slavery were narrower than adults; slave children journeyed the Atlantic in discrete capacities different from adults; freedom meant little to a liberated African child; and, finally, liberated African children faced greater obstacles as they sought to reintegrate into African communities.[9]

The six children entangled in the trial of *La Amistad* came from similar cultural and social backgrounds. Their distinct and separate journeys each began with their physical removal from villages in the Galinhas hinterland in what is today Sierra Leone. They took separate trans-Atlantic journeys over a period of six years. During the late 1830s their paths crisscrossed and intersected, until they were united before a judge in Connecticut in 1839 at the opening arguments of the now famous trial of the survivors of *La Amistad*. After the conclusion of the court case in 1841, with varying shades of volition, they went in different directions. Their paths through enslavement, various forms of liberation incommensurate to adult freedom, and post-enslavement dependency, however, were shaped by many different political and economic forces, which were part of the grand transformations sweeping the Atlantic world in the early to mid–nineteenth century.

We know about the lives of these children—only six of the many tens of thousands transported illegally during the "progressively increasing" trade of the 1820s, 1830s, and 1840s—because of a curious and unlikely historical accident: the revolt aboard *La Amistad*. The children's experiences reveal to us the internal dealings of the clandestine world of illegal mid-nineteenth-century Atlantic slave trading from the highly unusual perspectives of the children themselves. The children's voices are preserved in their own words, in letters, witness statements, and testimonials. Their personal narratives and desperate pleas for assistance usher us from rural West African family life situated in kola nut forests and rice paddies into the dismal world of child enslavement, re-enslavement, sale and resale. Each child endured multiple experiences of enslavement, guardianship, apprenticeship, and ownership, and all lived at the mercy of numerous African, European, and American owners, guardians, captains, and masters. And each child sought the protection of powerful individuals against the unpredictable and violent vicissitudes of their journeys. Were it not for this brief episode in the history of Caribbean slavery and illicit Atlantic slave trafficking, the six children would never have come together as a unit.[10]

This book is an experiment in what Rebecca Scott and Jean Hébrard have described as "micro-history in motion," insofar as a carefully chosen event, or set of personalities viewed at the ground level, reveals broader regional dimensions. At its most expansive, *Amistad's Orphans* demonstrates that when our attention is directed away from adults and toward the qualitatively different experiences of African slave children, a prevailing wisdom about the nineteenth century begins to lose its luster. The details of the children's lives, contextualized with a wide spectrum of diverse evidence from the epoch, support two general, mutually situated, observations. Not only did slave traders actively seek children in increasing numbers during this period, but also child enslavement provided both slave producers and consumers with specific capacities not afforded by adult slaves to avoid detection and continue their illicit economies. Dispensing with the misidentification of the epoch as an age of abolition reveals the early nineteenth century as the beginning of an age of child enslavement.[11]

A CHILD'S VIEW OF THE WORLD OF *LA AMISTAD*

For some readers, the story of *La Amistad* may be very familiar and the narrative easy to follow. But for others the many personalities discussed in this book may become confusing. A synopsis of the general Amistad story is thus in order to set the stage for understanding the remarkable lives of six African children. In the summer of 1839 a U.S. government vessel detected a schooner, crewed by Africans, off Long Island. The boat was escorted to New London, Connecticut, whereupon the Africans were imprisoned in New Haven. The arrival of three girls (the alleged slaves Mar'gru, Kag'ne, and Te'me), and two boys (an alleged slave, Ka'le, and the slave cabin boy, Antonio), along with many adult males, attracted the attention of the recently established Connecticut Anti-Slavery Society. Various parties filed a series of suits, including libel of salvage under admiralty law, either to claim ownership of or to release the Africans. A grand jury convened to consider whether to indict the Africans for murder of the captain, Ramón Ferrer, and piracy. Competing suits were filed, and among the first issues debated was whether the Africans were legally cargo or people recently illegally smuggled from West Africa. Whether they were cargo or people rested in turn on whether they were slaves, which hinged on whether they were enslaved legally. Depending on which court had ultimate jurisdiction and how it ruled, various laws and treaties would direct specific outcomes.

In preparation for the court hearing, an Amistad Committee formed, made up of prominent New York and New Haven abolitionists Lewis Tappan, Amos Townsend, Timothy Bishop, and others. It raised funds for the welfare of the Africans; hired lawyers, including Roger Sherman Baldwin; and engaged university faculty and students, such as Josiah Willard Gibbs and George Day. Most important, it located an African sailor, James Covey, in the Royal Navy who was a liberated former child slave. Via the translation skills of Covey, the Africans were able to tell their story in their own words in court. In January 1840, Judge Andrew Judson of the federal district court in Connecticut ruled that the Africans aboard *La Amistad* were free because they were not born in Cuba but had been illegally smuggled into Cuba in violation of international laws and treaties. The U.S. government appealed to the Supreme Court, effectively on behalf of the purported slave owners, José Ruiz Carrías and Pedro Montes (who fled to Cuba to avoid the trial), and the Spanish crown. The defense team deployed former president John Quincy Adams to argue for the Africans' liberty. In March 1841, as Justice Joseph Story delivered the court's verdict affirming their freedom, the cabin boy Antonio escaped north to Canada. In April four of the children relocated to Farmington, Connecticut, where they attended school and church, in preparation for their return to Africa as part of a new missionary endeavor. And in November Mar'gru, Kag'ne, Te'me, and Ka'le, along with the interpreter Covey sailed for Freetown, Sierra Leone, arriving in January 1842.

The story of *La Amistad* is but the backdrop for understanding the broader contours of the lives of six remarkable children: Ka'le, Mar'gru, Te'me, Kag'ne, Covey, and Antonio. All six began their lives in West Africa, most likely in the Galinhas region, today in southeastern Sierra Leone close to the Liberian border. More information exists about some than others, and in some aspects Covey's narrative is the most detailed. Covey was born circa 1825–26, kidnapped from his parents' home as a small child, and sold into slavery in Africa as a young boy. He worked on a rice paddy for several years near the Galinhas coast before being sold to a European slave trader and put into a slave hold. The British West Africa Squadron captured the ship transporting Covey, aged about nine, and he was taken to Freetown and placed in a mission school for about five years. In 1838 he was apprenticed to the Royal Navy ship *Buzzard*, and in 1839 he sailed into New York City. After serving as the primary translator for the trials, he fell into poverty in 1840. Eventually he persuaded the advocates of the

Amistad survivors to fund his return to Africa. In Sierra Leone he lived with the mission for several years but later absconded.

Information for the other five is more fragmentary. Antonio was likely also born in Sierra Leone sometime around 1825–26. His path to enslavement remains unclear, but he was transported to Cuba circa 1835–36, purchased by Ferrer, and served as his cabin boy for approximately three years, until the revolt. As he was never charged with a crime, he lived freely in New Haven during the trials, with the understanding that he would likely return to Cuba at some point and to Ferrer's widow. But as the case concluded, fresh claims were made about his status, and he fled to Montreal via the Underground Railroad in 1840, after which he disappears. Ka'le was nine or ten years old, and Te'me, Kag'ne, and Mar'gru were approximately nine, ten, and twelve, respectively, in 1839. They were likely born some distance inland between 1828 and 1831. They lived in familial compounds for several years and were enslaved in different circumstances, either by kidnapping or by being pawned for a debt. They were housed in a coastal slave prison, or barracoon, (from the Portuguese *barracão*) owned by the successful Spanish slave trader Pedro Blanco or his acolytes in early 1839, and they were transported to Cuba in March or April on the same vessel.

Ka'le, Te'me, Kag'ne, and Mar'gru spent at least a month in a slave prison in central Havana before being sold by Cuban traders and put aboard *La Amistad*, where they first encountered Antonio. In New Haven they lived in the homes of various individuals, primarily that of the jailer Colonel Stanton Pendleton, and encountered Covey for the first time. They were schooled by students from Yale, and after the trial concluded, and their liberty affirmed, they were moved to Farmington for further schooling before returning with Covey to Freetown in January 1841 in the company of several American missionaries, including William Raymond. In Sierra Leone, the five were more closely tied to the American missionaries than the adult males. After several months in Freetown, they participated in the establishment of a new compound in Mende territory, possibly within several hundred kilometers of one or more of their original villages.

Six children's lives make up the core of this collective narrative, and they share many commonalities, most importantly mobility. Each of the orphans of *La Amistad* was born in what is today Sierra Leone, West Africa, and began life in villages and chieftaincies inland, with varying degrees of proximity, from the swampy, riverine, coastal Galinhas region where many illegal slave operations were situated. All six were enslaved as small children, and each was put aboard an illegal slave ship, one of many that specialized in trading slaves between Galinhas and Cuba in the 1830s. Their journey from Africa to the United States is charted in figures I.2 (for Covey) and I.3 (for the other children). Amistad's orphans resided in numerous places, for shorter or longer periods of time,

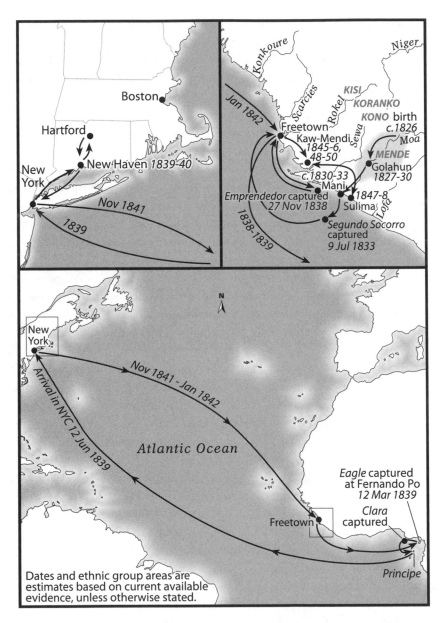

Fig. I.2. The journeys of James Covey, c. 1825–50 (Map by Don Pirius)

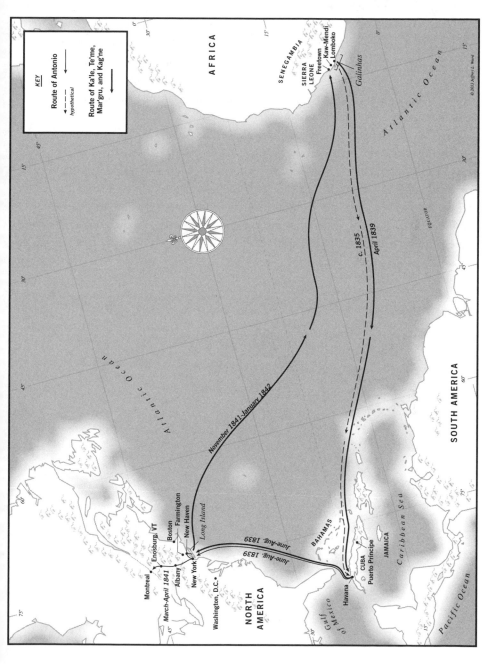

Fig. I.3. The Atlantic itineraries of Antonio, Ka'le, Te'me, Kag'ne, and Mar'gru, c. 1835–42 (Map by Jeffrey L. Ward)

spanning many years, and each place marked each child's life deeply. But their lives also differed enormously, and the information that survives about them is uneven. Their lives parted ways in five key aspects: in terms of how they were enslaved; in their experiences of enslavement, including the type of labor and service they were subjected to; in their experiences of transportation; in their paths to autonomy or liberty; and in their respective capacity to hold on to or rebuild family and kinship relations in the context of slavery. Each of these will be examined in subsequent chapters.

The six children whom I refer to collectively as Amistad's orphans are known in the historical record by names acquired during their journey through slavery and likely bear little relation to the names they acquired in infancy. Naming a child in West Africa was and indeed remains a sacred rite imbued with rich religious meanings and ancestral significance. The three girls are referred to by different names at different moments in time, but throughout the book I refer to them as Mar'gru (figure I.4), Kag'ne, and Te'me (figure I.5). The three boys also

Fig. I.4. "Marqu," pencil sketch on paper by William H. Townsend, c. 1840
(Beinecke Rare Book and Manuscript Library, Yale University)

Fig. I.5. The three girls (Kag'ne, Mar'gru, and Te'me), detail of a
lithograph by John Childs, c. 1839 ("Cinque Addressing His Compatriots,
on Board the Spanish Schooner *Amistad*, August 26, 1839"; reproduced
with permission of the Chicago History Museum)

have several names, accorded them at different moments in time inconsistently
and sometimes without adequate explanation; here I refer to them as Ka'le,
Antonio (figure I.6), and Covey (figure I.7). How and in what ways these names
relate to their birth names we shall likely never know. Anthropologist Mariane
Ferme describes how the process of naming a child transforms children into
"potential instantiations" of other family or kin.[12] Naming a slave, often in the
context of forced baptism and the torturous experience of branding by hot iron,
is an equally significant site of political, social, economic, gendered, and cultural meaning interwoven with incommensurable notions, such as proprietary
rights and entitlements.

Amistad's orphans were of different ages in 1839, but precise claims are difficult. The three girls and Ka'le were of a similar age when they first entered the historical record in 1839. The four had only recently left the West African coast, possibly the preceding spring. Of the three girls, Mar'gru was likely the oldest, but at the most by only a year or two. Antonio was about fifteen or sixteen when he arrived in Connecticut in 1839, but he had likely been removed from West Africa at a much younger age, and as he had been Ferrer's slave for at least three years, he may have sailed between Cuba and Sierra Leone on several occasions. Covey was the oldest of the six; he had traveled extensively in the Atlantic with

Fig. I.6. Antonio (center), detail of a lithograph by John Childs, c. 1839 ("Cinque Addressing His Compatriots, on Board the Spanish Schooner *Amistad*, August 26, 1839"; reproduced with permission of the Chicago History Museum)

Fig. I.7. James Covey (from John Warner Barber, A *History of the Amistad Captives*
[New Haven: E. L. and J. W. Barber, 1840])

the Royal Navy. When he appeared before the court in 1839 as interpreter, he
was likely just shy of maturity.

ORPHANS AND ORPHANHOOD CLAIMS

The title of this book, *Amistad's Orphans*, is provocation to rethink the relationships, strategies, and experiences of slave children whose identities are
too often determined primarily by their status as slaves. In order to uncover
the lived experience of children more broadly, I unite six historical lives into
one imagined slave ship family. The six children shared many experiences,
first and foremost the process of being bereft of family by their enslavement as
children. As an analytical term—a dynamic definition, if you like—"orphan"
emerges from actively and intentionally bringing into conversation the experiential insights bequeathed by six remarkable historical survivors: Mar'gru,
Kag'ne, Te'me, Ka'le, Covey, and Antonio. Of the six, some were identified as
orphans, some were not, and others made conflicting and contradictory claims

about their family and parents at different moments in time. The term "orphan" reminds us that the six children were once part of six families, but it also speaks to the disruption of family life by slavery and slave trading. To call them orphans is a deliberate political choice on my part, one that thrusts into the center of the analysis their dynamic kinship relations and their being denied a path to adulthood. Orphans, and relatedly, orphanhood claims, highlight the central role of intentional and accidental stages of a child's attempts to solidify, create, and reformulate kin-like relationship in the distressful and constantly changing "friendless" context of illegal enslavement.[13]

Orphan and orphanhood operate here as analytical devices to account for not only the inadequacies of scholarly explanations of enslavement that privilege the adult slave experience but, and more important, to think critically about the kinlessness characteristic of the child slave experience and the deliberate strategies of survival that build on the spectrum of kinlessness as experienced by children. I deploy the term "orphan" in an attempt to answer the omnipresent question directed at historical researchers who focus on children's history, namely, what exactly is a "child" in the various illegal enslavement contexts of the nineteenth-century Atlantic world. It is my response to those who would seek a concrete definition of child and/or child slave, something I find untenable.

The experience of orphanhood means different things to different people, but at the core of most definitions is the separation of a child from his or her parents. Separation may be permanent—such as that caused by the death of a parent—or temporary—such as that rendered by abduction or kidnapping followed by recovery and reunification. More often than not, however, the precise status of the erstwhile and possibly ongoing child-parent relationship of slaves is unknown and remains so. Unknowing is thus central. As historian Vincent Brown observed, "the struggles of slaves were not simply beset by the depredations of slavery" but were also "shaped and directed," implying "a politics of survival" and "existential struggle" in the context of incomprehension. It could be learned, individually and organically, or shared by others and acquired by observation or mimicry. Orphanhood claims ought to be situated within a larger strategy of resistance to the specter of alienation. Orphanhood claims are thus a social praxis of resistance to slavery by children for whom freedom is illusory, unimaginable, or unknown.[14]

The phrase "Amistad's orphans" directs attention to the dynamic relationship between identification and self-identification as experienced by the children and the many adults with whom their experiences intersect. No clear definition of "orphan" exists in part because of the great variation and changing nature of the experiences, agency, legal statuses, and economic-political contexts of "alienated" children. Perhaps, with the important exception of a court-ordered determination, no such fixity exists. Some recent historical and anthropological scholarship provides part of the scaffolding for a dynamic definition of orphanhood consisting of stages. Building on the scholarship of children and orphans, I propose a dynamic definition incorporating three stages.

Orphanhood has often been described as a catchall for a variety of alienated children and the attendant processes of alienation, including, but not limited to, those "bereft of kin" and those "orphaned by poverty." Alienation is thus an important element for establishing the first stage of the dynamic definition. The Amistad children were alienated from their homes and kin through various forms of enslavement; they became "bereft" of kin, often through violence or by poverty if pawned. The first stage was not always a complete process of orphaning but rather partial or piecemeal. Nineteenth-century orphans in Europe were rarely completely orphaned in a literal sense—that is, having two deceased biological parents. More often than not they were placed in government, parochial, or private institutions by one or both parents for a fixed or indeterminate period as a result of poverty, illness, injury, or destitution. Designating someone an orphan could be the first stage of a program to exert social control or a proprietary claim. Orphans were not always surrendered completely but could be reclaimed, like pawns, by parents who had regained economic security or found steady employment. The first stage of orphanhood thus emerges from the immediate first context of being bereft, but it is incomplete.[15]

The second stage of orphanhood was the completion of the physical and psychological separation from kinship and familial contexts. The Amistad children were completely orphaned in the sense that they lost contact with and support from their original biological or social parents once they were placed aboard the slave ship. The shifting terminology associated with the kinless child is just one in a series of fluid and changing conceptions of children and childhood. The childhoods of the orphaned and adopted are deeply articulated by global discourses, by international laws, and by the transnational processes associated with global mobility. The Amistad children's experiences were deeply embedded in a dynamic global capitalist system of labor exploitation that crisscrossed the Atlantic Ocean and often went far beyond. Thus in this second stage, a growing realization of the impossibility of returning to the family or hearth is coupled with the very traumatic physical processes of movement.[16]

The third stage of the dynamic definition of orphan is one of self-realization and self-awareness, often in the form of contesting adversity. In many ways the orphan operates as a social category, representing the destitute, the abandoned, the excluded, and the unwanted. But the problem with this formulation is that it still appears to operate from the outside, looking in. Self-realization involved physical and/or psychological dimensions. In the absence of specific forms of personal testimony, such as autobiography, psychological self-realization is difficult to evidence. In the narratives of Amistad's orphans, the psychological state of self-identification appears to be less substantiated than specific actions or statements seeking to create, sustain, or reestablish fictional kinship with possible protectors. Each of the individuals invoked various metonymic and analogous phrases and self-definitions conveying kinlessness, abandonment, or orphanhood; Covey, for example, uses the phrase "no mother, no father" in letters, seemingly in an effort to manipulate an emotional response by one of his protectors. In many ways, Amistad's orphans feared becoming destitute, abandoned, and unwanted. In this sense then, more than a term of fixedness and rigidity, the third of three stages in the dynamic definition of orphan focuses on how orphanhood operated as a metaphor of kinlessness and alienation within which potential patron-client relationships may be envisioned.[17]

By referring to the child slaves as orphans I am not seeking to sever them from the possibility of kin, parents, and friends. I am certainly not interested in resurrecting a "sentimentalist" child historiography and applying it to Africa, where it has no place until late colonialism, if at all. Orphanhood is not a precursor to or conduit for "adolescence," which remains as highly a problematic concept today as it was when Margaret Mead supposedly discerned its nonexistence. Orphaning did not result simply from the "withering away" of functional families and communities. Amistad's orphans were six children removed from any semblance of a childhood experience consistent with their erstwhile peer groups and age sets. The expansive and important "growing up" literature operates as a point of departure here, to highlight a methodology whereby children's experiences emerge from a close reading of the paraphernalia of childhood. Whereas "childhood" as a category of analysis is a site of fierce contestation between scholars highlighting variously agency, power, performance, and idealization, orphans and orphanhood offer an alternative, grounded in the lived experience of enslavement.[18]

Orlando Patterson famously described the "power relation" of slavery as a form of "social death" comprising three facets: physical violence, psychological influence, and cultural authority. Natal alienation was Patterson's attempt to explain the second, insofar as "the cultural aspect" of the slave-master relationship "rests on authority" and on "the control of symbolic instruments." Natal alienation thus operated as the mechanism whereby the slave became a "socially dead person," one who was "alienated from all 'rights' or claims of birth." Natal alienation was an expansive process that not only "denied" slaves "claims" to "parents and living blood relations" but also "all such claims and obligations on his more remote ancestors and on his descendants." Patterson distinguished between having a "past" and a "heritage" and observed that slaves were deprived of "formally recognized community" to distinguish the existence of "informal social relations." The "profound emotional and social implications" of the process of slavery with respect to the "loss of ties of birth in both ascending and descending generations" are summed up as the manufacture of a "genealogical isolate."[19]

At first glance, it would appear that aspects of Amistad's orphans' narratives sit comfortably with the expansive analytical category outlined by Patterson. They were wrested from their parents as young children, and only one or two, to the best of our knowledge, were ever reunited with biological family. These children were deprived of their genealogical context and lost all ties, at least with ascending generations. After their initial capture, they worked in a variety of capacities, often as dependent slaves. At the first moment of enslavement, when they were removed from their respective kin, the notion of family was not so distant that relocating them was completely impossible. But after the subsequent stages of movement toward the coast and across the ocean, their natal alienation became more or less complete. Amistad's orphans not only lost their cultural heritage and were stripped of all rights and claims of birth, but they also lost their birth names. At various moments during their respective captures, enslavements, and circumscribed liberations, they were renamed following an archetypal experience of slavery and liberation, one repeated time and time again throughout the Atlantic world.[20]

When thinking about the experiences of child slaves in general, and orphanhood in particular, social death at first appears a compelling analytical platform. And yet Brown, echoing Indrani Chattejee, recently observed, the "usefulness of social death as a concept" depends on what we as scholars are trying to explain. Indeed, the self-representation as parentless by one of Amistad's orphans, Covey, sits in tension with the framework theorized by Patterson and also with some of the narrower scholarship on orphanhood. Covey first claims he was kidnapped while his parents were still living. After arriving in the United States, instead of affirming the severing of genealogical ties, Covey embarks on a strategy to garner sympathy for his goal to be reunited with his family. He likely had no more information about his family than any other former child slave, but his claims resist the *totality* of "social death," as well as more capacious conceptualizations of orphanhood.[21]

The embedded assumption in Patterson's argument is that social death orbits exclusively around adult slaves, for how can a child slave, yet to start a family, be deprived of descending generations? Covey's recollection of his African name—and his insistence on the possibility of family reunification—further muddy the waters of genealogical isolation. Moreover, his manufacture of fictional kinship relations, coupled with the dogged persistence to relocate his family, blur Patterson's distinction between formal and informal community relations. And Covey is not the only one resisting categorization. Another of Amistad's orphans, Te'me, may have relocated her father in Sierra Leone in 1853. A third, Mar'gru, returned to the United States as an adult and then sailed again for Sierra Leone to work as a missionary where she also married. Antonio, for his part, complicates the picture yet further. He appears to have made several overtures to return to Cuba, seemingly acknowledging the proprietary interests of Ferrer's widow, before deciding to take flight and sever all ties with his former master.

Of the six members of this imagined slave ship family, no evidence has yet come to light that any one individual self-identified as an orphan. Rather it is within this metaphorical context that the imagined family unit of Amistad's orphans elaborates a broader self-preservation strategy against the cultural amputation of social belonging. Just as the survivors of the *Emilia* debacle found effective mechanisms of maintaining social relationships in Rio de Janeiro against political and economic pressures that should have made this quite impossible, Amistad's orphans constitute part of a virtual family unit born of trauma. But by identifying the six children as orphans, I am not simply employing a metaphor. "Orphan," "orphaning," and "orphanhood" all cohabit here as analytical terms; they are cognates of a dynamic definition articulating a social praxis resisting cultural amputation. Orphanhood instantiates specifically both real and fictional kinship and non-kinship relations sought by alienated children among themselves and between children and adults in the context of slavery and subsequent stages of subordination.[22]

The records demonstrate clearly that the imagined slave ship family I call Amistad's orphans were by any definition—physiological, legal, psychological—enslaved as children. But it is inadequate to rest there. Instead I propose a dynamic definition of "orphan" as a way of uncovering the experiential processes of identification and self-identification embodied by child slaves as a group. It is possible that in the eyes of other Africans they remained frozen in time as children because they never experienced the initiation rites of their respective natal societies via which they would be admitted into adulthood. But the children's narratives also provide a rich corpus of material with which to interpret how they perceived their predicament; how they struggled to reconcile, challenge, and alter their condition; and how they recognized the importance of the constantly shifting legal, social, political, and economic contexts of their status. In many regards Amistad's orphans never ceased to be children in the eyes of historical actors of the period and in the records preserved into the present; they are, quite literally, orphans of history.

ORPHANS OF HISTORY: MYTHS AND STRUCTURE

This book includes six chapters, which, when read as a whole, demonstrate that the nineteenth century was a pivotal epoch marked deeply by African child enslavement. The first chapter introduces child slavery and the nineteenth-century child slave experience more broadly, and the subsequent five narrative thematic chapters follow the geographical and chronological movements of the six children. Each thematic chapter begins with the disassembling of a myth and presents one part of a five-part argument that in the nineteenth century the experience of child slaves was qualitatively different from that of adult slaves. Chronologically each chapter encompasses an experiential period (namely, childhood, slavery, travel, liberty, and return) in the lives of the children, but as their experiences differed, there are important twists, turns, and overlaps in terms of time and place. Repetition of key events — but from different angles — is an intentional stylistic and methodological choice. I offer no rigid chronological structure and shuttle back and forth as needed across the Atlantic, chapter by chapter. And whereas the six children's experiences form the core of the narrative, I occasionally stray into discussion of a more generalized African child slave experience and draw on evidence from beyond the brief Amistad drama.

The six orphans' experiences were quite distinct from those of the adult males with whose lives they so deeply intersected. But the passage of time, the writing and rewriting of history, fads and preferences in scholarship and popular writing, and even the fame of *La Amistad* have all conspired to conceal the children's lives. The absence of documentation about children may once have been grounds for ignoring their contribution and their historical experiences, but my research has uncovered a rich vein of archival, oral, and ethnographical data. Making sense of this evidence, however, requires an additional step. Uncovering the children's qualitatively different experiences requires the development of a methodology whereby myths about slaves and slavery — rooted in the adult male experience, but concealing the boys' and girls' lives — are identified and dismantled. Great historical events create enduring myths. The literature on myth and mythmaking is expansive, but here I employ the term simply, to identify and describe a widely held but false belief, verisimilitude, or received wisdom. Five myths about the Amistad story occlude the children's experiences. And each myth emerged from the specific objectives of the survivors'

legal defense team and the wider network of supporters. Identified and dismantled, these five myths reveal important dimensions of the qualitatively different
African child slave experiences.

The following chapter, Chapter 1, examines the historiographical perimeters
of children and child slaves specifically and broader scholarly debates about
childhood. In it I argue that although the precise definition of "child" remained
unclear in the nineteenth century, slave traders increasingly identified children
as effective tools with which to circumvent new restrictions and prohibitions.
What precisely constitutes a "child" continues to fascinate historians, but child
enslavement remains a neglected area of research. The dimensions of child
enslavement in the context of the illegal nineteenth-century slave trade offer
insight into the interdependence of child enslavement and the expansion of
prohibitions on slave trading.

Chapter 2 argues that African child slaves do not have ethnicities and identities in the way that adult slaves may have, but geographical origins provide
some sense of their lived experience prior to transportation. The chapter begins
with the myth of "Mendi" identity spawned by the defense team's legal arguments and builds on scholarship on slave origins and ethnicity. The Mende
origin myth—embedded in the urgency of establishing the African origins of
the survivors—shrouds the much greater difficulties encountered in establishing the identities and origins of child slaves. This chapter examines the geographical, political, social, cultural, ethnolinguistic, and economic contexts of
the six children and identifies the Galinhas and its hinterland as their most
probable origin.

In Chapter 3 I argue that children are enslaved and subjugated in different
ways than adults. Here I first examine the mythology of free-born status that
looms large in the record of the trials. The free-born myth interfaces with ongoing debates about the modalities of enslavement in Africa and changes wrought
by abolitionism. Entrenched by the centrality to the defense team's argument of
the natural rights of man from birth, it conceals the narrowness of child-specific
enslavement practices in Africa. I consider the forms of slavery in the Galinhas
region in particular, the children's embarkation across the Atlantic, and their
reception in Cuba. I pursue the multiple passages of enslavement that each individual encountered to shed light on the episodic, interrupted nature of many
experiences of slavery.

Chapter 4 argues that African child slaves journeyed in different ways to
adults, and that the history of child slave mobility resides in discrete spaces. The
chapter opens with a discussion of the myth of a common Middle Passage on
the *Teçora*. The journeys of Amistad's orphans sit in tension with conventional

Middle Passage narratives. The common Middle Passage myth highlights a preference in current Atlantic scholarship for a linearity and alacrity of movement more appropriate to the adult experiences of forced migration. Embossed by a desire for certainty about and linearity in the survivors' itinerary, it occludes the many complex, irregular, and multidirectional movements of child slaves in Africa and the Atlantic world.

Chapter 5 argues that when emancipated, children are not really free in the sense as it is generally applied to adult slaves; freedom and childhood are in many ways incommensurable. In this chapter I begin with the myth that the Supreme Court freed all the captives to show that the legal statuses of Amistad's orphans differed significantly from that of the adult males. I explore the multiple and different mechanisms whereby each child attempted to end their enslavement while still children. The liberty myth reveals the obscuring influence of North American and European scholarly notions of freedom. Emerging from a mistaken interpretation of the import of the Supreme Court's decision, this myth disguises the incommensurability of any notion of child freedom.

The final chapter argues that liberated child slaves faced considerably greater obstacles upon return than adults. Indeed Amistad's orphans were in many ways imprisoned in a permanent state of childhood. Chapter 6 begins with a discussion of the myth about African family reunification. While several individual survivors reconnected with family members, the family reunification myth finds support in contemporary Pan-African nostalgia celebrating African resistance and African American survival. Grounded both in a romantic image of primordial Africa and a conscious disengagement with the social and psychological dislocation caused by enslavement, it masks the trauma, anomie, and the permanent state of childhood that encumbered liberated former child slaves when they return and attempt to reintegrate in their erstwhile homelands. The children's efforts to find natal homelands and kin groups were imperiled by the social and cultural deprivations resulting from their enslavement as children and narrowed by their experiences of formal education during liberation.

In the Epilogue, I return to my argument reconceptualizing the illicit slave-trading epoch. The enslavement of children during the nineteenth century escalated massively for a variety of reasons, some of which still remain unclear and require further research. It is possible to locate and identify child slave narratives. If the analytical framework of orphanhood speaks directly to the child experience of slavery and slave trading, perhaps a focus on orphans may have wider application for understanding what came after the closing of the trans-Atlantic trade, including, for example, expansion of plantation labor on the African continent, the role of children in colonial labor systems, and the dependency of the humanitarian industry on children's narratives. It is my hope that the experiences of Amistad's orphans will also facilitate a better understanding of the nature of contemporary child trafficking and contours of child slavery networks in the present era of child enslavement.

My investigation of the African children's experience of the Amistad story is informed by original archival, oral, and ethnographic research conducted in the United States, Canada, the United Kingdom, Sierra Leone, and Cuba, as well as the extensive research of a community of scholars with shared or overlapping goals. A range of documents from this familiar story, some well known and others unexplored, provide a rare window into the historical contexts of child enslavement and slave smuggling in the nineteenth century in contexts ranging from Africa to Connecticut. The testimonies of Ka'le and Mar'gru were what first drew me to this subject. These children left a thin historical record of their experiences, but enough material exists to partly reconstruct their lives and their worlds. These children wrote letters appealing for assistance and explaining their social and economic predicament. Others met with them and recorded their interactions.[23]

Evidence for the actual lives and experiences of the six children is piecemeal and inconsistent. The evidence I draw upon to reconstruct their journey from Africa to the Americas and back is primarily conventional and archival in form. References to the children are scarce prior to the shipboard revolt; the evidence is richest for the U.S. sojourn, 1839–41, and it is fragmentary and episodic thereafter. The first mention of Covey is from a ship's manifest in 1833. The first mention of the other five children is in 1838–39, in Cuban and U.S. documents about *La Amistad*, its cargo, and the imprisonment of the survivors in Connecticut. Interest in the children from 1839 to 1841 was intense among abolitionists and the U.S. public at large, and there exist many different perspectives for this period from white American participants, including personal letters and diaries. I have located no record of Antonio after 1841. After the remaining five returned to Africa, there are only occasional references in missionary reports. There exist brief fragments of the lives of Kag'ne and Te'me during the 1840s and 1850s but little else with the exception of an epistolary corpus from Mar'gru to her missionary sponsors into the 1850s. The last reference to Covey is 1850. Mar'gru may have lived longer, but it appears that Ka'le lived into his eighties or nineties and met Banfield in 1917.

Reconstructing the story of six children is possible today partly because of the several court cases in which they were embroiled. At the end of the book I provide a chronological timeline of events as it pertains to the children. There were multiple court cases and a series of trials and decisions, and so a brief summary is in order. The first case was a civil claim in a special session of a federal district court in Connecticut. Then a criminal investigation began and a federal circuit court impaneled a grand jury. The simultaneous case concerning salvage and libel in Federal Admiralty Court in Connecticut proceeded in fits and starts. Then followed a civil procedure in a federal district court, specifically a writ of habeas corpus seeking the release of some of the children, which contested the proprietary claim by Montes. In New York State a subpoena was issued to hold James Covey as a witness. A civil damages claim against Ruiz and Montes was filed in the New York State Court of Common Pleas. After the federal district court determined the Africans were not slaves, appeals wound their way via a federal circuit court to the U.S. Supreme Court. After the Supreme Court affirmed that the Africans were not legally enslaved, a second habeas corpus writ was filed in the New Haven Probate Court to seek custody of the children. A number of legal historians helped me navigate this labyrinth.

The majority of documentary evidence is located in public and private libraries, archival repositories, and national archives in the United States, Cuba, the United Kingdom, Sierra Leone, and Canada. Each chapter is supported by evidence from multiple sources and time periods. Much of the primary evidentiary basis for the reassembling of the lives of the six children is archival. Archival sources include court and tribunal records, pamphlets (particularly Barber's thirty-two-page booklet), published congressional records, period newspapers, official correspondence and diplomatic records, memoirs, personal and private correspondence, firsthand accounts sent or shared between and among key figures, diaries and journals, ship manifests, insurance records, published letters in missionary journals, and naval logbooks. Each of these primary texts has its biases and prejudices, and many must be interpreted in the context of their interwoven political, social, religious, or other interests and designs. The critical perspective I bring to the legal arguments undergirding the case, which provide the foundation for each of the five thematic chapters, extends to the individual primary documents; where appropriate I highlight or discuss how bias impacts or alters the understanding of the Amistad story.[24]

At times, however, the archival trace of specific children is thin or nonexistent. To connect the dots, fill in blank periods, connect individuals, postulate hypotheses, enrich the narratives and contextualize the experiences of the six, I draw on a variety of contemporaneous records, published and unpublished. Numerical data and shipping records contained in *Voyages* (the online Trans-Atlantic Slave Trade Database) provide the basis for assessing the statistical significance of children in the illegal slave trade and many more specific questions.

Lexicons and grammars from the period helped me decipher terms and concepts. Geographical and oceanographic treatises, surveys, and reports provide important ecological, agricultural, and environmental information. Travel narratives from participants and observers in the slave trade and the counteractions of the Royal Navy shed light on larger illicit networks operating during the period. Missionary correspondence and memoranda provide perspective about the role of children in colonization and proselytization efforts. Maps, charts, paintings, lithographs, photographs, and etchings provide a rich tapestry against which ideas and concepts may be imagined or visualized. Ethnographic data, oral interviews, and linguistic data collected during the period, and more recently by others and myself, facilitate the decoding of cultural, political, and social practices and institutions. These contextual sources are employed with caution and a heightened awareness of the preconceptions and prejudices of their time and production milieu. Firsthand accounts and ship data may be as valuable for what they exclude as for what they include. The structural biases of oral histories and the limitations of historical linguistics have spawned their respective subfields of inquiry.

The expansive critical scholarship about African slavery, slave trading, abolition, and related themes provides an additional, third layer to the evidentiary basis for the reconstruction of the lives of Amistad's orphans. I draw deeply on critical and insightful scholarship by historians, anthropologists, ethnographers, geographers, and sociologists of Africa, the Americas, the Atlantic, including published and unpublished work, and beyond to inform and develop my broader analysis and specific hypotheses.

⌃⌃⌃

"MOST FAVOURITE CARGOES":
AFRICAN CHILD ENSLAVEMENT IN
THE NINETEENTH CENTURY

The itineraries and biographies of Amistad's orphans are richly insightful as individual stories, but they also overlap in important ways. By reuniting them as an imagined slave ship family it is my hope that they may provide a template for understanding the broader contours of the nineteenth-century African child slave experience. From their enslavements in their natal villages, via their journey to the coastal prisons or barracoons, and then deep into the dark cavities of a slave ship, their collective experience echoed that of tens of thousands of others. And although these six children fortuitously avoided the ultimate destinations envisaged by their African and Cuban captors, the magnitude of child slavery—and indeed the expansive presence of children as domestic workers, as shipmates, and in sugar cultivation, all part of the buoyant Cuban economy in the last decades of the trans-Atlantic trade—is only beginning to be understood. In the 1830s, when Amistad's orphans were imprisoned in slave ships, children from Galinhas barracoons routinely accounted for 40 or even 50 percent of a Havana-bound ship's illicit "cargo." Unlike adult males aboard *La Amistad*, these six children were enslaved and forcibly relocated during the peak of Atlantic child slave transport. Whereas the adult narrative is relatively familiar, the story of Amistad's orphans is not; it opens the door to a richer understanding of an immense but often overlooked dimension of the trans-Atlantic slave trade: the place of children in the illegal slave trade of the nineteenth century.

Considering Amistad's orphans plunges us headfirst into the complex debate about the social construction of childhood. Because these particular child slaves may be analyzed from African, European, American, and Atlantic angles, oftentimes simultaneously, there are multiple dimensions to the processes of construction. Individually, each of the six children had his or her own childhood experience; these particularities and specificities are significant. From each child we garner important details about the possible meanings of their childhood and the traumatic effect of their journeys through enslavement. Those with whom they interacted during this journey also offer rich insight into attitudes about children and childhood.

Articulating precisely how the lives of six children can, and do, speak to the broader experience of tens of thousands of others is the core heuristic guiding this book. This chapter argues that although the definition of "child" was no clearer than in previous centuries, by the nineteenth century slave traders increasingly identified children as effective tools with which to circumvent new restrictions and prohibitions. This chapter thus explores the historically contextual perimeters of children and child slaves in the nineteenth century, set against scholarly debates about childhood more broadly. In it I grapple with such important questions as what constitutes a child and why child enslavement remains a neglected area of research. I consider the dimensions of child enslavement in the context of the illegal slave trade characteristic of the 1830s and 1840s and the relationship between child enslavement and the expansion of prohibitions on slave trading.

CHILDREN AND CHILD SLAVERY

What constituted a child in the mid-nineteenth-century Atlantic world is a subject of intense scholarly debate, and such definitions were linked to evolving ideas about childhood, particularly in Europe and North America, as much as they were to changing attitudes to slavery and slave trading in Africa and the Caribbean. Historian Wilma King drew attention to the difficulties of identifying children in the archive of slavery, and historian Erik Hofstee was among the first to observe that any attempt to establish a fixed definition of child or childhood during the entirety of the trans-Atlantic trade may well be a "fruitless" task. The most comprehensive resource for studying the trans-Atlantic trade, the web database *Voyages*, offers a cautionary note about reading too much into age definitions. They changed over time and among carriers, and slave traders and Africans employed a host of names and terms to disaggregate children based on perceived age, many of which filtered into Atlantic vernacular use.[1]

Collectively, the narratives that emerge from the lives of the Amistad orphans unsettle assumptions about the marginality, rarity, or insignificance of African slave childhoods and forcible child slave transportation. Although Hofstee's quantitative and qualitative research effectively demonstrated that children were a "deliberate target" of slave traders, scholarship arguing the contrary persists. Perhaps the most pervasive view diminishing the significance of children in the trans-Atlantic trade is that which routinely portrays children as a reluctant alternate choice of slave purchasers, as expendable space-fillers on ships, undesired by American planters and on the periphery of lineage and kinship networks. King argued persuasively that enslaved children in North America had virtually no childhood, but the experiences of Amistad's orphans blur the fixity and boundedness of such a capacious definition as it pertains to African child enslavement.[2]

Against such views—discussed further below—children were seen as possessing skills and competencies less accessible to adult slaves, including the powerful dependencies that quickly emerge from the emotional vulnerabilities of childhood. Slave traders realized that child slaves craved security and protection, as do all young children, and this made them ideal candidates at particular moments. Slave traders preyed on the emotional insecurities of children to strengthen the master-slave relationship and reshape it with the paternal dimensions of a pseudo-family. For example, the "spiriting away" of Ukawsaw Gronniosaw from his Bornu homeland underscored the naïveté of children; an initial reluctance to purchase him on the part of a Dutch slave trader dissipated as the benefits of the child's vulnerability and malleability became apparent. Slave children appear to have been highly prized, specifically targeted, and exceptionally valuable investments, at particular moments in time and in discrete geographical and economic contexts.[3]

During the *legal* trans-Atlantic slave trade, children appear in records identified as such, often because of their height, and four feet four inches was often the cutoff for children. The Royal Africa Company defined children as those judged to be under fourteen years of age but no doubt employed Eurocentric concepts of physicality in these determinations. Outward signs of puberty or inferences of sexual maturity also functioned as markers. But different countries and companies adopted varying standards, and they changed over time. Ships designed specific areas for boys and girls, and with what were considered appropriate measurements: on the *Brooks* it was "five feet by one foot two" for boys, and "four feet six by one foot" for girls." Children may be identified in records by the lower taxes paid on particular imports and also by the value of insurance paid for ship cargos. In terms of insuring cargo, three children were sometimes valued as two adults. In Dutch, French, Portuguese, Spanish, German, and English sources, different words are used to describe many different types of children, ranging from breast-feeding infants to infants able to stand by themselves freely to prepubescent girls, or boys with first whiskers, or children with first adult teeth. Indeed, deducing a definition of "child" for the purpose of understanding the extent of child participation in slave trades appears a Sisyphean task, as historians Gwyn Campbell, Suzanne Miers, and Joseph Miller appear to concede.[4]

Inductively establishing perimeters of childhood in the nineteenth century is also problematic but for different reasons. Because the trade was generally illegal, the social historian has to identify markers, shadows, or even palimpsests suggesting the previous presence of child slaves. During the illegal slave trade, insurance prices for unnamed cargo often concealed the sale of a child. As slave smuggling operations expanded after 1820, the redesigned sleeker, shallower, and swifter ships contained tighter spaces and concealed holds, into which sometimes only children could be stowed, as the missionary George Thompson's description explained. In Cuba, distinguishing between age grades and statuses was imprecise, and youths eighteen or twenty were often called children. But during the same period children became more visible, particularly in the court records of recaptives, where they are often identified by an estimated age and height and by physical marks, such as branding. Age estimates during the illegal phase focused on "sexual maturity as assessed by physical appearance" as the central criterion, which for most during this epoch would "probably occur in the mid-teens" but may vary "according to the diet prevalent in the areas from which Africans were drawn" and "according to the eye of the purchasers." Multiple copies of these records, in some instances, "often recorded slightly different distributions of the same group of slaves." The bounties paid to officers in the Royal Navy distinguished between males, females, and children. For these and other reasons, slavers and liberators of slaves had conflicting incentives to identify children clearly.[5]

In Africa, what constituted a child could be indicated by a specific appellation or nomenclature, membership of a social group, such as an age set or age grade, and also various initiation, scarification, and puberty rituals, including male and female genital cutting. In many African cultures age was calculated against events rather than by years. Just as slave traders distinguished between suckling infants, crawling children, and toddlers, so too African communities had distinct terminologies reflecting the incremental changes of social, psychological, and physiological growth. But these, and many other culturally specific connotations of children and childhood, may have been lost or abandoned throughout the processes and experiences associated with enslavement; they are certainly difficult to recover today. The Atlantic trade streamlined, simplified, and erased the nuance and complexity of African childhood. Enslavement practices in the African continent often, however, indicate attitudes to childhood. Child slaves were often not enchained in compounds or barracoons, and they performed labor appropriate to their age. To be sure, childhood in Africa did not cease suddenly, but rather it constituted an incremental process whereby one transitioned into youth and then adolescence and then early adulthood, both privately and publicly.[6]

The archival record demonstrates that Amistad's orphans met many of the historically situated and culturally determined definitions of children operating at the time. Evidence about ages recorded, prices paid, and treatment accorded all support the view that they were considered as quite distinct from the adults. From court records we know that Pedro Montes placed the "value" of a group of four at "one thousand and three hundred dollars." This sum situates them comfortably within what is known about prices for Cuban child slaves (ages one to fourteen) of the period. Antonio described "Mahgru, Teme, Kene, Cali" as "all small children." But even more important, Antonio affirmed that the children were "loose not chained," unlike the adult males aboard the ship. The fact that the girls were "not confined" and "walked about on deck, or went below, as they thought proper" and while still in the Havana dock "were never tied" underscores that they posed no risk of rebellion. By contrast, unfettering adult slaves aboard a ship was a highly risky proposition. Evidence about price and treatment, however, are only external markers of age and childhood. Toward the end of their sojourn in the United States, the girls were brought before courts as children and placed under the legal guardianship of adults.[7]

Beyond physiological and financial markers, in exploring contours of childhood in the nineteenth century, I am particularly concerned with the psychological, emotional, and situational behavior of Amistad's orphans that reflect what some—from humanists to clinical psychologists—call the "plasticity" of childhood. Building on some of the critical observations of the deeply personal, expansive "growing up" literature, it is possible to recover experiential insight through the archival fragments from the children themselves. But there are significant obstacles to such an approach with regard to African slave children. First, the textual record from the children themselves is very thin and fragmentary. Second, the terminology employed changes episodically and often illogically. In the court context, and afterward, all six were treated as children, and they were variously referred to as children, youths, or adolescents by observers and witnesses and other participants in the dramatic trial and its remarkable conclusion. And third, African historians routinely resist identifying African actors by the terminology accorded them by Europeans, and when children are described in proprietary terms, such an exigency would appear to be even more urgent. Whereas Hofstee argues conservatively for a textual consistency, a definition tied to the primary documentation, *Amistad's Orphans* embraces this complexity and takes an expansive view of the definition of children. Only by moving beyond prevailing biological, economic, and legal frameworks that situate and thus define the child primarily *as slave* is it possible to incorporate the emotional, psychological, and highly situational manifestations of childhood and childlike behavior that emerge in contexts of acute distress, such as enslavement.[8]

An expansive definition of childhood, tethered to emotional and psychological experiences, also addresses the longer-term manifestations of child enslavement. Although historical demography is a relatively new domain of study for nineteenth-century West Africa, it is not unreasonable to assume that most African children who survived infancy also lived long enough to become adults. All six of the subjects of this book attained liberty and lived adult lives: some shorter, some longer. We know a little about five of the six once they are legally adults, and yet even in adulthood they at times employed language, manners, and behavior more often associated with children. So, whereas one might argue from a biological perspective that childhood is a temporary stage, or that it is futile to compare the experience of a child with what transpired as the individual reached legal maturity, the experiences of Amistad's orphans suggest otherwise.

Several of the orphans continued to be treated as children in a variety of ways after they reached maturity. Similarly, individual actions at times suggest they deliberately invoked or engaged childlike language and behavior. In some respects they remained frozen in time as children because they had not experienced the initiation rites of African societies that would make them adults. Perhaps from a Western perspective one might argue they remained children because they never married or created their own nuclear families. If a young adult continues to behave as a child, is he a child or an adult? The implications of the liminal and temporary status of childhood loom large for scholarly accounts of the experience of children enslaved illegally in the nineteenth-century Atlantic world. In many regards, Amistad's orphans never ceased to be children in the eyes of historical actors of the period and in the records preserved into the present.

Notwithstanding these observations, with some noteworthy exceptions, nineteenth-century African child slaves have rarely been a direct focus of scholarly research. There are perhaps several reasons for this neglect, but two strike me as particularly worthy of critique: one is empirical, the other conceptual. First, child history and childhood studies have transformed sociohistorical praxis, but unevenly so. Historians of Europe blazed trails for research and questioned categories of analysis. But as King's study demonstrates, disaggregative trends in child history do not neatly match the invisible and silent categories child slaves occupy. Moreover, biographies by *former* child slaves, writing as adults— such as Frederick Douglass, Harriet Jacobs, Juan Francisco Manzano, and Gustavus Vassa (a.k.a. Olaudah Equiano)—continue to define the child slave experience.[9]

A second reason is surely the current scholarly attention to nineteenth-century emancipation, which has produced substantial new studies identifying the epoch as an age of abolition and asserting abolitionism as the defining ideology of the era. I know that I am not alone when I state that this view emanates largely from imperial, Whiggish, and Eurocentric circles and both puzzles African historians and insults advances in African historiography. The transformations wrought by the proliferation of abolitionist ideologies, including mission settlements, colonization, and the mischievously named "legitimate commerce," ushered in the single greatest expansion in the enslavement of Africans in human history. The nineteenth century spread new modalities of coercion and violence deep into the heart of the African continent, and women and children—the most vulnerable members of society—bore the brunt of these forces. Slavery expanded in response to new European markets for "legitimate" goods like palm oil (figure 1.1). The establishment of massive coastal plantations impressed whole communities into new production regimes. Far from being an

Fig. 1.1. Palm oil trading post at Sulima, by A. M. Dunlop, c. 1850
(© National Maritime Museum, Greenwich, London)

age of abolition—and if we must name epochs—the nineteenth century should more accurately be called the age of child enslavement. If I achieve anything here, I hope this book finally puts these two misplaced notions to rest.[10]

A focus on child slaves is an important undertaking for two reasons. First, it shifts the conversation away from slaves' capacities to "re-create" Africa in the New World, in the manner described by historians James Sweet and Walter Hawthorne and geographer Judith Carney, and returns a focus to the mechanics of survival in the context of trauma and distress. While I resist a revalorization of the "empty vessels" analogy of historians Kenneth Stampp and Stanley Elkins, children did not and could not hold and carry the depth of cultural knowledge displayed by adult slaves in South Carolina's rice plantations or Brazil's inquisition records. Second, the experience of child slaves also further disrupts the slavery/freedom dichotomy insofar as even when no longer de jure slaves, children were never free and autonomous. Instead they were variously wards of the state, apprentices, domestic servants, or cabin boys, and their paths toward liberty and autonomy erupted in fits and jerks, sometimes forward, sometimes backward. Indeed, scholarship on childhood in Africa is now beginning to build on the advances made by European, U.S., and world historians. Childhood studies as a subfield is grappling with the multitude of dependent statuses of children, including "rescued" former child slaves. Scholars of African children are now tussling with the complexities of recovering "multiple notions of childhood" from archival and oral records, but in this new scholarship the twentieth-century experience proliferates.[11]

Importantly, the six children at the center of this study were slaves in Africa *before* they were forcibly transported across the Atlantic. King observed that "differences in the times of their narratives matter, as well as the ages of the narrators along with the amount of time spent in slavery." When we encounter Amistad's orphans, however, their African origins reside at the core of the dispute and the substance of the trials of the survivors of the slave ship *La Amistad*. Rather than operating as a vindication of resistance or even a celebration of liberty, the narratives of Amistad's orphans are fragmented and incomplete and confound attempts at categorizing their genre. Their individual stories omit classic slave biographical tropes, such as attacking an overseer or rejecting a master's advances, and contain scant albeit tantalizing detail about their respective Middle Passages. Furthermore, unlike Douglass, Vassa, and Jacobs, who published autobiographies at the ages of twenty-seven, forty-four, and fifty, respectively, the lives of the six children ensnared in the trial emerge immediately in context of childhood. Different elements must be educed from documents produced by or with other individuals, who were often Anglo-Americans. These child narratives are genuinely unpolished and often unrehearsed stories, and until now they have remained scattered and fragmented.[12]

CHILD SLAVES AND THE ATLANTIC TRADE

The experiences of Amistad's orphans offer extraordinary and very personalized illustrations of the often overlooked but "dramatic increase in the proportion of children" in the mostly "illegal" slave trade of the nineteenth century. Whereas historians Stephanie Smallwood and Vincent Brown have shown that it was possible to transport "too many children," in the 1680s and 1790s respectively, from the early nineteenth century until the termination of the trans-Atlantic trade in the 1860s, the children among slave cargoes increased, by some estimates, from 22 to more than 50 percent. And although it may have once been acceptable to dismiss children as space-fillers or as marginal or undesirable, or to view the presence of children and infants in cargos as an indication of problems with supply, the research of Hofstee and others demonstrates that such a position is now completely untenable. Slavers purchased children for some of the same economic reasons they purchased adults, and they employed "deliberate choice." During the legal slave trade, some merchants appeared to specialize in children and infants. The numbers of infants appear to be consistently underreported in official records, and many children were misreported as adults. There is remarkable uniformity of data across slaving nations, and there was a strong market for children in the New World. The lack of substantive scholarship on children in the slave trade, until quite recently, in no way reflects historical reality.[13]

The experiences of Amistad's orphans took place at the very peak of Atlantic child transportation. As prohibitions on the slave trade expanded, slave traders turned to children in increasing numbers. These traders designed their ships with specifications "intended for children only," such as the "hellish nurseries" of the *Tragos Millas* and *Pharafoal*, with slave decks of fourteen and eighteen inches in height. Indeed, by the 1830s, boy children between the age of eight and twelve years were among the "most favourite cargoes." Girls featured less prominently in slave cargoes than boys, possibly because their acquirers in Africa valued their potential as bearers of children and did not sell them to Europeans. The peak period for child slave shipment, circa 1825–55, made it possible to specialize entirely in child transportation. In 1840, the *Jesús María* sailed from Sherbro near Sierra Leone for Havana with a cargo that was 98 percent children. Later in the decade, the *Triumfo* sailed with a cargo exclusively of children; all but 1 of its 105 Africans were between the ages of four and nine years. To be clear, these ships are not outliers. Many others existed for which we have no record. Despite the blockade of the Royal Navy, they operated with a "freeness and frankness" that surprised many.[14]

Ships transported ever greater numbers of children because markets like Cuba and Brazil demanded them, in spite of prohibitions on the trade. Whereas the British was the only naval power with the capacity to combat the illegal trade, the threat of seizure by the Royal Navy paradoxically appears to have ensured that a successful Atlantic voyage was "sufficiently profitable" to make it an inducement to Havana ship pilots, and one "not likely to be resisted." In 1840, a successful voyage with 500 slaves could net a profit of $120,000 to $130,000, according to one anonymous informant. The blockade created speculators and forced innovation in shipping technology and practice. Seized vessels offloaded huge numbers of children into Freetown, which the colony could not absorb, thereby creating a new supply of slaves for abduction and resale. The superabundance of liberated child slaves in Freetown in the 1830s, for example, meant that they were easy to seize and it guaranteed the kidnapper a quick £5 ($24) profit. The child's resale in Havana at $200 could produce a 700 percent return on the purchase price in Freetown or at the Galinhas barracoons. Even allowing for the cost of the voyage, the potential profit on child slaves was astonishing. Profits increased on both sides of the Atlantic for savvy and well-connected traders, and sellers often determined the prices of new arrivals because the clandestine nature of the activity ushered cartels into being. As African demand for consumer goods expanded in Galinhas, slavers could buy in the 1840s, by some accounts, three times as many slaves for the same quantity of tobacco or rum as a decade earlier. Witnesses like Jose Cliffe had any number of theories about why greater numbers of children appeared in slave markets in the 1830s, including that they were "smaller and pack more conveniently," endured "the effects of the voyage better," and consumed less food and water than adults. Regardless of the verifiability of such claims, it is important to consider the mechanisms of enslavement for children and the impact on children of the decline of adult enslavement.[15]

There are indeed multiple explanations for why children appear with increasing frequency in the context of the illegal trade. But among the most compelling arguments, that rise above the local and specific, is the view that children are more "malleable"—or as I prefer, more coercible. A quest for increased *coercibility* is a defining supra-characteristic of the shift from legal to illegal slave trading in societies and economies undergoing abolition. Slavers intentionally tried to circumvent accepted practices of enslavement and of emerging international law by filling ships with children because they were more readily coercible, a factor that mitigated the necessity for coercive action in slave markets and on board ships. The rationale behind this shift was multidimensional but deceptively simple. Children were more easily enslaved in Africa as abolition efforts shifted the nature and forms of enslavement and supply of slaves. They were more controllable in barracoons, less likely to jump from canoes and swim and escape, and more easy to control aboard the slave ship. As the sizes and shapes of ships changed in response to prohibition, slave holds on swifter clippers were sometimes smaller and often more secretive. Children were less likely than adults to rise up and overrun a ship. It may even have been more profitable to place two children in a space for one male adult on large steamers. And very simply upon arrival in Cuba or Brazil, one could quickly offload and sell a cargo of children: they were more easily concealed and moved from market to secondary locations; they were more easily coerced and less able than adults to contest their status as slaves.[16]

Only one of the vessels that transported Amistad's orphans is known, namely, the *Segunda Socorro*, carrying Covey in 1833. Covey's vessel comprised 53.1 percent children. The ship that transported the adults aboard *La Amistad* from Sierra Leone to Havana was typical of the period, insofar as the majority of its "cargo" was likely women and children. In an interview conducted by Yale Divinity School instructor George E. Day, through interpreters, Grabeau stated, "on board the vessel there was a large number of men, but the women and children were far the most numerous." Other reasons for the expansion in child slave cargos in this period identified by historian Jelmer Vos include decreasing shipping costs due in part to the introduction of faster American-built vessels, a reduction in crew size to cut costs, a fear of abolition on the part of Brazilian and Cuban planters, and possibly a belief that children could more easily be habituated to plantation life and were less impacted by changes in climate and nutrition. Recent studies on age differentials, disease, and mortality sustain this latter observation. Evidence about Amistad's orphans supports the view that their youth and dependency were partly responsible for them becoming "slaves" in Africa in the first place.[17]

Although African children seem to have been enslaved through many of the same tactics as captured adults, various forms of pawnship targeted children. Pawning operated in a variety of ways and was not always tied directly to enslavement, but it was considered "crucial as a way of securing credit" in slave-vending communities and thus functioned as a primary means for enslaving children. Historians Paul Lovejoy and David Richardson argue that in the town of Calabar in the Bight of Biafra "the use of human pawns to secure goods advanced against the delivery of slaves represented" an "extension of local credit arrangements to British ship captains enabling them to enforce repayment of debts in compliance with customary law." From Lovejoy and Richardson we have an impression that the very mechanics of the slave trade rested on securities afforded by pawns. But elsewhere pawning morphed from being largely a security to a "vehicle to generate slaves." Historian Roquinaldo Ferreira, describing indigenous practices in Angola and Portuguese attitudes more broadly, notes that certain groups targeted "disgraced pawns." Controlling the conversion of pawns was difficult because the practice was so "deeply ingrained." The habit of converting collateral into slaves was widespread enough that the Portuguese crown introduced additional penalties and punishments.[18]

It is often difficult to distinguish between like-minded entrepreneurs making credit arrangements and creditors who encouraged debt obligations with the knowledge that a likely unfavorable outcome might produce a slave. Eighteenth-century slave trader John Matthews noted that it was "customary" for "people of all ranks to put their children out as pledges" in the Sierra Leone River region in the 1780s. Presumably "all ranks" meant those with means and those who had pretensions, such as those Ferreira describes as desirous of "ridiculous *bagatelas*." In 1806, another Englishman, Francis B. Spilsbury, observed that "a king" might send "his wife, sister, or child, as a pawn, putting a tally round their necks; the child then runs among the slaves until exchanged" (see figure 3.1). But doubtless those of little means had the delusions of prosperity that produced unwelcome outcomes for peripheral members of their extended families. To be sure, conspicuous consumption remained a feature of coastal slave-trading communities. Pawning continued unabated after five of Amistad's orphans returned to Sierra Leone in 1841. An untold number of those sold into the trans-Atlantic trade were possibly once pawns.[19]

Traditionally only wives and children in West African society were subject to the potentially perilous transactions associated with offering family members as security for a debt. Historian Audra Diptee notes that famine and other hardships were often the cause of indebtedness leading to pawnship. Kag'ne's and Mar'gru's accounts of their own pawnship, which led to their being sold toward the coast and ultimately to becoming part of a cargo of illegal slaves, thus appear plausible and consistent with practices of the time. The two pawned girls came from large families. Girls were bonded or pawned in the context of famine and rural distress, but also because family members sought to acquire prestige items like clothing and jewelry. It is surely not inconsequential that the two children who began their journey into slavery as debt-pawns appear to be from two of the largest families among the Amistad survivors, suggesting that younger children in large families operated as a form of credit safety net. These circumstances point to abandonment of children as responses to drought and poverty in the late eighteenth century, particularly in western central Africa.[20]

The second path to child slavery in West Africa was violent abduction in contexts of conflict. Widespread sporadic internecine violence was the source of slaves for export as well as slaves for local consumption during the period of the illegal Atlantic trade in the nineteenth century. Lieutenant Frederick Edwyn Forbes of the Royal Navy described how, throughout much of the Galinhas and its hinterland, slave-trading chiefs, such as Siaka, Mana, and Amara Lalu, surrounded towns and villages and then enslaved and sold their entire populations. This second course was the fate of Covey, Ka'le, and Te'me and included capture in general wars and targeted kidnapping. Historian Mariana Candido notes that the "vulnerable situation" of women and children meant that in some instances they outnumbered men by a ratio of nine to one in war and targeted raids. Though whole families may have been enslaved together, it was probably rare for them to remain together throughout the entire process of enslavement, Middle Passage, and resale in the Americas. Ka'le was "stolen when in the street," perhaps because his community was experiencing raiding characteristic of that engulfing West Africa during a period when as many as twenty to thirty thousand slaves were shipped illegally to Cuba each year. Covey was stolen from his parents' home before being sold toward the coast. All but one of fourteen known slave autobiographers mentioning their capture in Africa left there as children.[21]

THE CONTOURS OF ILLEGALITY IN THE "AGE OF ABOLITION"

We know of Amistad's orphans because the ships they were transported on were captured and their "cargo" liberated. Were it not for this exceptionalism, Mar'gru, Kag'ne, Te'me, Antonio, Ka'le, and Covey may have remained nameless numbers in a database—or even more invisible and anonymous. The vessels forcibly relocating the children, and many others, were seized because they were evading the emerging international patchwork of laws and treaties banning slave shipments, first, in the North Atlantic and, shortly after, in the South Atlantic. Although slavery remained legal within the Spanish colonies and the southern United States, and a variety of forms of slavery were endemic to Africa during this period, Amistad's orphans were forcibly transported illegally in direct violation of international law, part of what historian Michael Zeuske calls the "hidden Atlantic." Put most simply, enslavement and slavery were legal in locations A and B, but there was no legal passage between A and B for those enslaved. This book thus drives a critical wedge in this important historical intersection, a period all too frequently misidentified as the "age of abolition."[22]

The nineteenth-century Atlantic world was the crucible of global abolition activities and anti-trafficking laws. The legislative, diplomatic, and military engagements characteristic of the so-called age of abolition speak volumes about European and North America attitudes toward Africa and the essentialized relationship imagined between Africans and slavery. Many Europeans and North Americans believed that Africa was a natural site for slavery and that enslavement was the natural condition of Africans. Propelled by these beliefs, Europeans and North Americans embarked on a series of initiatives to transform African societies and economies, beginning with the abolition of slavery. Indeed, from the era of the trans-Atlantic slave trade, via early imperial expansion, to the mature period of colonial rule, Africa has been the site of important experiments in antislavery legislation. Over the course of two hundred years, as the slave trades and slavery were progressively abolished in different regions of the globe, the African continent was often among the first regions to experience broad abolition experiments. And as the many stages of abolition transformed what was previously a legal economic activity into an illegal and illicit practice, new legislative responses were spawned. African social, political, and economic systems reshaped themselves in response to successive attempts to extinguish slavery and slave trades. Viewed this way, each wave of antislavery activity provides insight into nature of slavery as well as the legal framework of abolition.[23]

The narratives of Amistad's orphans suggest how nineteenth-century illicit slavers, like the Spaniard Pedro Blanco, reconceptualized indigenous practice to conceal their activities. In coastal African communities slave traders used slippery terms, such as "bonded person" or simply "adopted children," thus disguising illegal slavery as "cultural placement" when their activities or locations came under attack from missionaries or colonial officers. A pawn could be held for the length of a loan, and by working for a creditor or a creditor's lineage the pawn paid off interest on a loan. Pawns could be redeemed outright, or as was often the case with girls, they were married to their creditor and the bridewealth paid off the debt. Aside from a means of acquiring capital or providing security for debt, pawnship has been viewed by historians Toyin Falola and Lovejoy as a mechanism of constructing kinship. Falola and Lovejoy suggest the existence of a possible pawnship "belt" tied to the "spread of market forces." They also suggest that larger political structures may have been more reliant on slaves, while smaller, stateless groups depended on bonding and pawnship. The Galinhas region and its hinterland was occupied by various language communities, including Vai, Mende, Sherbro, and Krim speakers, who resided in polities that were somewhere between small states and acephalous (decentralized or state-less) and operated within dynamic local and regional trade networks. Blanco may thus have chosen the location because indigenous practices provided an additional cover for his illegal activities.[24]

Amistad's orphans found themselves caught in a web of illicit slave trading spun by four Spanish Cubans and their accomplices, with operations and investments in two hemispheres, three continents, and at least five countries and dominions. Like many thousands before them, the children were embroiled in an enterprise spearheaded by Blanco, operated by the Catalan Cuban José Ruiz Carrías, financed in part by the Spanish Cuban Pedro Martínez and his investors, and fueled by the shipowners Ramón and Damián Ferrer. In the 1830s, the Cuban economy was buoyant and expanding, and slave traders "could well afford to run some risks." Ramón Ferrer was involved in a complex interior Cuban trade, for which Puerto Príncipe was a primary entrepôt. He and others were exploring the development of new sugar factories and plantations in an area more traditionally known for cattle ranching. Blanco and another collaborator, the German Huguenot Daniel Botafeur, had been for some time in business with Ruiz, who was from a large family of merchant seaman, and had a cemented relationship supplying Martínez and Company with slaves from Galinhas. Galinhas was known to be a site of rice cultivation, containing many Africans skilled in the backbreaking work of preparing new terrain for cultivation. It was an area that provided discrete locations to avoid detection by the British. Ramón Ferrer turned to the Martínez slave vendors in Havana to bring slaves to Puerto Príncipe. Martínez and Company drew on Blanco for his primary supply, and Ruiz both captained vessels and engaged others, such as the Ferrer brothers and Hugh Boyle of Baltimore, to run the illicit gauntlet across the Atlantic from Galinhas to Cuba. In historian David Eltis's memorable phrase, Martínez and Company "adapted comfortably" to the pressures of the British navy blockade.[25]

Against the "impunity" of an "emboldened" Cuban Atlantic slave commerce, the centrality of illegality to the broader story emerges most vividly in the response of the attorneys or "proctors" for the Amistad Africans. In the richly tautological text of January 7, 1840, the "answer of S. Staples, R. Baldwin, and T. Sedgwick" to the "several libels of Lt. Gedney et al. and Pedro Montes and Jose Ruiz" the respondents retort,

> That they and each of them are natives of Africa and were born free, and ever since have been and still of right are and ought to be free and not slaves, as is said in several libels or claims pretended or surmised and that they were never

domiciled in the Island of Cuba, or in the Dominions of the Queen of Spain, or subject to the laws thereof, that on or about the 15th day of April 1839 they and each of them were in the lands of their nativity unlawfully kidnapped and forcibly and wrongfully by certain persons to them unknown, who were then and there unlawfully and piratically engaged in the slave trade, between the Coast of Africa and the island of Cuba contrary to the will of these Respondents unlawfully, and under circumstances of great cruelty, transported to the said island of Cuba, for the unlawful purpose of being sold as slaves, and were then illegally landed for the purpose of the aforesaid.

The multiple charges of illegality and actions to evade the legal regime of the Atlantic in this and similar court documents put the context of the illicit origins of Amistad's orphans in stark relief.[26]

Amistad's orphans were ensnared by the illicit Atlantic trade in spite of, and possibly because of, massive international efforts to abolish slave trading and slavery. The first acts of abolition were promulgated in Europe and North America, and their focus was on the origins of the trans-Atlantic slave trade in Africa. Anti-trafficking efforts extended outwardly both spatially and temporally from continental Africa. An examination of successive attempts to legislate abolition demonstrates the centrality of the West African region to anti-trafficking initiatives insofar as some advocates of legislative abolition, such as William Wilberforce, Thomas Clarkson, and Thomas Buxton, imagined ending slavery on the continent as the teleology of a larger ideological enterprise. Similarly, mechanisms to combat evasion of new laws banning the trade first focused on West Africa before being extended to other areas. For example, naval patrols, liberation courts, colonies composed of recaptives, and other physical realizations of legislative goals fanned out from West Africa across the Atlantic to the New World.[27]

In this context of expanding illegality, categories and identities emerged and were reinforced by subsequent legislation. Normative practices of enslavement shifted in the context of the emergence and expansion of international abolitionist legal frameworks in the Atlantic world from the early 1800s onward. After 1788, when Dolben's Act limited the number of slaves carried by British vessels by tonnage, thus raising transportation costs and diminishing the incentive for slavers to ship low-value slaves, such as children, the numbers of children temporarily declined. But soon after, women and children become increasingly visible as objects of enslavement and subjects of antislavery legislation because slavers actively attempted to circumvent controls on the slave trade. Indeed, Vos has argued that the proportion of child slaves grew after Britain withdrew from the trade and reached especially high levels during the illegal phase of trafficking in West Central Africa. At that time, practically one in two slaves sold in the Congo ports was under fifteen years old. Illegality was thus a defining element uniting the transportation experiences, if not the enslavement in Africa, of Amistad's orphans.[28]

The illegality of their condition is further underscored by the mechanisms whereby they acquired degrees of liberty and autonomy. Former owners did not free the six individuals, nor could the children purchase their freedom. Rather, liberation from illegal slavery resulted variously at the hands of naval officers, court judgments, and, in the case of Antonio, by fleeing north to Canada. Illegal trans-Atlantic slaving operated in the context of multiple, sometimes overlapping legal regimes. Amistad's orphans passed through at least six separate moments of illegality and eleven separate legal jurisdictions. When the ship transporting Covey, the *Segunda Soccoro*, was captured in 1833, it was one of several seized that year by the Royal Navy. Antonio entered Cuba on an unknown ship and thereafter served as Ramón Ferrer's cabin boy on Ferrer's several illicit runs along the Cuban coast, and between Sierra Leone and Cuba. By 1838–39, when an unnamed vessel carrying Kag'ne, Te'me, Ka'le, and Mar'gru, sailed from an illicit harbor on the Sierra Leone coast to Cuba, trade in the North Atlantic was completely banned to all parties.

The "illegal" North Atlantic slave trade operated under tightening legal constraints established over six decades between 1792 and 1867, but it remained chronically underfunded and lacked enforcement. The ban on British-flagged and American vessels transporting slaves came into effect in 1808. From about the same period the British used Freetown, Sierra Leone, as the command center for its antislaving naval patrol. A treaty in 1810 slowly eroded the Portuguese trade, which was then banned in the North Atlantic in 1815. In 1817, Louis XVIII decreed the abolition of the French slave trade, Portugal conceded to the British Royal Navy the "right of search" of suspected slave vessels, and the British established Mixed Commissions to regulate the trade south of the equator. A similar treaty between Spain and Britain abolished the slave trade north of the equator and was expanded to encompass the entire Atlantic effective May 30, 1820. In 1820, a U.S. law declared the American slave trade an act of piracy punishable by death. In these and other ways over several decades, the concept of illegality, via bilateral and multilateral treaty, if not the enforcement as such, fanned out across the North and South Atlantic.

Amistad's orphans transgressed this expanding illegality at six crucial points. Part of the zone on the African mainland whence the children came was off limits to export-oriented slave trading because it was the hinterland to the

British-protected territory of Sierra Leone; the North Atlantic transportation route itself was illegal under the international treaties in force, as was the sale of newly arrived Africans (*bozales*) in New World Spain (Cuba). The subsequent smuggling of four children from Havana, along the coast to La Guanaja near Puerto Príncipe (Camagüey today), aboard *La Amistad* was also banned. When Ka'le and Antonio were imprisoned, and the three girls placed under the guardianship of the New Haven jailer Colonel Stanton Pendleton and his wife, they were registered as Pendleton's slaves, which sat uncomfortably with Connecticut's Nonimportation Act of 1774 and the "gradual and piecemeal" law that had progressively ended slavery in the state from 1784, as well as federal law that deemed children to be "incapable" of "the crime of murder or piracy." Finally, Antonio's continued detention was in tension with the final judgment of the Supreme Court, a situation that must have greatly contributed to his being spirited away to Montreal before he could be handed over to the Spanish consul and returned to Ferrer's widow in Cuba.[29]

Ultimately the Supreme Court determined that *La Amistad*'s "cargo" comprised people "unlawfully kidnapped" in Africa "and forcibly and wrongfully carried on board a certain vessel," then illegally imported into Cuba (and crucially *not* illegally imported into the United States). The primary adjudicating documents with respect to the survivors—Pinckney's Treaty of 1795 between the United States and Spain pertaining to the treatment of parties, vessels, and cargo and the Adams-Onís Treaty of 1819—were deemed inapplicable. The Africans were not property and therefore not subject to the law of salvage; nor were they fugitives, murderers, or criminals. Rather, they were free individuals whose "lives and liberties" were to be restored.[30]

Amistad's orphans voyaged through and became subject to numerous legal and quasi-legal jurisdictions, some unique and others overlapping, during their multiple passages to and from the Americas. At each step their statuses changed and their civic personhood and access to social protections shifted. They had begun their lives in the familial legal systems of one of several different language communities inhabiting an area today known as Sierra Leone, Liberia, and Guinea-Conakry. Depending on their respective paths to enslavement, they were bonded or pawned, or kidnapped and sold, subject to local African systems of either pawnship or abduction and ransom. Subsequently, they were imprisoned in barracoons in the vicinity of Lomboko or neighboring settlements in the swampy coastal flat of the Galinhas region of West Africa, where they experienced their first European-style incarceration. As Spanish, Cuban, and Luso-African slavers operated the barracoons of Blanco, proprietary claims over "merchandise" were subject to Spanish monarchical or Brazilian imperial law, which prioritized, among other things, general commercial laws of property and recognized judges' authority to dispense royal privileges to particular slave traders. Upon sale to a maritime slaver, the children became subject to the almost absolute authority of the ship's captain or pilot within the wider realm of international maritime law, including the treaty obligations of the monarchical power whose flag the captain flew.[31]

Once aboard slave vessels Amistad's orphans' legal itineraries took many twists and turns. Covey's recapture and liberation from an Uruguayan-flagged vessel by the British in 1833 sent him via the Mixed Commission court in Freetown to a Church Missionary Society (CMS) school, then into the service of the Royal Navy as an apprentice, and finally under court-ordered subpoena into U.S. federal jurisdiction. Antonio likely entered Cuba illegally sometime in the mid-1830s and thereafter was purchased as a slave by Ferrer. The other four children upon arrival in Cuba in early 1839 became subject to the Spanish monarchical law prevailing in the colony, which guaranteed property rights conveyed through resale. Upon boarding *La Amistad* with Antonio in Havana harbor, they remained under Spanish law but were again subject to maritime law once the slave revolt diverted the schooner beyond Cuban waters.

Once U.S. authorities seized *La Amistad*, the five children, now including Antonio, became subject to international and U.S. interpretations of maritime laws of seizure and salvage in international waters. Upon landing in New Haven they became subject to Connecticut law, under the exclusions of the U.S. Constitution, and specified U.S. federal law; depending on their (as yet undetermined) standing as African persons or Spanish property, they were also subject to international agreements signed by the United States with Spain. Here they met Covey for the first time, and the six remained in close physical proximity until March 1841. As U.S. federal law was still relatively undefined, the Supreme Court ruling specifically focused on the interstices between the international law of nations and specific treaty obligations between the Spanish crown and the U.S. republic. After the decision, Antonio, a fugitive from justice (if not also from slavery), entered Canada a free individual via the illegal Underground Railroad. He disappeared into the illicit world of African and African American fugitive slaves in Montreal. The other five returned to Sierra Leone and were once again subject, first to maritime law, then to British colonial authority in Sierra Leone, and subsequently to informal western Christian jurisdiction that enveloped the missionary compound at Kaw-Mendi. They also again accessed the complex iterations of customary law operating in local communities and neighboring territories, including widespread initiation ceremonies, marriage, and even slave trading.[32]

Just as the illegality of their transportation impacted and indeed arbitrated all decisions about them and on their behalf, self-knowledge of their precarious condition may have informed the children's own actions. The children certainly had some awareness of the illegality of their circumstances. Mar'gru reported that some of the adult Africans had initially embarked from Sierra Leone aboard a ship that had been chased by the British navy. That vessel returned to the coast and hastily emptied its human cargo, whereupon the British seized the empty hull. The Africans were subsequently boarded into another unnamed vessel for Cuba. Indeed, all manner of subterfuge was employed to evade Britain's antislaving West Africa Squadron. Deception and duplicity resided at the very core of the illicit Atlantic traffic.[33]

With the requisite contextual information, the lives of Amistad's orphans can, and do, speak to the broader experience of tens of thousands of others enslaved during the nineteenth century. Whereas the definition of "child" remained unclear in many circles, by the nineteenth century slave traders increasingly identified children as a useful way to thwart restrictions and prohibitions imposed by European parliaments and international treaties. But slave traders did not suddenly stumble upon large supplies of child slaves in Africa. Rather, they intentionally sought out children informed with the knowledge that there were willing buyers in the Americas. Children were not space-fillers or afterthoughts but reflected an intentional strategy. By the 1830s and 1840s the significance of child slavery for the economic success of the massive illegal slave trade was undeniable.

Establishing the centrality of child slavery in the nineteenth-century Atlantic world is important for understanding both child slavery and child slave emancipation. It shifts the conversation to aspects that are relevant to children, namely, the mechanics of survival in the context of trauma and distress. African children did not bring with them to the Americas the depth of cultural knowledge displayed by adult slaves, but they had no less full and dynamic experiences during their ordeal. A focus on children also invigorates debates about the nature of liberty insofar as emancipated former child slaves were rarely truly free and autonomous. We must examine the successor statuses of former child slaves—as wards of the state, apprentices, domestic servants, or ship stewards. A child's exit from slavery was rarely linear; it was intermittent and interrupted and involved multiple mechanisms curtailing autonomy as the next chapters demonstrate.

2

THE ORIGINS OF AMISTAD'S ORPHANS

The dispute about the origins of the survivors of *La Amistad* resided at the heart of the trials in U.S. courts, 1839–41. In an effort to prove African origins, the defense team—Roger Sherman Baldwin, Seth Staples, and Theodore Sedgwick—developed sophisticated arguments built around information about the illegal African slave trade, Cuban slave systems, and African language, geography, and culture. Before the Supreme Court in January 1841, the expertise and evidence assembled appeared overwhelming. Justice Joseph Story observed, "It is plain beyond controversy, . . . that these negroes never were the lawful slaves of Ruiz or Montez or of any other Spanish subjects. They are natives of Africa, and were kidnapped there, and were unlawfully transported to Cuba, in violation of the laws and treaties . . . cogent and irresistible is the evidence in this respect." Notwithstanding the trenchant language, obtaining the evidence was hardly simple or straightforward. Establishing the African origins of the individuals was a product of arduous research, expert testimony, and data analysis, all deeply influenced by the interpretative perspective offered by Covey. But it also recast the identity of Amistad's orphans as "Mendi."[1]

Over the course of several months, from the initial discovery of the Africans on Long Island until the proceedings of the district and circuit courts in Connecticut, several theories were espoused and dismissed about the origins of the survivors. Africa was clearly the original embarkation continent in the opinion of the defense team, but where precisely was the subject of much discussion. Establishing which of the African "tribes" became a necessary first step. Speculation about the children's origins, identities, and languages ran the gamut of known slave sources and included Congo, Angola, Senegambia, Mandingo territory, and elsewhere. After Covey and Charles Pratt, cook on the *Buzzard*, joined the legal team as interpreters, a clearer picture of the adults' origins emerged. The precise origin of the children, however, was further complicated by the inclusion of Antonio.[2]

The complexity of the children's narratives was obscured by a concerted attempt to affix a Mendi identity onto the adult males in order to establish their West African origins and thus their illegal importation into Cuba. In this chapter, I first review the evolution of the Mendi identity myth and then examine how, in the context of the trial, the focus on origins embedded a Mendi identity within a grand unifying story grounded by an adult masculine metanarrative. My analysis of what I call the "Atlantic contextual argument" reveals how the defense team triangulated the origins of the Africans to establish the legal basis for their liberty. In so doing, however, they erased important details about the origins of some of the group and more or less abandoned discussion of the children. The supremacy of an adult, male metanarrative is a significant obstacle to understanding the complexity of Amistad's orphans' experiences.

It makes little sense to think of Amistad's orphans simply as Mende in the way many think of the adults, because the plasticity of childhood resulted in the temporary affixing of many and often overlapping "tribal" appellations. Indeed, current scholarly interest in establishing the ethnicities of enslaved Africans is so adult-focused that it becomes an impediment to understanding child slave origins generally. Revisiting the geographical data about the children's origins collected during the period with the benefit of more than a century of multi-disciplinary scholarship about this region and its history allows a hypothetical reconstruction of their possible origins, incorporating evidence about language, "tribe" or ethnicity, commerce, and geography. Ample evidence points to the region inland from the coast—a subregion identified as Galinhas and its hinterland—but evidence for Mende is more equivocal. Greater precision is possible for some of the individual children, and new evidence, such as a country marks, may yet enable further exactitude.[3]

THE MYTH OF MENDI ORIGINS

Before the Supreme Court in January 1841, Baldwin consistently referred to the adult males as "Africans" and as "freemen." But before he could do this with any certainty, their African origins needed to be established before the district court. Thus the prelude to the first trials was marked by a concerted effort to establish an African identity and origins with the assistance of translators. Within weeks of the Africans' arrival in New Haven, the received wisdom among the Amistad Committee became that the survivors were "from the Mandi or Mandy country." Gibbs, Tappan, and others repeatedly reinforced this notion, and they strove for homogeneity in news reports, fundraising pleas and pamphlets, and legal arguments. After Gibbs located Covey in New York and communication in the Mende language became possible, the need for using other languages spoken by some of the men (such as Gola, Temne, Kisi, Bandi, or Bulom) dissipated. Tappan and others remained cognizant of the existence of other languages and "tribes" among the group, and polyvocal narratives resurfaced after the Supreme Court decision. But from September 1839 until March 1841 the ethnic heterogeneity of the group was subsumed by the primary legal objective of winning their release. And in the view of the defense team, a single "tribal" moniker provided a more coherent basis for a legal argument about African origins and illegal importation to Cuba; an ethnographic argument had little value. As a Mendi identity for the adult majority congealed, a parallel Mendi narrative about the children emerged.[4]

Early press accounts exhibited a speculative tone about the specific "tribal" origins of the Africans, but a discernible shift unfolded as the trials approached. During the first unsuccessful habeas corpus hearing for the three girls in September 1839, a belief that the children were "Mandingo" and spoke a "dialect of Mandingo" soon gave way to "Mandi." During the same period, Tappan's newspaper sometimes employed the term "African," but more frequently it identified individuals by name. Pro-slavery papers, by contrast, routinely employed a variety of terms now often considered derogatory—including "blacks," "Negroes," or "niggers"—and referred to the imprisoned adults as "merry as crickets, and as satisfied as pigs in clover." References to "Mandi" and "Mendi" abounded during the September criminal case and civil trial in Hartford and New Haven, the October civil trial in New York, and the January trial in New Haven, and they began to filter into the press. When "Fulah" (Fuliwa) and Cinquez sued Ruiz and Montes in New York City for damages for battery and false imprisonment, the summonses to appear described them as Africans "of the Mendi tribe." Even anti-abolitionist newspapers repeated this description, while still employing more derogatory epithets. Not even Covey—the "Mendi interpreter"—was spared abuse in the heated public discussion.[5]

When Gibbs testified, he explained that "the great body of the prisoners speak the Mendi language," and he expressly omitted extended discussion of other tongues. As a professor of theology in Yale's School of Divinity, Gibbs was "much engaged in linguistic pursuits," according him the gravitas to profess a scholarly understanding of African languages, about which he actually knew little to nothing. Gibbs explained how he approached his task, situating it within the experience of the acquisition of a mother tongue. "I have spent a good deal of time in investigating the principles of language. . . . My knowledge of the Mendi language I have acquired from James Covey in the first instance, in the same manner as I have derived my knowledge of the English language from my parents. I have evidence that it is the English language from my intercourse with others." The Africans themselves also indicated that an inability to speak Mendi distinguished them from other non-Europeans of non-African origins, including the deceased Celestino, Ferrer's slave. On cross-examination, Cinquez stated, "The cook could not speak the Mendi language but used some words that they could understand."[6]

In addition to engaging the general public, scholarly and pro-colonization communities were mobilized. Gibbs took a role in disseminating the Mendi narrative in scholarly circles. In a letter reprinted by the American Colonization Society, Gibbs pontificated in the grandiose style of a mid-nineteenth-century explorer. "It is the practice of scientific travellers to give each nation or tribe the name by which they designate themselves. In conformity with this principle, we shall call these Africans *Mendis*, and their country the *Mendi* country." Gibbs later published the first scholarly articles about the Mende and Vai languages. The establishment of a Mendi identity was very effective. Once Judson's ruling cemented the survivors' African origin, the Mendi emphasis had served its immediate purpose.[7]

After the U.S. Supreme Court delivered its verdict, and the Africans relocated to Farmington, efforts to understand their background and origins continued. Records from the summer of 1841 show that Gibbs and others embraced the Africans' multilingual and multiethnic background. Gibbs knew that the "Africans of the Amistad" were "mostly of one tribe," namely, "Mendi." But he also revealed that five languages were spoken. "One of the Africans speaks the Bullom described by Winterbottom and Prichard. Two speak the Timmani of the same writers. The Bullom and Timmani countries are well known. One of the African speaks the Kissi of Prichard. The Kissi people are situated on the waters which flow into the Atlantic and south of the sources of the Niger. Another of the Africans speaks a language which I suppose to be the Gola or Gurrah." The polyglossia of the Africans was clearer to their interlocutors. One of their Farmington teachers, John Booth observed, "there are five languages spoken" by the Amistad survivors, "*viz*. Mendi, Bullom, Time, Kon-na, and Gora, some speak two, some three and some four of these."[8]

Notwithstanding these later concessions, in the wake of the initial trial, efforts continued to consolidate public opinion around a Mendi origin. The widely circulated pamphlet of John Warner Barber describing "information relative to the Mendi people and country" was sold to raise funds for their upkeep. The mystique accorded to the origin myth by Yale student Benjamin Griswold resonated with a nineteenth-century public fascinated by the "dark continent." He explained, "Never has it been visited, so far as we know, by a white man." Griswold took his audience on an armchair voyage of discovery. Other explorers had passed north, south, and east, but "these Africans tell us they have never seen a white man." Griswold explained the dress of the Mendi, the "painful process of tattooing" and the "incision of the knife," and the practices of tooth extraction and sharpening. He described the physical layout of the Mendi village, and burial and funeral rituals. And a brief discussion of gender and marital relations revealed how the Mendi woman is "made to feel inferior to her husband." The difficulty of safeguarding the Africans' liberty was tied to knowledge of the "Mendi language," which "so far as we have been able to learn, has never been reduced to writing." Furthermore, as "the natives" have no "characters by which they retain and transmit a history of passing events," the education of the Africans and the acquisition of linguistic knowledge were portrayed as a collective community project.[9]

Close scrutiny of Griswold's account reveals the complex interplay between the different ethnic and language groups of the survivors. Griswold, for example, appeared to cite the tooth extraction of the Kono speaker "Konoma" as an example of a Mende custom, seamlessly connecting it with other rites, such as tattooing and scarification. But even when apparent disagreement emerged between the adults about the ethnic meaning of a specific custom or practice, Griswold's narrative reinforced the homogeneity of Mende origin and language. "The observation was then made, you say 'yes' and you say 'no' here is a contradiction; do you both tell the truth? Fuli after a moment's delay replied, 'Merica all, all, all' extending his right hand and turning round through half a circle, 'so Mendi, all, all, all,' accompanying the words with the same gesture and motion of the body. The idea he wished to convey was this: 'America is a great country, so is Mendi; and because a custom is prevalent in one part of it, it is not necessary to conclude that it is universal.'" In Griswold's narrative the unintelligibility of what might today be considered multiethnic pluralism was swiftly silenced by an accusation of lying. The heterogeneity of the Amistad survivors' origins and languages was thus erased by a commitment to reproducing a coherent Mendi myth with profound consequence for the origin of the children.[10]

THE ATLANTIC CONTEXTUAL ARGUMENT
AND A MASCULINE METANARRATIVE

In the opinion of the defense team one issue could conceivably resolve all legal questions. If it could be established that the Africans were *born* in Africa, it would quash debate about whether they were legally slaves in Cuba, regardless of whether they were transported legally before the prohibition of the Atlantic trade. In order to advance a coherent argument, the defense moved to privilege one place of origin. After the Amistad Committee debated the conflicting stories from the adult survivors, the defense team settled on the "Mendi country" and "tribe" as the most accurate representation of origins. The Mendi myth formed the backbone of the assertion that the Amistad survivors were African. The defense focused on proving the origin of the Africans by attempting to pinpoint the languages of the men, collecting their narratives in their own words, and setting them against what was known about slavery in Cuba and the illegal African slave trade. The strategy employed in court in New Haven consisted of affirmative claims triangulating the Africans' identities, what I describe as an Atlantic contextual argument. One unforeseen consequence, however, was the emergence of an adult metanarrative that further obfuscated the children's origins.

The Atlantic contextual argument consisted of three components. Gibbs and his team of students worked closely with the Africans after locating several translators, and he testified himself in November 1839 and January 1840. The Irish abolitionist, medical doctor, and former judge Richard Robert Madden, learning of the case while in Jamaica, stopped on his way to London, was interviewed by Judge Judson, and provided a written submission about his "examination" of the adults, set against his West Indian experiences. American author and Atlantic traveler David Francis Bacon also testified in November and January, although by 1840 Judson had already "remarked that he was fully convinced that the men were recently from Africa." The three aspects of expertise complemented one another, providing the Atlantic contextual argument and triangulating the African identities of the survivors. The argument also erased inconsistencies that had emerged as a result of the collection of multiple narratives from different individuals.[11]

Gibbs testified in person twice. His team had worked with the survivors since August 1839. The information assembled by Gibbs and his team of students and alumni is known today through primary sources and published fragments. To date, no personal notebooks have been found. The primary sources comprising this information include miscellaneous correspondence, Barber's 1840 pamphlet, publications by Gibbs in the *American Journal of Science,* and the record of the trials in the circuit and district courts, where Gibbs testified on November 19, 1839, and January 7, 1840. Gibbs's testimony was designed to emphasize the African origins of the captives by highlighting information that they could only convey if they were Africa-born. At that moment all manner of theories were circulating about their individual backgrounds. The goal was to undercut the impression, created by the attorneys for Ruiz and Montes, Ralph Ingersoll and William Hungerford, that they had been legally imported into Cuba.[12]

Gibbs described an interactive, collaborative, and deductive methodology that operated within a wider language documentation project. He distinguished language from dialect. "I made out a vocabulary of the Mendi language from James Covey, and I am now able by means of it to converse with twenty or thirty of these Africans. They cannot speak the Spanish language. There are among them several different dialects." In his account, "Mendi" was the Africans' language, while "Bullom" and "Timmani" were reduced to "dialects." Gibbs's contribution comprised basic linguistic documentation of a form still very much in its infancy.[13]

The modus operandi of Gibbs drew on the activities of missionaries, such as Henry Brunton and Gustavus Reinhold Nyländer, who sought to translate Christian texts into indigenous languages in order to aid proselytization. But Gibbs was approaching language documentation from an alternative perspective; it was not so much a mechanism to spread "the word of God" to African pagans, but rather a means to spread the "proof" of their African origins to receptive audiences. Gibbs discerned the Mendi identity of some of the captives by constructing a basic numerical vocabulary within which he located Covey and Pratt. The data subsequently collected were informed by a central assumption that resonated with a receptive audience: such information could not be elicited if it were not true.[14]

What Gibbs ultimately accomplished was a basic form of language documentation, but the press did not uncritically accept his "competency" as "a linguist." Yet he held his own and pushed back on cross-examination. In his first written deposition he had declared, "From the language and manners of these negroes I have formed a decided opinion that they are native Africans and recently from Africa." In January 1840 he expanded his explanation of the importance of language to a determination of whether the "captives" were recently arrived from Africa or had resided for years in Cuba, as their documents indicated. He observed that regardless of the Spanish names in the documents, the names they had given themselves each corresponded to a place, object, or thing "in Mendi," and he added his own scholarly twist: if they had been in Cuba for years, their names would have been "corrupted" in form and sound. Judson interrupted Gibbs's second oral testimony by stating that he was "fully convinced that the men were from Africa, and that it was unnecessary to take up time in establishing that fact."[15]

Similar to Gibbs's testimony, the information conveyed to the court by Madden consisted of an oral interview and cross-examination in November 1839 and a "deposition" read in court in January 1840. Madden's knowledge base was quite different, however, and his contribution focused on the Caribbean dimensions. The information he provided might be more accurately portrayed as participant observation. In contrast to the knowledge of African language and culture conveyed by Gibbs, Madden focused on undermining assumptions about slavery and the experience of African slaves in Cuba. The objective in deploying Madden was not so much to prove African origins as to substantiate how entirely dependent the Cuban economy remained on the importation of slaves, *illegally*, from Africa.

Doubts surfaced about the survivors' African origins because of the fragility of the defense team's linguistic premise. Opposing counsel first raised questions about the language-based argument in September. Under cross-examination during the habeas corpus trial of the girls, James Ferry (identified as "Perry" in the record) asserted that he "had an opportunity of speaking the Gallinas language once or twice a-week when he could get a chance of visiting a [West Indian] plantation, where the natives were Gallinas." Attorney Hungerford seized on this. He observed "that they were unable to speak the Spanish language, is not strange. They have a large number of slaves on a plantation—a small colony—they are put on a plantation and remain there for years, entirely ignorant of all language except their own, which is continued by the mother of the children. This is the case with a great portion of the younger part of the slaves in the Island of Cuba. Nor does it appear, from any evidence before the Court, that they were not imported from some other island." He thus cast doubt on the linguistic argument and raised the possibility that the Africans were imported into Cuba from another island, possibly Spanish or French, where slavery was still legal, in spite of the fact that such an act was in itself illegal. But Ferry had distinguished between learning the Gallina language initially while "a good while" in Gallina territory "better than a year," and then keeping "up his knowledge of the Gallinas language, by opportunities of talking with persons who have come from Africa." This important distinction was not lost on those with language expertise and knowledge of Cuban slave systems.[16]

In the preliminary hearing in November this argument resurfaced in a modified form, namely as the idea that Africans maintained their language for many years after arriving in Cuba. Madden's experience was thus introduced to foreclose this avenue and to shift the focus to Cuban slavery and its dependence on illegal slave imports. He stated, "The native language of the Africans is not often continued for a long time on certain plantations. It has been to me a matter of astonishment at the shortness of time in which the language of the negroes is disused, and the Spanish language adopted and acquired." Baldwin used Madden to substantiate the argument that the captives were new to Cuba and to evidence that slave smuggling was ongoing, building on the advances made by Gibbs. His testimony thus undermined the opposing hypothesis. On cross-examination *in camera* he was quite unyielding.[17]

Madden's expertise on slavery was indeed considerable. He was familiar with Caribbean slave systems, the origins of slaves, the nature of the slave trade, and the conditions in which slaves lived on ships and on plantations. Employed in the British civil service from 1833, Madden served as a justice of the peace in Jamaica and was one of six special magistrates overseeing Jamaican emancipation, according to the terms of the 1833 Slavery Abolition Act. From 1835 he was Superintendent of the Freed Africans in Havana. In 1839 he became the investigating officer into the slave trade on the west coast of Africa. But this background also exposed him to accusations of bias. Elements of his affidavit circulated in the press in November 1839, prior to it officially entering the court record in January 1840, and attempts were made to discredit him.[18]

Indeed, it was perhaps fortunate for the defense team that Madden was not available for a more public cross-examination. In writing, Madden had conceded that he "was not acquainted with the dialects of the African tribes." But he nonetheless used every opportunity to reinscribe the depth of his expertise. He declared, "I speak this, from a very intimate knowledge of the condition of the negroes in Cuba, from frequent visits to plantations, and journeys in the interior; and, on this subject, I think I can say my knowledge is as full as any person's can be." By regularly inserting his experience into his narrative he amplified his credibility. He was thus able to describe the conditions of Cuban slaves, corroborating the survivors' accounts. He visited a Cuban *barracón* (barrack or jail) and claimed to have spoken to the owner of the depot where the sale of the very same Africans had taken place. He described how Cuban authorities "winked at the slave trade in return for $10 to $15 a slave," used fraudulent documents to deceive inspectors, and would without hesitation kill the Amistad blacks should they be returned to Cuba.[19]

Madden's expertise rested on his observation and participation. He furnished the Atlantic contextual argument with a Caribbean perspective that made the captives' story plausible. He also had legal stature, having served in an international court—the "Mixed Commissions" that operated in Sierra Leone, Cuba, and Brazil, examining, and liberating smuggled African slaves. He was familiar with terminology employed by Spanish Cubans to describe different types of slaves, and he observed, "From my knowledge of oriental habits, and of the appearance of the newly imported slaves in Cuba, I have no doubt of those negroes of the Amistad being *bona fide* Bozal negroes, quite newly imported from Africa. I have a full knowledge of the subject of slavery—slave trade in

Cuba; and I know that no law exists, or has existed since the year 1820, that sanctions the introduction of negroes into the island of Cuba, from Africa for the purpose of making slaves, or being held in slavery; and, that all such Bozal negroes, as those recently imported are called, are legally free; and no law, common or statute, exists there, by which they can be held in slavery." Madden importantly declared that having examined the Africans, he could say with "tolerable certainty" they were recently from Africa. After examining the *traspasso* (or movement permits) granted to Ruiz to transport the forty-nine adult males, he described the use of the term *ladino* as "totally inapplicable."[20]

Because of his extensive experience examining Africans released from seized illegal ships, and the documentation often accompanying such illegal importations, Madden's testimony more closely resembled that of a forensic document specialist. He noted, "To have obtained these documents from the governor, for *bona fide* Bozal negroes, and have described them in the application for it, as ladinos, was evidently a fraud, but nothing more than such an application and the payment of the necessary fees would be required to procure it, as there is never any inquiry or inspection of the negroes on the part of the governor or his officers, nor is there any oath required from the applicant. I further state, that the above documents are manifestly inapplicable to the Africans of the Amistad." Madden's testimony not only jeopardized the documentary record produced by Ruiz and Montes, but he also raised the curtain on government corruption in Cuba and American collusion with illegal Cuban operations.[21]

The final installment in the Atlantic contextual argument was the testimony of Bacon. Like Gibbs, Bacon testified in November 1839 and again in January 1840. Although Judson had declared himself convinced of the African origins of the purported "cargo," Baldwin continued with the introduction of new testimony, partly to underscore the extent of the illegal operations in the late 1830s. Bacon is recorded as stating that he most recently left the West African coast on July 13, 1839. "He knew a place called Dumbokoro by the Spaniards: it was an island in the river or lagoon of Gallinas. There is a large slave factory or depot at this place, which is said to belong to the house of Martinez in Havana; there are also different establishments on different islands . . . he had seen American, Russian, Spanish, and Portuguese vessels at Gallinas. The American flag was a complete shelter; no man-of-war daring to capture an American vessel." Bacon's testimony interwove the economies of Cuba, the United States, and West Africa, and it further corroborated the survivors' narratives.[22]

Historian Joseph Yannielli describes Bacon as a "tragic figure." As some of the captives appear to have recognized him in court in January 1840, he was clearly much more involved in the slave trade than he had conveyed to Baldwin. But like Madden's uncompromising abolitionist view, Bacon's history of slave trading did not surface in court. He stated that the slave trade "is the universal business of the country, and by far the most profitable, and all engaged in it who could raise the means. Extensive wars take place in Africa, for obtaining slaves from the vanquished. Different towns and villages make war upon each other for this purpose. Some are sold on account of their crimes, others for debts. The slaves are all brought on to the coast by other blacks, and sold at the slave factories, as no white man dare penetrate into the interior." Although Judson was already convinced the Africans were legally not slaves, Bacon's statement was important because it helped consolidate the various, and at times conflicting, accounts of the enslavement experience of the Africans.[23]

Bacon's testimony may also have been an intentional dramatic misdirection. Bacon, "a young gentleman of high scientific attainments and estimable character," gave public interviews and addresses about his travels. In a letter to the editors of New Haven newspapers "in connection with the report of the evidence," Bacon stated, "a few circumstances explanatory of the manner in which I became possessed of the facts to which I testified." He continued: "I was three times in Gallinas during my long wanderings on the coast of Western Africa. . . . On each of these visits I was the guest of Don Pedro Blanco, long famous for his large share in the slave trade. From him and all of his agents, . . . I received the most unbounded hospitalities. While thus an inmate of their houses, I became familiar with all the details of their business, which was carried on before me in the confidence that I would not abuse their hospitality as a spy; though they had been cautioned that from my connections I might be dangerous in this way." Via Bacon, Baldwin thus delivered a powerful internal record of the illicit world of illegal slave trading, as if it indeed were the product of espionage. Bacon himself seemed to relish the self-presentation as a double agent. With Bacon's testimony, the centrality of the Atlantic contextual argument and an adult narrative was firmly established. Unwittingly, however, the defense strategy privileged an adult male metanarrative that obfuscated the narratives of the children.[24]

SPECULATION ABOUT THE CHILDREN'S LANGUAGES AND ORIGINS

The Atlantic contextual argument seamlessly connected the economies of West Africa and Cuba and shifted the attention of the public and the courts to the enormous scale of slave smuggling. This shift effectively whitewashed the differences between the experiences of the children and those of the adults. The subordination of the children's narratives to an adult male metanarrative was profound and complete. This erasing of difference is ironic, because from late summer 1839 speculation had been rife about the origins of the children, and the three girls had been the subject of a separate habeas corpus writ and hearing. After the dismissal of this writ on September 23, 1839, however, the defense team appears to have streamlined and simplified the narrative. Notwithstanding this historical erasure, speculation about the children provides fascinating insight into their possible origins.

Questions about the girls' origins arose in August and September 1839 partly because they were subject to a separate proprietary claim. Pedro Montes claimed the girls and Ka'le as property, and the defense team filed a habeas corpus writ to seek their custody. In his testimony, Madden referred to the four children, declaring that Montes's permit for them was "wholly inapplicable to young African children, who could not have been acclimated, and long settled in the island." An additional factor set the girls, Ka'le, and Antonio apart. The adult males were being investigated by a grand jury for possible murder and piracy charges; the five children were "not implicated in the criminal charge" but were detained as witnesses. These two factors combined to generate great interest in the children, their fate, and their unknown origins.[25]

The contemporary press provides an excellent overview of what was publicly known, about the girls in particular. A September 1839 edition of the stridently anti-abolitionist *New York Morning Herald* claimed to provide "the only correct list of the slaves that has yet been published" and "their African names." It listed forty-five individuals, some with descriptions of "figure" and "countenance" and included "Females: Serne, 13, Kine, and Naugru." The paper implied they were from Angola and stated they "were stolen between Nova Redonda and old Benguela, on the coast of Africa." Other papers suggested alternative origins. The mouthpiece of the abolitionist Tappan, the *New York Journal of Commerce*, published a letter by the erstwhile publisher stating, "The four children are apparently from 10 to 12 years of age. The boy and two of the girls (who appeared to be sisters) are Mandingos, and the other girl is from Congo. They are robust, are full of hilarity, especially the Mandingos. . . . The children speak only their native dialects. . . . The district of Mandingo, in the Senegambia country, is bounded by the Atlantic Ocean, and is directly north of Liberia. Two or three of the men, besides one of the little girls, are natives of Congo, which is on the coast just south of the equator." As the trials continued, speculation continued unabated, but a vagueness about the girls' origins appears to enter the record. The *Colored American* and the *Richmond Enquirer* referred to them as "African girls."[26]

The shift in language was partly a reflection of the new details uncovered once several interpreters (Augustus M. Hanson, Ferry, Pratt, and Covey) had begun to communicate with the captives. The statement of one adult, and the only one to speak a smattering of English, "Bahoo of Bandaboo," was translated by John Ferry and introduced into court in September. "I knew Marngroo and Kenyee, two little girls, now in prison in Hartford; they were born in Bandaboo, in Mandingo, and came over on the same vessel as I did to Havana, as did Penna and the little boy Carre. . . . I know these children are the same that came over from Africa, and that Marngroo and Kenyee were born in the same place I was, which was Bandaboo." The commentary of John Ferry was added to "authenticate" this statement. Ferry explained that "Bahoo is Mandingo, but speaks Gallinas" and that he "was present when the forgoing affidavit was taken and translated . . . from the Galena to the English language." Thomas Hopkins Gallaudet, who claimed to have "been conversing with him, by signs," further supported Bahoo's testimony.[27]

In addition to translating Bahoo's affidavit from "Galena," Ferry provided his own statement, which brought "Teme" into the picture. Ferry's statement claimed that "the said children are all Africans by birth and that Teme is of the Congo nation, and that Kagne and Margui are of the Mandingo 'tribe' or nation as this deponent verily believes from the language spoken by the said children." Another African, Hanson, "of the Accra Tribe," also provided testimony. His affidavit, by contrast, stated, "that he has [seen the] African children named in the above entitled writ—that they cannot speak Spanish or English [and] this deponent has no doubt that they are native Africans and believes them to be Foulah Mandingoes and this belief is deemed from the language spoken by the [said] African children." This is amusing because it is unlikely the "Accra" Hanson spoke Fulani, as he most surely originated on the Ga-speaking coast of present-day Ghana, possibly passing through the Danish slave fort at Christiansborg. And whereas the "Congo" claim did not enter the court record, elements of the testimonies of Hanson and Ferry had clearly filtered into the press.[28]

The tension between the framing of the children as "African" and the deployment of a specific "tribal" or ethnic epithet reflects the shifting and at times conflicting objectives of the defense team. Establishing what today would be described as ethnicity was essential if useful accounts of their travails were to be elicited. The solicitation of the girls' narrative demonstrates this conundrum. Neither Ferry nor Hanson could speak with the girls properly, and Bahoo's version of the girls' story was twice translated, from "Mandingo" via "Galena" to English. Informed by the statements of Hanson, Ferry, and Bahoo, the habeas corpus writ attempted to tidy up the confusion by simply affirming the girls as "African natives." The writ stated, "the three African Girls, named in this writ of habeas corpus . . . are not now and never were slaves . . . they are natives of

Africa" and belong "to Senegambia in Africa aforesaid." At the same time, the
defense team sought to establish that the child survivors would surely be able
to speak Spanish if they were truly born in Cuba and not illegally imported.
Staples asserted, "This, at their tender age, is decisive." Trenchantly he claimed,
"they speak a language spoken no where else but Mandingo." Oblivious to its
vacuity, he cited Ferry's interpreting work as proof that "their whole language is
a dialect of Mandingo. They have no knowledge of the Spanish language." In
this manner, as the hearing wore on, the defense, vacillated between "tribal"
appellations, labeling them as speakers of Mandingo, and the vague category of
"African race."[29]

From the evidence, it is clear that there was great debate and disagreement
about the children's origins in general—but for a limited time only. The confusion about the girls' origins was sidelined by the arrival of Covey and Pratt in
mid-September 1839. Covey and Pratt began working with the adult males and
recording their narratives under the supervision of Gibbs, Day, and Griswold.
The public's attention returned to the riveting story of rebellion and murder on
the high seas. With Judge Thompson's dismissal of the habeas corpus writ on
September 23, 1839, the girls ceased to be a focus. Speculation about the origins of the children was eclipsed by the Mendi myth and the male masculine
metanarrative at the center of the Atlantic contextual argument.

"MENDI COUNTRY" REVISITED

Gibbs's claim—to have "succeeded in settling three points, which, when
taken together, determine[d] with sufficient precision the location of the Mendi
country"—is intriguing. Because no explorers who had ventured inland were
available for cross-examination, precise geographical data played a marginal
role in the legal dispute. Whereas geographical and ecological markers were intellectual stepping-stones toward African origins, victory for the defense rested
on language, translation and the Atlantic contextual argument. Notwithstanding, between 1839 and 1841 Gibbs and others collected "pains-taking" ecological
and geographical data. In light of a century and a half of exploration, research,
and scholarship, it is worth revisiting Gibbs's geography of "Mendi country."
Gibbs's claim to have identified the "native country" of "Mendi" was sidelined
in the dispute over origins, but the details he collected about the coast, agriculture, and rivers point to the origins of Amistad's orphans in the Galinhas region
and its hinterland.[30]

Gibbs attempted to locate Mendi vis-à-vis known coastal communities. The
three evidentiary components to his claim were based on interviews with Covey

and others: namely, the "waters of the Mendi country" come from "Gissi," including the Makuna and Keya Rivers, which flow into the Moa Rivers; a "principal river" of Mendi, the Moa, flows into the Vai country; and another Mendi "principal river," the Sewa, flows into the Bullom country. Because the coastal "Bullom and Vai" lay "between Sierra Leone and Liberia" and were "well known," it followed that Gissi was the source of the rivers that ended in the Bullom and Vai regions, although he was unable to identify the Moa and Sewa Rivers precisely. Therefore, Gibbs concluded, "The Mendi country lies between Gissi on the north, and Bullom and Vai on the south." Gibbs cross-referenced the captives' narratives with published accounts but observed that the captives "came from towns and villages not visited by European travellers, of course not known to geographers and not marked on our maps." In Gibbs's description, the region consisted of several "countries," some "well known" and others less so. In this way, he elevated Mendi to the status of a "country" of "Upper Guinea," and a tentative map was made available for circulation among supporters of the Amistad Committee.[31]

Although most of Gibbs's imagining of Mendi was based on the adult male narratives, geographical and ecological data also marked descriptions of Amistad's orphans, but unevenly so. Covey's personal narrative included a discussion of rice farming. Prior to his transportation aboard the *Segunda Soccoro*, Covey lived among Buloms working a paddy. Ecology informed Madden's expertise when he declared that Montes's "traspasso" for ownership of Kag'ne, Te'me, Mar'gru, and Ka'le were "wholly inapplicable to young African children, who could not have been acclimated, and long settled in the island" of Cuba. But Antonio's personal story provides no land markers or descriptions about West Africa. Descriptions from the adults were more detailed. But aside from Bahoo's claim that two of the girls were from his village, there is little evidence to confirm or deny that the children originated in the same area as the adult males.[32]

It is hardly surprising that Gibbs's geography of Mendi was so tentative. Slave traders' journals of the eighteenth century make no mention of Mende. The first reference is in the journal of Swedish botanist Adam Afzelius, wherein the Mende came no closer to the coast than the Jong River. Indeed, few geographers of the period mentioned Mendi, and the writings of those who did, such as Malthe Conrad Bruun, were perhaps not widely accessible. Nineteenth-century geographical descriptions of West Africa were generally at the macro level. Terms like "Upper Guinea," "Grain Coast," "Kru Coast," "Rice Coast," "Windward Coast," and other supra-geographical terms tied to commerce were preponderant. Knowledge of coastal geography was generally limited to

Fig. 2.1. View of the Galinhas River lagoon from the Atlantic Ocean
(Édouard de Bouët-Willaumez, *Description nautique des côtes de l'Afrique
occidentale* [Paris: Robiquet, 1848]; © The British Library Board)

"maritime" towns and settlements associated with the slave trade, antislavery skirmishes, and recent colonization efforts by liberated slaves. The zone was littered with swamps, lagoons, and rivers, including the Kerefe (Galinhas), the Moa, the Kittam, and others. Anecdotal details from the male adults referenced "high mountains," "small streams," wild animals, fish "as large as a man's body," and "hoes, axes, and knives" made from "iron obtained" in "Mendi country." But interpreting these anecdotal accounts must have seemed like throwing darts at an empty map to Gibbs and Tappan. "Upper Guinea" may have extended inland 150 to 350 miles, but the "interior" was "almost entirely unknown."[33]

Like the adults, all the children spent time in coastal barracoons, but the coast offered few physical markers beside the outlets of many rivers. Historian Walter Rodney asserted that "the most striking physical feature" of the greater region was "its numerous rivers." The coastal barracoons of the Galinhas region were located among the constantly changing "fresh channels" caused, according to Royal Navy Second Master Frederick Evans of the *Rolla*, by the "impelussity of the Currents during the Rainy Season." The "low, muddy" riverine environment was "thickly studded" with dense mangroves and "nothing but extensive swamps." Missionary Sigismund Koelle's account of his canoe trip to Bandakoro along the Bisuma (a tributary of the Moa River) in the 1840s describes the riverine region as "more properly called a lake" and the water "quite stagnant." Other accounts, such as that of the slave trader Theophilus Conneau, described the Kerefe (Galinhas) as a "sluggish river" oozing "lazily into the Atlantic." The estuary environment was "an innumerable mesh of spongy islands. To one who approaches from sea, they loom up from its surface, covered with reeds and mangroves, like an immense field of fungi." His contemporary, James Hall, echoed this description thus: "The land in the vicinity is very low and marshy, the river winds sluggishly through an alluvion of Mangrove marsh, forming innumerable small islands."[34]

Exploration of the region was in its infancy and rarely strayed beyond the coast, but Gibbs had little access to new contemporary descriptions. Seaman James Finlaison surveyed the region from the HMS *Tartar* in the 1820s; he observed that the "coast is very low, and covered with trees. It has a fine sandy beach all the way," a view reflected in an etching of mangroves and baobabs from the French admiral and governor Édouard de Bouët-Willaumez (figure 2.1). Several of the adults originated or sojourned in the maritime zone, including Berri, who lived as a slave in "Genduma" (Gendema) on the "Boba" River, "nine miles from the sea." Very few Europeans ventured up river, however. Geographer Hugh Murray noted that some rivers were navigable for short distances, but many were low flowing and their outlets to the ocean were replete with silt and sediment; he never personally visited the region. British naval surveyors described the Sulima or "Solyman" (the Moa), for example, as "inaccessible except through the narrow opening into the lagoon." And the Kerefe (Galinhas) was "accessible only to small vessels, in consequence of a spit of sand and shoals at its mouth." Contemporary accounts of the inland or interior region were scarce. Gordon Laing and Réné Caillié conducted expeditions inland from Freetown, although neither traversed Mende-speaking regions. Indeed, geographer James Bell noted "of the interior of the Grain country little is known to Europeans."[35]

The brief data on agriculture collected by Gibbs provide a firmer basis for pushing further inland beyond "the heads of rivers" to identify the origins of Amistad's orphans. Rice was "customary food of the region," according to slave trader Matthews. Slave traders knew they could supply their vessels with rice in Galinhas. Contemporaneous geographers considered the region "as fertile as in any part of the world." Brun observed that "the coast produces an abundance of rice, yams, and manioc." In addition to Covey's narrative, several adults self-identified as planters of rice, and one planted mountain rice. Most communities in the maritime region and much of the interior were rice farming. Indeed, farming was synonymous with rice cultivation in Mende. In the 1960s, agronomist Athanasius Njoku identified two primary systems, upland and inland valley swamp rice: the former was "traditional," household-run, and more widespread, and the latter was more labor intensive, often producing twice as much rice per acre. The specific nature of the labor possibly performed by Amistad's orphans in the rice paddies that monopolized the regional economy will never be known. But it may not be insignificant that one of two annual downtimes in rice cultivation occurred between February and March and the first heavy rains in May or June. During this period labor of all kinds was in low demand; it was also when several of the ships carrying the Amistad captives left the Galinhas coast. It would seem reasonable that the early child identities of Amistad's orphans emerged in the context of familial rice cultivation.[36]

The rice cultivation systems in operation today in the primarily Mende-speaking region distinguished between ownership and use, and ownership among Mende speakers was tied to patrilineal descent. Nkjoku describes the land tenure of rice farms as the "instrument" that bound "kinship together." And throughout the Mende region farms and paddies visited in 2012 were still family owned and managed (figure 2.2). Although the context of descent groups and family life of Amistad's orphans will likely remain opaque, ethnographic scholarship provides some insight into acephalous (that is, decentralized or stateless), patriarchal, gerontocratic village authority. John Davidson's work in the 1960s noted that the fundamental unit of organization among Mende speakers continued to be the *mawe* or *mahei*, a household or extended family. Although the size of the *mawe* varies even today and is partly dependent on the number of wives, larger *mawe* group together a number of brothers, descendants, and dependents. The *mawe* head coordinated and supervised farm work and settled disputes. Kenneth Little's description of a *mawe*, comprising several round mud-brick houses built in a circular formation, resonated with accounts from the African adults. A number of *mawesei* constituted a *kuwui*, or kindred-group compound or village; a *kuwui* was a geographical aggregation with a single kinship group nucleus, *ndehun-bla*, composed of closely related patrilineal kin descended from the *kuwui*. The "big man" of the *kuwui* was called the *kuloko*, although the region has a rich tradition of female chiefs too. Multiple *kuwuisia* together constituted a town. Bulom social structure was similar to Mende, but lineage patterns were basically matrilineal. Among the neighboring Gola communities, organization in "conical" units may have been defined in terms of genealogical distance rather than kinship per se. In many cases individuals and groups are attached by links other than kinship, particularly ties of clientship and previous enslavement. The two girls who came from the same rice-cultivating town as Bahoo were possibly from different villages, or *kuwuisia*; otherwise he might have identified them more precisely as family or kin.[37]

Fig. 2.2. Rice paddies near Kenema, Sierra Leone, April 2012

Although nineteenth-century observers rarely ventured inland, a variety of sources provide a richer sense of the network of rivers, footpaths, and overland routes of the originating zone of Amistad's orphans. Mende and Vai communities in the Galinhas region lived in "strongly stockaded towns," as observed by Koelle in the 1840s and Thompson in the 1850s (figure 2.3). The area inland from the coast was crisscrossed by trade routes and dotted with hundreds of small villages with varying forms of association and many languages reflecting the fusion of Mel and Mande languages and what historian Warren d'Azevedo called the dynamic processes of "mobility" and "local cultural pluralism." The size of the natal villages of Amistad's orphans was probably quite small. In the 1960s the majority of Mende speakers lived in villages with populations under one thousand. Many of villages I visited in 2012 had between three hundred and five hundred inhabitants. Whereas the Mende as a cohesive group may have established their fullest presence in the Galinhas region only at the end of the eighteenth century, the many language and political communities among which they settled and cohabited were marked by a rich history of trade patterns between towns. Around the same period trade, routes moving salt, slaves, and kola from the forested regions inland toward the savanna shifted direction

Fig. 2.3. Fortified village with double perimeter wall, c. 1850 (George Thompson, *The Palm Land; or, West Africa, Illustrated* [Cincinnati: Moore, Wilstach, Keys, 1859])

toward the coast, interweaving with the trade in rice, palm products, and slaves. Consequently, in the 1700s and 1800s, settlements closer to rivers became popular.[38]

When Amistad's orphans were enslaved and brought to coastal barracoons, the riverine region of Galinhas and its hinterland was experiencing episodic warfare between chiefly rivals. War was, to be sure, symbiotic with trade; peacetime and wartime trade to the coast, along rivers and footpaths, comprised rice, cassava, game, and palm products, and slaves. Trade along the rivers was easiest during the rainy season, from May to July or beyond. Foodstuffs were sold at harvest time, often around September, whereas palm products were traded in the greatest quantities between March and June. Despite the general non-navigability of many rivers, traders penetrated upriver by foot and canoe and followed networks of streams and estuaries up and down the coast (figure 2.4). Much of the Galinhas coastal trade for slaves was influenced by the permanent presence of descendants of English trading families, such as the Rogers family, which maintained a headquarters on the west bank of the Moa at the beachhead (figure 2.5). It is plausible that itinerant traders and coastal middlemen, purchasing palm oil or dyewoods for trade, may also have purchased small numbers of slaves, who had the added benefit of being able to assist in moving heavier products to the coast. And by the mid–nineteenth century the expanding slave trade in the region forged a greater intensity of contact between the coast and the interior.[39]

Although Gibbs's geography was nonspecific, a closer reading demonstrates that the broader geographical origins of Amistad's orphans lay in a zone where slave trading, slave wars, and other economic activities were deeply interwoven. Paths interlaced through forests, rice paddies, and grassland, and canoes navigated rivers, streams, estuaries, and swamps. Although the Galinhas and its hinterland was indeed just such a place, it is not too surprising that Gibbs and others ventured no further than identifying the origin zone of the Amistad survivors as "Mendi country." As a name for a river or region, Galinhas was more or less unknown in the 1830s beyond very limited circles. Historian Adam Jones observed that the origin of the word lies most probably with the Portuguese for "chicken," and it was first recorded in 1485 because of the preponderance of guinea fowl. Europeans used the name vaguely and imprecisely, and it never entered American vernacular. As a name for a river, Galinhas was used to describe the Kerefe (also Kife), the Waanji, the Moa, and Mano, at different moments by different outsiders. Locals, however, called the zone *Jaialô*, or "mangrove country," and when they used this term it included the coast and inland chiefdoms, comprising over seventeen hundred square kilometers. The frequent movement of the meandering rivers, swamp sediment, and mangroves

Fig. 2.4. Trading post at Mano-Salija, by A. M. Dunlop, c. 1850
(© National Maritime Museum, Greenwich, London)

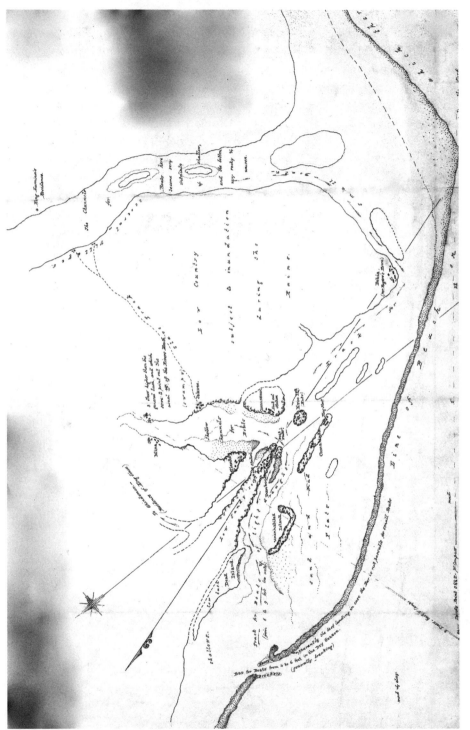

Fig. 2.5. Naval chart of Kerefe (Galinhas) and Moa River lagoon, as drawn in 1840 by Frederick Evans, indicating sites of barracoons (Detail from "Destruction of the Slave Barracoons, 1840," sketch by F. J. Evans, second master of HM

over centuries and the violent surf meant that European infiltration was minimal until the late nineteenth century. The lagoons of the region were and are expansive and constantly shifting, and as they can move one or two miles in the course of one rainy season, there is no way of reconstructing the precise geography of the Galinhas and its hinterland in the nineteenth century from maps or anecdotal accounts. Galinhas is not an ethnonym or even an established name of a language. Locals did not recognize Galinhas or Gallinas as a name of a people, according to the British colonial officer Stanley Despicht. The majority of communities in the period were related to several families, including Massaquoi, Kpaka, and Rogers. Whereas today most inhabitants speak Mende, in the nineteenth century Vai, Krim, Sherbro, Bulom, and many other dialects and lost language variants coexisted throughout Galinhas and its hinterland. Informed by this general discussion, we can now examine specific details about the origins of Amistad's orphans.[40]

THE GALINHAS ORIGINS OF AMISTAD'S ORPHANS

Establishing the specific ethnic origins of enslaved Africans has emerged as a dynamic site of scholarship. Although scholarship has advanced beyond the vague claims of Rodney about the "interior" origins of the majority of slaves exiting Sierra Leone ports, tying African personal names to ethnicity is deeply problematic; nineteenth-century names correlate most convincingly with geography. Although it may be tempting to fix an ethnicity to Amistad's orphans, closer scrutiny of their complex experiences is suggestive of the plasticity of childhood and the malleability of child identities. It is possible, as historians Herbert S. Klein and Francisco Vidal Luna assert for Brazil that children "never really grasped" the "meaning" of their ancestry or origin.[41]

Affixing a specific ethnic identity to the children is made difficult by the fact that at different times the children are accorded different names and identities. Indeed, as Jones has observed based on data of African children settled in Freetown and the surrounding areas between 1821 and 1824, many children "changed" their ethnic identity. Rather than reinforcing a belief in one specific identity, and because the children lived in the region only briefly before their Atlantic passage, it makes more sense to think of a region of origin, one that embraces the cultural, economic, and linguistic pluralism of a zone undergoing rapid and violent transformation, such as the Galinhas and its hinterland.[42]

The collective stories of the six children highlight the complexity of claims about slave origins. They also reinforce the importance of stepping back from the term "Mende." The Galinhas and its hinterland was not necessarily the *birthplace* of all six children, but it was a region they all likely passed through, and certainly resided in, for different lengths of time. The Galinhas is a small region of, at its core, perhaps a hundred miles east–west and north–south. But the hinterland feeding into it from many rivers—including the Moa, the Kerefe (Galinhas), the Kittam (Waanje), Moro, and many others large and small—is expansive (figure 2.6). Yet the multiple and overlapping identities affixed to the children by different actors in the Amistad drama underscore the plasticity of childhood, the fungibility of child identities, and the inappropriateness of the labels of "tribe," language, and definitive origin for children.

On an individual basis, it is possible to develop hypotheses with greater or lesser degrees of specificity. Individually, the children's experiences point to a common origin zone in the region inland from the mangrove-covered Galinhas coast and its hinterland, behind the coastal towns of Sulima, Mina, Gbandi, Medina, and others, where Mende, Vai, Sherbro, Krim, and many other languages were spoken. Although there are various possibilities for each of the children, it is useful to think of the Galinhas and hinterland as a site of origin, if not necessarily a collective homeland. After the arrival of Covey in mid-September 1839, "the means of communication" were "as good as could be desired." Tappan, Gibbs, and others identified Covey as Mende. But his origins were far more complicated and affixing an ethnic identity or "tribal" appellation is tenuous. Antonio could understand several of the Africans, and he communicated with the Africans and translated into Spanish. He was likely also from Sierra Leone and may possibly have spoken Mende. But establishing specifically Mende identities for any of Amistad's orphans is problematic for a number of reasons.[43]

KA'LE, TE'ME, KAG'NE, AND MAR'GRU

By September 1839, the *African* origins of Ka'le, Te'me, Kag'ne, and Mar'gru were widely accepted. Identifying them as Mende or by another ethnic appellation, however, is more tenuous; some evidence supports the Mende ethnic epithet with respect to the children, but it is not conclusive. The brief narratives of Gibbs published in Barber's account, in which the four children are enumerated (after the adult males), as 33, 34, 35, and 36, respectively, listed the English translations of children's African names as "bone," "frog," "country," and "black snake." These purportedly Mende translations emerged after Covey and Pratt began to work with the prisoners, translating their life stories. As the testimony of Bahoo exemplifies, however, translation is an acquired skill and hasty work oftentimes produces compromised results. Moreover, many Guinea

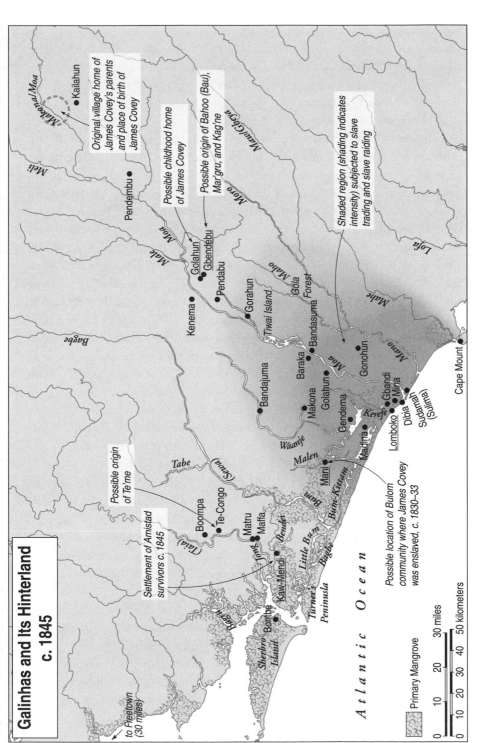

Galinhas and Its Hinterland c. 1845

Original village home of James Covey's parents and place of birth of James Covey

Possible childhood home of James Covey

Possible origin of Bahoo (Bau), Mar'gru, and Kag'ne

Shaded region (shading indicates intensity) subjected to slave trading and slave raiding

Kailahun

Pendembu

Golahun
Gbendebu
Pendabu

Kenema

Gorahun

Tiwai Island

Gola Forest

Bandasuma

Bandajuma

Baraka

Gonohun

Makona
Golahun

Ghandi
Mina

Gendema

Kerefe

Dibia
Sudamah
(Sulima)

Madina

Lomboko

Malen

Mani

Bum-Kittam

Waanje

Tabe

Possible origin of Te'me

Boompa
Te-Congo

Matru
Maffa

Kaw-Mendi

Settlement of Amistad survivors c. 1845

Sherbro
Bonthe
Island

Turners
Peninsula

Little Bum

Bagbe

Bendi

Jong

Bum

Bagru

to Freetown
(30 miles)

Bagbe

Meli
Male
Moa
Makona/Moa

Moro

Mani (Gbei)

Mabo

Moa

Mano

Mabe

Lofa

Cape Mount

Atlantic Ocean

Possible location of Bulom community where James Covey was enslaved, c. 1830–33

Primary Mangrove

0   10   20   30 miles

0   10   20   30   40   50 kilometers

Fig. 2.6. Galinhas and its hinterland, c. 1845 (Map by Phillip Schwartzberg)

coast languages share elements of their vocabularies; loan words abound. Indeed, alternative translations of the children's names circulated among their supporters, including "sabbath" for Te'me or Te'ne.[44]

At first glance Te'me's origin appears to be the most obscure and improbable. Earlier I fleetingly mentioned the early belief in August and September 1839 that Te'me was from Congo. Precisely how the Amistad Committee deduced she was from Congo remains unclear. And, as the above narrative demonstrated, once the trials gained momentum, interest in the origins of the children waned. In reality Te'me's origin may be concealed in plain sight, albeit embedded in circumstantial evidence. We know the children, like the adults, were repeatedly questioned as to their origins with varying degrees of success. If Te'me did use a word to describe her origin, she would quite logically have been referring to a village, not a country, "tribe," or nation. A young girl, recently abducted, would likely have very little sense of place or identity beyond knowing the name of her natal village. If she did use the word "Congo," she was possibly referring to Te-Congo, a predominantly Mende-speaking village on the Taia River (see figure 2.6). Te-Congo was in a constant state of conflict with its larger neighbor Boompa (or Boompeh) in the 1830s and 1840s. The towns' menfolk raided each other and enslaved whole families. The missionary George Thompson interceded to make peace between the rivals in 1850. But perhaps the most interesting detail comes from two letters after Te'me returned to Sierra Leone; these appear to suggest that Te'me was reunited with family when her father, or possibly an uncle, walked into the mission compound at Kaw-Mendi. The close proximity of Te-Congo to Kaw-Mendi makes this, and thus a Mende origin, conceivable.[45]

Returning to the purportedly Mende children's names, it is important to note that what may be translated into Mende may possibly be translated into another language, and differently. Ferry deposed September 20, 1839, "that he had seen and conversed with the three girls, and found that they spoke the Gallina language and no other." On only one other occasion, however, is language knowledge actually noted as it pertained to the girls. Gibbs observes that "Ka-gne" had knowledge of two languages: "She counts in Mendi like [the adult] Kwong, she also counts in Fai or Gallina, imperfectly." Maybe, like Ferry, she learned Vai (that is, Gallina) while in the region before her transportation. But the basis for the assessment of "imperfect" is unclear. This information may provide us with a clearer sense of her location prior to departure for Cuba, but spoken numeracy is by no standard unequivocal proof of origins. Neither Gibbs nor Ferry make any mention of Ka'le's language. From other sources, it appears that two of the girls shared a language and possibly other experiences, whereas the third spoke another and had a different passage to enslavement.[46]

The origin narrative of Mar'gru is further complicated by the later adoption of the name Sarah Kinson from 1842. Historical accounts of the Amistad story oscillate between Tappan and other abolitionists according her the name in Farmington and its emergence upon her arrival in Freetown. It is curious that she acquired this particular and highly unusual last name, while others took more jejune names, such as Maria Brown (Te'me) and George Lewis (Ka'le). One oral historical narrative collected in Fernando Po (Malabo, Equatorial Guinea) suggests a possible rationale behind this. According to local Fernandino lore, a John Kinson, son of Nathaniel Kinson, relocated from the Waterloo settlement outside Freetown, Sierra Leone in the 1850s. He claimed that the Kinson family included nine children, two of whom—a boy and a girl—were pawned for a debt. Both children were subsequently enslaved, sold, and shipped to Cuba. Legend has it that Mar'gru was told to "never forget her name" was "Sarah Kinson." She was separated from her brother in Cuba and never saw him or her family again. At some point during her ordeal in Connecticut, she conveyed this information and reasserted her name. During field research in Freetown in April 2012, I was unable to locate any Kinson family descendants in Waterloo.[47]

Assessing the plausibility of the story of Mar'gru's origins is difficult, but it adds fascinating dimensions. The "liberated" status of child slaves was often ephemeral; they were always in danger. Newly liberated children were whisked away from Freetown regularly and placed aboard ships for Cuba. British officials in Cuban freedom courts noted in the 1830s the curious phenomenon that many liberated slaves in Cuba spoke Creole (Krio) and/or a smattering of English. Thus, it is plausible that Mar'gru, living on the outskirts of Freetown, could have found herself sold across southeastern Sierra Leone, either up to "Bandaboo" or toward "Lomboko," and then out through the Moa River barracoons controlled by Blanco, a reverse of the paths described by historian Philip Misevich. Many slaves arriving in Cuba began at least one of their journeys in Freetown or the many settlements around it. Furthermore, having an Anglicized name (Sarah Kinson) in no way conveyed any speaking knowledge of Krio or English. Many families, especially Galinhas chiefs, in the southeastern quadrant adopted English names for a variety of reasons. Indeed, this oral historical narrative provides additional cement to the origins of Mar'gru. Mar'gru may have spoken one or several of the many language and dialects spoken in various central, southeastern, and southern parts of Sierra Leone.[48]

If two of the girls did share a language, what this language was we may never know precisely. Historical linguistics in the region occupied today by Sierra Leone, Guinea, and Liberia is an inexact science, and extrapolating backward in time to reconstruct language contact is deeply problematic. Bahoo stated, "Marngroo and Kenyee" were "born in Bandaboo," his hometown. In another record, Bahoo notes that his village was close to a large river called "Wo-wa," which is likely a variation of Moa. If Bahoo came from "Bandaboo," then there are a number of possibilities because several towns today and earlier (some of which are identified in figure 2.6), bore such a name. It may be Pendembu, a chieftaincy in the Kailahun district of the eastern province of modern Sierra Leone, where today the primary language is Mende. In the mid–nineteenth century, the many languages spoken in many of these villages, and others sharing the homophone "Bandaboo," are largely a matter of conjecture. Alternative spellings include Bendembu, Bandahu, and Ghendembu, and numerous villages and towns have such names. During my research survey in Sierra Leone, I tried to identify as many as possible, from historical and contemporary maps, that were on or are close to the Moa River. The homophone is relatively common, and reasons for this became clearer once I began my field trips. After making a list of various possibilities, I attempted to visit several of the towns on the east side of the Moa River. Those on the west bank were inaccessible because of the early arrival of the rainy season.[49]

Among the most promising candidates was the present town of Gbendebu, in the Dama chieftaincy, approximately forty-five minutes by four-wheel-drive vehicle south of the town of Kenema. A conversation with several inhabitants, including El Hadji Moussa Kpombai and the paramount chief of Dama, El Hadji Samdi Momoh Fowai, provided an additional tantalizing dimension to the possible location of the origins of two of Amistad's orphans. Investigations in Sierra Leone suggest that "Bandaboo" is likely a variation of the Gola root for "meeting place," *kpandui-a*. The Mende of this same word is *kpande-bu*. The name "Bandaboo" connotes a gathering place for male adolescents who then undergo initiation into *poro* societies. Informed thus, it became clear to me that identifying the actual village of Bandaboo, circa 1838, was likely impossible because almost every village and town in Mende country featured active *poro* societies.

The visit to Gbendebu was nonetheless fascinating. Today it remains the location of an active *poro* society, with a visible physical presence. Two elderly individuals, in the presence of several others, including a professional Sierra Leonean linguist, Ali Touray, explained that one of the original founding families of Gbendebu whose name was Vandi Bawoo-lo was known colloquially as Bahoo. Together with the Dasseh clan, the Bawoo clan settled Gbendebu during the era they identified as "the slave wars." Whereas today the village consists of one large central unit, El Hadji Moussa Kpombai and El Hadji Samdi Momoh Fowai explained that in the past, people lived in smaller village settlements in a circular pattern and came together during ceremonies at a central meeting place. In the presence of El Hadji Moussa Kpombai (figure 2.7), I visited and photographed the *kpande-bu*, the original center of the community (figure 2.8). Although it remains impossible to verify if "Bahoo of Bandaboo" and two of Amistad's orphans came from this same town, the proximity to the river, the origin of the name, and the settlement history of the region provide correlations to the piecemeal narratives from the children themselves.[50]

But it is possible to make yet another stab at the girls' origins by turning to current scholarly understanding of language families in the region. Descriptions of the girls, discussed earlier, suggest that while two of them communicated freely, one appeared linguistically isolated; this provides an alternative linguistic path to hypothesizing about their origins. They originated far enough apart so that

Fig. 2.7. Interview with El Hadji Moussa Kpombai (reclining), Gbendebu, Sierra Leone, April 2012, with Alie Mohamed Touray (seated left) and the author

Fig. 2.8. The *kpande-bu* (meeting place) of Gbendebu,
Kenema district, Sierra Leone, April 2012

they spoke different languages. Because they were enslaved as young children, they had yet to be exposed to the full spectrum of plurilingualism that marked the region so powerfully, as evidenced in Gibbs's descriptions of adult captives. How do we make sense of this? Two sub-branches of the Niger-Congo phylum or macrofamily occupy the region. The Central West Mande (Manding-Kpelle) languages, of the Mande family, include several languages spoken in Sierra Leone, among them Mende, Vai, Kono, and Kuranko. The Mel branch of the Atlantic group of the Atlantic-Congo languages (formerly identified as the southern branch) includes three languages spoken in the region, namely, Temne, Kisi, and Bulom. Thus if we begin with contemporary understandings of regional linguistic divisions, a narrative emerges.[51]

The wording of its public call for assistance indicated that members of the Amistad Committee had a very limited understanding of the relations between languages in the region. It observed, "The Mandingo dialects are spoken extensively, and it is said to be the commercial language of nearly the whole coast of West Africa. We found that the following words are nearly the same in the

Gallinas of the interpreter, in the Mandingo of the prisoners, in the Mandingo of Mungo Park, and in Jallowka of the German author Adeburg, *viz:*—Sun, moon, woman, child, father, head, hand, and foot. The numerals do not agree so well." Likely unwittingly, Tappan correctly identified the "Gallinas" (Vai) language as a coastal Mande language when he stated, "No person will be able to converse with them well until he can speak the dialect of Manding. Persons, however, born on the Galinhas River may be able to converse with some of them." Interestingly, Tappan hypothesized a relationship between Mandingo and Galinhas that has since been substantiated by linguistic scholarship. But we can move further if we pursue this analysis in terms of the relationship between mutual incomprehension and proximity. According two of the girls a Central West Mande mother tongue—say Vai—and the other a Mel language—perhaps Bulom—provides a working framework whereby physical proximity and linguistic difference may colocate, following d'Azevedo's analysis.[52]

And yet, one ought not to be too hasty. When informed by what little is known about the historical movements of the populations in the context of the trans-Atlantic slave trade, based on loan words, even this preliminary hypothesis falters. Literally dozens of languages, dialects, and dialect groups were spoken across the coast during the early nineteenth century, with a band of Atlantic languages broken up by a grouping of Mande, "part of a gradual process, stretching perhaps over hundreds of years." Furthermore, any linguistic reconstruction of the region—and the children—must also take into consideration the different roles of languages. Vai has been identified as a language of nineteenth-century commerce. Jones observed, the "adoption of Vai as a trade language seems to imply that there existed a seller's market for the goods in which Vai speakers dealt." Indeed, there were many coastal-oriented trade networks in the region, and a particularly large market for slaves, many of which converged with routes beyond the inland forest belt. Elements of the Vai language were spoken by several of the captives, including Ka'gne. But more instructively, at least five of the captives describe their enslavement and sale as being at the hands of a Vai speaker or being carried through Vai country. The addition of Vai thus adds another dimension to the linguistic complexity of the girls' (and Ka'le's) origins and derails the tentative hypothesis above.[53]

Word borrowing and language use are indeed complicating factors. To be sure, the linguistic complexity of the region was echoed in Tappan's public plea for assistance. He suggested a tone of desperation when he wrote, "The tribes in Africa are very numerous, almost every tribe has a distinct language, and it often varies, it is said, from village to village." But Tappan could not have foreseen the additional difficulties encumbered by modernity. Contemporary "language death" must also be added to this confusion; a number of Atlantic languages are now highly endangered, moribund, or extinct, making hypotheses about previous language relations tenuous at best. More problematic is that a number of coastal languages in the early to mid–nineteenth century were known by names no longer corresponding to contemporary linguistic family trees. One example is Bulom So, a moribund language sometimes identified as Mmani, Mani, or Mandingi. And thus, bearing in mind that Bahoo identified "Bandaboo" as being "in Mandingo," and Tappan referred to "the dialect of Manding," our brief historical linguistic detour brings us full circle—and no closer to identifying the girls' language or origin. To complicate things further, the term "Mandinga" represents 30 percent of the sample of African origins in the Havana-based Register of Liberated Africans. Mandinga was a way to indicate a slave was purchased in the Rio Pongo region. If this conjecturing demonstrates anything clearly, it is that sometimes terms used to describe languages during the early nineteenth century—such as Mandingo—may bear little or no resemblance to languages identified today—such as the unrelated Mel language Mandingi and the Mande language Mandinko.[54]

The potential of linguistic reconstruction is again resuscitated, however, when informed by additional data. Other possibly useful information about Ka'le and the girls' origins is contained in the description of their passage to the coastal entrepôt from whence they were forcibly relocated to Cuba. Ka'le was "about a month in traveling to Lomboko." Te'me was "a long time in traveling to Lomboko." Ka'gne was "many days in going to Lomboko." For Mar'gru we know nothing, although if she did indeed come from Bahoo's town, it was "ten days in going to Lomboko," which would have included canoe travel along the Moa River. (In Chapter 3 I discuss Lomboko and the enslavement experience more broadly.) At this point it is reasonable to hypothesize that, among the three, Ka'le traveled the greatest distance, and that constituted a month's walk. A month's walk from the Galinhas River point of departure would limit the origins of Ka'le to a region of approximately fifty to sixty miles from the coast. Ka'le's distance places him in historically Mende-speaking territory, and other data, including twenty-one variants of the spelling of this name from the African names project, supports the contention that he was Mende. Te'me's and Ka'gne's families possibly originated closer to the coast, and today the name "Teme" is a large Mende lineage in the Tunkia chiefdom, although there is no proven linguistic correlation between the two uses. With this information, we can possibly eliminate Kisi and Koranko from the two language groups, but narrowing it any further is difficult. Substantive circumstantial and overlapping evidence strongly suggests a Mende and/or Gola origin for several, but asserting a Mende origin without significant qualifications remains difficult. Instead I propose to settle for the broader general origin of Galinhas hinterland, where Mende cohabited with many other languages, with a nod to the compelling complexity of the historical linguistic and geographical data. In the words of Fuliwa, "The three little girls Teme, Kane, Mahgru, and Carli. They natives of same country [as me]."[55]

ANTONIO FERRER

Evidence about Antonio provokes a different set of questions about origins and returns us to language. Antonio is interesting because his assumed "situational identity" and assumptions about his origin shifted several times as the court cases wore on. From the first interview, conducted in New London in August 1839, Dwight P. Janes suggested, "he was brot [*sic*] to Havanna as a very small boy." But perhaps because of Antonio's association with slave trading— "he had made regular trips from Havana to Principe, with slaves"—Tappan and other advocates displayed little interest in Antonio's status from the outset, and Tappan appears to be the source of the claim Antonio was "was born in Havana." The correspondent of the *New York Morning Herald* put this simply: Antonio told "different stories at different times, but this is perhaps owing to his confusion and want of memory." In the records of the court prior to January 1840, Antonio is described in a number of different ways, including "a creole negro," a "black boy," "the slave of the Captain of the Amistad," a "Creole slave," a "boy," and as a "cabin boy." In his own words, he explained that he had been Ferrer's slave "since he was a very small boy." But during the January 1840 trial, as recorded by Barber, Judson apparently described him as "a Creole, born as he believes in Spain, recognized by the laws of that country as being the property of Ramon Farrar [*sic*], a Spanish subject." Of greater importance, however, is surely that no one during the trials made an affirmative claim that he was *born* in Cuba, unless Judson's reference to "Spain" was in fact an implied reference to Cuba. The Spanish vice consul in Boston, Antonio Vega, who claimed to be acting on his behalf, declared Antonio "the lawful property of the legal representatives of one Ramon Ferrer" and requested the court "return him the said Antonio Ferrer to his lawful owners in said Island of Cuba." Newspapers picked up the claim that he was "the undoubted legal slave of Captain Ferrer," but neither Vega nor anyone else ever explicitly claimed that Antonio was Cuban-born.[56]

Language renders Antonio's origins even murkier. Early in the case, he is referred to as "being able to speak only in Spanish," and he gave his testimony in Spanish, which was translated into English in the court. Furthermore, during the first habeas corpus trial of the three girls, Staples turned to Antonio in an effort to underscore that the girls were African. He observed, "Here is a boy, the first time he 'found himself,' very young, speaking Spanish. That shows those born there, begin very early to speak the Spanish language." Because the girls spoke only an African language, and Antonio spoke Spanish, Antonio was thus introduced as evidence to undercut the contention that children could be born slaves in Cuba and raised speaking African languages without knowledge of Spanish.

But this was a ruse, and Antonio's knowledge of African languages, and Mende in particular, had been evident from the outset. Janes's August 1839 interview in New London affirmed Antonio's ability to speak Mende. He stated, "Some say that the cabin boy, who is principal witness about the murder of the capt. can speak Spanish and African—when I saw him on board the schooner, as near as I could understand he said he was brot [*sic*] to Havanna when he was a very small boy—when 'asked' how long the negros had been there, he gave us to understanding that they had just come—if you can find some one who speaks Spanish you will perhaps be able to communicate with the blacks thro' this boy." Therein resides the confusion: in the urgency to learn the Africans' narratives, the story of Antonio's origin was buried. Finding a Spanish translator to work through Antonio may have compromised the case because he was likely to be a witness for the murder and piracy prosecution. Although he may well have spoken Mende, his capacity to translate was potentially deleterious.[57]

Claims about Antonio's African origins persisted for some time and emerged in different contexts. In one of the earliest newspaper reports, Antonio is described as "a cabin boy, new in the schooner, who speaks African and Spanish." In the first days of the trials Ruiz stated Antonio was "African by birth, but has lived a long time in Cuba. . . . [The rebels] would have killed him, but he acted as an interpreter between us, as he understood both languages." Cinquez also purportedly spoke to him (in what could only have been Mende) and "told [Antonio] to go on shore." Later, during the trial in Hartford, Bannah (Burna) was brought to the stand to contradict a particular claim regarding a recollection of events on Long Island. Henry Green, one of the salvage claimants, allegedly communicated with Banna: "My talk was with Banna—a word or two with others. I could understand many words of Banna; but not all—broken sentences." News reports of the trial noted that Antonio served informally as interpreter, insofar as "whenever a question was put to Bannah that he could not comprehend, he would appeal to Antonio, who was present." This is certainly not conclusive proof that Antonio was Mende, however; Gibbs noted that Burna had "lived in a small town in the Mendi country" but observed Burna also "counts in Tim-ma-ni and Bullom."[58]

Other elements of the narrative support the contention that Antonio knew Mende, Temne, and/or Bulom. In the struggle aboard the boat, some accounts suggest one of the Africans, "Llamorni" ("Nga-ho-ni" in Gibbs's list?), was "very cruel to the cabin boy" and wanted to kill Antonio, mirroring the fate that befell Ferrer's other slave, the cook, Celestino. One of the Africans, "Dama" (Bannah/Burna?), was "a great friend of the cabin boy," interceded on Antonio's behalf, and "saved" his life. Antonio himself stated that when he was tied to the schooner's "anchor," "Burna cut me loose." The trust born of this struggle had other later consequences. Bannah testified that "Antonio, the cabin boy, gave him a little money to keep, and he tied it up in a stocking." Their ability to communicate such confidences would likely necessitate an original knowledge of Mende. If this were the case, Antonio would possibly have been identified as "Gangá," the prevailing term in Cuba. But to date, no reference to a Gangá identity has been uncovered.[59]

A final set of two anecdotes provides an additional dimension framing his likely knowledge of Mende and/or other African languages. First, in a *New York Sun* account of a visit to the ship by Americans in August 1839, Cinquez purportedly delivered one or two speeches, surely in Mende, of which Antonio translated the gist. Tappan's mouthpiece also reported the speeches and Antonio's translation. The fiercely anti-abolitionist *New York Morning Herald* interviewed one of the alleged slaveholders, Ruiz. It challenged the account and declared "that he [Cinquez] made no speech whatever; and that if he had, there was no one who could translate what he said; the cabin boy knows nothing of the language, as asserted by the 'Journal' and had he been able to tell Mr. Hyde, according to the 'Journal's' account, Mr. Hyde knows nothing of Spanish, and the boy cannot speak English." Whether the reported speech occurred or not is unclear.[60]

A second, and equally interesting, consideration is Tappan's claim (long after Antonio had left the United States) that Antonio had been branded. Tappan wrote, "The Spaniards took Antonio, the cabin-boy, and slave to captain Ferrer, and stamped him on the shoulder with a hot iron, then put powder, palm oil, et cet., upon the wound, so that they 'could know him for their slave.'" If this is accurate, it adds an additional dimension to him being either originally from Africa as Janes stated, "as a very small boy," or born a slave in Cuba. Slaves smuggled during the illicit period may have been less often branded than during the legal trade, to insulate slave traders from seizure. By having unbranded Africans aboard (and sometimes unshackled immediately prior to boarding by a Royal Navy vessel) slave traders sought to conceal their cargo. Alternatively, Antonio was born in Cuba, and Cuban-born slaves were routinely branded in childhood, adolescence, or early adulthood.[61]

What is now becoming clearer, however, as a result of research conducted by historians Michael Zeuske and Orlando García Martínez, is that Antonio was embedded in a larger illicit slave-trading and smuggling operation that spanned the Atlantic at the center of which was Ferrer. Antonio testified that "the Sch[ooner] Amistad had carried slaves before—every two months [it] made [a] trip." He implied that Ruiz had run the Atlantic gauntlet too (as indeed he had) when he said he "had before carried slaves." Antonio himself reported that he had been in the service of Ferrer for "upwards of three years." Additional comments belied his deeper knowledge of the clandestine trade and his own experience of the illicit traffic in the service of Ferrer, who owned at least three ships and made multiple visits to Spain and West Africa. Antonio, when he was "told that the negroes would perhaps be sent to their own country, . . . laughed and said they would be caught and carried back to Havana again in less than six months."[62]

With a command of Mende (and possibly other African languages) and Spanish, Antonio would have been an ideal cabin boy for Ferrer's frequent Cuban trips and occasional Atlantic crossings. Although not as unequivocal or abundant as for the girls and Ka'le, the evidence for Antonio's African origin is undeniable, and his knowledge of Galinhas languages, if not a Mende ethnicity, is on a reasonable footing.

JAMES COVEY

Establishing Covey's origin is more complex and yet more feasible because of the multiple and sometimes conflicting accounts of how he came to be in New York in September 1839. Although Covey was celebrated for his Mende conversation skills, he claimed "his father was of Kon-no descent, and his mother Gissi." If this was accurate, it is important because the ethnolinguistic origins of Covey and his parents are suggestive of major political transformations and population movements during the early nineteenth century, partly caused by the expansion of wars for the purpose of slave trading. The precise location of Covey's birthplace remains hypothetical, but other childhood places of residence are discernible, based on the references to Kisi, Kono, and Mende and based on geographical and ecological descriptions collected by Gibbs.[63]

Gissi (today Kisi) is a Mel language, of the Atlantic branch of Niger-Congo, the closest relatives of which are Sherbro, Mani, Kim (Krim), and Bulom

(Bom). Kono, by contrast, is in the central branch of the Central West Mande family, the closest relative being Vai. Although the precise early nineteenth-century sociopolitical relationship between Kono and Kisi peoples is unclear, the linguistic familial relationship of Kisi to Bom, Mani, and Kim are important. Covey's mother's Kisi community resided inland toward the east (today's borderland of Sierra Leone, Guinea, and Liberia). At the time of his birth little was known about the Kisi. A contemporary geographer, James Cowels Prichard, observed, "The Kissi are a people of whom we know nothing, except that they inhabit the mountainous country about the sources of the Niger, to the southward of Sulimana and Sangara."[64]

In approximately 1825–26, when Covey was likely born, however, the Kisi had yet to cross the Makona River. Furthermore, as Tucker Childs, an applied linguist who studies endangered West African languages explains, "there were two historical movements of the Kisi people," the first a larger migration of Atlantic language speakers precipitated by Mande expansion, and a second involving only Kisi, from the coast inland. In earlier scholarly parlance the Kisi would constitute a "truly segmentary society." They share similarities in terms of political fragmentation with other Mel language groups and the nearby Bijagos, Baga, and Diola, who speak related Bak languages. Today scholars refer to them as acephalous, like the Balanta, which conveys the notion of decentralized authority and different forms of power distributed among lineages and families. The northeast migration was thus part of the political, socioeconomic makeup of a "highly decentralized ethnic group." Thus "half-Kisi" Covey was among a select group with important sociopolitical traditions and ethnic attributes throughout the Atlantic, including possibly linguistic exogamy.[65]

Covey's Kono father helps frame his origins. Kono is closely related to Kuranko, and both are part of the Central West Mande group of the Mande family. In the 1700s, southern Mende displaced Kono farmers, who subsequently relocated to Kuranko. According to oral traditions, Kono women were sometimes referred to as "salt wives" by Mende, Vai, and Bulom. Because Kono moving to the coast in search of salt often risked enslavement, Kono men began bringing women with them to the coast, selling them for salt, and returning with profits, thus avoiding capture and sale themselves. The slave trade–era Kuranko, and refugee Kono, inhabited centralized, defensively constructed chiefdoms. Some of these were "natural, impenetrable" barriers, and others were manufactured, including "hilltop forts protected by entrenchments," mud walls fifteen feet thick, "stockades of living trees," and "winding entrances." The precise relationship between early-nineteenth-century Kuranko and Kono, however, is almost impossible to recover.[66]

An additional component in Covey's origins concerns the appellation "Mende." Exactly how and why Covey highlighted Mende can be explained by two developments: his parents' relocation to Mende territory during his infancy and his first experience of enslavement among the Bulom. The only record of one of Covey's "African" names comes from Gibbs, who observed that his "original name was *Kaw-we-li*, which signifies in Mendi, *war road*, i.e., a road dangerous to pass, for fear of being taken captive." It is impossible to corroborate the name's ethnicity, but some context here is valuable. In the Gola language, the importance of which is discussed below, *ka-wi* may be translated as "let's go." *Kaw-we-li* may be thus possibly a variant or extension of a Gola root verb. In Mende today, there exists no suggestive correlation. Interviews conducted in several locations elicited only that *ka-we* meant "dustbin." There is, however, no record of Covey himself using this name or even referring to a Gola or Mende name. The name "Covey" may be a variant of a Bulom Sherbro word *co-vi* for "pot" or "cover." In Mende *co-vi* also means "cooking pot." If this correlation is more than mere coincidence, it may further anchor his enslavement experiences discussed later.[67]

In terms of ecology and geography, Covey's descriptions of his infancy provide significant clues to origins. Gibbs claimed that Covey's "parent's house" was in "Go-la-hung, whither they had removed when [he] was quite young." In his New Haven deposition, Covey stated, "I was born in the Mendi country, in a place called 'Gho-roun' and the Mandi is my native language." In a third instance, before the district court, Covey mentioned "Berong" and stated that "Barton has been in my town, Gorang," likely John B. Barton, a Methodist missionary, originally from Georgia, who was in Monrovia in 1831. Furthermore, the distance from the coast to Covey's next location is anchored around his statement that "one man carried us two months' walk." A survey of nineteenth- and twentieth-century maps revealed five possible candidates for Covey's parent's home—two villages called Gonahun, one town and one village called Golahun, and one town called Gorahun—all of which are broadly within Mende territory today. Assessing which of these is most likely is advanced by knowledge of settlement and resettlement histories and a common preference for naming a community after the origins of its first inhabitants. Covey's multiple testimonies include references to the Moa (Mua) River. A fourth text noted his birthplace as "Go-raun, by the river Mo-a, in the Mendi country." Covey also noted that *La Amistad's* captives "speak of rivers which I know." All five locations are relatively close to the Moa, only one is conceivably "two months' walk" from Mani, Covey's last residence before his forced ocean migration. And at least three can be eliminated because they are newer settlements named Golahun possibly after the earlier settled community near the Moa River.[68]

A more detailed geography comes from Gibbs's interviews with the three interpreters, Covey, Charles Pratt, and John Ferry. Gibbs recorded, "Some of the principal towns in the Men-di country, according to Covey and Pratt, are Dzha-e-ve-fu-lu, Go-raun or Go-la-hûng, Bai-ma, Se-bi-ma, Si-ma-bu, Gna-ya-hung, Gong-a-bu . . . and Ben-der-ri. The principal rivers are (1.) Mo-a, which runs into the Vai country; (2.) Sewa, which runs into the Bullom country; (3.) Ma-wu-a, which comes from Gissi, where it is called Ma-ku-na, and joins the Mo-a; (4.) Ma-le, which flows by Dzho-po-a, and joins the Mo-a." So with reasonable certainty we can assign Covey a childhood residence in Golahun, in the southeastern-most portion of Kenema district, a village approximately twenty miles west of Liberia's border and at the time likely in the thick of the Gola forest. Of five communities in Mende territory with similarly spelled names, it is the oldest in terms of settlement. The village was likely part of a chieftaincy in the vicinity of what is today the Tunkia chiefdom, and was two months' walk to the coast, just under one hundred miles, squarely within what Misevich identified as an "average" distance. Today Mende is a lingua franca, but Gola is also spoken. Covey may have spoken Kisi with his mother; if he spoke Kono with his father he had lost most of it by adolescence. It is possible that Covey's parents were themselves enslaved and brought to Golahun, as Mende and Gola people enslaved Kissi people, whose descendants live there today. Perhaps those who captured him in Golahun were Gola speakers. And he spoke Mende both with his future slave owners and kidnappers and with the African captives in New Haven.[69]

A final dimension concerning Covey's origins emerges from his experience of rescue from the slave ship *Segunda Socorro* in July 1833 and involves the term "Cossoo." When the *Trinculo* escorted Covey's ship into Freetown harbor, it contained an additional 102 boys as part of its illicit cargo. The arrival in the Liberated African Yard of so many boys provoked agitation on the part of the acting governor, and he wrote immediately to the Church Missionary Society (CMS) head, Reverend James Frederick Schön, expressing his "anxious desire" to place "103 Cossas under their charge and to have them educated" at the CMS school in Bathurst. The "Cossoo boys lately seized by His Majesty's Sloop, 'Trinculo'" were described as being in excellent health because they had been on the ship for only a few days. The CMS willingly took the boys of "the Cossoo nation" under their care, after negotiation of terms (Chapters 5 and 6).[70]

The origin of the term "Cossoo" or "Kossa" is unclear, but at various points "Kosso(h)" was used by Mende to describe themselves and their land. Misevich believes it may have been a Temne word for Mende, and although in the 1830s it was a derogatory term, by the 1840s it was "deprived . . . of any offensive meaning." Misevich cites a slave dealer interviewed by Schön who said the slaves "were cheap, but that they were Cossoos, and that Cossoos were mere cattle, and more should not be paid for them." Gibbs seemed unaware of its pejorative nature when he wrote Tappan, "They call themselves *Mendi*. Perhaps they may be better known on the coast of Africa under the name of kosso, and their country under that of Longobar." Several months after the Supreme Court verdict, John Pitkin Norton, a teacher, wrote to Tappan, "Kinna has just been here and says that their country is known by another, *viz*. Cossa. I find on the map a Cossa River, apparently 30 or 40 miles north of Gallinas river and also Benda river 30 or 40 miles still further north." Two days later Norton wrote to clarify: they "say Kossa is not their name, but a term of reproach, a name applied to them by the English and by those who enslave them."

Although today there appears to be no river known by the name Cossa, it may at the time have marked a physical boundary between Temne-speaking and Mende-speaking chieftaincies. Robert Clarke observed that the "Kussoh country" was to the "east and far north-east of the Vye nation" and was a populated by a "turbulent people always at war among themselves, and against their neighbors, the Timmanees." Sierra Leone's lieutenant governor William Fergusson wrote to the Amistad Committee in the 1840s to explain that the "rather extensive" Kosso country "nowhere infringes on the sea side, but lies immediately behind" eastward of Sherbro country. North and south Cosso territory, however, "share nothing in common except the language." Regardless of the fact that Covey never appears to have self-identified as Cossoo, it provides an additional dimension to his origins.[71]

CONCLUSION

The origins of Amistad's orphans can be reconstructed by scrutinizing various data embedded in the children's narratives and those of others in whose circles they moved. The trial records are a very important source of details about the African captives, but the trial itself contributed to the obfuscation of the identities and origins of the children. The defense attorneys developed a sophisticated argument drawing on expertise from scholars, travelers, and practitioners. Their team's strategy was deliberate and intentional, and it was guided by the goal of establishing African origins. But in so doing, in what I identify as the Atlantic contextual argument, it created a mythology of Mendi origins, and an adult masculine metanarrative. Whereas there was initially great interest in the children's identities, once the focus shifted to the adults, the complexity of the children's experience was marginalized: the powerful and persuasive Atlantic contextual argument erased the different experiences of the children. In many regards, however, it was a legal ruse. Even Baldwin appeared to admit as much when he wrote to the Amistad Committee after the Supreme Court decision, "They seem to have some knowledge of—or at least to have heard of Sierra Leone, which is probably nearer to their native region than any other part of the coast." But by the time the Africans returned to Sierra Leone, Mendi was so cemented that Rediker refers to it as the "apotheosis of their long-standing fictive kinship."[72]

The plasticity of childhood and the multiple and shifting claims and statements about the children make establishing any identity frustrating, and it diverts attention from the experiential narratives of the children. Indeed, affixing a static ethnic identity to specific children is deeply problematic. But by reuniting the Amistad's orphans it is possible to develop a very rich narrative about broader origins. In this chapter I focused on the linguistic, ethnographic, and geographic data. By cross-referencing what was known and unknown about the children in order to undercut the assumption that the children were Mende, it is possible to imagine a location for all the children in one region. By locating Amistad's orphans in the Galinhas and its hinterland we arrive at a tentative picture of their earliest experiences prior to transportation, including their likely agricultural activities and village life.

Cross-referencing the claims and counterclaims of, by, and about Amistad's orphans with current scholarly knowledge and debates about language and ethnicity points with varying degrees of precision to possible sites of origin. While it may be tempting to assert a Mende identity for several individuals, much of the evidence is circumstantial and speculative. But more important, the affixing of specific ethnic appellations makes little sense with respect to children whose identities and personalities were still developing. Instead of focusing on Mende, it is more illuminating to contextualize their origins in Galinhas—a geographical *and* linguistic term that highlights the overlapping cultures, languages, and economic practices that deeply shaped the region and the period. The specific details pertaining to each individual provide greater or lesser certainty, to be sure, but it is difficult to resist acknowledging the role of the Galinhas region in shaping the early lives of all the children, including Antonio.

3

THE ENSLAVEMENTS OF AMISTAD'S ORPHANS

In September 1839, at the first of the several trials of the survivors of *La Amistad*, the defense team forcefully asserted that the Africans were "born and still of right" free. Free-born status featured in the first habeas corpus hearing for the girls. During the civil proceedings in New York in October 1839, the Spanish Cuban claimants ultimately admitted the Africans were originally "free-born" and not "property." And in subsequent cases, establishing not only the "domicile" of the Africans in Cuba but also a law permitting their being held as lawful slaves became crucial to the case. In Justice Story's decision, the significance of free-born status loomed large. He wrote: "It is not only incumbent on the claimants to prove that the Africans are domiciled in Cuba, and subject to its laws, but they must show that some law existed there by which 'recently imported Africans' can be lawfully held in slavery. Such a law is not to be presumed, but the contrary. Comity would seem to require of us to presume that a traffic so abhorrent to the feelings of the whole civilized world is not lawful in Cuba. These respondents, having been born free . . . have a right to be everywhere regarded as free until some law obligatory on them is produced authorizing their enslavement." The Amistad survivors came before the Supreme Court "as freemen," according to defense counselor Baldwin and acknowledged by Story. Freedom and free-born status were themes revisited time and time again over the course of the trials in numerous writs and petitions.[1]

From a court with a slaveholder majority, and from the perspective of antebellum American slavery, the affirmation of having been "born free" was an important closing argument in a long sequence of legal proceedings. U.S. law did not recognize the reduction to slavery of free-born individuals within the United States, black or otherwise. Many southern states still had statutes permitting the re-enslavement of former slaves as punishment, or voluntary re-enslavement, but free-born individuals could not be constitutionally deprived of free-born status. The legal strategy adopted by the defense required pushing back the initial instance of illegality into the Atlantic and beyond, into West Africa, thus criminalizing the entire experience of enslavement and transportation endured by the Africans. If it was indeed true that they were all born free, then birth status as one path to their hypothetical enslaved status in Africa was eliminated. But the insistence that all the Africans were born free was sleight of hand on the part of the legal team, and it obscured the multidimensional complexity of the enslavement experiences of all the survivors, and Amistad's orphans in particular.[2]

Amistad's orphans experienced a wide spectrum of acts of enslavement spanning a decade, beginning with the first instance in the Galinhas region and its hinterland, continuing with their sale to European slave traders and their embarkation across the Atlantic, and concluding in mid-nineteenth-century Cuba, their ostensible destination and intended final slavery context. A child's experience of enslavement is qualitatively different from that of an adult for a number of reasons, not least of which is that even when ostensibly free, as children they remained dependents and wards of others. The stories of Amistad's orphans show that the paths into enslavement for children were often narrower than for adults, particularly during the period of the illegal slave trade between Galinhas and Cuba. And although brief, the children's truncated Cuban slavery provides a window into the expanding use of child slaves in the rapidly industrializing island economy. A focus on child slavery muddies scholarly debates about African slavery, which draws heavily on adult experiences. Deliberately separating the children's experiences from their Atlantic mobility (Chapter 4) directs attention to the complex and varied instances of enslavement encountered during childhood. Each of the children experienced several different acts of enslavement as they were transferred. And their individual experiences of enslavement overlap with their later ostensible liberations insofar as all the children were held against their will in some form of court-ordered guardianship.

The myth of free-born status that anchored the Supreme Court's basis for the adults' claims originated, ironically, in the first habeas corpus hearing pertaining to the children. Despite their free-born status, the children shared experiences of initial enslavement in Galinhas and its hinterland, including pawnship, kidnapping, and violent seizure. The multiple passages of enslavement that each individual encountered shed light on the interrupted and discontiguous nature of their slavery experiences and those of their contemporaries. In this chapter the incremental processes that immediately follow their initial enslavement, resulting in their imprisonment in barracoons in the Galinhas region, are examined from the perspective of the enslaved child. And why, intentionally or otherwise, were the children enslaved? The percentage of children in illegal slave cargoes entering Cuban ports rose dramatically over the course of several decades. To understand the rise in demand, we must also consider the changing nature of slavery in the intended final destination of Amistad's orphans, the Spanish colony of Cuba.

THE MYTH OF FREE-BORN STATUS

The origin of the free-born status narrative embedded in the Supreme Court decision is convoluted and complex. The first questions to come before Circuit Court Judge Thompson concerning the adults detained in prison pertained to criminal charges—namely, murder and piracy. Yet free-born status was a powerful dimension informing District Court Judge Judson's verdict, as demonstrated in his draft ruling. Unraveling the origin of the claim of free-born status requires disassembling the multiple libels and claims made by multiple parties at the onset of the trials. It also necessitates turning briefly to a lesser-known episode in New York City: the suit for damages, caused by false imprisonment and battery, brought by several of the Amistad survivors against the purported slave owners Ruiz and Montes.[3]

In adjudicating the status of the Amistad survivors, the Connecticut judges were torn between two poles—claims that the Africans be put on trial for piracy (for which a grand jury was convened for the circuit court), and alternatively that they be treated as property and thus returnable or salvageable. Claims of mutiny and murder were swiftly dismissed by the circuit court on the grounds that the acts took place outside U.S. waters. In the wake of the dismissal of the criminal elements, six different claimants delivered writs of libel for the cargo of the ship, including the Africans. The Spanish claimants consistently described the Africans as property, subject to the terms of Pinckney's Treaty of 1795. In insisting that the case was subject to the treaty, the Spanish claimants were invoking a hotly contested issue, namely, Article VI, Clause 2, the Supremacy Clause, of the Constitution, by which any treaty supersedes all state laws, in this case those of Connecticut and New York. Formal argument was held over until January 1840, and the decision of Judson and subsequent appeal is, at least for historians, now familiar terrain.[4]

In the interim, Tappan and members of the Amistad Committee filed charges of false imprisonment and kidnapping against Ruiz and Montes before the New York Court of Common Pleas. The writs of summons demanded that Ruiz and Montes present themselves before the court "to answer to FULAH" and "to answer SINQUAH, an African of the Mendi tribe in a plea of trespass and assault, for falsely imprisoning, beating, ill treating and wounding the said plaintiff to his damage two thousand dollars." Accordingly, the sheriff accompanied Tappan, and the two "gentlemen were marched to prison, and locked up." When the case was presented for review, Ruiz insisted that he "did not know the plaintiff was an African by birth, and now does not know it. That he purchased him in the same manner in which all other slaves are purchased in Havana, and thus legally acquired property in him." In reply, Tappan and others filed their own affidavits, with Covey's translation assistance, stating that they believed Cinquez and Fuliwa "to be native born Africans." The plaintiffs made no claim at this point to be free-born.[5]

As the case continued, the attorney for the detained, John B. Purroy, appeared to concede that the Africans might not be Cuban-born slaves. But he insisted that Ruiz and Montes bought the slaves under the impression they were legally slaves. They could not, he argued, be prosecuted for a tort. Purroy stated, "Ruiz cannot be sued in an action in the form *ex delicto* unless it be proved or alleged that he knew them to be Africans when he purchased them; the animus must be proved; if he purchased them bona fide they cannot bring an action of false imprisonment, upon the ground that the negroes could not be sold in Havana as slaves." Chief Justice Jones and Judge Oakley ultimately lowered the bond for Ruiz to two hundred dollars and released Montes without guarantee. Montes and Ruiz skipped bail and returned to Cuba, where they resumed their many clandestine activities.[6]

In deciding thus, Jones and Oakley determined that the motivation for the suit was not really "damages" but "liberty." They appeared to accuse Tappan of trying to circumvent the pending suits and ongoing Connecticut proceedings, and the failed habeas corpus writ for the children, in order to acquire the liberty of all the Africans. Oakley found no basis for the alleged crimes and stated, "I can draw no inference from any quarter except the affidavits themselves, and it appears to be very doubtful whether the forced embarkation and the imprisonment of the plaintiff[s] did not take place under the coercion of other individuals, whose names are not given." Because Cinquez himself had stated that "he was brought to a village one day from Havana, where he kept five days when he was taken to another village, where stayed five days more," it was more likely than not that neither Ruiz nor Montes had deprived him of his freedom. He concluded that "the plaintiff was bought fairly and openly in Havana without any knowledge of his being fraudulently in slavery," regardless of the actual legal status of Cinquez. Oakley drew on New York precedent to observe that while the intention of liberty may be earnest, this was not an appropriate venue for a damage claim. This brief but fascinating episode suggests disagreement about legal strategy between Tappan and others. But what it also highlights is that deprivation of liberty and free-born status were still concealed within an additional set of claims and complaints.[7]

And so whereas the Connecticut suits pertaining to the adults proceeded apace, there appears little evidence that a specific claim of free-born status originated with the adults. The free-born argument appears in the "answer of S. Staples, R. Baldwin, and T. Sedgewick" to the "several libels of Lt. Gedney et. al. and Pedro Montes and Jose Ruiz" from January 1840, quoted at length (in the introduction). It then appears in Judson's ruling and in the determination of the Supreme Court. But when did it *first* make an appearance? The answer lies in the short-lived and ultimately unsuccessful attempt to release the three girls from prison. Because Tappan, Sedgwick, and others observed that the girls were not being charged with murder and piracy (though Ka'le was included in the initial charge with the adults), they sought to have the three released into the custody of a guardian and protector. Furthermore, they knew from the outset that the girls could not have been imported legally into Cuba because the latest date for legal importation was 1820. The girls were young and could not have been born before 1830. Therefore there was no need to engage with the complex issue of legal importation into Cuba.[8]

After close scrutiny, it appears that the free-born claim, as a separate statement and a distinct line of defense against the alternative of slave status, originated with the children's habeas corpus hearing in September 1839. In three different versions of the draft affidavit prepared for the writ of habeas corpus for the girls, Sedgwick stated, they are "not now and never were slaves as is most unjustly and untruly set forth," language later echoed by Story. More important, free-born status featured prominently in the actual hearing pertaining to the girls. In an account of the proceedings from the abolitionist newspaper, *The Colored American*, we learn, "T. Sedgwick, Esq., read the answer [on the] return of the Marshal, and was ably sup[por]ted by Mr. Baldwin of New Haven. He [. . .] tended that the children who were of the ages 7, 8, and 9, were not slaves—nor ever had been—they were free born—illegally captured, and taken to Havana where they were sold contrary to the laws of nature and humanity. [. . .] the laws and ordinances of Spain, in existence long before the birth of these children. [. . .] contended that the capture of them was illegal, felonious and piratical." In the eyes of many today this brief trial may appear marginal to a more complicated process. To be sure, the habeas corpus hearing was unsuccessful, and the continued detention of the children in Pendleton's home and other "evil influences" distressed many abolitionists. Tappan and others continued to press for their release in May and October 1840. But closer scrutiny of the record reveals that language informing the rulings of Judson and Story first appears in the habeas corpus trial of September 1839.[9]

Several months after the Amistad survivors arrived in Sierra Leone in 1842, the myth of their free-born status continued to make waves in legal and constitutional circles. A short article in the *Long Island Farmer* noted, "We are, perhaps not yet done with the poor captive negroes of the Amistad." The paper reminded its readers that Colonel Pendleton had "represented as slaves" thirty-seven individuals under his care in the New Haven jail. Indeed, of the total Connecticut population of 310,014 in the 1840 census, 54 were listed as slaves. As the Amistad survivors had "been declared by the United States Courts to be freemen," the paper argued they should be counted as such in the appointment of congressional seats. "If the apportionment bill, allowing one representative to every 92,000 passes," it continued, "the correction, which ought to be made, counting these thirty-seven not as slaves, but as freemen, will entitle the state to an additional representative."[10]

In hindsight, the irony of the free-born claim is that although it originated in the girls' habeas corpus hearing, there was little if any credible basis to assert that any of Amistad's orphans were free-born. Indeed, since historian Suzanne Miers and anthropologist Igor Kopytoff first advanced the notion that African slave status must be positioned on a continuum of kinship systems—wherein lineage heads cultivated rights-in-persons, and where children and women were generally the most vulnerable to the implementation of such rights—scholars have developed a richer and more nuanced understanding of the role of subordination, hierarchy, patriarchy, and lineage in the lives of African children. It may be an overstatement to assert that the status of free-born was inconceivable to a child in mid-nineteenth-century Galinhas. Nevertheless, recent scholarship has highlighted the role of environment and culture in shaping ideas of childhood, and the lives of child slaves in particular. Scholars are increasingly cognizant of the parameters of childhood, the responsibilities and labor of children, and the demands placed on them by lineage and family superiors. To understand the context of their enslavement, it is important to resituate the Amistad's orphans in their socioeconomic milieu in the nineteenth-century Galinhas.[11]

CHILD SLAVERY IN NINETEENTH-CENTURY
GALINHAS AND ITS HINTERLAND

The context in which the slave status of Amistad's orphans was embedded was far more complex than their American legal advocates could ever have realized. Although freedom was a powerful cry in the republics of the Western

Hemisphere, from the perspective of an enslaved African in a Galinhas barracoon in 1839, an assertion of free-born ancestry would likely have generated
little interest on the part of the slaveholder or his associates. Before their temporary incarceration in a Lomboko barracoon, all the survivors of La Amistad had
been enslaved, via one mechanism or another, consistent with African practices
in the Galinhas region, ranging from warfare and debt seizure to kidnapping or
punishment for a crime. The vast majority of slaves transported across the Atlantic, before and during the nineteenth century, was enslaved as a result of what
Lovejoy described as the massive "intensification of political violence," which
in turn gave rise to a "spectacular surge" in the capacity to enslave people.
Although one contemporary observer alleged that hereditary slave status constituted 90 percent of the population in Cape Mount (the immediate adjacent
territory to Galinhas) in 1848, today the percentage of slaves whose identity
was tied to slave-born status is probably unknowable. But the status accorded
Amistad's orphans immediately before transportation was only one snapshot in
six individual stories of enslavement with many twists and turns.[12]

Children in Galinhas and its hinterland in the early to mid–nineteenth century were extremely vulnerable to enslavement and transportation across the Atlantic to Cuba. First, consistent with the widespread socioeconomic system in
operation, as very junior members of lineages, children were highly susceptible
to the operationalization of rights-in-persons, wherein claims on their labor,
their future labor capacity, or other valuations made them expendable. Second,
in addition to the illicit trans-Atlantic trade, there were highly buoyant shorter-
and longer-distance trade routes throughout the region, wherein children were
increasingly desirable mechanisms facilitating exchange, credit accumulation,
or debt obligation. Third, as smaller, lighter, weaker individuals, children were
more susceptible to violent seizure, kidnapping, and capture in conflict, and
later transportation to the coast. And fourth, the environment and geography
of Galinhas provided an ideal site for the relocation and continuation of trans-
Atlantic trade in the face of attempts to end it by the Royal Navy, enabling traders to tailor their barracoons to shifting demands in Cuba.[13]

How Antonio was first enslaved remains unclear, but evidence from five of
the Amistad's orphans suggests that the paths to enslavement were somewhat
narrower for children than for adults. Like adults, children could be captured
in warfare and targeted raids. Children could be separated from kin and family
very easily in the context of conflict. Like adults, children could be enslaved as
punishment for witchcraft or as part of a broader "catastrophe" inflicted against
a family group as the result of trial by ordeal. Children were also given as settle-

ments after the conclusion of a palaver, and they could operate as proxies for adult crimes, as Koelle's account of his travels among the Vai in 1847 demonstrates. But children were unlikely to be accused of infidelity or adultery and punished with enslavement. Adults, particularly males, were rarely used as pawns for credit or debt. Adult males had greater capacity to fight back against attempts at violent seizure. And all healthy adults, male and female, had a better chance than any child of evading capture by fleeing and hiding.[14]

Notwithstanding the paucity of information about their formative years in their natal villages, Amistad's orphans entered the trans-Atlantic trade through two primary enslavement vehicles, kidnapping and pawnship. Participation in enslavement networks was universal among the communities in the region, as slavery operated as tool for the reinforcement and transformation of social and political order. But some ethnic groups feature particularly frequently as slave traders or slave purchasers in the region. What is clear from the accounts of other African survivors of the Amistad is that African slave traders and slave purchasers operating in Galinhas region bought and sold children and adults promiscuously and resold them into complex and shifting networks operating in multiple and different directions.[15]

ENSLAVEMENT PRACTICES AND SLAVE TRADING IN GALINHAS

Amistad's orphans were born during the first decades of the *illegal* trans-Atlantic trade, but in a region and time where *legal* enslavement of men, women, and children was customary for a wide variety of social, political, and economic functions. The children may have been born into servitude or into some form of dependency; alternatively, they may have been raised by parents who never experienced significant social or economic bondage. Generally, enslavement could result from many different social and political actions, ranging from raids and warfare to punishments and trial by ordeal. But in the Galinhas the forms of slavery and the paths to child enslavement were more limited than those available to adults. The enslavement and slave-trading context that resulted in Amistad's orphans imprisonment and sale in Lomboko was intimately tied to the historical practices of the Bulom-, Mende-, Sherbro-, and Vai-speaking communities and other language groups found living or temporarily traversing the Galinhas region. Slavery and slave trading were universal among the ethnic groups inhabiting the region both before and after the children's sale at Lomboko. The long history of trans-Saharan trading was certainly a factor in the persistence of particular slave sale networks in the supra-region, but it was of marginal significance in the Galinhas. By contrast, domestic forms of slavery and regional slave-trading practices are very important for understanding the context of the children's enslavement.[16]

Domestic slavery was all-pervasive and unchallenged in the Galinhas region in the 1820s and 1830s, one facet of a spectrum of intermingled labor relationships shaped by lineage and land access that contributed to the early experiences of Amistad's orphans. Although we know little of the family context of the six children, there is a high probability that their families, like most others, were engaged in agriculture, either for subsistence, for local resale, or a combination of both. Before their kidnapping or pawning, the children may each have experienced domestic subordination or bondage intimately tied to their marginal position in a lineage and family. Their status was also dictated by the status of their parents, who may have worked their own small farms and drawn on the labor of their children and other kinsmen. Their parents' successes or failures may have led to credits or debts—and even to the pawning of children, like Kag'ne. Or whole families may have relocated from one community and sought refuge in another, like Covey's parents, and requested access to land as strangers. Upon arrival in a new locale, refugee families supplicated themselves before the chief of the community, exchanged gifts in the context of a palaver, and established a patron-client relationship. Regardless of the tasks performed—farming, hunting, fishing, salt making, domestic chores, or small-scale trading—as young children, Amistad's orphans, occupied a tenuous position in a lineage, rivaled in vulnerability only by the most elderly.[17]

The majority of slaves living in Galinhas villages worked in agriculture. Among some communities possibly close to 50 percent of the population were slaves. Agricultural production throughout the supra-region of Senegambia and Guinea, according to historian Boubacar Barry, was based on a "degree of collectivism" whereby activities were tied to one's lineage and extended family ties. Rice cultivation in this tropical environment operated on a two-season cycle, and for labor during peak periods rights-in-persons were accessed through lineages. Children performed a variety of tasks on their family farms and also on farms of extended lineage kinsmen to whom their parents owed labor. Some children, like Covey, worked on larger farms, closer to barracoons, which supplied rice, yams, and other foodstuffs for slave ships. By the early nineteenth century, some coastal regions were beginning to experience the precursor to the economic transformations later described as the transition to "legitimate" commerce, such as the expansion of highly labor-intensive organized plantations. But larger-scale slave owning was a privilege of the more rich and powerful, like the Bulom chief and his wife in Mani, mentioned by Covey.[18]

Vai, Mende, Sherbro, and other groups in the region measured wealth in people, not in goods. The many language communities residing in the Galinhas region were structured into ranked descent groups, which were relatively fluid and subject to change amid the endemic warfare that gripped what Adam Jones called the "Galinhas Kingdom" in the 1820s and 1830s. Slavery both reinforced and transformed social and political order. The number of individuals whose services were under one's control was a primary mechanism of the structure of power. Koelle, visiting Vai communities in the 1840s reported, "I was told, that the wealth of a man is estimated by the number of wives he can have on the Sandbeach to prepare salt." Whereas historian Walter Rodney's assertion that slavery did not exist in the region prior to European contact has been the subject of extensive dispute, this particular debate is moot for the enslavement contexts of Amistad's orphans. All six children were born and raised in a world profoundly transformed by more than three hundred years of trans-Atlantic trade. The children were not free-born but were embodied and invested with the claims of others from birth and possibly before. The children's first few years unfolded in a world where a variety of junior and senior lineage members as well as larger corporate groups could claim access to the "intricate transactions" associated with rights-in-persons.[19]

The context for initial enslavement of some of Amistad's orphans resonates with anthropologist Svend Holsoe's discussion of three forms of servitude among the Vai, namely, indentured laborers, pawns, and domestic slaves. Indentured laborers were individuals who incurred a debt and labored to pay this off. Adults frequently incurred debts for material goods and political and spiritual services. Mar'gru may have been enslaved because her parents failed to fulfill their debt obligations. Indeed, paying off a debt was rarely simple in a community interwoven with kinship and lineage obligations. Raymond, living in the region in 1845, observed that by offering a wife to the debtor once the debt was repaid, one could resaddle a debtor with obligations and social distance diminished. Children worked without remuneration, but their labor serviced the interest on the debt.[20]

Pawnship and domestic service were common forms of slavery and often affected children. The male head of the patrilineage could pawn nieces and nephews, and Holsoe suggests that lineage heads could refer to them as "my servants." Girl children of patrilineal sisters might be subjected to a form of pawnship that lasted a lifetime. The master of the pawn would be responsible for housing, clothing, and feeding, and the social distance among members of the household was "scarcely noticeable," with the result that they resembled a biological family. Kinship and ritual ties of pawns were sustained with their original families, and "unpawned" and pawn cohabited. Domestic service was a form of slavery to which stranger groups, like Covey's parents, were frequently subjected. Domestic slaves may have originated as strangers or pawns, subsequently slipping into a form of irrecoverable debt and domestic slavery.[21]

Once children were enslaved via such mechanisms, they were susceptible to being traded locally or regionally and thus removed from their family or natal village. The nature of slave trading among Vai communities in the Galinhas region provides important insight into the formative experiences of Amistad's orphans. Vai traders occupied a privileged place among slave traders in the region for a number of reasons. As members of a Mande-speaking group, Vai traders were able to maintain relationships with slave traders via linguistic ties to the wider Mande communities, many of whom traded along the coast or north and northeast into the interior. The Vai migrated toward the coast over several centuries, and by time the trans-Atlantic trade was illegal they occupied key positions in the coastal geographical zone that enabled them to compete for a leading role in slave purchasing and resale.[22]

But Amistad's orphans were bought and sold in the context of wider regional networks connecting local agriculture to regional trade. Some, notably Covey, were exchanged several times by different traders, possibly for manufactured goods or agricultural products. Réné Caillié observed the connection between European trade goods on the coast and regional demands for labor. He witnessed a group of slave merchants on their way to purchase slaves for resale in Kankan, their caravans replete with wares "destined for this infamous traffic." He noted that African slave traders were motivated to acquire "twelve or fifteen slaves, whom they employ entirely in agricultural labor." Longer-distance commerce, such as that Caillié witnessed, crisscrossed the entire region. Historian Martin Klein observed that the market for "older children" was competitive because locally they were in demand, and because the sale and resale of older children procured the "sustenance" to "keep other slaves alive" as they were marched to the coastal entrepôts. Slave traders visited regularly established markets to acquire newly enslaved children. And Jones observed that goods on credit or "trust" made Galinhas traders' movement inland, in search of slaves for sale, possible. When the *Wanderer*, the *Rolla*, and the *Saracen* destroyed the eight "Spanish-owned barracoons" at the "mouth of the Gallinas River" in 1840, British officers estimated that the Spanish loss of between £100,000 and £500,000 was coupled to "a claim on 13,000 slaves already paid for to the local natives."[23]

Slaves sometimes operated as a form of currency in the Galinhas, "and the supply of every want" and "every article" was "estimated, by its proportion, to the value of a slave." But with the official prohibition of the Atlantic trade from 1807, the dynamics of slave trading shifted dramatically. As British antislavery action in the Rio Pongas and Rio Nuñez areas north along the coast from Freetown made it difficult for interior polities and traders, such as those centered in the Futa Jallon, to dispose of slaves, Vai communities tapped into the existing interior-coast trade of local products, such as salt and kola and manufactured goods like guns and cloth, for slaves and then expanded it with a massive influx of locally acquired slaves. As the risks accompanying slave trading rose, so too did the price of slaves.[24]

During the formative years of Amistad's orphans, there was a massive upsurge in slave trading and slave capture among Galinhas communities. One contemporary observer calculated that of a total Vai population of twelve to fifteen thousand, possibly as many as three-quarters were slaves. Holsoe argued that as a result of these market changes, the Vai economy shifted in the 1810s and 1820s to a system focusing on the "collection" of slaves. The Sierra Leone Commissioners provided a vivid account of the slave purchasing economy in 1823. "The course of the trade at Gallinas . . . is to contact with the King or chief headman, Siaca, for the supply of the total number of slaves wanted and to deliver to him the goods paid in advance for the purchase of them. He makes subordinate contracts with the interior headmen and with slave dealers of the vicinity who undertake to furnish scores or dozens of slaves according to their means." This account suggests that the trade was orchestrated from the coastal-dwelling communities familiar with the needs of slave traders. Slavery expanded among the Vai communities as new mechanisms were sought to increase the numbers of slaves available for export. Indeed, slave trading became such a staple element of the Galinhas economy that later attempts to suppress the trade by treaties with chiefs fomented conflict and renewed slave wars.[25]

KIDNAPPING, VIOLENT SEIZURE, AND PANYARRING

Three of Amistad's orphans—Te'me, Ka'le, and Covey—indicated that their first enslavement experience was a form of kidnapping. Violent seizure in context of conflict, including capture in general wars, and targeted kidnapping were a primary vehicle for child enslavement in Galinhas. Child enslavement may have resulted from intra- or inter-ethnic strife or reprisal attacks, or it may just as easily have resulted from an incidental or opportunistic moment. A distinction between children engulfed by warfare and targeted seizures merits consideration; warfare was often circumscribed by weather or seasonal considerations, but kidnapping could take place throughout the year. Kidnapping could take place anywhere, but it may have been more prevalent on the political borders or ecological frontiers. In some instances enslavement of children was accompanied by the capture, sale, and subsequent dispersal of entire families. Some kidnapping victims were immediately sold to itinerant slave traders, and others were transported to the coast for sale directly to Europeans. Kidnapping could take place during the daytime or at night. Whereas a number of the adult victims aboard the Amistad indicated they were abducted during the day, kidnapping of children may have been more common during the night.[26]

Te'me explained that she was a victim of an evening attack on her home. She was living with her mother, an elder brother, and a sister; her father may have passed away or relocated. She stated that "a party of men in the night broke into her mother's house, and made them prisoners." Te'me was enslaved with her family members. Her brief narrative is somewhat ambiguous, but she appears to indicate that she was separated from her family members more or less immediately. Te'me lived an unknowable distance from the embarkation point in Lomboko, but it is reasonable to assume that she was separated at the initial act of enslavement, before the transactional re-enslavement experience of being sold to Europeans at the Galinhas coast. Although whole families may have been enslaved together in the violence widespread in Galinhas in the 1820s and 1830s, it was probably rare for them to remain together throughout the entire process of enslavement, Middle Passage, and resale in the Americas.[27]

Ka'le was "stolen when in the street," but it is unclear whether this took place in a village or in the bush, at nighttime or during daylight hours. Opportunistic abduction occurred in villages, towns, and in fields and along footpaths. Slaving gangs' attacks on homes and villages were supplemented by opportunistic seizures. Gangs of slavers might lie in wait in bushes or under the steep grass thatch eaves of huts. Although he had two parents and at least two siblings, Ka'le's brief narrative indicated that he was enslaved alone and transported immediately to the coast for resale. The context of his kidnapping is frustratingly vague. He may possibly have fallen victim to some type of reprisal action against the community, about which he was completely unaware. Kidnapping and seizure for "honour" injury spanned "many generations" and greatly contributed to general insecurity. His community may have experienced a raid like the one Paramount chief Foday Kai described to anthropologist Carol Hoffer Mac-Cormack: upon raiding a village, each "victorious warrior" claimed the "goods and persons inside each house he broke into." Ka'le's letter to John Quincy Adams seems to have indicated as much.[28]

A rare contemporaneous account by an erstwhile slaver echoes Ka'le's narrative. While traveling between the villages settled by recaptives in Sierra Leone in 1834, British traveler Harrison Rankin met a liberated "Ibbo" slave in the town of Regent. "Pointing to a child who was revelling in the dust near a cottage by the roadside," the man explained to Rankin, "Were he in his own country and found the boy thus unwatched by his mother, he should bandage its mouth and put it into the large wallet which his countrymen constantly wear at the side for this specific purpose, and sell the little wretch for a few dollars." In this unusual display of candor, the man explained that just as he "felt pride in the number of victims" he had captured, a "treacherous friend" seized him in a similar manner.[29]

Covey provides the richest detail about the experience of child kidnapping, and we have tantalizing particulars of the context of his first enslavement. Covey was the victim of a planned raid conducted under darkness that resonated with Foday Kai's description above. Conflicting accounts of the precise nature of the seizure party exist. Gibbs wrote that Covey "was taken by three men" from his "parents' house" and "in the evening." By "parents' house" Gibbs meant the location identified as Golahun, in the easternmost portion of the Kenema district. If this were the case, Covey was likely the victim of a targeted raid by a professional or purpose-oriented operation. Before the district court in Hartford, Connecticut, however, Covey complicated this narrative. He explained, "I was stolen by a black man who stole ten of us." There was no suggestion that any of his family members were also captured, so the other nine were possibly victims of similar illicit nighttime abductions. It is hard to imagine how one man alone could seize and hold ten captives. Thus it is highly likely that Covey was the victim of a professional targeting endeavor, a for-profit kidnapping company directed by a leader or captain, and not an opportunistic or incidental account.[30]

Two of Covey's "African" names provide possible additional contextual anchors. "Covie," the name recorded in the Liberated African Register, may be a variation of a Bulom Sherbro word, according to anthropologists Esther Mokuwa and Paul Richards, in which case it may further anchor his enslavement to the Bulom "Ba-yi-mi." Although Gibbs claimed (without irony) that his "original name was *Kaw-we-li*, which signifies in Mendi, *war road*, i.e., a road dangerous to pass, for fear of being taken captive," to date no new information has come to light to corroborate this explanation, and there is no record of Covey using this name or referring to a Mende or Cosso name in any other context. Furthermore, whether or not the words are indeed Mende, or another language, or a complete fabrication, is probably unanswerable. It is perhaps more appropriate to view the signification of this "original name" within the context of the Amistad Committee's effort to identify the African survivors' origins, which involved translations and transliterations of most of their African names. If this was a name used to describe him or even used by Covey himself, he may have acquired it during his first enslavement or during his subsequent sale and enslavement in the Bulom community in "Mani" (discussed below).[31]

Other, more familiar enslavement narratives echo the experience of these three of Amistad's orphans. Kidnapping and violent capture in conflict featured in narratives from eighteen of the thirty-two adults among the adult survivors of the Amistad. Forty-three of Koelle's informants (30 percent) stated that they had been "kidnapped" into slavery. Several identified being kidnapped while traveling or on business, and one of these ("Musewo, or Toki Petro of Freetown [a SONGO] born in the town Bopunt") was kidnapped as a child at the age of fifteen. Several of the thirteen slave autobiographers discussed by historian Jerome Handler were kidnapped. Belinda described being kidnapped "before she had twelve years" by "men, whose faces were like the moon, and whose bows and arrows were like the thunder and lightening [*sic*] of clouds." John Joseph was kidnapped at around the age of three, in the context of a "deadly war" during which "a great many" of his community were "taken prisoners." Ottobah Cugoano, Archibald Montieth, and Sibell were "duplicitously enslaved" as children, having been "innocently enticed to accompany someone they or their parents trusted." The most famous kidnapped child is Gustavus Vassa (a.k.a. Olaudah Equiano), who claimed to have been abducted with his sister by unknown men who broke into the family compound.[32]

Raids specifically for the purpose of kidnapping children were likely regular occurrences because children were easy to capture and could be sold immediately to a prospective purchaser. Although Matthews protested he had "never heard of such a practice" as kidnapping, that no "word in their language" existed "expressive of such a custom," evidence suggests otherwise. Francis Spilsbury witnessed an incident in Sierra Leone in 1806, which suggests an opportunistic kidnapping raid and an ideal type. "A man will lay in wait until he can seize a boy or girl who is prime, that is four feet four inches high; this he hurries down to a factory or ship, and sells." In this fascinating description, a specific measurement often cited as the uppermost threshold for a child (four feet four inches) is described as a visible measure of childhood. What often operated as a distinction between child and adult also appeared to function as an index for would-be kidnappers.[33]

But the ease with which children could be kidnapped was only part of the picture. As Spilsbury indicates, the hasty sale of the recently kidnapped child was the basis for an increasing monetization and an expanding market economy, which together produced an upsurge in slave supply on the coast. "With the purchase of his villainy he goes into the country and purchases more slaves;

these he sells again, and goes on trading until he brings a string of them. By this time, the negroes have perhaps found out who stole their child; they then lay in wait for him, seize him and all his newly acquired slaves, and retaliate by selling the whole. [A slaver] Mr. Wilson declares he frequently bought the slaves and the kidnapper this way." From Spilsbury we thus have compelling evidence of the key role child kidnapping played in undergirding the wider enslavement economy. Regardless of the ultimate goal of slavers, children were particularly vulnerable to enslavement in active kidnapping raids.[34]

At its broadest, the process of enslavement described by Te'me, Ka'le, and Covey resulted from social and political instability. Their experience of enslavement had a long and rich history in the region, but enslavement practices changed over the centuries. Much earlier, Europeans and Africans led raiding parties from coastal islands. An English slave merchant and pirate, John Hawkins, described one of these raids in the 1560s, the goal of which was to seize the slaves owned by other Africans. By the time the three Amistad children were kidnapped, European-led raiding parties were not necessary. The supply side of the trade had become firmly an Africanized activity. An account from the mid–nineteenth century demonstrates how monetization undergirded the practice of kidnapping and violent seizure. "The manner of obtaining and shipping slaves at Gallinas may be described in a few words. Intelligence is sent abroad, through the country, that 'slave money lives on the beach'; that is, that merchandise is offered for slaves. The 'mercenary' chiefs and the head-men of all the tribes are made such by the fact that money awaits the production of slaves, at once fit out expeditions to the nearest defenceless towns; which they surround and fire in the night time, making prisoners of all fugitives. These, without exception, are now slaves, and are brought down to Gallinas and sold. Nine-tenths of all slaves are thus obtained." By the time the three of Amistad's orphans were kidnapped, intentional acts of warfare and kidnapping in the Galinhas region had a direct relationship to the presence of barracoons and the regular arrival of ships.[35]

The seizures of many kidnapping victims have left no record, and others remain difficult to define. Kidnapping was not restricted to the wealthy or powerful. To be sure, many of the slaves in barracoons had likely been enslaved, redeemed, escaped, and re-enslaved multiple times. One complex form of kidnapping was "panyarring." The sense of "panyar" is to grab, seize, or steal, with purpose, and the word may come from the Portuguese *penhorár* (literally, "to pledge") or from *apanhar* ("to catch" or "to grab"). As a term, it originated among coastal Luso-African communities throughout West Africa and quickly spread beyond Portuguese speakers to describe a subset of targeted kidnapping practices, some of which were tolerated politically and culturally. The term itself does not appear in nineteenth-century Sierra Leonean sources pertaining to *La Amistad*. It may have come into use because of its Portuguese origin and the extensive presence of illicit Lusophone trading communities in the region. While very difficult to define, in some historical sources the term "panyarring" is invoked to describe the specific communal action of kidnapping; at other times it applies to the almost quasi-legal basis of illicit seizure for retributive justice.[36]

Whether something actually resembling panyarring existed in Galinhas is a matter of speculation. Oral interviews conducted by Richards in the 1980s and 1990s suggest the possibility of a local vernacular term. The most compelling evidence for the existence of a form of panyarring is found after the Amistad survivors return to the region. As the internecine conflicts took their toll on the small mission community in 1844, the settlement leader, Raymond, sought help in understanding the situation. He explained, "It is not uncommon to resort to the custom of the country and catch some people. He first informs his land lord of his interest and then if his debtor has slaves he takes as many as he is able to catch if the debt is due and keeps them in custody until the debt is paid. If the debtor has no slaves he then catches people belonging to the same town as his debtor whether bond or free and keeps them in custody until the debt is paid." Panyarring, if it existed in Galinhas, was but one of several forms of enslavement in the context of kidnapping.[37]

Certainly, there is no way to completely distinguish such accounts from seizures and attacks in the context of warfare. European and American narratives of violence and African plundering no doubt obscure the complexity of the practice. But if panyarring could be prohibited, as historian Robin Law suggests, while at the same time kidnapping continued unregulated and unabated, then it operated in the interstices of African customary law and retributive justice. Falola and Lovejoy suggest that pawnship operated possibly "as an alternative" to panyarring insofar as it established a specific good or chattel that served as security for a debt.[38]

PAWNSHIP, BONDING, AND DEBT SEIZURE

Pawnship, bonding, and debt seizure constitute a second widespread group of interrelated mechanisms for child enslavement. In historical records, commercial debts feature prominently as the reason for pawning a child. Those who self-identified as being sold by family members were often first pawned after the incurring of a familial debt. Prepubescent girls or young unmarried women were considered most pawn-worthy because the credit could be forgiven by converting the pawn into a prospective bride or actual wife. When a liberated slave boy "ran away" from the Kaw-Mendi mission compound in 1845, Raymond accepted a chief's son as pawn until the boy was returned to the mission. For two of Amistad's orphans, Mar'gru and Kag'ne, pawnship was an important first step in the beginning of a much longer process of enslavement.[39]

Amistad's orphans were born into a sparsely monetarized economy, one in which economic activity expanded cautiously in the context of limited credit. Child kidnapping was one way to procure funds from which a larger enslavement enterprise may arise. Pawning, by contrast, was a slower process, and it shifted the risk away from the adult, the debtor, and onto the person of the pawn. Kag'ne provided a frustratingly compact description of her initial path into enslavement when she stated that "she was put in pawn for a debt by her father which not being paid, she was sold into slavery." We are left wondering many things, including how long she was pawned, who initiated the sale of the pawn, and at what point. Mar'gru's narrative was almost identical and similarly economical in detail: "she was pawned by her father for a debt, which being unpaid, she was sold into slavery." We can only speculate about the nature of the debts a father might incur. Possibly he had to purchase food for his family, new agricultural tools, or new weaponry, or he owed labor to an elder or chief. The appearance of new consumer products along the coast with the arrival of each European ship provoked a constantly shifting set of economic relationships within which children were readily moveable goods.[40]

The pawnship experienced by Kag'ne and Mar'gru was, however, distinct from the form most often referenced in European sources insofar as it was between two Africans. The pawnship invoked more frequently in European sources from the coast of West Africa concerns pawns between African slave vendors and European slave purchasers and their African staff and assistants. Pawning operated as a means of securing crucial credit in slave-trading communities when new goods appeared. Children or young women could be placed under the protection of the trader as a temporary placeholder. When creditors failed to return with the requisite goods or liquidity, enslavement ensued. Indeed, evidence suggests that the very mechanics of the coastal Atlantic-oriented slave trade in Calabar and the Gold Coast rested upon pawn-based securities.[41]

Bonding operated primarily as means of making labor available to service a debt, whereas pawning made new credit available for future commercial transactions. Pawning and bonding were options open to parents, guardians, or lineage heads, whereby they could intentionally release children or dependents from their control as collateral via debt service or credit for a family obligation.

European accounts of bonding often conflate it with sale by parents. And from the perspective of a child, there was surely little discernible difference. It is likely that the majority of bonding was temporary, and surely most bonds left no historical record. Pawning for new credit, however, was much riskier. It increased in usage throughout West Africa in the eighteenth century as the supply of alternatives, such as gold, diminished. It could more easily result in enslavement and removal from the community. For these reasons Lovejoy and Richardson describe pawning as enveloping the slave trade in a twofold dimension. By tying local credit arrangements to the slave trade, pawnship exposed people to the risk of enslavement and undergirded the market in slaves.[42]

In the wider Sierra Leone coastal region, of which Galinhas was part, the prevalence of children among the pawned was unmistakable. In the 1780s, the slave trader Matthews described how pawnship provided a pool for prospective slave traders. "It is customary, indeed, for people of all ranks to put their children out as pledges, but then they are careful either to redeem them in time or to pawn them to the resident traders or established factories; and these pawns are generally considered as a protection for your property . . . but are equally as liable to be sent off, if not redeemed in due time, as the pawned slave." By "sent off" Matthews meant that pawns were enslaved and shipped away as part of a slave cargo. But his narrative subtly distinguished between slave sellers seeking credit and slave purchasers using their own children and other commercially active individuals. "Another method which they make use of to dispose of their slaves is, to put them in pawn either to shops and factories, or the native traders, for a limited time; and if they are not redeemed at the expiration of that time, they become slaves to the person to whom they were pawned." This second group of traders appeared to be seeking credit for the acquisition of consumer goods or other services with slaves they have acquired previously.[43]

Discerning precisely who was a pawn, and who was not, was not easy. A physical marker was sometimes used, but it could not be permanent, like a branding mark. When Spilsbury visited Tasso Island in the Sierra Leone estuary in 1806, he observed that a trader, king, or chief seeking to procure "articles which [he] is not at the time able to pay for" will put "a tally round" the "neck" of a "wife, sister, or child." Spilsbury's account provides the sole image of such a tally (figure 3.1). The pawn resides with the trader but is still discernible as a pawn, and not a slave. He noted, "The child then runs among the slaves until exchanged; and it is an invariable custom never to take these pawns away. . . . At Tasso Island, I saw a great number of pawns with their tallies." Pawning continued unabated after the African survivors returned to Sierra Leone. It would be remiss not to mention the curious corollary between the tally for pawns and

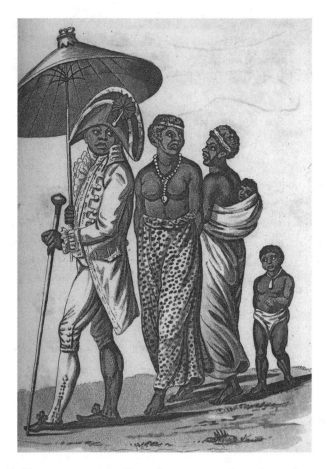

Fig. 3.1. Child wearing a pawn tally in the presence of an African slave trader and family, c. 1800 (Francis B. Spilsbury, *Account of a Voyage to the Western Coast of Africa* [London: Richard Phillips, 1807]; © The British Library Board)

the "tin ticket" worn by Liberated Africans in Freetown streets in the 1830s and 1840s. Historian Allen Howard has cited numerous examples in the hinterland of Sierra Leone from the 1850s onward and well into the early twentieth century.[44]

Precisely why a specific child might be pawned at any one time—whether in their original natal village or on the coast as part of an Atlantic transaction—is a matter of conjecture. Raymond, writing from Kaw-Mendi in 1845, appeared to consider both sexes equally vulnerable and identified money as the primary motivation. "It sometimes happens when a native has taken money, and is unable to pay he gives the trader a boy or girl in pawn for the debt. It not infrequently happens that they are never redeemed and consequently they are held as pawns alias slaves." Raymond thus reinforces Lovejoy's and Richardson's analysis. But gender distinctions were important. There are few records of adult males beginning a life of slavery in the Atlantic world as pawns for credit. Wives and girl children were more often subject to the potentially perilous transactions associated with offering family members as security for a debt. Child betrothal and marriage was a mechanism whereby a girl might be released from a natal into a marital context via pawnship. Matthews's account of child marriage suggests that this was a contractual relationship among "Bullams, Bagoes and Timmaneys." But no evidence suggests a defaulted marriage contract was a factor in funneling two of Amistad's orphans into the Atlantic trade.[45]

Mar'gru and Kag'ne, by their own descriptions, came from large families. Kag'ne's parents were still living and had eight other children—four girls and four boys. Both of Mar'gru's parents were also alive, and she had six siblings, among them four sisters. Young girls were pawned in the context of poverty, famine, and other calamities. As Diptee notes, "Not only would these parents be putting newly enslaved children into a circumstance that guaranteed them food and shelter, but the money obtained from the sale of their children also enabled the purchase of provisions for the rest of the family." Whether or not their parents regarded Kag'ne and Mar'gru as expendable we do not know; but it is surely not inconsequential that these two girls who began their journey into slavery as debt-pawns were from the two largest families, at least insofar as they were described by the survivors of the Amistad ordeal. Their narratives point to abandonment of children as a response to poverty and insecurity.[46]

To what extent the experience of Kag'ne and Mar'gru mirrored that of others is hard to say because the pawns most often referenced in European sources in the context of Atlantic slave purchases were not likely relinquished for marital, ecological, or economic reasons. The use of pawns on the coast of Africa was an extension of a long-established African transactional relationship to a new economic circumstance. Along the coast, pawns were collateral for a debt between traders, and pawnship took place between economically active and engaged parties. The pawns and pawnship practices bequeathed by the historical record in these contexts were the troublesome cases involving violation of the pawnship arrangement. When a specific agreed-upon time passed and the debt remained unpaid, the pawn was seized as collateral. When ships sailed, slavers exchanged pawns they were holding for slaves on another ship, and in so doing passed on the debt.[47]

A third aspect of child enslavement thus emerges from the shadows of Amistad's orphans' description of pawning: debt seizure. Debt seizure had a rich history in the region, and non-kin children could be seized for debts and enslaved. Debt seizure operated at the quasi-legal interstices of kidnapping, panyarring, and pawnship. Seizures could take place by Europeans or Africans in accordance with "the country law" that "warranted this mode of redress." Sometimes local community leaders regulated it "on the principles of African justice," and in some accounts it appears to have operated as a free-for-all. Debt seizure was an intermediary stage, whereby a creditor could seize a debtor or other persons or objects. But its arbitration required the intervention of the community leader. Matthews observed, "Debts are commonly contracted for a limited time; that is, there is such a length of credit given. If the debtor refuses or delays payment when the debt is due and demanded, the creditor applies to the king, or chief, for his assistance; who sends to the debtor, desiring him to pay the debt. If after this notice from the king, he refuses to pay it, or to satisfy his creditor, the latter gets the king's consent to seize the person of his debtor, or any of his slaves or people." If the debtor fled, the creditor could legitimately seize any person "who resides in the same town" in order to compel the townspeople to pay the debt.[48]

What Matthews described appears to be a legal proceeding, in which the case is taken to a "king," who in his judicial capacity issues a decision. With this decision the creditor is provided enforcement powers, but it is unclear how a European could accomplish enforcement without the king's militia. If this description also concerned debts between local vendors, it is similarly vague about enforcement. And whereas he affirmed that this mechanism was "founded on the first principles of jurisprudence, which are generally adopted by all nations," Matthews was at pains to point out that enslavement opportunities applied only to Africans, for "in their disputes with white men they are not very rigid observers of justice." Raymond's account from 1845, which blurs the grounds between debt seizure and panyarring, confirms that debt seizure was still happening in Galinhas after the Amistad survivors returned.[49]

Irrespective of the protocol, a child seized in such a manner was in a perilous position, not simply because the legal basis for the enslavement was doubtful, but because children lacked the agency to initiate a "palaver." A child thus seized would likely have little capacity to understand the nuance of the experience. Did the legal basis reside in African customary law insofar as it was tolerated, and was chattel redeemable if the debtor presented himself? Or was it an extra-judicial economic artifact for which no legal remedy existed? These questions mattered little when the seizure was a child. Once the seizure had been effected and the child shipped away, there was no legal formula whereby the pawn might be redeemed. The frequency with which this mechanism was used is unclear. The eighteenth-century British slave trader Richard Rogers suggested some parameters were understood. The foreclosure of a debt and seizure of a pawn in satisfaction of that debt was a method whereby pawns were converted from persons (meriting respect and, in the case of children, protection) to disposable objects.[50]

Whether pawned, bonded, or seized to recover a debt, the child became part of an enslavement system funneling boys and girls toward the coast for sale to European slave traders. At some point in the 1830s Antonio possibly met a fate resembling that of the other children, and an African likely sold him to a Spaniard in a Galinhas coastal barracoon. The initial enslavement in a village or town, or in the bush or rice paddy, was only the first stage in a sequence of exchanges, sales, and resales.

SERIAL TRANSACTIONS AND COASTAL BARRACOONS

Regardless of whether a child was kidnapped or pawned, the initial experience of enslavement was but the first in a series of perilous transactions spanning months or years. Whereas the mechanics of seizure, capture, or pawnship are relatively well documented, the economic transactions whereby Amistad's orphans were funneled toward markets and barracoons are less well understood. Identifying and analyzing the stages of commercial transaction as slaves moved toward the coast is an important aspect of the child's experience of enslavement. For adults, many of whom participated in the slave trade, the transactions may have been a known unknown. But from a child's perspective, the constantly shifting ownership status, as they were passed on and resold, was daunting. Age, however, could not prepare anyone for the experience of the barracoon.

The serial transactions involved in the travel to the coast were terrifying, exhausting, and disorienting (Chapter 4). Three of the children gave precursory details of the transaction that resulted in their arrival at the coastal barracoon but no details of their sale or resale. The mortality rate from capture to arrival at the coast and boarding a ship was, conservatively, 15 or 20 percent, sometimes as high as 40 percent, but death rates in barracoons are difficult to estimate. Ka'le spent a month traveling to Lomboko after being captured. Te'me and Kag'ne were also in the slave pen within a month or so of their initial enslavement. For Antonio and Mar'gru there is no record of their arrival in a coastal slave port. None of the children mention being shackled, tied, or imprisoned.[51]

Other contemporary accounts help make sense of the debilitating ordeal. The sequential transactions were rapid. As Samuel Crowther explained, "In the space of twenty four hours, being deprived of my liberty and all other comforts, I was made the property of three different persons." Thirteen-year-old

Louis Asa-Asa was "sold six times over, sometimes for money, sometimes for cloth, and sometimes for a gun," according to the tale retold by the abolitionist Mary Prince. Asa-Asa was "sold at every place" he "stopped at" over a period of about six months. Other Amistad survivors echo the multiple stages of Asa-Asa's move toward Lomboko. Cinquez indicated that after being captured and tied up, Mayagilalo sold him to Bamadzha, "son of Shaka" the king (Vai: *siaca*) of Gendema in the Vai territory. He was then sold by Bamadzha "to a Spaniard" at Lomboko. Berri was also "sold to Shaka" and then to a Spaniard. Grabeau was sold to a Vai man who sold him to Laigo, a Spaniard. Kimbo was first taken slave by his king, after the death of his father. The king gave Kimbo to his son, Banga, who in turn sold him to a Bulom man, who sold him to a Spaniard at Lomboko. Gnakwoi was sold to a Vai man after being seized and then sold to a Spaniard name Peli. Sessi indicated that "he was sold twice before he arrived at Lomboko." Fakinna stated that "after being a slave to the man that took him, less than a month," he was brought to Lomboko. A number of others explained that the Lomboko barracoon was only one stage in a series of transactions spanning days, weeks, months, or years.[52]

None of Amistad's orphans provide information about being chained or tied up during their move to the barracoon. Binding male adults was surely necessary to prevent their escape on short or long journeys, but children and women were also chained or placed in neck braces or other wooden or bamboo devices to prevent them escaping slave coffles. Asa-Asa explained that he was captured and tied at the feet. The most vivid description comes from Crowther, who explained that as a young boy, one of the greatest discomforts came from being chained together with adult males. He wrote,

> Men and boys were at first chained together, with a chain of about six fathoms in length, thrust through an iron fetter on the neck of every individual, and fastened at both ends with padlocks. In this situation, the boys suffered the most: the men sometimes, getting angry, would draw the chain so violently, as seldom went without bruises on their poor little necks; especially the time to sleep, when they dress they draw the chain so close to ease themselves of its weight, in order to be able to lie more conveniently, that we were almost suffocated, or bruised to death, in a room with one door, which was as soon fastened as we entered in.

The ordeal lessened only slightly when the "number [of adults] was increased, and no more chain to spare; we were corded together, by ourselves."[53]

We know little about the food they ate or where they slept. The paucity of detail about this stage in their enslavement is frustrating, but it can surely be explained from the perspective of a child. Very young children would have little sense of who owned them at different points during the passage from the interior to the coast. It is unlikely that they had any direct interaction with the leader of a slave-purchasing gang or the owner of a barracoon. During this period the closest and most memorable relationships would have been between the children and other adult slaves, with whom they rested, walked, ate, and slept.[54]

Covey's experience, which involved a sequence of temporary slave statuses, provides rich insight into different aspects of the serial transactions involved in enslavement. He was not kidnapped and brought to the coast, sold, and shipped to Cuba in one continuous process. Rather, after his initial capture he was "sold as a slave" and enslaved in a coastal community for several years. Gibbs noted, "He was carried to the Bullom country, and sold as a slave to Ba-yi-mi, the king of the Bul-loms, who resided at Mani. He lived there for three years, and was employed to plant rice for the wife of Ba-yi-mi, who treated him with great kindness." At the time of Covey's enslavement at Mani, pockets of Bulom-language speakers inhabited many parts of the coast, including areas today identified as predominantly Sherbro, Bom, and Krim. Bulom settlements were scattered from the Scarcies Rivers, south along the low-lying islands to Liberia. Mani was possibly a small Bulom community settled by Mani speakers (a dialectal variant), approximately five to ten miles inland from the coast in the mangrove-covered region of interwoven waterways. But as there are several candidates for Mani on maps of the region from the epoch and more recently—and probably many additional settlements that have left no historical record—its precise location will likely remain unclear. Bayimi was likely a variation of a Bulom phrase "Bay Yeome," meaning "king" or "highest headman." The titular epithet "Bay" or "Bai" is still used today in Temne-speaking and Bulom-speaking regions. For several years after his initial kidnapping, Covey lived among a Bulom family, as part of an enslavement community of varied peoples farming rice.[55]

Covey's narrative sheds important light on the transactional nature of slavery in the Galinhas region in the early to mid–nineteenth century. Instead of following a path to the coast, such as that indicated by Asa-Asa's story and those of many others, some individuals were retained as slaves for long periods in a variety of capacities and locales. Because of their adaptability and the relatively low cost involved, children were likely highly desirable. Covey's experience is mirrored by several of the Amistad adults, including Pungwuni, who, after being "taken in the night," was sold to "Galobá who had four wives." Pungwuni worked a rice paddy for two years. Although many slaves were brought hastily to the coast, placed in barracoons, and then sold, many others worked among these slaves in Galinhas. The food grown and prepared for slaves in barracoons

Fig. 3.2. West African slave barracoon, with a man being whipped, c. 1845
("Slave Barracoon," *Illustrated London News* [April 14, 1849], 237)

was likely the work of slave women and children. One barracoon raided by the British in 1844 had thirty tons of rice in its stores.[56]

The residential dimensions of the barracoon experience are important. Grabeau described Lomboko as a "prison" where slaves were "chained together by the legs" in twos. None of Amistad's orphans provided information about their physical experience in the barracoons, but describing the barracoon as a "kind of prison" is not unreasonable. Men were kept in confined enclosures (figure 3.2) and whipped. Sometimes they were chained in pairs. Women and children were usually unshackled. How this affected children, compared to adults, is unclear. One contemporary observer, Robert Clarke, stated, "In the case of children the injury then done is not so much felt afterwards, because, they are not confined, but allowed to run about and amuse themselves, except in stormy weather, when the hatches are battened down." But he seems to have detached the physiological from any possible psychological damage.[57]

To guard against possible escape, many of the barracoons, such as those in the Galinhas lagoon and estuary were on islands. Spilsbury's visit to two barracoons on Crawford's Island (one of the Îles de Los), in the early 1800s, suggests women were never chained. Amistad's orphans may also have been allowed to roam freely within a delimited space. But islands also made escape difficult when the Royal Navy attacked barracoons. Whether on islands or the mainland, all barracoons were filthy, disease-ridden, mosquito-plagued enclosures open to the elements, although they were sometimes depicted in a more congenial manner (figure 3.3). Within the enclosures slaves carried out daily activities, such

Fig. 3.3: Highly sanitized interior view of Guinea Coast hacienda-style slave barracoon, c. 1845, showing the preparation of food and the dancing (possibly exercise) of slaves prior to trans-Atlantic transport (Édouard de Bouët-Willaumez, *Description nautique des côtes de l'Afrique occidentale* [Paris: Robiquet, 1848]; © The British Library Board)

as cooking and physical exercise. In addition to the several Europeans present, those securing the barracoons were generally adult slaves, "hired natives," and Kroomen. The enslaved may easily have been under the control of several masters by the time they arrived in the barracoon. African "men-servants" or "gromettas" had been used to guard slaves for centuries.[58]

Enslavement in the Lomboko barracoon rarely lasted more than a month or two. Covey indicated that after three years of farming rice, he resided in the barracoon "about one month." Cinquez was in Lomboko for two months. Sessi "was kept about a month" after he arrived at Lomboko. Among the Amistad survivors, Burna appears to have been the longest in Lomboko, "where he was kept three and half moons," possibly because he was quite old and partially blind. Raymond, writing in 1844, described the ongoing slave trade and explained that once the Spaniards had paid for the slaves in goods, the Africans had two months to produce the slaves. Residence in the barracoon was relatively brief for a number of reasons, one of the most important being that it was close to the sea and highly vulnerable to attack. An African slave trader on Crawford's Island, Betsy Walker, explained to Spilsbury that, "when she saw our [Spilsbury's] vessel in the offing, she had resolved to collect the slaves, and remove the property into the woods, as she before had been twice obliged to do when the French affected a landing, by which she means she preserved the effects of her friend from plunder. She was continually on the watch with a glass . . . liable every moment to brutality from the attacks of the corsairs, or a whim of the petty kings of the opposite coast." And the Spanish and Portuguese traders on the coast knew of the insecurity too. They maintained both coastal facilities and other separate concealed compounds and barracoons inland within a short walking distance. Foni, for example, was kept in Luiz's barracoon in Bembelaw for two months, only one day's walk to Lomboko. Slave traders, African and European, moved their slaves into the more vulnerable coastal barracoons at what was hoped to be an optimal moment.[59]

The Galinhas slave barracoons were numerous and the slave supply voluminous. Frederick Edwyn Forbes, who sailed with the West Africa Squadron aboard the *Bonetta* in 1848, claimed the Galinhas barracoons housed as many as six thousand slaves at one time. In a contemporaneous trial of a slave trader, Sergeant Talfourd described the barracoons as "extensive buildings of themselves; and the buildings, necessary for the parties to live in to attend to the slaves, are numerous. At Dumbocoro there may be fifty or sixty houses, storehouses, and places." Another account describes the facilities as "swarming with slaves of all ages and characters, from the sullen stalwart warrior chained by the leg, who may have defended his town to the last, down to the infant at the mother's breast; the aged and decrepid [*sic*] grandfather and toddling younker, some coupled together, others strung on poles, or if helpless, at loose in the wattled yards." The barracoons comprised many enslavers as well: "hosts of straggling armed natives were lounging or prowling about the factories."[60]

Although barracoon locations may have been "permanent," the buildings themselves were constructed and laid out to evade detection by rival slavers and the Royal Navy. Because they had to withstand tumultuous weather, they were constructed of local pliable materials like bamboo and acacia, as well as materials brought from Cuba expressly for that purpose. The floors were designed to provide protection against insects, and the walls for air circulation. In the trial of Pedro de Zulueta, barracoons were described as "large barns" containing "five or six hundred slaves sometimes." Many comprised multiple enclosures on neighboring islands. Theophilus Conneau explained that slave prisons, of which there were "ten or twelve[,] . . . contained from one hundred to five hundred slaves." Barracoons were highly fortified, which suggested that they were built in anticipation of regular attack. Conneau explained that each was "made of rough staves or poles" and then "clamped together" by "iron bars." And "two or four Spaniards or Portuguese" guarded each barracoon from "watch-houses" equipped "with loaded muskets." Africans and Spaniards would brutally flog rebellious slaves and any suspected of planning insurrection.[61]

The style of defense Conneau described was modeled on that of the neighboring towns and villages, which likely developed in response to the slave-related violence engulfing Galinhas. Berri described coming from "a large fenced town," and Ngahoni described his town as "formerly fenced around, but now broken down." From Koelle's description of Datia, in the Vai country, in the 1840s a town "could not easily be taken with guns." He noted, "The proper stockade consists of piece of wood, half a foot or a foot in diameter, which are rammed into the ground so closely together, that each touches the other. Generally, only one, but sometimes two, three, and more such pieces of wood, form the thickness of the stockade. Above these sticks, which are about twelve or fifteen feet high, there is again a regular fence of the same height, but consisting of much thinner sticks. On the other side of this stockade . . . there is a girdle, fully four feet broad, consisting of sharp-pointed sticks three feet long, which are rammed into the ground with their points upward." In addition to these remarkable defenses, the town had "strong gates" that were locked every evening with an imported European lock or a big piece of wood or both. The "outermost" defenses comprised "a light wooden fence, about twenty feet high," and "between it and the properly protecting stockade, there is a walk [space] all around the circular town of about three or four feet in breadth."[62]

Fig. 3.4. View between two perimeter defensive fences
of Mende Town, c. 1890 (Thomas Joshua Alldridge, *A Transformed
Colony, Sierra Leone, as It Was, and as It Is; Its Progress, Peoples,
Native Customs, and Undeveloped Wealth* [London: Seeley, 1910])

Koelle explained that "all the other" towns in the region "were fortified in the same way" on account of the wars enveloping the country. Raymond found the town of Malaga to be "barricaded" by a "thick mud wall." And his successor, George Thompson, provided a sketch of a wood fortress in the 1850s (see figure 2.3). Thomas Joshua Alldridge, a British colonial officer, took the only known images of such fortifications about 1890, before such construction was prohibited in Mende territory (figure 3.4). Because they were made of wood, the main tactic of attack, by rivals or the Royal Navy, was to burn them to the ground, as illustrated in the spectacular cover image adorning historian Richard Huzzey's book. But because they were wooden, they could easily be rebuilt. Although Blanco had reportedly "renounced slave trading" in October 1840, by 1845, "attempts" had "been made to rebuild barakoons at Gallinas," and the rights to the territory sold for five thousand dollars. And the site was again under siege in 1849.[63]

The precise location of the barracoon that housed Amistad's orphans will probably remain unknown, but from Covey's narratives and Charlotte Cowles's conversation with Kag'ne we know that they both passed through Lomboko. Lomboko was only one of many establishments in "this remarkable spot, this modern Tyre, this den of iniquity." Jones asserts that Lomboko was Lombokoro, also known as Dumbokoro. Rediker claims to have seen almost twenty variations of the spelling, and may have located the island in 2013. Lomboko and Dumbocoro may be one and the same, or two distinct but neighboring facilities of the same supra-compound. Because of the remarkable cartographic skills of Frederick Evans, second master of Her Majesty's brig *Rolla,* who partook of the British navy attack on Dumbokoro and neighboring Kamasun and Taro, we know its precise location (see figure 2.5). But his map indicates (in red on the original) five sets of "slave factories" or barracoons. Lomboko's notoriety was firmly established by the presence of Pedro Blanco, but none of the Amistad captives claim to have personally met him. Years later, after the return of the survivors, Raymond identified a Spaniard by the name of "Luiz" as "the very man that bought and shipped most of the Amistad Africans."[64]

The concealed and temporary barracoon compounds were an innovation forced upon illicit slave traders by the Royal Navy's Anti-Slavery Squadron patrols. One of the legendary operators of this illicit trade was Pedro Blanco of Galinhas. When most of the Amistad captives were shipped from Lomboko in 1838–39, Blanco's operations were winding down; by the early 1840s he had more or less shuttered his barracoons, and other Spanish traders were moving into his territory. Although there are few records of Blanco's activities in Sierra Leone today, aside from isolated references in oral historical narratives in the Galinhas region, archival records in Cuba provide a vivid picture of the extent of his contraband operations. Records of commercial disputes extend our knowledge of his activities back to the 1820s and 1830s and provide a context for understanding the role of the Galinhas barracoon in the illicit slave trade between the region and Cuba. In one particularly important episode, Blanco sued Guillermo Salguela before Havana's Tribunal de Comercio in 1832 about obligations stemming from the Galinhas trade. The tribunal was the primary site for resolving commercial disputes between Cubans, including those operating abroad, and in this particular episode, Blanco sought indemnity for contracts signed in Havana for debts incurred in commercial enterprises originating in Galinhas. In the tribunal records a variety of financial interactions are referred to by numerous euphemisms, and the expansive operations in Galinhas are attested to in detail. But "slaves" and "slave trading" never appear in the more than forty pages recording the long-running dispute.[65]

Slavers visiting Lomboko examined slaves in the barracoon at the time of sale, finalized the deal with the leader of the enterprise (Blanco), and then returned to Blanco's residence or to their own ship. The slave offered for sale "passed" an examination for what in a horse or other animal would be called "soundness." Each of the Amistad's orphans had this experience. Blanco, from Malaga, relocated from Cuba to Galinhas in 1824–25. He was not the first dealer to operate in the region, only one of several, and he built up his empire after the slow withdrawal of John Ouzeley Kearney, who had been particularly active in Galinhas between 1812 and 1820. Blanco improved on Kearney's methods; whereas Kearney filled ships with "300 or 400 slaves" when they were available and personally accompanied the vessels to Havana, Blanco had to contend with the "increasing efficiency" of the Royal Navy by the 1820s and 1830s. Blanco's main innovation was to build multiple barracoons at the coast, from which ships could be hastily filled with slaves in a matter of days or even hours. Under Blanco, Galinhas "became, not only the centre of an extensive and lucrative traffic, but the theatre of a new order of society and a novel form of government," of which he "was the head, the autocrat. Over all, his authority was absolute, acquired and maintained, not by his wealth alone, but by his will, energy, ability and address." To acquire a cargo of slaves from a barracoon, slave traders moored their ships in deeper water adjacent to a slave "factories." Indeed, in 1835 as many as twelve ships were "lying at anchor" at Galinhas at any one time. Blanco allegedly claimed that if only one in three vessels made it through to Havana, the trade was profitable. And contemporary reports confirmed that "the profit" was "so enormously large, that the traders could well afford to carry on," despite the "heavy losses from capture and other causes." In 1844, exchanging one hogshead of tobacco for twelve slaves, and reselling them in Cuba for an average of $350 each, could conceivably produce a profit of $4,080. When he employed Conneau, whose biography is a primary source for Blanco, his "two large factories monopolized this lucrative trade."[66]

Antonio's and Covey's lives were part and parcel of Blanco's wider operations. José de Inza purchased Covey in early 1833 in Galinhas during his fourth visit to the region. Ferrer purchased Antonio at some point in the mid-1830s, and because of his ties to Pedro Martínez and Blanco this transaction quite possibly took place in Galinhas. Ferrer and de Inza worked closely with the Havana-based establishment of Martínez and Company, and they traded directly with Blanco and others operating the region. Martínez had stakes in as many as thirty slave-trading vessels. Of the Galinhas slave traders who worked with Martínez and Company, the three "most active" contraband traders of the "new trans-Atlantic and hispanocuban elite" were Pedro Blanco, Pedro José de Zulueta (on trial in London in 1843), and Julián de Zulueta. Conneau noted that Blanco's residence was far from the barracoon. Blanco's "solitary and pestilential domain" was located "on several . . . marshy flats. On one . . . he had his place of business or trade with foreign vessels, presided over by his principal clerk. . . . On another island, more remote, was his residence . . . this man . . . dwelt in a sort of oriental but semi-barbarous splendor." Blanco and others like him, such as Don Miguel at Cape Montserrado farther along the coast, likely came down to the coastal barracoon only to interact with important traders, such as Miguel Oliver Moll, Ramón and Damián Ferrer, and José de Inza.[67]

Many Cuban traders, among them the Ferrers and de Inza, would have been the guests of Blanco during the 1830s. Francis Bacon, who testified in the Amistad trials, also resided with Blanco, but he avoided directly implicating himself in slave trading. The final deals and prices would be haggled over during long meals and drinking sessions. How much was paid for Amistad's orphans is unclear, as prices fluctuated. In 1830 children were kidnapped and exchanged for £5, and when they reached Cuba, they sold for $150 to $200. But in 1844 one hogshead of tobacco was exchanged for a dozen slaves in Galinhas. These accommodations were replete with food, wine, and sex slaves handpicked from the barracoons. Blanco's influence was so powerful that Richards and historian Christopher Fyfe believe his impact entered the local Mende vernacular dialect. Richards recounted in an interview with Bemba Gogbua, young men in Sembehun were invited to "taste the high life on board the European ship" and then "kidnapped into slavery." Bemba insisted on using the word *panyamô*, meaning Spaniard, rather than *puumôi* (white person).[68]

Amistad's orphans, however, would not likely have seen the residential compounds. After their humiliating physical examination, their penultimate defining experience, before being marched to the beach and taken aboard an Atlantic vessel, was the painful process of branding. Covey was branded with a *B* on his "left arm," as was almost every other man, woman, and child disembarked from the *Segunda Socorro*, indicating they were owned and sold by Blanco. Kag'ne explained that she was branded with a "pipe bowl" in Lomboko, and Charlotte Cowles inspected the scar and described it as "exactly the size and form of a pipe bowl." The Wesleyan newspaper, the *Watchman*, described an 1846 cargo of Brazil-bound slaves from Galinhas aboard the *Paquete do Rio* with various letters marking their purchasers, such as J, P, A, RJ, and others, variously on the left or right shoulder or breast, and "two inches in length." Whereas private traders at Galinhas and elsewhere routinely branded their slaves *before* boarding them to reflect that they were purchased in advance under contract, the illicit trade ushered in changes in technique. Historian Arturo Arnalte demonstrated that Cuban traders tried to conceal the advance purchase brand by burning it behind the knee or on the inner thigh. An account of Antonio's branding is more ambiguous, as to whether he was marked as a slave in the Galinhas or in Cuba. Tappan wrote to Joshua Leavitt (long after Antonio was in Canada), "The Spaniards took Antonio, the cabin-boy, and slave to captain Ferrer, and stamped him on the shoulder with a hot iron, then put powder, palm oil, et cet., upon the wound, so that they 'could know him for their slave.'" Tappan's account appears to imply Ferrer branded Antonio, perhaps to avoid any possibility that he could claim to be free, but whether it took place in Cuba or Africa is unclear.[69]

The *Segunda Socorro*, captained by de Inza, moored off the coast of Galinhas in June 1833 and filled its hull with slaves, including a young boy by the name of "Covie." In spite of its seizure, de Inza sailed the *Solitario* from Havana to West Africa again in February 1834. In April 1835, he was again in West Africa, piloting the *El Esplorador*, anchored at Ouidah, which was co-owned with Pedro Blanco. It was likely that Ferrer resided with Blanco while his ship, the *Bela Antonia*, filled its cavities with slaves for one of its many voyages across the Atlantic, including some of the adult survivors of the *Amistad*. Brother Damián may also have resided with Blanco while filling his steamship the *Principeño* with more than a thousand Africans. Antonio had likely traveled back and forth a number of times aboard the *Bela Antonia* and other vessels owned by the Ferrers. By the time Mag'ru, Te'me, Kag'ne, and Ka'le found themselves imprisoned in the barracoons awaiting transportation in late 1838 or early 1839, a number of Cuba-bound ships were seeking to fill their holds, including one owned by Pedro Martínez, called *La Bandeira*, under the captaincy of a certain Rodrigues. And why the Cuban economy craved such a volume of children is the final component of the enslavement narrative of Amistad's orphans.[70]

CHILD SLAVERY AND NINETEENTH-CENTURY CUBA

Had everything gone according to the plans laid by Cuba's slaveholding merchant community, Amistad's orphans would have become slaves in Cuba and swiftly disappeared into the expanding slave economy. Covey was initially part of a shipment destined for Havana, aboard a vessel captained by a trader who had multiple encounters with antislavery courts. Covey, along with more than 150 other children aboard the *Segunda Socorro*, would have been sold quickly to small-scale traders and dispersed around the island. Antonio likely arrived some time in 1835 or 1836; he was one of approximately 20,000 African children disembarked in Cuba during a two-year period and sold permanently into slavery. Ferrer purchased him, possibly directly from a vessel or from one of many Cuban *barracones* in Havana or Santiago de Cuba, the two ports that he most frequented. Antonio was placed aboard a slave-trading vessel and served Ferrer directly. And Kag'ne, Te'me, Ka'le, and Mar'gru were destined for resale, along with the adult males, at Puerto Príncipe (today Camagüey), the site of an innovative sugar production complex. Although the Cuban slavery episode endured by the six orphans lasted only a combined total of approximately forty months, their temporary Caribbean stopover offers an opportunity to reflect on important economic transformations in the island's economy and the increasing dependency of Cuban slavery on African child imports.[71]

Over a period of six years, spanning 1833–39, the African enslavement of each of Amistad's orphans in Galinhas gave way to a Caribbean enslavement experience. The six at some point formed part of at least three separate slave cargos bound for Cuba, of which one was captured and taken to Freetown. The other two landed illegally in Cuba, whereupon their cargo immediately became slaves under Spanish-Cuban law and were resold. The Galinhas-to-Havana route was a regular itinerary for Cuban and American slave traders during the illegal trans-Atlantic trade, and many of them operated under the veil of Portuguese identities. Galinhas children were in great demand by Cuban slave traders, and new arrivals from Africa commanded a "high price." As the Royal Navy blockades took a toll on suppliers, and because the demand in Cuba remained so intense, the capacity to profit from a single successful trans-Atlantic voyage rose dramatically. Furthermore, of the slave cargoes arriving in Cuban ports in the 1830s approximately 40 percent or more were children. Of the more than 70,000 African children entering the Cuban slave economy in the 1830s, approximately 23,600 passed through Havana alone. The brief Caribbean sojourn of Amistad's orphans thus opens a window to a better understanding of the expanding role of children in Cuban slave systems, which in turn helps make sense of why the children were enslaved and transported in the first instance. The children's likely labor purpose also contextualizes the expanding presence of children in nineteenth-century Cuban imports.[72]

When Antonio arrived in Havana in 1835–36, and when four of Amistad's orphans landed in mid-1839, they entered what contemporary observer and sailor Robert Walsh described as the "great inlet for slaves." The girls and Ka'le arrived earlier than the majority of adult males aboard *La Amistad*, possibly in late April or early May 1839. After being disembarked by a small launch craft, they were immediately imprisoned inside a *barracón* by the harbor's edge. Madden, after personally conducting research, noted that "public promenade" was "exclusively devoted to the reception and sale" of newly arrived Africans. Indeed, Cuba's merchant elite displayed such crude "poise" and "power" during the 1830s that it was not unheard of for new arrivals from Africa to be walked through the Havana streets and auctioned in public. An account of the arrival of the four children from "Bahoo of Bandaboo," however, suggests a more surreptitious disembarkation. When the three girls and Ka'le "landed on the coast, at a little place, near sunset," they stayed "until night and walked into the city" of Havana, where there were put "in an old building, and fastened."[73]

There is no way of telling how long Antonio resided temporarily in a *barracón*, but Mar'gru, Te'me, Ka'le, and Kag'ne were imprisoned for approximately one month before their resale. An imprisonment of one month is consistent with Madden's description "where[in] they commonly remain two or three weeks before [being] sold." Ferrer may have purchased Antonio upon the boy's arrival in Havana, or even earlier, during one of the several trans-Atlantic voyages of which he likely took part, aboard the *Bella Antonia*, *El Esplorador*, or the *Aguila Vengadora*. The adult Amistad survivors, with the possible exception of Bahoo, were imprisoned in a *barracón* called *La Misericordia*, supervised by Francisco Riera and owned by Pedro Martínez. This particular *barracón* was a substantial facility, and when Madden visited, "carpenters and other persons" were refitting it. The precise name of the facility housing the four children purchased by Montes in June 1839 remains unclear, but it may have been part of the warehouse run by Martínez and Company or possibly Ferrer's business partners, José Antonio de Hecheverría and Juan Ricas. Montes appears to have purchased one girl separately from the three other children. Madden's "diligent inquiry" uncovered the fact that the first three children were bought from "Xiques" by "Montez" and then "1 little girl" was purchased from a certain "Azpilaca" (Azpillaga?). "Xiques" was quite possibly Felipe Xiques of "los Sres Xiques y Compañía," with whom Ferrer had several dealings, including the vessel *Vapor Principeño*. The transactions were distinct from the purchase of the "49 Bozales" by José Ruiz, a.k.a. José Ruiz Carrías, on behalf of his uncle Saturnino Carrías, who were destined for resale at Puerto Príncipe.[74]

When the children were sold, they would have been physically inspected, much as they had been in Lomboko. There is no account of the children's remembrance of this intrusive and unpleasant experience, but one of the Amistad adults provided some indication. Grabeau reported in court, "Soon several white men came to buy them. . . . Ruiz, selected such as he liked, and made them stand in a row. He then felt each of them in every part of their body; and made them open their mouths, to see if their teeth were sound, and carried the examinations to a degree of minuteness of which only a slave dealer would be guilty . . . [and] they were separated from their companions who had come with them from Africa." The experience of Amistad's orphans, with the exception of Covey, would likely have been similar. And to be sure, their experience was echoed by many of the 161,000 African children imported during the illegal era (1819–66).[75]

Whereas it was once argued that the Cuban slave economy was of decreasing profitability by the nineteenth century, and that the mechanization of sugar production was incompatible with continued dependence on slave labor, subsequent studies have dispelled these erroneous ideas. Historian Rebecca Scott demonstrated that in sugar-growing regions where technology was employed, demographic data supported the contention that slavery remained vital and important until abolition. Historian Laird Bergad and others studied statistical data for the market in both Cuban-born and African-born slaves in Cuba from the late eighteenth century to the abolition of slavery in 1886. Bergad demonstrated that slavery was increasingly profitable in the nineteenth century by analyzing data from more than 23,000 slave sales recorded between 1790 and 1880. For the key period of 1817–30, which marked the first two decades of the illegal trade, the domestic slave market was confident and reliable. Although Eltis discerned a small dip in Cuban slave prices in the mid-1830s, in Cuba, as well as Brazil and the United States, prices rose faster than the price of raw commodity exports from the 1820s into the 1860s. And on the eve of the arrival of four of Amistad's orphans, between fifty to seventy ships left Cuba annually for the African coast.[76]

From the period of legal slave importation into and including the period of illegality (the focus of this book), several important observations are noteworthy. Gross data on the arrival of slaves in Cuba from 1790 until the end of legal importation in 1820 are estimated at 325,000 slaves, which is 18 percent higher than official Cuban government records. During the final four legal years alone, 1817–20, at least 70,000 slaves arrived. Significantly, this demonstrates that Cuban slave importers had developed sophisticated strategies for evading import duties and taxes during the legal phase, which suggests in turn that estimates for the illegal phase should be treated with caution. During the period that forms the focus of this book, 1831–40, approximately 180,000 slaves were imported from Africa "to satisfy the labor needs of a relentlessly expanding sugar economy." By the 1830s, the import trade was firmly in the hands of Havana merchants. Nevertheless, it remains difficult to accurately assess the extent of the illegal enterprise. Zeuske and García Martínez identified a variety of mechanisms employed by trans-Atlantic traders to evade taxes and import duties during this period, most notably intentionally labeling slave cargo as *en lastre* (ballast) and the creation of fraudulent *trespassos* (or traspassos), labeling new African *bozales* as Cuban-born *ladinos*. Contemporary records also suggest that coastal and regional slave traders, like Ferrer, labeled slave cargoes as bulk cargo (*bultos*), charcoal, or coal. Slavers regularly changed the flags, papers, and names of their ships, operated themselves under noms de guerre, and were aided and abetted by sympathetic Americans, such as the U.S. consul in Havana, Nicholas Trist.[77]

Amistad's orphans were enveloped by a transforming Cuban economy and emboldened political class. From 1790 to 1835 there was a clear shift toward the sale of younger slaves, as Madden witnessed. Bergad states that the 1820s and early 1830s were characterized by the most intense purchase of younger slaves in the history of the Cuban slave market. Of Cuban-born slaves sold, 29 percent were under fifteen years between 1790 and 1800, 35 percent for 1801–20, and 42 percent for 1821–35. African-born slaves mirrored this pattern: from 1790 to 1820, 8 percent were under fifteen years, but for 1821–35, 18 percent of Africans were under fifteen. Bergad suggested that a shift toward younger purchases can be explained by anxieties about the impact of the 1817 treaty banning the trade, and the role of younger slaves in guaranteeing a future labor supply via reproduction. There was a particularly steep decline in sales of Africans aged fifteen to forty in favor of children. And until at least the mid-1840s, African slaves dominated the slave market in Cuba. Between 1821 and 1835, 64 percent of slaves sold were born in Africa.[78]

During the period of transportation of Amistad's orphans, from 1833 to 1839, the Cuban slave economy was experiencing important changes in terms of the prices of slaves, the gender ratio of imported slaves, and the age of imported slaves. On average over 18,000 Africans were imported annually between 1834 and 1841. Whereas slave prices were subject to short-term fluctuations, the average price during the period did not surpass 400 pesos. The island's slave market, until the 1840s, was conditioned by "the strong demand" for slaves in sugar, coffee, and urban services. Large-scale European immigration (including Ferrer and Blanco) in the 1830s also spurred the demand for slaves. David Turnbull noted that at least 6,500 new white immigrants arrived in Cuba in 1836 alone, and many would have purchased slaves for household service. The high volume of African trade and resulting labor market saturation, in spite of rising labor demands, caused static or slowly declining prices during the 1830s. The price of male and female slaves was largely equal during the decade of the 1830s, with sharp periodic changes. In 1839, the year of sale for four of Amistad's orphans, the average price in Cuba of 38 males aged one to fourteen was 225 pesos, and of 54 females, 232 pesos; the average price of 24 African children was 225 pesos. This resonates with the insurance value of $1,200 to $1,300 recorded in court papers in Connecticut, as both currencies were tied to the gold standard and almost at parity. Although the children were sold in Havana, I have not identified any records for the sale of definitively African children in Havana in 1839. The Havana average price, however, of 37 African adult males was 382 pesos, and of

18 adult females, the average price was 381 pesos. Average assessment values for slaves in Havana and Santiago de Cuba, also, underscore this data. The average assessment value for ten children and for nineteen Africans was 350 pesos.[79]

That Amistad's orphans arrived in Cuba principally via the port of Havana speaks directly to the central significance of this port to the importation of African children. Although Antonio's original entrance point is unclear from the historical record, Covey would have landed in Havana had the *Segunda Socorro* not been captured, as it originated there. Child slave imports during the illegal period (1819–66) numbered over 162,000 for the entirety of Cuba, or approximately 31.3 percent of total slave imports. Imports to Havana during the same period comprised a similar percentage (29 percent) of a total of 122,000. Over time the numbers of children entering Cuba via Havana increased. During the 1820s, children were 32 percent of imports. By the 1830s, however, Havana became the central location for African child slave imports entering the Cuban economy. In the 1830s children comprised 44 percent of African slave imports in Havana but only 37 percent at all other ports. For the period 1835–39, 47 percent of Africans entering Havana's port were children. When Pedro Montes entered the *barracones* of Havana to purchase Te'me, Mar'gru, Kag'ne, and Ka'le, he may well have seen facilities that were 50 percent children. Although the demographic data is imprecise during certain periods, the 1830s and 1840s marked the peak period for the importation of African children to Cuba via Havana.[80]

The final part of the puzzle to unraveling the significance of Amistad's orphans to the wider Cuban slave economy of the mid–nineteenth century concerns their intended destination in Puerto Príncipe and the small settlement of La Guanaja, "the point of intersection" between the cattle-raising region of Puerto Príncipe—a huge plain in the center of Cuba—and "the Northern Sea," as Cubans called the Gulf of Mexico and the Atlantic Ocean. Although Amistad orphans never arrived in Puerto Príncipe, regional notarial records attest to the extensive business operations of Ramón and Damián Ferrer in the city, of which the movement of fifty-four slaves was but part. The Ferrer brothers were independently wealthy Catalan merchants with financial operations in several islands and coastal entrepôts, including Puerto Rico and Caracas, and deep roots in both Havana and Puerto Príncipe. Zeuske and García Martínez demonstrate that Ferrer owned or part-owned at least five ships, including the *Bella Antonia* and *La Amistad,* and his brother also captained several vessels implicated in slave trading, including the massive steamship *Principeño*, which carried over 1,200 Africans. They were also key players in a larger "veiled history" of illicit slave traders, which included several U.S. merchants, such as Hugh Boyle, whose eponymous vessel Zeuske and García Martínez believe to be the elusive *Teçora.* Cuba played a crucial role in the expansive illicit slave smuggling operations into the U.S. South during the 1830s and 1840s, particularly to Florida and South Carolina. Although it is beyond the scope of this book, evidence from Cuban archives is beginning to undermine the received wisdom that intrastate slave trading constituted the primary antebellum source of new slave labor in the Deep South.[81]

The Ferrers' trans-Atlantic slave-trading operations were only part of a multidimensional investment portfolio comprising land, capital, and labor. If the Cuban government was "terrified" of abolition elsewhere in the Caribbean as historian David Murray claimed, it was not apparent in Puerto Príncipe and the dealings of Ferrer. The Ferrers embraced the Carrías family's vision of Puerto Príncipe as a new experimental sugar-growing region. Sugar plantations were booming in Cuba, and sugar output grew by 5 percent annually between 1830 and 1850. Today Camagüey is known more for its cattle ranching, but in the 1830s Carrías, Ferrer, and others worked hard to attract investment from Havana-based entrepreneurs and the wealthy elite of Puerto Príncipe to develop the outlying regions in a manner replicating the "remarkable economic growth" and expansion of sugar into Matanzas and Cárdenas. Records from the Tribunal de Comercio in Havana show that the Ferrers invested in steamships, canal construction, and a variety of enterprises broadly incorporating as naval transport modernization.[82]

The Ferrers, the Carrías, and others shipped large numbers of slaves to the region over several decades to perform the backbreaking work of draining swamps and clearing virgin territory for new sugar plantations or *ingenios.* Perhaps they held the belief that Africans from the Galinhas region, familiar with rice and the burdensome tasks associated with clearing and maintaining paddies for risiculture, were ideally suited to preparing new territory for sugar cultivation. With more detail of the large investments in the Puerto Príncipe region we may yet be able to make better sense of this growth and its relationship with the Galinhas trade. Ferrer drew on his trading relationship with Blanco and others in the Galinhas region. Had his ship not been seized in 1833, Covey and the more than 150 children aboard the *Segunda Socorro* would likely have spent their lives clearing virgin land for sugar. Several years later, Ka'le and the three girls would have joined them. They may have planted and harvested sugar, or they may possibly have become domestic servants to the increasingly urbanized and industrialized economy of Puerto Príncipe and its outlying network of towns, or even servants to other children.[83]

Thus when Amistad's orphans set sail for Cuba they constituted a tiny part of a massive illegal importation scheme funneling Africans into rapidly advancing

sectors of the Cuban economy, including expanding sugar and coffee plantations, and an increasingly industrialized and urbanized population with a growing need for domestic labor. The economy grew eastward during this period,
into the forested and swampy central regions, aided by a railroad beginning in
1837. Slavery remained the bedrock of sugar monoculture. Whereas the price of
slaves in Cuba from 1830 to 1840 declined marginally, the exportation of sugar
increased significantly. This suggests that per slave capita profits were increasing during the period, and indeed they continued to grow into the 1850s until
a sharp jump in slave prices imperiled the sugar expansion. Isolated incidents
had overblown impact; for example, a major cholera epidemic in 1833 killed as
many as twenty thousand slaves, possibly contributing to an uptick in the price
of slaves in 1835 and a trend toward purchasing reproductive-age females. But
by and large, during the period when Amistad's orphans were sold, they were
part of a vibrant slave-based economy that craved new African imports constantly and expanded rapidly on the backs on the massive importation of slaves,
many of them children.[84]

CONCLUSION

The myth of free-born status obfuscates the complex nature of the multiple
enslavement experiences of Amistad's orphans. The six children were enslaved
over a period of approximately a decade, and attempts were made to transport
them during a period of approximately seven years, from 1833 to 1839. Although
we will never know whether the children were born free in Galinhas, we have
a rich sense of the many stages of their enslavement experiences from the moment they left their natal family context and concluding with their arrival in
Cuba. The enslavement experiences of Amistad's orphans disrupt the adult-
centric narrative that prevails in much of the literature of African slavery and
the Atlantic slave trade.

Whether Amistad's orphans were free-born or born into a form of bondage,
lineage dependency, or servitude is a distraction, which belies much more sophisticated examination of the increasing importance of slavery and the slave
trade in Galinhas communities during the era of illegality. As the abolition of
the slave trade restricted the export and import of slaves to smaller numbers of
ports on both sides of the Atlantic, the massive increase in profitability thrust
Galinhas communities into the center of a commercial exchange focused on
Cuba. Revisiting the enslavement experiences of Amistad's orphans sheds important light on the role of slavery to both reinforce and transform the social
and political order of coastal communities in the 1820s and 1830s.

The free-born mythology also beclouds the narrowness of the paths to enslavement for children. A child's experience of enslavement is qualitatively different from that of an adult for a number of reasons. Adults were vulnerable to enslavement by mechanisms to which children were not susceptible. The first experience of enslavement of many children, and of Amistad's orphans in particular, was often one of two mechanisms—either violent seizure/kidnapping or pawning. Indeed, during the illegal slave trade, the greater emphasis on child enslavement in Galinhas and child slaves in Cuba contributed to social and cultural shifts. Turnbull connected these two forces seamlessly when he wrote, "The well understood difficulty of breaking in men and women of mature age to the labours of the field has produced a demand at the barracoons for younger victims, so that it is not, as formerly, by going to war, but by the meaner crimes of kidnapping and theft, and the still baser relaxation of social ties and family relations, that these human bazaars are supplied." Kidnapping and a variety of related practices were widespread in the Galinhas. Contemporary accounts provide a rich vein of narratives with which we can make sense of Ka'le, Te'me, and Covey. Pawnship, by contrast, operated in two distinct spheres: between Africans seeking credit, and between coastal Africans and European slave traders, as security. The parents of Kag'ne and Mar'gru pawned them, but most historical sources focus on the second form of pawning for security.[85]

Kidnapping and pawning were the gateway to a much longer and complex series of transactions leading inexorably toward the coastal barracoons. Amistad's orphans spent between one and two months in one of many prison compounds scattered along the coastal zone. In the barracoons there were many children and many adults. They may have been guarded and tended by other African slaves and also European merchants. But the small numbers of Spanish and Portuguese who resided in this locale kept close ties with the traders from Cuba and Brazil. As British naval cruisers patrolled the waters, many slaves were kept inland a short distance or concealed in fortified barracoons in mangroves. The slave traders brought forth their slaves only when word came of a vessel awaiting cargo. But because the demand for young African labor was so unquenchable and the potential profits so handsome in Cuba in the 1820s and 1830s, African slavers ensured a steady supply of young slaves. Young Africans were highly desired in Cuba as the economies expanded rapidly eastward. The ample supply of child slaves in the Galinhas meant that Havana-bound slave traders increasing turned to the region as a primary supplier.[86]

4

THE JOURNEYS OF AMISTAD'S ORPHANS

Of the five myths silencing the experience of Amistad's orphans, perhaps the most material or physical is that of a common Middle Passage on the *Teçora*, the elusive slave ship that purportedly transported all the Africans to Cuba. The *Teçora* appears in numerous accounts of the ordeal of *La Amistad*, in print, online, and in film, from the nineteenth century to the present day. The *Teçora* is a veritable *Flying Dutchman*, sailing the oceans, riding across cinema and television screens, but never making port, never docking. The illusory vessel formed a fundamental component of the narrative of illegality assembled by the Amistad Committee. Its central role quickly expanded, based on circumstantial records and anecdotal accounts, but its identity, its crew, its origin and ownership, and indeed its very existence were imputed but never proven by the legal defense team. To underscore its intangibility, as of 2014 the ship does not appear in the Trans-Atlantic Slave Trade Database.[1]

The myth of a common Middle Passage emerged from the court argument that the Africans were transported to Cuba illegally. Today the complex experiences of transportation are the foundation of a prolific branch of slave-trade scholarship, but in 1839, the attention of the legal team was focused narrowly on violation of bilateral treaties and international law. In the context of the court, presenting a straightforward and homogenous story of transportation—persuasive and simple to comprehend—was more important than exploring the lived experience of the children. As a result, the legal team focused its energy on the massive scale of the illicit trade. Individuated stories of the Middle Passage may make great cinema today, but they were relatively unremarkable in 1839.

The role of the *Teçora* in the myth of a common Middle Passage is particularly ironic, because despite its contested existence, there is no evidence that any of Amistad's orphans traveled aboard the ship. From the children's words and those of adult survivors, it is very clear that five of the six children arrived in Cuba before the adults, on different ships, and spent longer in Havana. The Middle Passage of Mar'gru, Te'me, Kag'ne, and Ka'le—while certainly no less traumatic—was possibly shorter than that of the adults and certainly predated it. Covey's journeying began much earlier and took a very different path. Antonio's trans-Atlantic passage was also distinct from that of the adult males. Even in the unlikely case he was aboard the *Teçora*, he would have been a member of the crew, not held in chains in the hold. It is quite possible he traveled many times around Cuba in the service of Ferrer and several times to and from Africa.[2]

There are several reasons why so little is known about the voyages of Amistad's orphans. The legal defense team was focused on big questions, such as the African origins of the survivors and the massive scale of the trade. The lives of four African children must have appeared unexceptional to many at the time, resulting in a thin documentary record. Unlike the adults, the children were not characterized as murderers and pirates by the press. Five of the children were detained as possible witnesses, in the event that charges were supported by the grand jury (they were not), and Covey served as translator. After the failure of the habeas corpus writ, the children were under less legal scrutiny. Their movements were not deemed central to the subsequent legal question, the origin of the Africans. And after several months' imprisonment, several of the adult Africans were learning English and telling and retelling their stories, contributing to the erasure of a distinct child experience.

But concealing the full details of the children's narrative may also have been intentional. The defense team realized that the age of the children, were they African-born, meant they could not have been imported legally into Cuba prior to 1820. But as it became clear the children had arrived at least a month before most of the adults, this fact compromised the legal coherence of the slave-trafficking argument. The defense team sought to win in court and also in the court of public opinion, and the stories of the children's voyages, like their identity, origin, and background, however, had the potential to unravel the comprehensible, digestible story the defense team sought to convey about the Amistad Africans.

The myth of a common Middle Passage, much of it borne by the adult transportation aboard the *Teçora*, served a useful purpose in the context of the trial of the survivors of *La Amistad*. But it belies the dependence of the illicit trade on child slaves. Using the journeys of Amistad's orphans as a vehicle, in this chapter I disentangle myth from reality in order to investigate the complexity of child mobility in the nineteenth-century Atlantic world to advance two arguments. I first argue that adult journeying narratives obscure the complexity of children's mobility in context of the illicit Atlantic nineteenth-century slave trade. By identifying the mechanisms and modes of mobility of Amistad's orphans, as they traveled from West Africa to the Americas and back, I then argue that the histories of child mobility inhabit discrete spaces, such as serving in a ship's crew or unaccompanied migration. After providing an overview of the multidirectional mobility of Amistad's orphans over a period of almost two decades, during the 1830s and 1840s, I explore key sites of child mobility.

Children featured prominently in the illicit slave smuggling operations of the nineteenth century, and the volume of child smuggling increased over several decades. The plasticity of childhood meant that boys and girls offered both pro- and antislavery actors important opportunities to specialize and finesse their operations. Young boys, whose minds and capacities had yet to be fully shaped, were highly sought after for crew on ships, both illegal slavers and legal commercial and naval vessels. And empathy for the plight of orphans, vulnerable girls in particular, meant that children were targeted by humanitarian enterprises for engagement in migration and resettlement schemes. Amistad's orphans' journeying—contextualized by the mobility of other Atlantic Africans and numerical and statistical data from slave-trading vessels—demonstrates how children traveled and moved in different ways, ones that did not always parallel and were often concealed by adult movements.

THE MYTH OF A COMMON MIDDLE PASSAGE

The existence of a vessel capable of making a trans-Atlantic voyage was an essential element of the narrative of kidnapping, illegal transportation, and illicit Caribbean human smuggling, which formed the core of the cohering story disseminated by the Amistad Committee. The ship today known as the *Teçora* makes its first appearance as *La Facora* in an account of an interview between Tappan and Antonio in early September 1839. In the Westville, Connecticut, house of the jailer, Pendleton, in the presence of Baldwin, Gibbs, and several others, and with the translation assistance of John Ferry, we learn that "Antonio said the brig that brought the negroes from the coast of Africa was under the Portuguese flag, and was call La Facora." It is important to note that, whereas Antonio, or "Anthony," as he was often referred to, volunteered the name of the mysterious vessel, the information was conveyed in the context of an interview in which Tappan had some sense of what he was seeking to uncover. The following sentence is instructive in this regard. Tappan noted, "It will probably be proved that one of the Spaniards has said in this country that he bought the slaves from a slave ship, on speculation," by which he is referring to his hope that a New London witness would shortly testify under oath to this effect. "Speculation" perhaps referred to the notion that that the slaves were to be transferred for resale inland, with the assumption that profits would result. As Antonio had worked for Ferrer for several years, he possibly knew more about both the internal Cuban and Atlantic trades than he let on.[3]

Furnished with information about "La Facora" or "La Forcora," Tappan and others began a two-pronged assault on the argument of Ruiz and Montes that they were legally moving Cuban slaves from one port to another. Central to cementing the abolitionists' narrative about an illegal transportation of slaves, of which the survivors were victims, was illustrating a comprehensive picture of the ongoing illicit trade from Africa. To do this, Tappan and his colleagues focused on convincing the general public of the certain existence of a ship. No one besides Antonio and the Africans claimed to have seen the vessel, but that did not stop Tappan from running articles in his newspaper affirming its existence. "The examination of the Africans, which has now embraced nearly all of them individually, established very fully the fact that they were all, with the exception of Antonio, shipped in the same vessel from Lanboro by Petro [*sic*] Blanco, the Spanish trader, whom the interpreter [Covey] from the Buzzard knew." In this public forum, hypotheses became facts. And by furnishing a skeleton argument, the newspaper also connected otherwise unrelated aspects of the story, including Antonio with Africa and James Covey with the infamous Blanco. Furthermore, the legal team claimed the papers of *La Amistad* contained hidden details of a second ship.[4]

The second line of attack on Ruiz and Montes involved affirming the name of the ship, drawing on the sketchy information relayed by Antonio. Some survivors of *La Amistad* had spoken of another ship, which brought them to Cuba several months earlier, but it remained unnamed. There are very few means whereby slaves inside a ship, largely illiterate and unfamiliar with Spanish, could know the name of the transporting vessel. The only solid "fact"—that the vessel captured off the coast of Connecticut was not an oceangoing schooner and could not itself have made a trans-Atlantic voyage—was an entirely erroneous notion. Tappan sent out inquiries far and wide, knowing well that the most likely source of reliable information would be those who had served or were currently serving in the Royal Navy's West Africa Squadron or other abolitionists active in the Atlantic context. Tappan's inquiries were at least partly successful. The name *Teçora* first appears in the United States in the context of the trial, but in writing, spelled "La Tecora," it is found in the United Kingdom in a November 9, 1839, letter from John H. Tredgold of the British and Foreign

Anti-Slavery Society, informing Lord Palmerston of the "vessel under Portuguese colours." The "forty Africans and upwards" aboard La Amistad "chiefly from Mandingo and Congo" were originally aboard "La Tecora" and part of a "large cargo of men, women, and children" taken "from the coast of Africa" directly to "the Havana."[5]

Whether or not a ship ever sailed under the name Teçora is less interesting to a study focusing on children than why it has remained so difficult to locate the ship in archival sources. The answer to this latter question drives at the very heart of the subterfuge and deceit shrouding the illicit mid-nineteenth-century trade, of which children were such an important component. Ship name changing was very common, particularly in the 1820s to 1850s, as traders sought to evade detection and seizure on both sides of the Atlantic. Ships might depart Havana or Bahia under one name, arrive in Galinhas or Bonny under a second name, depart Africa under a third name, and return to port under yet a fourth name. Changes in captaincy could result in the changing of ship names, and captains also used different noms de guerre. Obscuring the relationship between various alternative names was the very intention of illicit slave traders, but the Hispano-Cuban mercantile elite still needed to keep track of its investments, the single most valuable component being the ship itself. Insurers operating in Havana, a port that Zeuske and García Martínez describe as the "principal center of the illegal slave traffic," required concrete proof of routes and transactions, particularly when claims were lodged. Attempts to unravel this web of illegality gained traction recently with the discovery, in the Cuban National Archive, of a ledger belonging to Pedro Blanco, which provides lists of ships operating in the Atlantic and in the Caribbean and their alternative names. This ledger was an authoritative guide for Blanco in Galinhas and others in Havana, facilitating their contraband activities and also ensuring that investors' dividends reached the correct individuals. Based on an analysis of this ledger and other documents, Zeuske and García Martínez have asserted that the Teçora was in fact a ninety-eight-ton vessel owned by Hugh Boyle of Baltimore, operating at times under the name Hugh Boyle.[6]

Back in 1840, however, such information was not publicly available. Establishing the plausibility of the existence of a hypothetical ship was made easier by the abundant evidence of deceit perpetrated by Montes and Ruiz. The most striking example of fraud concerned the names of the Africans themselves and the documents produced by Montes and Ruiz as proof of their legal purchase and transportation. Zeuske has argued that the main problem confronted by slave traffickers in the 1820s and 1830s in Cuba and the Spanish territories concerned "assigning an official presence" to that which was both "a human body" and "a commodity." Traders arrived from West Africa with lists organized by age and sex but omitting any names. In Cuba the slaves were accorded Christian names in place of the numbers in the ship's documents. In this way new Africans (*bozales*) were "converted" into Cuban-born slaves (*criollos*), but a paper record was created of the process. Subsequently, the intra-Cuba smuggling operation of Ferrer, Ruiz, and Montes was furnished with a *licencia* to move the *negros ladinos* (ostensibly Spanish speaking and born in Spanish territory, thus "cultivated" or "latinized Blacks") slaves along the coast. But as the Amistad Africans called themselves by African names and appeared to have no knowledge of the Spanish names accorded them in the ship's papers, the ruse unraveled.[7]

Whereas the existence of a ship is no longer in dispute, the manufacturing of the narrative surrounding the *Teçora* raised an almost impenetrable barrier to understanding the journeys of Amistad's orphans. Evidence collected by Tappan and others demonstrates that the journeys of the children differed significantly from those of the adult males. Although Antonio's precise origins remain undetermined, data about the remaining five enable the mapping of their physical movements from the Galinhas and its hinterland and into the Atlantic. Covey's travels began earlier than the other five, and involved returning to Freetown, apprenticeship in the Royal Navy, and the seizure of several slave vessels. The girls and Ka'le likely arrived in Cuba on the same ship. Antonio's mobility in the Atlantic predated the departure of *La Amistad* from Havana, but there is scant detail about his enslavement to Ferrer and service aboard his ships. The five sailed together to Connecticut where they encountered Covey. In the United States, Amistad's orphans moved between New York, Connecticut, and Vermont. In liberty one traveled to Canada, and the other five returned to resettle in West Africa. The diversity and complexity of their mobility is astonishing—more so because of its hidden nature.

In *Many Middle Passages*, Emma Christopher, Marcus Rediker, and Cassandra Pybus argue that the value of the metaphor "Middle Passage" transcends its traditional Atlantic framework. They assemble a collection of common stories of forced migration spanning more than three centuries that bring punishment, enslavement, forced labor, and gender into conversation. The result is a powerful united narrative that demonstrates the expansive role of coercibility in the broader imperial projects of settlement, colonization, and industrial and agricultural production. Building on these accounts of adult mobility and the alternative networks they navigated and focusing on the discrete spaces inhabited by six children provides an opportunity to begin to bridge a divide in the scholarly narration of the Middle Passage and regional itineraries on both sides of the Atlantic.[8]

THE MOVEMENTS OF AMISTAD'S ORPHANS

Amistad's orphans traveled considerable distances by foot and by boat, on land, by river and sea, in bondage and liberty. The prevailing account of the adult Amistad captives parallels some aspects of the children's experiences, but the greater part of the children's journeying in bondage and liberty was not in the physical presence of the Amistad adults. The mobility of Amistad's orphans may be divided into several parts: namely, the movement to the coast of West Africa; westward movements across the Atlantic; movements within the Americas; and the eastward return voyage across the Atlantic.

Covey's journeying began earlier than that of Mar'gru, Te'me, Kag'ne, and Ka'le. Antonio's movements remain relatively unknown, but new research on Ferrer may yet reveal details of his purchases of his slaves, including Antonio, and their service in the illicit Atlantic trade. All six children resided within close geographical proximity for a period of approximately eighteen months beginning September 1839. After March 1841 they were never again together as a group, moving to different countries and continents.

JOURNEY TO THE COAST

Identifying the stages of movement toward the coast is important to understanding a child's experience of enslavement. For adults, the passage toward the coast may have been a known unknown, somewhat unfamiliar yet navigable; insofar as many spoke several languages, they more easily could elicit information from their enslavers or passers-by, and they may have themselves participated in the trade and enslavement of other Africans. Furthermore, some of the adults had friends and family members who were captured, shipped, liberated, and subsequently returned home to retell their story. But for young children, with little experience of slavery or long distance travel, the passage to the coast was an alien ordeal of nightmarish proportions. It was certainly dangerous, and many perished. Some estimates suggest that between 10 and 40 percent of captives might have died during a journey from the interior to the coast.[9]

The geographical paths taken by Amistad's orphans—regardless of their differing experiences of enslavement—converged as they moved toward the coast and the common point of departure at the Lomboko barracoons. Slaves departing from Lomboko and neighboring Galinhas barracoons in the nineteenth century may have traveled, on average, approximately one hundred miles. The Galinhas ports' hinterland catchment area was expansive and extended beyond southeastern Sierra Leone to include parts of modern-day Liberia, Guinea, and possibly Mali. Jones's analysis of more than six hundred African names of recaptive slave children resettled in Sierra Leone between 1819 and 1824, representing one-third of the total number of children, provides some guidance. Of the 638 named children, 215, or approximately one-third, had names possibly from language communities relatively close to Galinhas ports, including 108 identified as Cosso/Mende, 23 Gola, 15 Kpelle, 13 Kisi, and 12 Bulom/Sherbro. These data are consistent with the fact that of the twelve ships with Sierra Leone cargoes that were captured and escorted to Freetown during this period, nine embarked from Galinhas ports. Understanding the average distance traveled by slaves exiting Lomboko and neighboring barracoons is complicated by the fact that those originating from the region are underrepresented in recaptive African data because it was much easier for them to return home. Only a more careful scrutiny of the African names of 4,522 slaves shipped from Galinhas ports and landed in either Freetown or Havana between 1818 and 1847, will enable a clearer sense of the catchment area for Galinhas.[10]

Precisely how long the journey took for Amistad's orphans depended heavily on the terrain and the route. Overland movement during the dry or wet season—following a combination of established roads and narrow bush paths—was slower than travel by canoe. As historian John Davidson reminds us, many "trade roads" were "simply paths through the bush" along which goods were transported "walking in single file." Water travel—via small river dugouts or purpose-built large vessels for estuary and coastal movement—was swifter and covered long distances. As much of the region featured swamps and mangroves, a combination of the two was to be expected. George Thompson, writing in the 1850s, claimed that one of the adult Amistad survivors, Fabena, could travel 150 to 200 miles in seven days, an average of 21 to 28 miles a day. But travel overland as part of a slave convoy was probably considerably slower than an individual's intentional journey from one town to another. Fabena's journey is thus no indication for those of Amistad's orphans, who were individually likely part of larger convoys. Covey, for example, said he was one of a group of ten when he moved to the coast. Furthermore, death rates were likely higher among children moved to the coastal barracoons primarily by foot, and the mortality rates likely necessitate the exclusion of the very small.[11]

Precisely how Amistad's orphans were physically relocated from the point of capture to the coastal slave barracoon remains largely conjecture. At first glance, three of the children appear to imply that their passage to the coast was primarily overland before arriving in Lomboko, but there was clearly more to their stories than what was elicited. Ka'le, Te'me, and Kag'ne indicated that soon after their enslavement they were moved to the coast. Ka'le stated he was "about one month in traveling to Lomboko." Te'me was "a long time in travel-ing to Lomboko" but provides no further information. If she came from Te-Congo, she could have covered more than one hundred miles. And Kag'ne was "many days in going to Lomboko," by which she may have meant less than a month, but it is unclear. Covey, however, asserted that "one man carried us two months' walk," which adds an additional dimension insofar as the term "car-ried" conveys that he was moved with adults, and possibly that small children were moved in ways other than by foot.

Amistad's orphans were probably traded by professionals with considerable experience in the business of slave transportation and connections in many towns and village. Captured slaves could be conducted by members of the original raiding party, but it saddled the trader with the maintenance costs of the team, including food, water, and purpose-built shackles with which slaves were coffled together. Rival chiefs blocked roads, and individual warriors built stockades, charged tolls, and plundered goods, including slaves. As a result, slaves were often passed on from one trader to another, multiple times, over hundreds of miles by land and water. During the early nineteenth century, with the exception of Siaka and a few others, it was improbable that any one leader controlled more than a handful of towns, according to Jones. Siaka created a confederacy built on warfare and kinship. Amara Lalu was also well established regionally, commanded a powerful reputation, and had deputies working for him throughout the Galinhas and its hinterland.[12]

Moving slaves by either method brought risks and benefits. Traders met infor-mally along paths or in villages, or in established secondary exchange centers, like Mattru or Maffa, on the Jong (Taia) River. Canoe travel was often the remit of professionals familiar with the complex inlets and estuaries, who guarded their turf enthusiastically. Overland passage ran the risk of reprisal attacks or sei-zure by rival enslavement gangs or family members of the enslaved, but greater numbers could be moved collectively. Travel by canoe along rivers could re-sult in drowning and accommodated smaller numbers than when coffled and walked, but it was often swifter during more hospitable weather.[13]

Although none of the children's narratives referenced movement in canoes as such, vessels of varying sizes likely played a prominent role. As Davidson ob-served, the existence in the Galinhas region of an inland system of waterborne communication and the absence of a readily accessible harbor made for an ideal slave-trading setting. Movement by canoe along most of the larger named rivers—including, but not limited to, the Bagru (Gbangbar), Jong (Taia), Sewa (Bum), Kittam (Waanji), Moa (Sulima, Solyman), Kerefe (Galinhas), Mano, Sangara, Keya, Boba, Makona, and Bendei (Benda)—was generally by swift shallow dugout canoe. Although most Western accounts of canoe travel post-date the enslavement of Amistad's orphans, several models likely played a role in their mobility. A shallow river craft was used to navigate swamps and estuaries and could carry small numbers of people. Koelle, traveling in the Galinhas region in 1847, observed that the canoe "was so small, that everyone had to sit right down on its bottom, and not to stand up again" for fear of "upsetting." Thompson, writing a decade later, explained that the effort to keep one's balance was sometimes "much more tiresome" than walking, but there was no avoiding canoe travel. In May 2012 small dugout canoes were still a primary means of transportation along the Moa River (figure 4.1).[14]

Established trade routes that required crossing rivers could also use wide log rafts, a rudimentary vessel that Thompson describes as a "country ferry-boat," pushed by poles or propelled by paddles (figure 4.2). A much larger canoe was manufactured for longer distances among estuaries, inlets, lagoons, and along the entire coast. Thompson explained that the larger canoe, which could hold fifty to one hundred men, began as a dugout but was then "spread open" and "timbered as a boat" with a "raising" of one to two feet atop the tree cavity. Such vessels were constructed from massive trees found along the tributaries of the Rockel or other rivers, and they were between thirty and sixty feet long, four to eight feet wide, and three to five feet deep. They often had one or more

Fig. 4.1. A canoe on Moa River near Kenema, 2012

Fig. 4.2. Small watercraft of the Galinhas region, c. 1850 (George Thompson, *The Palm Land; or, West Africa, Illustrated* [Cincinnati: Moore, Wilstach, Keys, 1859])

masts, sails, and were equipped with four to ten oars. Thompson observed Soso canoes moving from Sherbro along the coast past Freetown to bring slaves to the peanut plantations inland (figure 4.3). The slaves were "made to sit in the bottom" and "lashed" with "long pieces of bamboo," in a description that resonates with novelist Martha Mary Sherwood's narrative of Dazee who was "shut down under hatches," suggesting it was based on a story collected by a missionary. Amistad's orphans may have traveled in smaller vessels or on rafts initially, and then by larger craft as they reached coastal lagoons, the heads of rivers, and brackish estuaries.[15]

The captors of Amistad's orphans likely had a desired distance to cover each day. As children moved more slowly than adults, it would be inaccurate to extrapolate a journey for children based primarily on adult accounts. Scant accounts from children exist with which to gauge how their mobility differed from that of adults. In the marvelous tale of Sherwood, a party of men who traveled upriver by boat with slaving as their objective seized Dazee at the age of about fourteen in the "Mountains of the Gazelles" of Sierra Leone. He was immediately "dragged" aboard the boat, which then glided "smoothly down the river" toward the ocean over a period of four days and nights. The testimony of Augustino, a boy brought to Brazil in about 1830, when he was about twelve, provides important context for understanding the mobility of children. He observed that he traveled for a fortnight, at about three Brazilian leagues a day, or approximately four miles. Augustino explained that the group of slaves and their captors always traveled by night, "because they were afraid to travel by day," lest they be attacked by "relations" of those enslaved. Whereas Augustino described mobility by foot at four miles per day, the narratives of Amistad's orphans are ambiguous; they mention only "traveling." Amistad's orphans would almost certainly have been moved by land and water and passed through many towns and villages of varying size and significance.[16]

The exact routes of Amistad's orphans are unclear, but they may be viewed in the context of the wider trade patterns of the region. Thompson provides a glimpse of the interior geography, including roads, paths, and trading routes.

Fig. 4.3. Coastal slave transport craft of the Galinhas region, c. 1850
(George Thompson, *The Palm Land; or, West Africa, Illustrated*
[Cincinnati: Moore, Wilstach, Keys, 1859])

"Big roads" would be "cut" between villages and towns for the purpose of trade. The Galinhas hinterland, feeding into the Lomboko slave barracoons, was interwoven with footpaths, established roads, and trade routes, all of which assisted the navigation of a web of rivers, streams, estuaries, and swamps. One of the reasons Jones gives for the success of Blanco's enterprise was that he, unlike the local chief Siaka, was able to guarantee the provision of slaves by drawing on established routes. Davidson demonstrated that the lands occupied by speakers of Mende, Sherbro, Vai, Kissi, and other languages, were a dynamic commercial zone, with a complex regional network of trade routes. Although the Mende-speaking region did not feature regular market cycles, other parts, such as Kisi, had periodic markets. Market goods, including powder, guns, salt, iron, kola, and other products, moved along routes linking Monrovia and Bopulu in Liberia to Kisi territory, and Freetown and the Futa Jallon with the Niger River. Wealthier towns were fortified, usually with a wooden stockade, but sometimes, like Madina, by thick mud walls and a ditch. Other important mid-nineteenth-century trading centers included Dodo and Kuniki, and many concentrated at particular points, such as the heads of rivers, like Makona and Bandajuma. Mandingo, Fulbe, and Susu merchants controlled much of the longer-distance trade. The Galinhas region was a source of fine cotton cloth and salt, both of which moved inland, often exchanged for slaves and cattle. And many traders situated along the Galinhas coast had connections reaching into inland Mende-speaking regions, which today might be as far inland as Kenema.[17]

The stages of movement, contextualized by the enslavement experience in Chapter 3, support the view that most of the captives traveled overland and by canoe. Many slaves during the same period passed overland first and then boarded small canoes down the Moa River. Slaves terminating their trek at Lomboko made a final overland journey toward Blanco's barracoons in the swamps and lagoons of the Kerefe (Galinhas). Here they were branded, or as Kag'ne explained, "burnt upon the shoulder with a hot pipe." In follow-up interviews conducted in summer 1841 before their return to Sierra Leone, several of the Amistad survivors explained that they "were brought the last day of their journey down the Moa in a boat, to Lomboko." And as preparations to return the survivors to Sierra Leone gained traction, several individuals attempted to locate original natal villages by calculating the distance traveled. They consulted colonial officers in Sierra Leone about terrain, re-interviewed the survivors, and drafted sketch maps.[18]

Because the region was an expanse of "marshy flats," with swampy terrain, it is very likely that the journey to the barracoon involved land and water travel. The most precise map from the period, charted in November 1840, shows a web of waterways and overland paths, including a "slave track" connecting "several villages" along the edge of the Moa River via the "swampy" area surrounding Jakree to the "shallow channels for boats" that ran between five barracoon sites at Tiendo, Dombocorro, Comassoon, Comatinda, and Jakree, all of which were located in the Kerefe (Galinhas) inlet lagoon system (see figure 2.5). Although we learn of Mar'gru only after she arrived at the coastal barracoon and was purchased by a slave merchant, and we know nothing of Antonio's journey to the coast, if indeed he made such a journey (he may have been born at the coast), it is likely all six traveled by foot and by canoe at various stages before boarding a trans-Atlantic vessel.[19]

WESTWARD MOVEMENTS ACROSS THE ATLANTIC

The journeys across the Atlantic took place in several stages, beginning with a movement to the beachhead and then by ocean canoe to a slave ship moored off the coast beyond the breakers. As the barracoons were often located in swampy areas, sometimes as much as a day inland, the march to the beach was arduous. Major Henry J. Ricketts explained that "hundreds" of slaves were "marched together considerable distances," and "dozens" died of thirst, "being whipped up to the last moment." If the Royal Navy squadron was operating elsewhere along the coast on the day the orphans were loaded on their respective vessels, "terrific horrors" were avoided. If, however, their experience mirrored that of the Amistad adults—boarded on an ill-fated vessel, the *Cirse*, then unloaded hastily and moved back to the barracoon until a second ship became available—their ordeal may have lasted many days or weeks. When the "blockade" was "kept up," barracoon operators and *grumettas* would move up and down the sandbars and seacoast, looking for "more convenient places of shipment."[20]

When the ocean was free of Royal Navy vessels, boarding began in earnest, conducted by a coastal community of people referred to as "Kroo" or Kru. Wherever the slave trade flourished, Kru established villages. Accounts from the period observed that slaves awaiting "the arrival of a vessel" would be transported over the dangerous breakers by large purpose-built canoes, with seats "so high a man can walk underneath" (figures 4.4 and 4.5). These enormous multistory canoes were powered by crews of forty of more Kru rowers, usually "hired directly by the captain" of the slave vessel, and were quite unlike the shallow dugout canoes that ran up and down the Moa River and throughout the swampy mangroves of Galinhas. When a ship appeared, a Kru lookout signaled "either to come in" or "go to windward or leeward," according to the "danger" from the British navy. If the way was clear, the slaver ran in, to receive

Fig. 4.4. Crossing the surf and sand bar at Kerefe (Galinhas) River, c. 1845
("Crossing the Bar of Gallinas River," *Illustrated London News* [April 14, 1849], 237)

Fig. 4.5. Section of a two-story slave embarkation canoe, c. 1845
("Section of Embarkation Canoe," *Illustrated London News*, April 14, 1849), 237)

her cargo immediately. Canoes servicing the boats could carry between two
and five hundred slaves at once, and the entire process from land to ship could
run from two to twelve hours depending on weather and currents. But passage
was dangerous because the British navy could see such large canoes from a
considerable distance. Once a boat was filled, the Kru canoe crew stayed on
watch until the ship left with its cargo. In urgency, some slave traders would use
"tiny Kru canoes," more suitable for the inlets and rivers. In bad currents and
weather the smaller canoes "invariably capsized," and "hundreds" of Africans
"would be devoured by sharks." Rankin reported a conversation with "a Kroo"
in Freetown, which appeared to convey a belief on the part of the Kru that they

were equal and codependent economic partners with slavers, because "white man no slave, Krooman no slave." But this idealization ignores the fact that many Kru were enslaved and transported across the Atlantic. Moreover, Luiz and Blanco were entirely at the mercy of Kru communities who professed "no sympathy" for particular Europeans, and ill treatment or abuse could produce a boycott of particular traders.[21]

Like many children, Amistad's orphans were probably housed separately from male adults on slave ships. Once aboard the trans-Atlantic vessel, Mar'gru, Te'me, and Kag'ne may have been placed in a part of the ship specifically constructed for girl children and women, or they may have remained unfettered on deck. Covey, Ka'le, and Antonio may have been placed in an area solely for boy children, or with the men, or with the girls and women. It is a common misconception that children were routinely used simply as space-fillers for ships that were otherwise at capacity with respect to adults. Close scrutiny of the internal architecture of slave ships demonstrates that they often included areas designed to hold children, smaller spaces that could not hold adults. Among the most widely circulated images of the internal structure of a slave ship during the *legal* slave trade is the diagram of the *Brooks*, which demonstrated two specific areas likely designated for children and youths. But during the *illegal* slave trade, evidence of separation by age is more equivocal. Robert Walsh's illustration of the *Veloz* headed for Brazil in 1829 shows a considerably smaller area for slaves, with a height of three feet three inches (figure 4.6). The *Veloz* had only two slave sections, a larger hold for males and a small hold for females.[22]

Whether a ship was purpose-built for trading in children or whether it was refitted to accommodate a mix of slaves is another factor in the experience of Amistad's orphans. Some ships specialized in children. Forbes observed several "hellish nurseries," such as the *Tragos Millas* and *Pharafoal*, with slave decks of fourteen and eighteen inches in height, respectively, "intended for children only." The *Triumfo* had no slave deck, but when captured it had 104 slaves between the ages of four and nine years "stowed on the casks." The *Veloz*, seized in 1829, appears to have been a retrofitted vessel. As a direct result of subterfuge, slaves were experiencing increasingly cramped conditions. Walsh noted, "The slaves were all enclosed under grated hatchways, between decks. The space was so low, that they sat between each other's legs, and stowed so close together, that there was no possibility of their lying down, or at all changing their position, by night or day." The *Veloz* "crammed" 226 women and girls in an area twelve by eighteen feet. Nearby 336 men and boys were imprisoned in a space forty by twenty-one feet. The males had on average twenty-three square inches, and the females, including pregnant women, thirteen square inches. When Madden

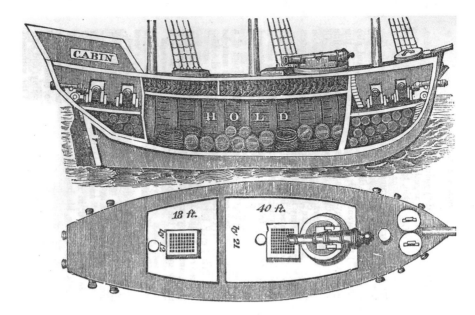

Fig. 4.6. Views of a slave ship, c. 1830 (*Thompson in Africa; or,
An Account of the Missionary Labors, Sufferings, Travels, and Observations
of George Thompson in Western Africa, at the Mendi Mission*, 9th ed.
[Dayton, Ohio: Printed for the Author, 1857; orig. printed 1852], 19;
used with kind courtesy, from collection of Marcus Rediker)

examined the *Eagle* (captured by the *Buzzard* in 1838), he found it "allowed" for 350 individuals "but two feet six inches." Other vessels had as few as eighteen inches height.[23]

No accounts exist of the dimensions of the ships transporting Amistad's orphans. But the Royal Navy surgeon Peter Leonard left a detailed account of the "infernal apartment" inside the *Primeira*, whose specifications possibly resembled those of the seized *Segunda Socorro* carrying Covey in 1833. Like the *Veloz*, the women and children were "separated by a wooden partition from the other slaves" and occupied the after part of the deck. In "filth" and "suffocating heat" the men "were bound together in twos, by irons rivetted around the ankles." He observed that "the small space in which these unfortunate beings" were "huddled together" was "almost incredible." The *Primeira* was 130 tons, and "the slave deck only two feet two inches high," so that the Africans could "hardly even sit upright." Although the tonnage of the *Segunda Socorro* is unknown, it and the *Primeira* operated along a similar route and had a similar total capacity.[24]

Although details of the Middle Passage experience of Amistad's orphans are scant, it is possible to get some sense of the ordeal of Mar'gru, Ka'le, and Kag'ne from the "affidavit of Bahoo" of "Bandaboo." Bahoo stated that Mar'gru and Kag'ne "came over in the same vessel that I did to Havana, as did Penna and the little boy Carre [Ka'le]."[25] Bahoo described his passage as "tight together, two and two chained together by hands and feet, night and day," but he was likely referring to his own experience as women and children were rarely shackled during this period. How cramped the boat was is unclear, but Bahoo explained that there were "good many in the vessel, and many died." If the "Penna" he referred to was in fact "Kinna," it is possible to extrapolate further. In Kinna's account, during his trans-Atlantic voyage "they were brought up to decks to take fresh air" in "the full blaze of the tropical sun," and "this was so intolerable that they often begged to go below again." As for Antonio, contradictory statements confound details of his possible Middle Passage." There is no record that Te'me ever recounted her trans-Atlantic experience.[26]

The degree of discomfort experienced by Amistad's orphans depended on variables, including the ships' size, tonnage, and number of masts. The *Veloz*, the *Primeira*, and *Segunda Socorro* were not the slave ships of the legal era but rather ships that attempted to disguise and conceal their purpose. Various innovations sought to accomplish this. Ships might have larger holds for "legitimate" activities and cramped mezzanines for concealing slaves. Because the slave holds were often smaller than in previous decades, captains had to bring their live cargo top-deck more often simply to keep them alive, despite the risk of rebellion. When the overcrowded *Paquete do Rio* was seized a month after leaving Galinhas, it was "totally impossible" to assemble all 547 slaves on deck; many had to be left in the hold "in profuse perspiration and panting." Some vessels during this period were swifter and lighter, with copper bottoms, like *La Amistad*. Others, such as the Ferrer brothers' *Principeño*, were enormous steamships capable of holding over 1,200 individuals. The provisioning of the vessels with food and water was the responsibility of the captain and crew. Because they often had to load quickly, they may have acquired food and water in advance. But it was just as possible that once full, they were forced to immediately set sail, without adequate food and water provision, to avoid pursuit by the Royal Navy. From Kinna we learn that three of the children had "scarcely any water" and that when they fell sick, they were "forced to eat." To be sure, Africans transported by slave traders with more experience of the Atlantic passage likely had a better chance of survival.[27]

Unlike the other five, Covey's Middle Passage was brief, a fact that contributed significantly to the physical health of the entire group of approximately

162 children once they were disembarked in Freetown. Covey had been placed aboard the *Segunda Socorro*, under the control of José de Inza, on or around July 6, 1833, with 306 others. After two days at sea, de Inza realized the Royal Navy vessel *Trinculo* was pursuing him; he was captured on July 9, 1833. The *Trinculo*'s log recorded a journey from Galinhas to Freetown lasting four days, two days out and two days under escort to Freetown. There are no accounts of the disembarkation of Covey's vessel, but Leonard's account of the *Primeira* can give us an idea of his experience. The *Primeira* was captured with 311 slaves about a year before the seizure of the *Segunda Socorro* with 307. Leonard's demographic description closely mirrors that of the *Segunda Socorro*. He noted that the ship contained 111 men, 45 women, 98 boys, 53 girls, and 4 "infants at the breast," including 1 born since capture. They were disembarked in large purpose-built canoes; the men first, the women second, and the children last. The canoes were large enough to carry between 50 and 80 each time, so that after several trips over two hours the whole group was on shore. Whereas the *Primeira* was fired upon, and several Africans killed, Covey's first Atlantic ordeal ended quickly, with no canons fired, after which he was taken to the Liberated African Yard in Freetown. Here he waited with the other boys while the British decided his fate. Together the boys suffered "from want of a proper supply of food."[28]

The Middle Passage experience of Amistad's orphans was shaped by the ship on which they traveled. Vessels varied in size, tonnage, and the volume of the hold, depending on their origin and destination (ships headed to Brazil, for example, needed more food and water). Data for fifty ships from Sierra Leone locations, including the Galinhas region, during the period 1833–39, show that the slavers carried 15,961 departing Africans and averaged 100 tons, thus 319.2 slaves per vessel, or 3.1 slaves per ton. Data for the same period for vessels from the Galinhas region alone indicate a significantly higher average of slaves: approximately 384. A total of 9,983 slaves embarked on twenty-six voyages, with a similar average tonnage of 102, thus 3.7 slaves per ton. Thus we can reasonably conclude that Amistad's orphans traveled in vessels considerably more cramped than those from other regions. There were few large ships carrying large numbers during this period, and the ships likely carrying Amistad's orphans were smaller craft, such as schooners and pilot-boats, designed to outrun British navy cruisers on their way to Cuba, with an optimal capacity of 350 to 450 slaves, with extremes of fewer than 200 or more than 600.[29]

The length of the voyage of Ka'le, Kag'ne, and Mar'gru contributed to their discomfort level, but it is difficult to ascertain how long they were at sea. Bahoo claimed his voyage (and that of Ka'le, Kag'ne, and Mar'gru) took two months (approximately 60 days). But his recollection differed from that of the other adult survivors. For the entire slave trade from Sierra Leone to Cuba, based on nineteen ships, the average Middle Passage was 41.2 days. Data exist for sixty-four voyages from Sierra Leone to Cuba during the illicit period of transportation (1819–66), but of these only eight also include the length of the Middle Passage. For this period the average journey time was shorter, at only 37 days, perhaps reflecting the swifter vessels, such as Baltimore Clippers, that formed "the greater part of the vessels" traveling to Cuba, according to one of Madden's anonymous sources. Thus a voyage of two months would have been an unusually long journey.[30]

Children aboard slaving vessels endured chronic dehydration and malnutrition. They were routinely fed and watered at half rations. Ricketts witnessed the disembarkation of a "cargo of children" and noted they were "mere skeletons, in a complete state of exhaustion." They were exposed to numerous diseases, such as trachoma, dysentery, smallpox, and horrific skin lesions. The physician Thomas Nelson described the "disease, want, and misery" of 360 slaves liberated in Brazil in lurid terms. The mortality of those who traveled with Amistad's orphans speaks to their experience of the Middle Passage. Bahoo's claim that "many died" may appear vague, but with some additional considerations, a sense of the voyage mortality is possible. If the voyage's length was as long as two months, then mortality would likely have been higher than average. For the entire period, the average mortality between Sierra Leone and Cuba, based on seventeen ships, was 13.4 percent. The average mortality for ships departing Sierra Leone for Cuba during the illegal period was higher, at 15 percent. But as records exist for only nine ships, it is difficult to establish how accurately this reflected the larger enterprise. Havana's slave merchants operated with the assumption of a 20 percent loss, according to one of Madden's anonymous sources. But the length of the voyage had a direct impact on the mortality rate. As the length of the Middle Passage increased, mortality generally increased at an equal ratio because mortality was closely tied to endemic disease. Children were particularly susceptible to disease as they lacked the natural immunities garnered by age and exposure. Thus, if Bahoo was correctly reporting the voyage length of two months, it is plausible that mortality on the ship carrying Kag'ne, Mar'gru, and Ka'le to Havana was 20 percent or higher, particularly if endemic disease was rampant.[31]

Fifty to seventy ships left Cuba for Africa annually in the late 1830s, and it may never be established which ship transported the four children to Cuba. The scant information about ships during this period provides for a very limited speculation. There are no reliable dates, although Sedgwick claimed that the girls were removed from "some place in the district of Senegambia" by Pedro Montes or "his agents" on "the 20th of April last past," without providing an explanation of how he calculated this claim. Furthermore, much of the available information must be viewed within the context of the many techniques of illicit travel and illegal commercial activities. Indeed, the district attorney in the first habeas corpus hearing remarked, "Nothing is more common than for a slave vessel to sail under false colors." Notwithstanding these complicating factors, if all the variables considered above are combined with specific data about traders and firms operating between Galinhas and Cuba, there are three possible candidates for the vessels that may have brought the children into Havana. The *Primogenito*—owned by Blanco—arrived in Cuba in 1839, with 467 slaves, after 100, or 17.5 percent, perished. Another Blanco vessel, the *Firme*, also arrived in Cuba on an unknown date in 1839, with 440 African survivors, of an original 535, a similar mortality rate. A third ship, *La Bandeira*, left Cuba in November 1838 and returned to Havana with 229 slaves in February 1839. Pedro Martínez, the director of the eponymous Cuban firm of which Blanco was an associate, owned *La Bandeira*, but it flew the Brazilian flag.[32]

Discerning which vessel may have transported Mar'gru, Ka'le, and Kag'ne is complicated by the fact that some of the Amistad survivors were first placed on a ship, which was "chased by a British cruiser." It "returned" to the coast, "landed the cargo of human beings," and was then "seized and taken to Sierra Leone for adjudication." The unknown individuals were placed aboard a second vessel. Several ships were seized empty and condemned during this period, including the *Bela Fiorentina*, the *Maria Theresa*, the *Catalana*, the *Rebecca*, the *Goliubchick*, the *Hazard*, and the *Iago* or *Caroline*. Perhaps the best candidate is Blanco's ship, the *Cirse*, which was seized by the *Buzzard* (with Covey aboard) in late 1838, after it had offloaded its slaves. If this were the case, it provides for a fascinating historical moment whereby Covey just avoided encountering the soon-to-be Amistad rebels.[33]

It is also possible that Te'me arrived in Cuba on a separate fourth ship, because Bahoo explicitly excluded her from his accounts, and the other adult Africans noted they met all the children in Havana. At various points Te'me was described as originating in the Congo, but the most likely explanation is that this referred to the town of Te-Congo. And although the fact that she could talk to the other girls makes it unlikely she originated in Central Africa, it is not entirely implausible and thus merits further exploration. Between 1831 and 1840 more than 13,000 slaves came from eight different West Central African ports to six Cuban ports (table 4.1). Several vessels disembarked slaves in Cuba in 1839 from West Central Africa, including the *Casualidade* and the *Dichosa*. Many more likely secreted their clandestine cargos on remote or deserted beaches, in the manner described by Arturo Arnalte. Importantly, however, Te'me herself appears never to have claimed to be of Central African origin. Perhaps as the

Table 4.1. Cuban Slave Imports from West Central African Ports, 1831–40

West Central Africa port	Cuban port							Totals
	Bahia Honda	Guanimar	Havana	Mariel	Santiago de Cuba	Trinidad de Cuba	Not specified	
Ambriz		540					1,445	1,985
Benguela				307		401	490	1,198
Cabinda			3,209				673	3,882
Coanza River							29	29
Congo River	505		1,281				267	2,053
Loango			1,011				659	1,670
Mayumba			210					210
Luanda			845		167		1,001	2,013
Totals	505	540	6,556	307	167	401	4,564	13,040

Source: *Voyages: The Trans-Atlantic Slave Trade Database* (http://slavevoyages.org/tast/database/search.faces?yearFrom=1831&yearTo=1840&mjbyptimp=60700&mjslptimp=31300)

youngest, she was most terrified and reluctant to speak to anyone until she achieved an appropriate level of comfort.[34]

Whereas Te'me, Mar'gru, Ka'le, Kag'ne, and (likely) Antonio concluded their first Atlantic passage in Cuba, the final installment in the initial westward Atlantic journey of Covey took place in the context of an apprenticeship with the Royal Navy West Africa Squadron, beginning November 1838, after a hiatus in Freetown and Bathurst (Chapters 5 and 6). Once apprenticed aboard the *Buzzard*, Covey was thrust center stage into the dramatic context from which he had been liberated barely half a decade earlier. The *Buzzard* was a ten-gun, 233-ton, Cherokee-class brigantine-sloop, with a crew of thirty-seven officers and men, ten "boys," and eight marines, launched in 1834. The *Buzzard* had been active along the coast for several years. The only known image of the ship shows it capturing the slaver *Formidable* in December 1834 off the Old Calabar River (figure 4.7).[35]

With Covey aboard, the *Buzzard*, under the command of Captain Charles Fitzgerald, sailed from Freetown to Fernando Po, Principé, and into the Niger River delta. Fitzgerald and other West Africa Squadron captains operated under the doctrine of the "right of visit." The *Buzzard* first seized two ships in 1838 off the coast of Sierra Leone: the empty *Cirse* of Blanco and the *Empreendedor*, with 467 slaves aboard. In early January 1839 Fitzgerald boarded the American-flagged *Traveller* to examine her papers. And in March the *Buzzard* intercepted two vessels flying U.S. flags, the *Eagle* and the *Clara*. The *Eagle* presented a conundrum for Fitzgerald and the Royal Navy. It began its journey from an unspecified Bahia port in September 1838. When captured in March 1839, Fitzgerald believed it was "Spanish property," and "the American flag was only hoisted to cover that vessel from being taken by an English Man of War whilst empty and that on her receiving on board her slaves for which purpose she was equipped, the American flag would have been hauled down and the Spanish flag hoisted." The *Clara* left Havana July 1838. It had no slaves when seized July 1839, but Fitzgerald considered it, like the *Eagle*, a "Spanish Schooner with slave fittings." The *Buzzard*'s seizures were part of a "brief period of confusion" tied to illegal slaving, and the *Eagle* and *Clara* were but two vessels servicing slaveholding nations flying U.S. flags.[36]

TRAVEL WITHIN THE AMERICAS

After surviving the Middle Passage, Antonio, then, in 1839, Ka'le, Kag'ne, Mar'gru, and Te'me arrived in Cuba, where they were "secretly and privately landed." Although Antonio's precise arrival is unclear, in 1835, when he likely

Fig. 4.7. HMS *Buzzard* capturing *Formidable*, December 17, 1834, by John William Huggins
(© National Maritime Museum, Greenwich, London)

set foot in Cuba, the authorities routinely overlooked the illegal arrival of *bozales* in Cuba, both in Havana and in small villages on the coast. Once they arrived, they were all "taken to a secret place," housed in an illicit coastal slave facility, and made available for immediate purchase. They would likely have been taken by small launch craft—such as the *Criolla* or the *Catalana*, owned by Ferrer—to a *barracón* (Spanish for barrack) facility by the harbor's edge. Again, Bahoo provides the detail for the experience of the majority. He explained that they "were landed on the coast at a little place [near Havana], near sun set—stayed until night, and walked into the city, put them in an old building, and fastened them in." Here the children probably had their first substantial food and water for several months, primarily to prepare them for resale. But they would also have been inspected for diseases and the very sickly separated. The precise facilities housing the children would likely have been proprietary buildings owned by Martínez and Company, or Señor Xiques and Company, or one of Ferrer's collaborators, all of whom had close dealings with Blanco and others on the Galinhas coast.[37]

There were *barracones* throughout Havana, and the Cuban authorities made no attempt to regulate them. They were replete with new arrivals from Africa. Madden noted that "five such 'slave marts' were situated within a 'pistol shot' of the Captain General's home and only one and half miles from the walls of Havana." David Turnbull, a British consul traveling in Cuba in 1840, observed "two extensive depots for the reception and sale of newly imported Africans" recently constructed near the Paseo in Havana, "just under the windows of his Excellency's residence." Turnbull estimated that one could house 1,000, and the second 1,500 Africans. More important, during his visit, they were "constantly full." The volume of slaves coming into Havana in the late 1830s was indeed considerable. During the ten-year period from 1831 to 1840, 144 ships arrived in Havana, carrying 51,607 Africans (table 4.2). This means that at any one time, individual *barracones* contained slaves from between three and five ships, or more, from any number of different origin points, including Sierra Leone and Congo ports. However, this number represents only the known ships. Many more sailed from Havana to Africa and back undetected. One anecdote suggests thirty-six ships left Havana every year in the late 1830s. If the data for fourteen vessels per year, with an average cargo of 358 disembarked, are adjusted to thirty-six vessels a year, the number of Africans entering Havana ports in the 1830s would be 128,880.[38]

A *barracón* operated as a halfway station where newly imported Africans were taken before being removed to the different parts of the island. The Havana *barracones* served the purpose of marketplace and prison, to "save the expense

Table 4.2. Slave Imports, Havana, Cuba, 1831–40

	Total slaves	Number of vessels for which data exists	Average
Slaves disembarked	51,607	144	358.4
Percentage male		7	74.3%
Percentage children		7	44.0%

Source: *Voyages* (http://slavevoyages.org/tast/database/search.faces?yearFrom=1831&yearTo=1840& mjslptimp=31312)

of advertising in journals." Madden noted that among the "largest dealers and importers of the Island of Cuba in African slaves" was the "notorious house of Martinez and Co of Havanna." During his residency in Havana, where he served as judge on the Mixed Commission in Cuba, Madden had visited specific *barracones*. "These barracones outside the City walls are filled up exclusively for the reception and sale of *Bozal* negroes." The new railroads into the interior, including to Matanzas, flowed directly out of the facilities. The local Cubans considered such facilities to be, in Turnbull's words, "the lions of the place," by which he meant that "on the arrival of strangers, they were carried here as to a sight which could not well be seen elsewhere."[39]

Amistad's orphans likely remained in the *barracones* two or three weeks before being sold. On the day of sale, street callers and local papers, such as *El Diario*, publically announced the sale of "negroes." French traveler Étienne-Michel Massé provided a lurid account of this process in the "deplorable markets." He witnessed firsthand how the men were brought forth with nothing on their bodies but a "pantalon" and "chemise" of cotton. He compared the lines waiting for the sale to commence to a "queue" outside a *boulangerie*. He described the hustle and bustle as buyers jostled to see the prospective purchases. Women were particularly badly treated, and Massé witnessed the "despair" on their faces as they were touched and examined. He saw brothers separated from sisters, and children "un peu grands" crying as they were separated from their mothers. Once purchased, the "unfortunate Africans" were supplied with a "chemise" upon which was written the name of their new master and sometimes even their own new slave name. They were sometimes given a cigar as a "consolation."[40]

Shortly before *La Amistad* sailed from Havana, in a spectacle like this, Pedro Montes purchased the girls and Ka'le from Xiques and Azpilaca, two slave traders associated with Ferrer. At the point of sale, they were subjected to yet another unpleasant bodily inspection. There are no accounts of the purchase of the children, but Cinquez provides a sense of the intrusive physical nature of the pre-purchase examination. On cross-examination he stated, "When they first landed there they were put in prison. Were not chained. Pepe [Jose Ruiz] came and felt of them. [Jingua here described how Pepe felt of the Africans to ascertain if they were healthy and sound.] He then said, 'fine,' that is, good, and that he would take them." The children were purchased before the adult males, and the adults described first seeing the children unchained on the deck as they themselves were brought on board and imprisoned and chained in the hold. Antonio witnessed them come aboard.[41]

La Amistad left harbor on June 28, 1839, at approximately four o'clock in the afternoon. On board the children were treated differently from the adults. Antonio was the cabin boy and therefore crew. He was entitled to crew rations of food and water and slept in the crew's cabin. The other four—Kag'ne, Mar'gru, Te'me, and Ka'le—moved about the deck with considerable liberty; they had open access to fresh air. They slept at night on the deck on boards or makeshift beds, with some of the crew and half of the adult Africans. They were not imprisoned and chained in the hold, which measured only six feet six inches at its highest point. Daytime on the deck, likely crowded with adult males, would have been very unpleasant for three young girls. Although food and water were scarce and the ship was supplied with only six casks of water, the children were on smaller rations. Soon after departure, the water ration was cut in half to a teacup a day, half in the morning and half in the evening. Cinquez stated that they "were kept short of provisions. They [the Cubans] gave them 'half eat and half drink'—one plantain and two potatoes." The children rapidly became dehydrated, exacerbating their malnutrition from the trans-Atlantic voyage. Soon after departing Havana, the ship encountered a squall.[42]

As conditions deteriorated on the ship, the adult slaves mounted an insurrection and seized control of the vessel. Documentation of African remembrances of the violent insurrection appears richer than for the Middle Passage, and there are several reasons for this. First, the revolt captured the attention of the U.S. public and the courts, and understanding the context was central to the outcome of the case. The survivors were questioned about their Middle Passage only later. Second, the Cuba–Connecticut voyage was likely longer than the Middle Passages for all concerned. Third, the Cuba–Connecticut voyage involved a successful insurrection, itself a result of brutality, deprivation, and taunts and thus a cause for celebration. And fourth, the story of the *Amistad* was told and retold over and over again before the trials to journalists, in the context of the trials, and again after the Supreme Court victory.[43]

Notwithstanding these observations, Amistad's orphans were likely marginal to much of the violence, a defining element of the celebrated Amistad story. A few scant details of the children's experiences provide some sense of their ordeal as they sailed toward Connecticut. Although five of Amistad's orphans endured the shipboard revolt, they surely had different recollections of the violence. The children first encountered Antonio when they boarded the vessel, but they likely had their first serious interactions with him only after the revolt. The Africans seized rudimentary weapons and killed first Celestino Ferrer, the cook, and then Ferrer himself. As Ferrer's slave, Antonio surely feared for his life. He had made "regular trips" with Captain Ferrer during the previous three years. He fled upward into the rigging shrouds. After being lured down from his initial refuge in the mainstays, one of the Africans, Burna, forestalled his summary execution. He was then tied up with the surviving slave traders, Ruiz and Montes, on the deck.[44]

Antonio later provided, in Spanish, one of the most detailed accounts before a special district court session held aboard the seized vessel in August 1839. His dramatic narrative, however, omits any reference to the other four children. Although they had not been chained, they must have been terrified and probably hid in some part of the ship. Mar'gru, Te'me, Kag'ne, and Ka'le likely watched the violence unfold from a discrete location, but we cannot be sure, as accounts of the events are vague and conflicting. One of Madden's multiple accounts infers that the girls assisted the revolt, "true to their sex," and may have helped the adults locate the machetes and cane knives. A news report identified Kag'ne as the "principle companion" of Cinquez and suggests she sought at his side physical protection from others.[45]

For all five of Amistad's orphans, conditions worsened after the seizure of the vessel. The children no longer had to witness whippings or blood being washed from the decks, but the continuation of their Atlantic journey involved new physical and emotional tribulations. Food was scarce, water scarcer still. Antonio was deprived of food and water and kept under guard throughout. The other four children fared slightly better. Tappan reported that Cinquez "would not drink any [water], nor allow any of the rest to drink anything but salt-water." But he "dealt out daily a little to each of the four children." *La Amistad*, with the five children, sailed northward, instead of west, and after two and a half months ran aground off the coast of Long Island. It was then towed into New London harbor in August 1839, and all the Africans were imprisoned.[46]

By September, Amistad's orphans were all within relative proximity for the first time, and their itineraries converged until March 1841. Antonio, Ka'le, and the three girls were detained in Connecticut, under the watchful eyes of the U.S. marshal, the New Haven jailer Pendleton, and the hastily assembled

Amistad Committee. They were shuttled from New London to New Haven to Hartford and back to New Haven for various hearings. Unaware of the events, James Covey sat on the Staten Island docks with other African naval apprentices until Gibbs encountered him. In early September Covey came to New Haven under the supervision of Gibbs and resided with Timothy Bishop, one of the Amistad Committee. After the first habeas corpus trial and the dismissal of the murder and piracy charges, the five other children were relocated to Pendleton's home in Westville. For most of their time in Connecticut the children were together, quite apart from the adults. Antonio and Covey were free to move back and forth and visited the adults in jail regularly.

Although Antonio was prohibited from studying with the girls and Ka'le in Westville, Amistad's orphans must have spent many long hours together between October 1839 and March 1841, when the girls and Ka'le were relocated to Farmington and Antonio fled to Montreal, joining the many thousands of fugitive slaves who made Canada their home. He sailed from New Haven to New York City aboard the steamer *Bunker Hill*, then traveled overland through Vermont accompanied by several "conductors" of the Underground Railroad. Covey moved to Brooklyn for several months. The four in Farmington continued their studies for several months. Ka'le traveled in May with a group of the adults to Philadelphia, Boston, and New Jersey in efforts to raise funds for their return to Sierra Leone. A half-baked plan to relocate one of the girls, unnamed, to the home of Mr. Weld in New York City was abandoned after the girls' guardian, Amos Townsend, objected that they "would feel deeply grieved at a separation."[47]

EASTWARD MOVEMENT ACROSS THE ATLANTIC

The final stage of the Amistad's orphans' journey was their return to Africa. Throughout the summer of 1841 Tappan and others had deployed a small group of the adults and Ka'le to cities along the Eastern Seaboard in an effort to raise funds. The Amistad survivors gave public speeches and performed acrobatics. Preparation for the voyage began in earnest in September and October 1841 and included the purchasing of agricultural implements, teaching aids, clothing, and food. Antonio lived out the remainder of his adolescence in Montreal, Canada, but the other five began their final sea voyage as children in November 1841.[48]

The five children, along with the other adult males, departed New York City aboard the *Gentleman* on November 25, 1841. The ship manifest included thirty-nine Africans; two black abolitionists, Henry R. and Tamar Wilson; and three white missionaries, James Steele and William and Elizabeth Raymond. Covey was a last-minute addition to the trip. Ka'le and Covey roomed with the adult males in steerage, although they were free to move about the ship. In a disquieting echo of the slave trade practice of counting three children as two adults, Tappan tried to put the three girls in the cabin at the cost of two adult passages. The three girls traveled in relative comfort with the missionaries. Linda Brown-Kubisch has observed that "the Africans became suspicious of their white traveling companions fearing they would be returned to slavery," but I have seen no substantive evidence to support such a claim. As the passage took a little longer than anticipated, when the *Gentleman* docked in Cape Verde, they traded some tools for food. Covey was instructed by Tappan to report to the commanding officer of the naval squadron upon his arrival in Freetown. Tappan provided a letter of introduction and explanation. But Covey does not appear to have returned to Her Majesty's service.[49]

For the next eight years the five child migrants remained in close proximity. Shortly after their arrival, newspapers in the United States printed brief details of their resettlement. The *New York Tribune* noted, "from Sierra Leone, letters have been . . . [from] the Missionaries who accompanied the Mendians to their native land. They had been one month at Sierra Leone, and in excellent health." They resided in Freetown for about one month, and the girls endured significant torment at the hands of Cinquez and others (Chapter 6). Steele made a preliminary trip to Mende territory in the company of Covey and others. The missionaries quarreled, some quit, and the remaining team relocated the group to York, along the peninsula, in March 1842. After several years in York, William Raymond negotiated with local chiefs for land for the establishment of a settlement, in an area named Kaw-Mendi (a.k.a., Komende), on a square mile along the south bank of the Bendei River for $80 and an annual fee of $150.

The girls, Ka'le, and Covey relocated again by canoe, a journey of between three and ten days, "according to the weather." They settled in Kaw-Mendi in March 1844. Covey drifted in and out over several years, but the other four remained tied to the mission.[50]

CHILD MOBILITY IN THE
NINETEENTH-CENTURY ATLANTIC

Amistad's orphans featured prominently in three forms of Atlantic mobility: namely, as slaves, as ship crew, and as migrant settlers. First, certain slavers in West Africa specifically sought out and specialized in children for purchase, and as the nineteenth century wore on the percentage of children in cargoes from

Sierra Leone to Cuba increased dramatically. Cuban slave traders desired children, and the prices paid for them suggest children were valuable commodities in industrializing Cuba. Second, children provided the navies and merchant marines of the Atlantic with a steady stream of manipulable and coercible labor. Whether as shipmates, cabin boys, apprentices, or in other capacities, both the military and private enterprise drew heavily on coerced child labor to staff their vessels. And third, children became increasingly important vehicles for missionary enterprises and migrant settlement schemes. Building on the successful early missionary schools in West Africa, which filled their schoolrooms and church pews with "redeemed" and "rescued" African child slaves, missionaries began to view children also as ideally suited to the rigors of the frontier experiment that defined the global nineteenth-century proselytization project.

CHILDREN AS OBJECTS OF TRADE

Both enslavement and the slave trade–based economy were increasing in the region in which Amistad's orphans lived in the early to mid–nineteenth century. Although it may be tempting to see the small number of children aboard *La Amistad* as an index of the marginality of children in the Cuban import trade, or to view child slaves as peripheral to the Atlantic mobility of the 1830s and 1840s, it would be a gross mischaracterization. Closer scrutiny of the data for ships operating during this period demonstrates that they were part of an expanding child-based illicit slave economy in general, and a dynamic relationship between the Galinhas region and Cuba in particular.

The ordeal of Amistad's orphans took place when the slave economies of Sierra Leone and Cuba were most closely aligned. If, as Bergad and others once noted, Cuba generally had "no preference for any particular nationality," by the 1830s economic, political, and geographical realities reshaped the market. A majority of vessels during this period were destined for Cuba. During the illegal slave trade, the relationship between Sierra Leone and the Americas, and with Cuba in particular, was in flux. Embarkation data for the first illegal years, 1807 to 1829, indicate that Sierra Leone ports constituted only 37,381, or 0.27 of 1 percent, of total exports of 1,381,636 across the Atlantic. Of 58,459 slaves arriving in Cuba for the same period, 9174, or 15.6 percent, originated in Sierra Leone. During the last decades of the trade, 1830 to 1866, the percentage of slaves from Sierra Leone ports rose to 0.39 of 1 percent of total numbers in the illicit trade. But the dependency of Cuban ports declined over time, and only 14,823 of the 168,663 slaves for whom the embarkation region is known originated in Sierra Leone ports, 1830–66. The role of Sierra Leone ports for Cuban slaves waxed and waned over the six decades of illegal transportation. The 1820s to the 1840s marked the peak of Cuban interest in Sierra Leone ports. In the 1820s, 17.8 percent of Cuban slaves whose embarkation point is known originated in Sierra Leone. In the 1830s, 11.5 percent of slaves originated in Sierra Leone. In the 1840s, Sierra Leone provided 20 percent of slave imports.[51]

Contemporary anecdotal evidence supports the view that Amistad's orphans' Atlantic itineraries took place at the zenith of the Cuba–Sierra Leone relationship. The British merchant Joseph Corry, who visited the region at the behest of the British government in 1805–6, estimated the annual number of slaves departing the region of Sierra Leone, which includes the "Rio Noonez" (Rio Nuñez), Rio Pongo, Sierra Leone River, and adjacent regions; the Sherbro River; and the "Gallunas" as approximately 9,500 slaves. Corry appraised the value of slave exports from the region to be a modest 190,000 pounds sterling. By the 1830s, however, the expanding role of the "rivers in the neighborhood of Sierra Leone" in the "increase of the illegal slave-trade" ports was widely recognized by British colonial officials. Walsh witnessed numerous Sierra Leone vessels departing laden with slaves in 1829, some to Brazil, most to Cuba. The number of slave vessels seized off the coast of Sierra Leone spiked significantly in the 1830s, to at least one a month, but Blanco claimed that profitability was assured if only one of three ships reached their destination. If this was the case, it marked a noticeable discrepancy with Alexander's claim that only one of every eighteen vessels crossing the Atlantic was captured. When Amistad's orphans moved clandestinely across the Atlantic in the 1830s, they were part of an expanding Cuba–Sierra Leone trade in an increasingly contested Atlantic passage.[52]

In addition to being part of an expanding Sierra Leone–Cuba trade, Amistad's orphans were part of an expanding trade in children from Sierra Leone. Embedded within the data about the increase in traffic from Sierra Leone is specific evidence about the expanding role of children. From 1563 until 1856, 1,108 ships sailed from Sierra Leone ports with 239,021 slaves. The percentage of children is known for 188 voyages, spanning the years 1681 to 1848. Over many decades, the percentage of children in the trade from Sierra Leone increased significantly (table 4.3). Whereas at the beginning of the eighteenth century, children constituted roughly 15 percent of slave ship cargos and individual slavers purchased occasional child slaves at Sierra Leone ports, by the end of the century it was closer to 25 percent. The nineteenth century, however, marked the peak period in child transportation from Sierra Leone. For the first quarter of the nineteenth century, 38 percent of slaves shipped from Sierra Leone ports were children. By the second quarter—and the period of Amistad's orphans—children were, on average, 41.5 percent of slave ship cargos. The *Empreendedor*,

Table 4.3. Children in Slave Ships from Sierra Leone, 1681–1848

Time period	Percentage
1681–1700	5.8
1701–1725	14.7
1726–1750	25.0
1751–1775	34.5
1776–1800	24.6
1801–1825	38.4
1826–1848	41.5
Average	30.0

Source: *Voyages* (http://slavevoyages.org/tast/database/search.faces?yearFrom=
1514&yearTo=1866&mjbyptimp=60200)

seized in 1838, carried 43 percent children. Galinhas was a location frequented
by those who specialized in children. The vessel that attempted to carry Covey
to Cuba was 53 percent children. The *Gertrudes* sailed in 1839 and carried
84.5 percent children. And the cargo of some, such as the *Triumfo*, consisted
entirely of young children.[53]

The increase in the number of slaves transported from Sierra Leone over
the course of the nineteenth century is of interest when set against evidence
of the consistent demand for children during the illegal period from a wider
zone, including the neighboring regions of Senegambia and the Windward
Coast. Over a period of twenty-three years—from 1807, the first year of abolition, to 1830—81,359 slaves were disembarked alive, and of the sixty ships with
age data, children were 38.8 percent of the total (table 4.4). Extending the time
frame to 1856, 115,379 slaves were disembarked alive on 542 voyages. Of these,
39.8 percent were children, based on records of eighty-five vessels (table 4.5).
The consistent demand for child slaves until the complete cessation of the slave
trade is striking.[54]

The point of embarkation for Amistad's orphans was an important site for the
sale of slave children throughout the history of the Atlantic trade. The six children departed from Sierra Leone, specifically from the Galinhas River region
and the barracoons and factories owned and run by Blanco, Luiz, and Martínez
and Company. The Galinhas region was the site of many important slave factories, but boys were among its primary exports. From 1730 to 1856 (the inclusive

Table 4.4. Slave Exports from Sierra Leone, Senegambia, and Windward Coast, 1807–30

	Total slaves	*Number of voyages*	*Average per voyage*
Slaves embarked	91,968	430	213.9
Slaves disembarked	81,359	426	191.0
Children		60	38.8%

Source: *Voyages* (http://slavevoyages.org/tast/database/search.faces?yearFrom=1807&yearTo=1830&mjbyptimp=60100.60200.60300)

Table 4.5. Slave Exports from Sierra Leone, Senegambia, and Windward Coast, 1807–56

	Total slaves	*Number of voyages*	*Average*
Slaves embarked	129,909	546	237.9
Slaves disembarked	115,379	542	212.9
Children		85	39.8%

Source: *Voyages* (http://slavevoyages.org/tast/database/search.faces?yearFrom=1807&yearTo=1866&mjbyptimp=60100.60200.60300)

dates of known vessels), 40,990 slaves were purchased at the Galinhas coast. The data show a dramatic spike in supply from Galinhas after 1801 and suggest that the area emerged as a successful embarkation location as the trade became illegal (table 4.6). The age breakdown is available for 24 of 141 voyages. For the entire period children constituted 42.4 percent of shipments from Galinhas, a rate more than twice that of the overall Atlantic trade average of 20.9 percent, representing 4,219 of 33,366 known voyages, spanning 1514–1866.[55]

Children were a particularly important commodity in the Sierra Leone ports of Galinhas, as well as in the neighboring region of Sherbro, during the illegal phase in the nineteenth century. Between 1808 and 1839 (the year of *La Amistad*'s capture), approximately 50 percent of slaves leaving Galinhas ports were children, significantly higher than the overall average (table 4.7). Of a total forty-eight voyages, nineteen departed Galinhas, and sixteen from Sherbro. By contrast, during the same period, children constituted 33.9 percent of the entire trans-Atlantic movement, 35.9 percent of exports from West Central

Table 4.6. Slaves Purchased in Galinhas, 1730–1856

Time period	Number of slaves	Number of voyages
1730–1750	843	6
1751–1775	920	3
1776–1800	770	3
1801–1825	14,594	68
1826–1850	23,324	60
1851–1856	539	1
Total	40,990	141

Source: *Voyages* (http://slavevoyages.org/tast/database/search.faces?yearFrom=1514&yearTo=1866&mjbyptimp=60208)

Table 4.7. Children in Ships Departing from Sierra Leone Ports, 1808–39

	Sierra Leone ports					Sierra Leone average
	Galinhas	Îles de Los	Rio Pongo	Sherbro	not specified	
Percentage	49.5	14.4	29.7	66.3	30.2	42.6

Source: *Voyages* (http://slavevoyages.org/tast/database/search.faces?yearFrom=1808&yearTo=1839&mjbyptimp=60200)

Africa, and 34.2 percent of exports from the Bight of Benin. Within the Sierra Leone and Windward Coast subregion, only the ports of Sherbro had a higher percentage of children during the same period. Outside of West Africa, only Southeast Africa and the Indian Ocean islands had a comparable one-to-one ratio of adults to children. One possible explanation is that as the Royal Navy successfully ended exports from the Îles de Los, Rio Nuñez, and neighboring regions north of Freetown, the enslaved children that once supplied these areas were redirected via Galinhas and Sherbro. Further research may yet establish how supply channels changed during the illegal phase of the Atlantic trade. These data underscore the earlier observations about slave traders operating in the region who specialized in children.[56]

Amistad's orphans' voyage from Galinhas to Cuba speaks to the island's specific relationship to Sierra Leone and to the Galinhas region in particular.

As historian Oscar Grandio Moraguez observes, Galinhas, along with Lagos, emerged as a major player during the first decades of the nineteenth century. Data about the embarkation port for 248,244 slaves imported into Cuba during the trans-Atlantic trade establish Sierra Leone as the fourth most important embarkation region, after West Central Africa, the Bight of Biafra and Guinea Islands, the Bight of Benin, and equal in importance to Southeast Africa and the Indian Ocean islands. For the entire trade, of the 239,021 slaves from Sierra Leone, for whom we have data on embarkation origin (185,136), 145,188 or 78 percent arrived in the Caribbean region. And during the same period, slaves from Sierra Leone ended their journeys in Cuba with a higher frequency than every other Caribbean port except Jamaica. Within this data, moreover, Galinhas features very prominently. Of the slaves arriving in Cuba, 16,957 are identified as coming from the specific ports of the Galinhas region. Only Bonny, Congo River, São Tomé, and Mozambique had a larger share of Cuban imports.[57]

By the time trade into Cuba was illegal, 1819–20, the preeminence of Galinhas among Sierra Leone disembarkation points was unmistakable. Between 1820 and 1866, departures from Galinhas to Cuba dwarfed slave shipments from all other ports in Sierra Leone (table 4.8). During the same period Galinhas was the fourth most important individual embarkation port for slaves arriving alive in Cuba, of the 211,657 slaves whose disembarkation port is known (table 4.9). To what extent demand was shaping supply, or vice versa, is very difficult to determine. Galinhas was perhaps increasingly favored by some traders for cost and logistic reasons, insofar as once connections between Galinhas and Cuba were established, the costs of that particular trade route were probably lower and the

Table 4.8. Slave Exports from Sierra Leone Ports, 1820–66

Ports	Number of slaves
Côte de Malaguette	273
Galinhas	16,957
Rio Nuñez	300
Rio Pongo	3,038
Sherbro	1,373
Sierra Leone, port unspecified	562
Total all ports	22,503

Source: *Voyages* (http://slavevoyages.org/tast/database/search.faces?year
-From=1820&yearTo=1866&mjslptimp=31300&mjbyptimp=60200)

Table 4.9. Principal Embarkation Ports for Cuban
Markets, 1820–66

Port	Total slaves
Congo River	34,430
São Tomé	27,654
Mozambique	23,837
Galinhas	16,957
Whydah	14,094
Bonny	12,077
Lagos, Onim	9,786
All other ports combined (50)	72,822
Total	211,657

Source: *Voyages* (http://slavevoyages.org/tast/database/search
.faces?yearFrom=1820&yearTo=1866&mjslptimp=31300)

returns higher for certain particular slavers. Its environment offered security against the British navy not available elsewhere, for example, mangroves, shallow creeks, and secluded lagoons. But whether slavers specialized in children, or purchased from available supply, and how these matters were affected by demand is beyond the scope of this study.[58]

Just as children were a major export from Galinhas, they were also highly sought after imports in Cuba, and Havana in particular, where 44 percent of imports in the 1830s were children. Children were desired commodities in Cuba in the 1830s and 1840s, and the demand for children in the Americas may even have altered the experiences of children in Galinhas and beyond. Turnbull witnessed firsthand the slave barracoons in Havana, with their large numbers of children. He connected the two dynamics powerfully when he wrote that "the demand at the barracoons for younger victims" contributed to the "baser relaxation of social ties and family relations." Turnbull was perhaps alluding to pawnship and kidnapping of children.

In light of Turnbull's observation, the experience of Amistad's orphans is more emblematic of the period than previously recognized. The percentage of children in the slave trade leaving the Galinhas coast was higher than other regions for much of the slave trade. The percentage of children leaving Sierra Leone ports increased steadily over the course of several centuries until it peaked in the 1840s and 1850s. The role of Galinhas ports in Cuban imports outweighed that of most other ports. And the demand for children in Cuba was consistently high.[59]

Oceangoing vessels are a second significant site for understanding child mobility in the nineteenth-century Atlantic. Male children were highly prized for service in the Royal Navy, and every ship in the West Africa Anti-Slavery Squadron sailed with Africans, many of whom were recaptive slaves rescued by the very same squadron. African children were a cost-effective way to outfit a naval vessel; unlike merchant ships, the navy paid Africans less than white Europeans, and they did not qualify for any bounty payments for seized slaving vessels. As boy sailors were apprentices or recaptives, they were relatively easy to recruit in Freetown, Jamaica, Rio de Janeiro, and other places where captured slave vessels had disgorged their cargo. There is little doubt that some welcomed the opportunity to see the world and potentially make their fortune.[60]

The Royal Navy's West Africa Squadron was established in 1808 after Parliament passed the Slave Trade Act of 1807. Its home base was Portsmouth, England, but from 1819 it established a naval station in Freetown. Covey's apprenticeship in the squadron was rooted in a several-decade-long tradition of "disposing" of liberated boys and men in military and naval service. Historian Suzanne Schwarz has demonstrated that as settlements around Freetown began to appear overpopulated with liberated Africans, the Liberated African Department began seeking new outlets, including the Royal Africa Corps (R.A.C.) and later the "West India Regiments." Pencil notations in the Freetown-based Register of Liberated Africans from 1814 and 1815 indicate about thirty-four male recaptives were enlisted in the R.A.C. Records from 1808 to 1812 contain more detail on apprenticeships, including one of the first references to a boy being placed on a Royal Navy vessel. Sennama, Jeddo, Maca, and Coomba, aged between ten and eleven, were rescued from the slave ship *Lucia/Albert* in 1810 and almost immediately "Entered on board His Majesty's Ship *Crocodile*." Around the same time, Sara, a boy of six, was apprenticed to Lieutenant Scott of "His Majesty's Ship *Myrtle*," possibly in a personal steward capacity. Evidence from this period also attests to the first apprentices in the antislavery squadron. Tom, aged eight, released at Freetown on November 24, 1808, was swiftly apprenticed to the sloop *Derwent*. Thong, also aged eight, was similarly placed aboard the *Derwent* under the command of Captain Frederick Parker, along with another eight-year-old boy released from the *Two Cousins* only a day after Tom's ship was seized by the navy. In 1822, when the *Myrmidon* captured the

Portuguese vessel carrying Samuel Crowther, the system of apprenticeship was still informal. Crowther recalled, "In a few days we were quite at home in the man of war; being one six in number we were soon selected by the sailors for their boys, and were soon furnished with dress." These anecdotes contextualize both Covey's specific story and, more broadly, the extent of the dependency of the Royal Navy on apprentices courtesy of the Sierra Leone Liberated African Department.[61]

The circumstances of Covey's naval service are unclear, which suggests a continuation of certain informalities. After five or six years under the control of the Church Missionary Society (CMS) missionaries, Covey's apprenticeship abruptly shifted in 1838 and he was put aboard the *Buzzard* with twenty others. Oral and written reports attest to Covey's naval service, although the *Buzzard*'s ledger makes no mention of him by name. It is not surprising, as African crew were usually not named but feature more commonly as anonymous boys, cabin boys, and mates. Although Gibbs stated that Covey "was enlisted as a sailor," Covey himself was more circumspect. In his first deposition Covey stated simply that he was "a sailor on board the British Brig of War Buzzard." Before the district court, however, he claimed he "was put on board a man-of-war one year and a half." Although impressment of Africans was illegal, transferring an apprentice from one location to another was commonplace. And the CMS routinely "apprenticed out" underperforming students from their schools on a quarterly cycle, as only the best students were retained for training as ministers.[62]

Records of the apprenticeship of African boys in the West Africa Squadron are sparse. One of the earliest descriptions come from Maria Graham in Rio de Janeiro in 1821. Although she did not distinguish "free blacks" from those subject to apprenticeship, in her journal she observed, "It seems that the English ships of war on the African Coast are allowed to hire free blacks to make up their complement when deficient. There are several now on board the Morgiana, two of them are petty officers, and they are found most useful hands. They are paid and victualled [*sic*] like our own seamen. The negroes for any kind of labour, for six, eight, or ten months, sometimes for a year or two." Graham may have misunderstood the financial arrangements. By the 1830s, apprenticing "free blacks" was de rigueur. Leonard appears to suggest that the "custom" originated "with the liberated African department," rather than with the navy. The department routinely put "on board our ships of war a number of African lads recently emancipated, to be employed, as may be deemed fit, by the officer commanding." Leonard explained the practice in terms of cost and benefit: "They receive no pay, are supplied with two-thirds of a ration daily, and are scantily clothed from the store of the department at Freetown." Thus whereas boys liberated in Freetown and sent into an apprenticeship locally would incur the department a debt of one and half shillings a day, at sea, there was no such expense.[63]

Leonard believed the African apprentices were better sailors than many of the English ship boys. Once "they had been taught a seaman's duty" they "were infinitely more expert and active aloft, than the white boys of the ship." They "did their duty" with "so much zeal and alacrity, that their behaviour called forth the most unqualified praise." Captain Charles Fitzgerald may well have felt similarly. Among the "twenty blacks" Fitzgerald added in Sierra Leone in October 1838 were at least six new recruits, including Covey and Pratt, the cook. Fitzgerald nonchalantly described the process of staffing a squadron vessel. "The two young men from the Buzzard who acted as interpreters of the captured Africans of the Amistad at New Haven, have been in the asylum, where they learn to speak and write the English language. The Buzzard was allowed six of these African boys, beside 8 Kroomen, and 4 boys who have served some years." The *Buzzard* had a crew of "20 black and 50 white men and boys," and Fitzgerald explained that Africans are "favor[ed]" over "the white part of the crew" on account of the "climate." As there were between sixteen and eighteen vessels operating in the mid-1830s, approximately two to three hundred African boys were part of the squadron at any one time, many of them likely recaptive apprentices.[64]

Recaptive African apprentices aboard Royal Navy vessels, such as Covey, performed a variety of tasks. They were carpenters, sailmakers, rope makers, and blacksmiths. Fitzgerald alluded to a seamless connection between the rescue of boys and the staffing of rescue vessels when he stated, "The liberated slaves received into the asylum here under British authority, they are cleansed, and in a short time many of them were located in different villages. Pains are taken to teach the young, to put them to trades, and some of the boys are employed on board the cruiser." The number and age of the recaptive apprentices varied. Leonard counted eleven aboard for upward of twelve months, and fifteen more for shorter periods; in age, they ranged from fourteen to nineteen. But whereas the boys Leonard met were just off slave ships, "recently manumitted," and "unable to utter a word of English," Fitzgerald and other captains preferred boys who had some schooling and spoke a modicum of English. They may not have been the best students, but it appears the CMS schools and the Royal Navy developed an understanding in terms of expectations for students and potential apprentices. As late as 1852 the Royal Navy was still soliciting "Liberated African boys" of "the age of thirteen years to sixteen" from the CMS schools for service aboard the HMS *Wasp* and HMS *Penelope*. In May 1852, the HMS *Crane* took aboard Thomas Gobbet, aged about eleven, and Robert Beneley, aged fourteen.[65]

While many of those aboard the Royal Navy were apprentices, a good number were also born free and actively sought gainful employment. Alexander witnessed firsthand the critical role of Kru in the mid-1830s. He explained that frigates on the "African Station" always have "twenty Kroomen on board, and brigs and schooners about a dozen." Alexander described them almost as fortune hunters. "They are active, willing and obedient, and are called the Scotchmen of Africa: for they seek their fortunes out of their country; or return after a few years' service on board men of war with backases, as they call boxes filled with uniforms, cocked hats, and European clothing in general, and with which they doubtless make a great swagger among the crow-fair-mammies in Kroo country." Robert Clarke noted that the "broad-chested, muscular Kroomen" were "constantly employed" by the squadron. Aboard the *Buzzard*, Covey sailed in the company of eight "Kroomen." The reasons given by Alexander dovetail with the environmental explanation of Fitzgerald, namely, "to save the white seamen from exposure in boats, and in wooding." But whereas fortune hunting may have been important, some Africans may have joined the navy to exact retribution. The log of the *Black Joke* recorded the following: "I found . . . that the black cook had stowed away about two fathom of chain, promising that the first 'negro catcher' we had a palaver with should have it as a present from an African."[66]

In contrast with Covey's experience, Antonio's narrative provides a window into the secret world of illicit slave smuggling operations and how its dependency on African boys and male children expanded in the nineteenth century. Boys were equally important in merchant fleets, including legitimate commercial enterprise and illicit slave trading, and for many of the same reasons. African child sailors were often assigned more dangerous tasks than their white counterparts; if they died at sea or in combat, no pensions were payable to family members. An additional consideration for illicit slave traders was that if a vessel was captured, the master's cabin boy and ship slaves generally were protected from seizure. African boys provided a useful mechanism for all sorts of subterfuge in the trans-Atlantic game of cat and mouse.

Slave traders had long engaged African and African American male children and male adults, and historian Emma Christopher argues that "seamen with darker skin formed an integral part of the seafaring community." Africans were sought by slave traders as interpreters to mediate relations with slave merchants and ship captains. If they were more fortunate, they might become a captain's steward, like Baquaqua, but even that would not protect them from brutish

"corporeal punishment." As the slave trade became increasingly illegal, recruitment did not diminish. Historian Jaime Rodrigues assembled a list of three
hundred African seamen by name, operating on slave ships between Brazil and
West Africa from 1790 to 1860, and sixty-one Brazilian vessels seized between
1812 and 1863 containing African crew.[67]

Not every reference to a boy meant the boy was actually free. Slave traders pretended boy slaves were crew, but the slavers' subterfuge was sometimes
uncovered, as in the case of the *Eliza Davidson* seized off Galinhas in 1840.
And not every reference to a "boy" necessarily constituted a child; "boy" was
frequently used to identify Africans or to distinguish white from black, and not
necessarily in a derogatory fashion. African males—adults, youths, and boys—
opted for service in European merchant marines for any number of reasons,
and escaped slaves and manumitted slaves found sea service as a site of security.
Matthews reported that "instances of desertion" were rare among the Africans
used as "domestic and sailors" by "white people resident in Africa" because
they were treated better by them than by "black masters." And for some African
slaves, such as Denmark Vesey, or possibly Gustavus Vassa (Olaudah Equiano),
the cabin boy experience may have proved formative in their political awaken-
ing. Henry Louis Gates describes one ten-year-old cabin boy from Cuba who
went on to later organize a colonization scheme in Liberia for free black people
from Mexico and the West Indies.[68]

An African aboard a slave ship was in a potentially perilous position. Ship
captains feared the involvement of black sailors in slave revolts. Free African
seamen could be sold as slaves, and many occupations, such as cook, were
easily refilled on either side of the Atlantic. Slave crewmen were at risk of pirate seizure and resale. To be sure, it was perilous for anyone—cargo and crew
alike—to be on a slave ship. The crew was exposed to all the diseases infecting
the ship and its cargo. Many slaving vessels had slave crew and that crew had life
opportunities much greater than those of field slaves. Some ships were crewed
almost entirely by slaves. Slave crew did much to distinguish themselves from
slave cargo, including tattoos, language, and dress. They were highly valued for
their skills as sailors. Some held higher rank than "free" crew. Some were paid
better. And in exceptional cases, slave crew could be awarded insurance payments and damages.[69]

Antonio had been in the "service" of Ferrer for approximately three years
when the adult Africans seized control of *La Amistad.* The numerous terms
used to describe his status—including "slave," "servant," and "cabin boy"—
speak to the many jobs performed by African boys on vessels. Aboard slave ships
and other merchant vessels, African boys were cooks, servants, apprentices, and

"waiting boys," the latter category exclusive to slaves. The term "boy" was often a byword in the eighteenth and nineteenth century for any and all service men who were "black." Of the three ranks of enlisted men—able seaman, ordinary seaman, and boy, each with multiple classes—Africans were routinely accorded the latter, among the "lowliest occupations afloat." Historian Jeffrey Bolster explained that boys coiled rigging, held the log-reel, and unfurled sails. They learned hitches, bends, and knots and rudimentary sailing and navigation. In the nineteenth century slave boys were operating on oceangoing vessels and also on many coastal schooners operating out of New Orleans, Baltimore, New York, and elsewhere. Historian Martha Putney identified 135 African American children, ranging in age from seven to thirteen: ninety-four worked on boats registered in New Orleans alone. Twelve black children worked on ships with their fathers, and one family had three generations working aboard vessels operating between Baltimore and New Orleans. Underscoring the informality of many of the arrangements, Putney found a variety of different terms in use, including "bound boys" and "small black boy," the former used exclusively for slaves. The multiple terms highlight the plasticity of childhood as well as the spectrum of child-specific tasks.[70]

In the context of the revolt, Antonio was highly vulnerable, but somehow he survived. The white crew of *La Amistad* knew their likely fate and fled the vessel in a small craft. Ferrer ordered Antonio to throw bread to the revolting slaves, but the slaves refused it and killed another black crewmember, the cook Celestino. After coming down from the rigging, Antonio was tied up and treated "very cruelly" by one of the Africans, but another was "a great friend of the cabin boy" and may have "saved" his life. Antonio's survival was not unique, but mirrored other contemporary accounts. The cabin boy was the only crewmember to survive the insurrection aboard the *Virginie* in 1831, described by Leonard. The several accounts of the Amistad revolt suggest different possibilities as to why Antonio was not killed. Sweet argues that Antonio's multilingualism was key to an "overlapping, shifting, and situational identity," whereby he played for time, assisting the Africans in their attempt to sail home and thus gaining their "trust," but switching sides as he saw fit. Rather than a means to an ends, however, Antonio's survival was perhaps, to echo Hawthorne, "an end in and of itself." Drawing on his analysis of the survivors of the *Emilia*, I think a more compelling reason resides in the notion of shipmate bonding. If Antonio was originally from the Galinhas region, his survival strategy emerged from the importance the Amistad captives placed on immediately reestablishing very intimate, personal bonds with kinsmen who shared a common experience.[71]

A final important consideration for understanding Antonio—and perhaps as an aid for locating other such individuals—is the role played by African crew, "boys" in particular, in the subterfuge characteristic of the illicit maritime slavery of the 1830s. It is possible that his slippery identity was a product of the illicit context of slave smuggling. Regardless of whether Antonio was a slave cabin boy, such a status was not the same as a slave who was cargo. This distinction is important because slave crew were legal, depending on who owned them and whether or not they remained on board. If a ship were seized by the navy and found to have no slaves in the hold, the absence of proof often resulted in the release of the ship and its crew, such as the *Traveller* boarded and released by the *Buzzard*. Occasionally ships boarded seemed to have many more African crew than necessary, and naval officers were suspicious that the slaves had been quickly unshackled and brought out as subterfuge. Sometimes even ships with slave cargoes briefly seized, such as the U.S.-flagged *Maria da Gloria*, were ultimately released. Observers speculated that crewmembers were actually slaves in disguise.[72]

Treaties between Britain and Spain and between Britain and Portugal led to the passage of edicts, such as Portugal's 1831 law, permitting the seizure of the property of persons implicated in the illicit trade in slaves. The applicability of such bilateral treaties in the United States was at the crux of the Supreme Court appeal by the defenders of the Amistad Africans. Pursuing this argument yet further, after the final verdict John Quincy Adams, arguing for the defense, insisted that Antonio was "entitled to his freedom," long after he fled to Canada. Antonio may or may not have been a legal slave, but he was certainly part and parcel of the complex world of intrigue and subterfuge of the illicit world of nineteenth-century Atlantic slave smuggling.[73]

CHILD MIGRANTS AND CHILD SETTLERS

Amistad's orphans also provide a window into the important role of children in migration and its connection with missionary settlement and fundraising. At first glance, the phrase "child migrant" may appear an oxymoron in the context of the nineteenth century. On one hand, the word "child" implies minority and thus a diminished capacity or complete incapacity to convey consent. Children are almost always wards, guardians, or even the property of adults. The very notion of child freedom is deeply contested. On the other hand, the word "migrant" conveys a voluntary process, an experience to which one subjects oneself by choice. Whereas many contexts of such decision making may appear to offer little volition or discretion (war, flood, and famine all come to mind), migration is a physically deliberate act. Drawing together the words "child" and "migrant" forces us to scrutinize the narrowness of many definitions of both.

The experiences of Amistad's orphans push the stories about nineteenth-century child migration and settlement from familiar into unfamiliar territory. The phrase "child migrant" suggests both a personhood challenging prevailing legal and social conventions about childhood and a mobility operating at the interstices of coercion and liberty. The rich documentation of the experiences of children—black and white, slave and free—traveling accompanied by parents or kin or unaccompanied in the United States and beyond has been a site of important research. Just as children may have been more vulnerable to kidnapping than adults in the antebellum era because slavers escorting kidnapped children encountered less physical resistance, the plasticity of childhood provided many opportunities to conceal a child seeking to escape slavery, insofar as chaperones could describe the child as kin and deflect questioning and scrutiny.[74]

Antonio appears to have made the choice to move north to freedom rather quickly in March 1841, but adults accompanied him all the way to Quebec. Antonio fled to Montreal because his precise legal status exposed him to continued jeopardy. Early in the proceedings, the advocates for the Amistad survivors displayed little interest in Antonio's status. Tappan's primary news vehicle referred to Antonio as the "undoubted legal slave of Captain Ferrer." When Judge Judson sustained the slave status of Antonio, Baldwin and Tappan registered no significant objection. Secretary of State John Forsyth instructed U.S. attorney William S. Holabird to appeal Judson's decision but insisted "that part which concerns the slave Antonio is not to be disturbed." But by the conclusion of the trial, there was no longer unanimity of opinion about Antonio's status. And because the northern states were no safe place for young, unattached, able-bodied black youths, Townsend, Tappan, and others counseled Antonio to seize his destiny in liberty. Antonio thus joined the small but significant refugee migration of children north to Canada in the 1840s, which by the 1850s, with the passage of the Fugitive Slave Act, had swelled to a flood. After 1850 the black population grew rapidly. Between thirty and sixty thousand slaves fled to Canada. Canada was not entirely safe: indeed, free blacks were kidnapped in Toronto and taken back to the United States. But in Antonio's chosen destination of Montreal the free blacks were "a small and closely knit refugee community," with high visibility.[75]

If northbound slave refugee children constitute a relatively familiar subject, less familiar are rescued former child slaves who migrated and settled as part of nineteenth-century missionary endeavors. The missionary compound is a fascinating site for locating children, particularly former child slaves, but familial narratives often conceal the child subject. In its early years, the Mendi Mission, as it became known, drew heavily on the training and education Ka'le, Mar'gru, Kag'ne, Te'me, and Covey received before leaving the United States as it sought to gain traction in the wider community. As the Raymonds, like many missionaries in tropical West Africa, had no children of their own, they turned to the children to create a simulacrum of family. The turmoil of resettlement took its toll on the children, and the Raymonds "watched over them continually with parents' care," in an expanded parental role. Raymond wrote to Tappan, "They look to us as children do to their parents, and I am happy to say they are dutiful and obedient." The Raymonds regularly referred to the mission compound as their "mission family" and spoke of Amistad's orphans as their "adopted" children. Tappan and the American Missionary Association (AMA) appeared to view them as the Raymonds' children, as the children were supported with William Raymond's salary.

The children were ideal subjects for the missionary endeavor on two accounts. Their experience of enslavement as children had stripped them of their capacity to reconnect with kinship networks and families. And their training and education had narrowed their capacity to become true adults by cultural and social standards operating among the indigenous population in the Galinhas and throughout Sherbro- and Mende-speaking communities in the 1840s and 1850s.[76] Five of Amistad's orphans settled within the missionary compound, and four of them remained there for most of their adult lives. Updates from Raymond and others to Tappan demonstrate that whereas most of the adults disappeared from the mission quickly, Amistad's orphans were quite solid stalwarts. Tappan and others had assumed the adults "had been converted long before leaving" the United States, but as time passed the children were revealed to be more reliable participants. Raymond struggled with the adults because in his view they had few "habits of industry" and instead viewed "labor as disgraceful." By contrast, the children were reliable and performed a variety of tasks, including taking "care of the mission house."[77]

Reports from Raymond in the 1840s underscore the centrality of the children to the mission. Covey was "still at work" in July 1845. Kag'ne (now Charlotte) and Te'me (Maria) were doing "very well." Marg'ru (Sarah) was "an active growing Christian"; and Ka'le (known by then as George Lewis) was a "good boy" but "not yet converted." By August 1845, Raymond had "discharged and sent away all the Africans of the Amistad" because of "their general bad conduct," except Ka'le and the three girls. Of the five child migrants aboard the

Gentleman, Covey was to prove the least reliable. After being booted from the compound he went "to the Gallinas to assist in taking some slaves for" a certain local slave trader, a Mr. Tucker.[78]

In addition to the five children who returned aboard the *Gentleman,* Raymond and the American missionaries who followed him actively sought children in order to expand their influence in the region. Raymond sought to remove children "entirely away from their parents" and bring them up under the sole influence of the mission. After expelling the few remaining Amistad adults and Covey, Raymond went around the neighboring territories seeking to acquire children. He wrote to Tappan, "How many children I shall be able to obtain I cannot tell." Raymond sought to fill the mission school with children, many of whom were former slaves. By 1846 the school had thirty-nine students, including six girls. Twelve of the boys were accorded "apprenticeships" as carpenters, sawyers, and blacksmiths. In one account, he explained how five children were about to be redeemed by him, but they were weak and sick. Only one, whom he named Margaret, survived and was redeemed. In another letter he described rescuing a boy from being murdered as "punishment," and he redeemed a girl from "slavery" by a boatman.[79]

Raymond viewed the Amistad migrant children as success stories because of their rescue from American slavery, their subsequent education, and their ultimate Christian redemption. He sought to extend this microproject more broadly. By 1847, "one third of the children in school" were redeemed former slave children. The "expense of saving some" was not "as much as one dollar, while one was $35." And the "average expense" was "about $16." Raymond explained that thus, at an expense of $800, "fifty immortal beings" were "saved from Slavery, and some from immediate death." He admonished critics who questioned the perverse economic incentives embedded in the notion of purchasing children and encouraged him instead to send them home to their parents. "Whatever may be your opinion as to the propriety of redeeming them, you would have me turn them loose upon the world, to be again reduced to slavery. . . . If I send them away without sending them to [slave traders], the sword would find them. If I send them away, where shall I send them? You say, send them home. Some of them have no home, and those who have are liable to have it destroyed any night by war. If it was a time of peace[,] your plan of sending home part of the children might do, but as it is I am unwilling to take the responsibility of doing it." The AMA came to his defense, stating that "the mission premises are looked upon as a refuge for the slave" and that Raymond had "never yet failed to secure the freedom of every slave that has fled to him for protection." Even Ka'le assisted Raymond in the redemption of child slaves.[80]

The AMA defended Raymond's approach because it began to see the value of children and child narratives in fundraising for missionary endeavors. The utility of employing children's narratives would blossom in the late nineteenth century. But early records from this period demonstrate that Tappan and others were becoming aware of the potential value added by the presence of children in the mission. Albert Bellows, the superintendent of a Baptist church, sent five dollars from the children of his "Sabbath school" to the Amistad Committee in May 1841. He explained that after he had told the story of the Amistad to the children, the accompanying "freewill offering of nearly two hundred warm little hearts" was collected, and "the children said on giving their money 'send it to the Mendi children.'" The AMA appeared to grasp the promise of child narratives, and later issues of the *American Missionary* were designated to acknowledging the "contributions of children." When Thompson went to Sierra Leone after Raymond's sudden death, he continued the focus on children, proclaiming, "The children of the country are the hope of our labors." Redeeming children was continued in order "to save them from death, or American Slavery." He published a book of his letters to raise further funds.[81]

CONCLUSION

Amistad's orphans journeyed farther and longer than most children of their age. They traversed the Atlantic multiple times and in different capacities, and each of them inhabited several different legal statuses. But more important for this story, they did not follow the itineraries of the adult males of *La Amistad* for most of their experience. At times they paralleled the mobilities of the adult males, but the adult narrative of a common journey aboard the *Teçora*, and the myth of a common experience arising thereof, occludes the complexity and diversity of child movement. The story of the *Teçora* is important for understanding the experience of the Amistad survivors, but the ship itself had little relevance for Amistad's orphans. The subterfuge enveloping this mysterious vessel, however, speaks volumes about the illicit world inhabited by the many tens of thousands of children smuggled yearly into Cuba and elsewhere, such as Brazil.

The Middle Passage of Amistad's orphans sheds light on the experience of many thousands of African children during the period of illegal Atlantic slave trading. Their journeys across the Atlantic likely represented the average length of travel and mortality for a vessel during the 1830s. But their incarceration in the bowels of the vessels was unlike many of the popular descriptions of slave passage, because the increasing enforcement by antislavery patrols during the illegal period transformed the lived experience aboard the ship. The ships were smaller, swifter, and faster. They were filled more quickly and the space for slaves was considerably smaller than before abolition. Ships carried other products and concealed their slaves in compartments that were not designed for humans. Although the children may or may not have been shackled during their trans-Atlantic passage, the deprivations of water and food and the heightened vulnerability of children to violence and sexual assault were important factors.

In this chapter I have argued that understanding the divergent experiences of the children begins with a dismantling of the myth of a common Middle Passage. To be sure, there were many Middle Passages for Atlantic Africans, slaves and free, but too often the adult experience overshadows the discrete locations of child mobility in the context of the illicit Atlantic trade. From the perspective of a child, mobility in the Atlantic was disorienting, debilitating, and traumatic. With a shorter life experience prior to enslavement, they likely had less capacity than adults to understand what was happening to them. And as they were usually much smaller and physically weaker than their captors, they had less ability to resist their condition or change its course. Amistad's orphans traveled as slaves, as sailors, as prisoners, as students, and as migrants and settlers. Children were highly sought after for slave transportation from the Galinhas region of Sierra Leone, abundantly represented in slave cargoes from Sierra Leone, and valued commodities in Havana's barracoons. Their journeys were unique and their itineraries child-specific. And they occupied the three primary spaces identified—slaves, seamen, and settlers—primarily because of the plasticity accorded by their minority.

5

THE LIBERATIONS OF AMISTAD'S ORPHANS

In deliberating the legal status of the captives found aboard *La Amistad*, the Supreme Court wrestled with U.S. law and U.S. treaty obligations with Spain. The defense team, comprising Baldwin and Adams, argued forcefully that upon setting foot on Long Island, the Africans were legally free. In the court's landmark ruling, Justice Story drew heavily on Baldwin's arguments. He quoted liberally from Baldwin's statements: "They appear here as freemen. They are in a state where they are presumed to be free. They stand before our courts on equal ground with their claimants; and when the courts, after an impartial hearing, with all parties in interest before them, have pronounced them free, it is neither the duty nor the right of the executive of the United States, to interfere with the decision." The judgment of the majority ended the legal proceedings in January 1841, and accordingly the captives found aboard *La Amistad* were set free. From Story's interpellation of Baldwin's narrative a fourth myth was born, namely, that the Supreme Court's decision conveyed blanket freedom to all the captives.[1]

That the Supreme Court's decision constituted the final word on the freedom of the Africans remains as popular mythology, even today. Whereas evidence from New England months after the decision demonstrates that the court's suzerainty was strongly contested in some circles, and that the importance and implications of its decision remained unsettled, especially as it pertained to Amistad's orphans, the notion of blanket freedom is as powerful and attractive today as it was in 1840–41. The blanket freedom myth takes several different forms, ranging from the simple formulation—the uncritical restatement that the Africans were all freed by the court's decision—to the more complex and implausible notions that the case in some way paved the way for the infamous Dred Scott ruling, or that it constituted the first civil rights case for African Americans. Furthermore, the return of the Amistad Africans to West Africa is still celebrated as a touchstone of the nostalgia undergirding visual and written accounts of the North American slave experience because the freedom teleology provides a finite and incontestably tangible coda, anchored by notions of justice, equality, and humanitarianism.[2]

The experiences of Amistad's orphans in the wake of the Supreme Court determination were complex, painful, and likely traumatic. In some regards Ka'le fared the best: he was released with the adult males shortly after the ruling and relocated with the majority to Farmington, a small village on the outskirts of Hartford, Connecticut. For the remaining five, however, liberty was often an elusive or ambivalent status. For several months after January 1841, correspondence demonstrates that Pendleton, the New Haven jailer, met the Supreme Court's decision with circumspection and disregard with respect to the girl children. The Amistad Committee was forced to go to court in March to gain their release. The girls themselves were also unsure about the promise of liberty, and their experience highlights the ambiguity of free status for children. To the consternation of the abolitionists, the court appeared to sustain Antonio's enslavement. At different moments over the course of almost eighteen months, Antonio had expressed conflicting desires, including returning to Cuba or returning to West Africa, but ultimately he fled to Canada. And Covey, ostensibly liberated at the age of nine, but first apprenticed and then detained in the United States under subpoena, was more or less abandoned by the Amistad Committee. Over the next ten months he struggled to reestablish his place among the Amistad "family" in order to assure his return to Sierra Leone.

The Amistad orphans experienced multiple contexts of liberation; but the concept of freedom, and indeed the status of "free," likely meant little to the six children. Contrary to the beliefs of the blanket freedom myth, the Supreme Court ruling had little impact on their status. The complexity of their encounters with autonomy and liberty began well before January 1841. Like the adult captives who had revolted during the summer of 1839, the passage toward liberty and autonomy, if not freedom per se, for Amistad's orphans was not a linear trajectory. Moments of increased liberty were short-lived and followed by the recurtailment of autonomy. Liberation conveys a process and incorporates the multivalent, interrupted nature of the six children's experiences with autonomy. And focusing on liberation evades the many problematic ideological and conceptual issues embedded in the adult-centric slavery and freedom binary.[3]

THE MYTH OF BLANKET FREEDOM

The origins of the blanket freedom mythology lie partly with the ambiguous language employed in the ruling of 1841 and partly with the historical sequence of trials and court appearances between September 1839 and March 1841. On one hand, the 1841 ruling regularly referred to the survivors collectively as "Africans," it only rarely mentioned them as individuals, and it implied that "the dreadful acts" perpetrated aboard the ship resulting in the deaths of several individuals represented a single, collective act restoring a freedom unlawfully negated by illegal enslavement. By this logic, the decision not to sustain the claims of libel by the Spanish-Cuban pair, Ruiz and Montes, was extended to the entire African collective, including the children. On the other hand, the verdict of the court was but a concluding phase in a sequence of arguments that began with the first habeas corpus trial of the three girls. It cannot be overlooked that whereas the freedom determination in some ways originated with the children, further action was necessary in order that it be extended to those same children.[4]

The first appearance of the "free-born" claim was in the unsuccessful habeas corpus trial of the girls in September 1839. Although the hearing failed to gain their release, it subsequently became the foundation for the argument of the defense team in January 1840. The declaration cited in Chapter 1 merits repeating, wherein advocates for the African adult males in court declared:

> That they and each of them are natives of Africa and were born free, and ever since have been and still of right are and ought to be free and not slaves, as is said in several libels or claims pretended or surmised and that they were never domiciled in the Island of Cuba, . . . they and each of them were in the lands of their nativity unlawfully kidnapped and forcibly and wrongfully by certain persons to them unknown, who were then and there unlawfully and piratically engaged in the slave trade, between the Coast of Africa and the island of Cuba contrary to the will of these Respondents unlawfully, and under circumstances of great cruelty, transported to the said island of Cuba, for the unlawful purpose of being sold as slaves, and were then illegally landed for the purpose of the aforesaid.

This powerful declaration of freedom resonated with Judson, who affirmed that the "the burden of proof" of slave status rested on the shoulders of the Spanish consul representing the purported slaveholders. Judson rejected the idea that the *licencia* (license) or *traspasso* (movement permit) conveyed ownership, and stated that "possession is only one indici [sic] of property." "When the right is disputed" a simple statement of ownership "is not enough."[5]

The complex argument rejecting slave status and asserting freedom was personalized and emboldened by a masculine heroic master-narrative. According to Justice Story, "Cinque, the master-spirit who guided them, had a single object in view," namely, "the deliverance of himself and his companions in suffering, from unlawful bondage. They owed no allegiance to Spain. They were on board of the Amistad by constraint. Their object was to free themselves from the fetters that bound them, in order that they might return to their kindred and their home." In this version of the history of the survivors' ordeal, Cinque's behavior was recast as that of the legitimate action of a dispossessed leader of a larger community. The leader thus symbolized an entire community's struggle to return home. In the eyes of many, a decision in Cinque's favor encompassed the entire collective. And thus a blanket freedom emerged simultaneously from both the absence of proof and from an act of defiance.[6]

And whereas the Supreme Court's decision did result in the swift release of the adult males from the New Haven jail, freedom did not automatically extend to Amistad's orphans. The six made up a group with differing and conflicting claims to autonomy and complex histories of liberty. It included Covey, who was initially liberated at the age of nine, when the Royal Navy captured the ship transporting him; in Freetown, the Court of the Mixed Commission ordered the immediate liberation and apprenticeship of all aboard the *Segunda Socorro*, including Covey. Covey's liberty, if we can call it that, was short-lived. After mandatory schooling in the village of Bathurst for five years, he served in the West Africa Squadron. The group also included Antonio, the cabin boy and slave of the murdered captain, Ferrer. Even though evidence points to the possibility that he was born in West Africa, he had certainly served as Ferrer's cabin boy for three years, and during this period he constituted slave property in the eyes of many. Why most of the advocates for the Amistad captives abandoned attempts to extend the Supreme Court ruling to Antonio remains shrouded in mystery.

A final consideration in understanding the persuasive impact of the blanket freedom myth is the attitude today toward the Supreme Court. The anachronistic notion of immediate freedom is perpetrated by the contemporary wonderment and awe with which all determinations from the hallowed body echo across the nation. Indeed, current scholarship about the case rarely captures the conservatism and modesty of the early nineteenth-century court. In its place is projected an assumption of the centrality of Supreme Court decisions to the national body politic that only began to develop in the 1850s. In this anachronistic view the news of a controversial decision speeds around the young nation with the alacrity usually accompanying a declaration of war.[7]

Unlike the adult males, the Supreme Court did not free Amistad's orphans as such. As a term, "freedom" likely meant little to the six African children. Rather, it makes much more sense to conceive of child encounters with liberty and autonomy as nonlinear and interrupted and to focus especially on the spaces and fora that give rise to these experiences. There were several contexts wherein the autonomy and liberty of the children waxed and waned. The children's experiences were not uniform but involved a variety of contexts, including the Royal Navy's West African antislavery patrols, the liberation court in Sierra Leone, the federal courts in the United States, shipboard revolt and the Underground Railroad in North America, and the decision to participate in a return migration (the Sierra Leone missions operated by the Union Missionary Society, examined in Chapter 6). Over the course of several years Amistad's orphans first embodied and then eclipsed various gradations of autonomy, some of which more closely than others resembled freedom. And yet throughout most of their ordeal, largely because of their minority, they always remained legally, socially, and economically subordinate to others.

CHILD "RESCUE," APPRENTICESHIP, AND THE WEST AFRICA ANTI-SLAVERY SQUADRON

Were it not for the antislavery squadrons patrolling the Atlantic in the 1820s to 1840s, we would likely have little knowledge of Covey or the many thousands of children like him. From 1807–8, it became increasingly dangerous to export slaves from West Africa as the prohibition on new imports into the United States took hold. But in this context of increasing illegality, the slave trade swelled dramatically from 1815 and the end of the Napoleonic Wars. The profitability of slave trading rose too. The Royal Navy's antislavery patrols represented one side of what historian George Brooks characterizes as a complex symbiotic relationship between slave trading and legitimate commerce.[8] The navy ships captured slavers and brought them into Freetown. But many of the participants in the patrols had equally complex personal relationships with slavery: the ships were sold and their cargo "liberated," but slave traders were rarely imprisoned or sentenced, and former slaves were subjected to a mandatory apprenticeship, ranging from as few as five to as many as seventeen years. Child apprentices, moreover, experienced a wide spectrum of jeopardy.

Covey first appears in the historical record as a direct result of actions by the West Africa Squadron. In his district court deposition, Covey stated, "I was sailing for Havana when the British man-of-war captured us." He indicated that the captured ship returned to Freetown within four days with no slave deaths. The Trans-Atlantic Slave Trade Database lists twelve ships that meet some of the parameters described by Covey, but only one neatly fits, namely, the schooner *Segunda Socorro*. Records in the British National Archives include the captured ship's log, which indicates that José de Inza recognized the

Trinculo was in pursuit after only two days at sea. The *Trinculo* captured de Inza's vessel at 6°30′ N and 12°12′ W on July 9, 1833. The *Segunda Socorro* was bound for Havana, carried 307 slaves, flew the Spanish/Uruguayan flag. Covey's narrative is complemented by the ship's log, which recorded a journey from Galinhas to Freetown lasting four days, meaning two days out and two days under escort to Freetown. Data also indicate that whereas no slaves died during the brief journal, at least one boy, named Saso, aged eleven, died several months after disembarkation.[9]

The *Segunda Socorro* was the *Trinculo*'s first seizure after it arrived in the area from Mauritius via Fernando Po and Ascénsion in May 1833. The *Trinculo* was to become a very active antislaving vessel. Shortly after the condemnation of the *Segunda Socorro*, it assisted the *Despatch* in its capture of the slave schoo- ner *Rosa*, near Accra. In September en route from Bonny to St. Jago de Cuba, it seized the Spanish slave schooner *Caridade*, piloted by Antonio Fortunato, with 112 slaves on board. In December bound to Príncipe from Cape Lopez, the *Trinculo* captured the Portuguese slave schooner *Apia*, piloted by Chris- tovao Xavier Vellozo, with 54 slaves and the *Santiesimo Rosario a Bom Jezuz*, mastered by Francisco Silvestre. In 1835–36 alone it seized five ships originat- ing in Bonny, namely, the *Isabella Segunda*, alias *Cuatro*, with 374 slaves on board; the Spanish vessel *Feliz Vascongada*; the Spanish brig *Maria Manuela*; the Spanish schooner *Eliza*; and the Spanish brigantine *Diligencia*. The *Trin- culo* returned to Portsmouth in May 1836 with 2,300 ounces of gold dust and 309 elephant tusks. From the debut of commission in April 1832 it logged 82,900 miles in 914 days "under canvass." It never lost a man by accident, and only three deaths occurred onboard, all from fever. By some accounts the crew had seen "as much, in boats and otherwise, as any vessel in commission."[10]

The *Trinculo*'s operations in the 1830s unfolded during the more mature phase of antislavery patrols. Earlier, in the wake of the Napoleonic Wars, the antislavery squadron struggled with enforcing the antislavery treaties to which France, Portugal, and Spain had been subjected by the United Kingdom. The squadron in the 1820s rarely comprised more than six ships, and very few of the "old tubs" were faster than the slavers of the period. A short-lived collaboration with the U.S. Navy collapsed. As Brooks demonstrates, the patrols were ham- pered by a number of factors, including failure to agree on reciprocal rights of search, the requirement that slaves be found in situ aboard a ship for it to be held in violation of the treaties, and a large loophole allowing the transportation of "domestic slaves" from one Portuguese territory (Guiné) to another (Cabo Verde), actively utilized by slave traders who carried false documents.[11]

To incentivize seizure the British government paid a bounty to officers and servicemen in the squadrons for each slave disembarked alive in Freetown, what historian Padraic Scanlan has described as the "monetarization" of abolition. The bounty began in 1807 at £60 for a male, £30 for female, and £10 for a child. In 1824 Parliament lowered the bounty to £10 a head, and by 1830 it had dropped further still to £5 per recaptive. Historian Christopher Lloyd argued that because officers were paid more for full slavers than for empty ships, a perverse incentive meant officers might be tempted to wait until a ship was filled with "cargo." And whereas British and U.S. law viewed slave trading as "piracy," a capital crime, there was no incentive to prosecute such cases, for to do so the squadron officers would forfeit any bounty.[12]

By the time the *Trinculo* joined the squadron, however, funding and support for the antislavery patrols was rising again. Covey's legal liberation did not really take effect at the moment of capture, but only when he was physically removed from the ship in Freetown harbor. A romantic illustration from the late nineteenth century shows a group of recaptive slaves, including women and children, having their shackles removed on the beach by British colonial officers (figure 5.1). Whether Covey was shackled, and if so, under what conditions, is unclear. Records from the Sierra Leone Mixed Commission indicate that all slaves were disembarked alive from the *Segunda Socorro*. Recaptives disembarked in Sierra Leone were often identified by name. Records of the Sierra Leone Commission in the British National Archives list one boy, age nine, with

Fig. 5.1. Slaves liberated on a beach, c. 1840 (Emily Durrant, *The Good News in Africa, Scenes from Missionary History* [London: Seeley Jackson, 1883])

a height of four feet nine inches, named "Covie," branded "B" on his left arm, as slave number 27094, disembarked from the *Segunda Socorro*. This individual can also be found in the Trans-Atlantic Slave Trade Database. He is the only African boy with such a name in the database and quite possibly the future youth who was to be baptized "James" and anglicized as "Covey."[13]

Further support for this contention emerges as a result of a curious twist in recordkeeping concerning "Liberated Africans." The Registers for Liberated Africans were copied in multiple places; there are sets in Freetown and copies in the British National Archives, and it is not entirely clear which set is the original. Philip Misevich has observed that the Freetown-based records contain additional details about the freed slaves, most noticeably an indication of how some individuals were disposed of after liberation. This important information was kept infrequently and is not available for most liberated people. One page of one of the two Freetown-based registers identifies "Covie" with the number "42643" and repeats the details of height and branding (figure 5.2). But more important, these registers indicate that this person was at least initially placed with a group of other boys, all ages nine, ten, and thirteen, scheduled to go to the liberated African settlement of Bathurst in the Mountain District outside Freetown, on September 3, 1833, as part of a mandatory apprenticeship (figures 5.3 and 5.4). Like most so-called liberated recaptives, Covey was subject to a court-ordered apprenticeship, usually between seven and fourteen years in the mid-1830s. Correspondence from Robert Dougan, private secretary to the governor of Sierra Leone, to the head of the Christian Missionary Society

Fig. 5.2. Detail of Freetown Register of Liberated Africans, 1833,
showing listing for "Covie" (Sierra Leone National Archives)

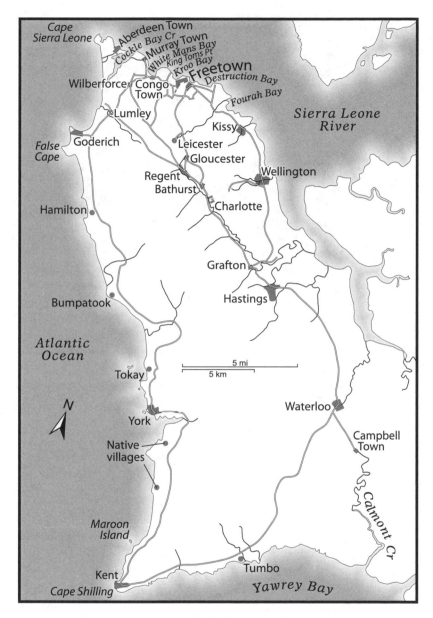

Fig. 5.3. Sierra Leone peninsula, c. 1835 (Map by Don Pirius)

Fig. 5.4 Village of Bathurst, lithograph, c. 1835

(CMS) mission in Freetown, specifically addressed the welfare of "a number of Cossoo boys lately seized by His Majesty's Sloop, 'Trinculo' and who having been for a very (limited time) short period in slavery, are in excelent [*sic*] health and . . . not at all tainted by the baneful and demoralizing influence" of "a long continuance in that state." And thus there is compelling grounds to believe that Covey was one of approximately "103 Cossas boys" resettled in Bathurst under the supervision of the Reverend and Mrs. John Weeks, and assisted by a young Samuel Ajayi Crowther, who relocated from Gloucester to Bathurst expressly for that purpose.[14]

Whether apprenticeship constituted liberation per se is a matter of perspective. Once the Africans from the *Segunda Socorro* came ashore their future was adjudicated by a court, which usually ordered their apprenticeship. But there are sparse records of this stage pertaining to the ship, aside from a report describing it as a "lawful and good prize" and its subsequent auction, or for Covey, aside from his "emancipation" on July 17, 1833. For Gibbs, the capture of Covey's ship by a "British armed vessel" was enough to educe that "Covey thus obtained his freedom." Gibbs continued, Covey "remained in this place five or six years, and was taught to read and write the English language, in the schools of the Church Missionary Society. . . . His Christian name, James, was given him by Rev. J. Weeks, a Church Missionary, at Sierra Leone." In New Haven, Covey himself declared, "I learned to speak the English language in Sierra Leone and have been taught to read and write"; in the district court he made a somewhat narrower claim: "I learned to speak English at Sierra Leone." Regardless of the exact circumstances, as a young, orphaned, "recaptured" child, Covey was the ideal vessel John Weeks sought.[15]

When Covey arrived in the CMS-run school in Bathurst, it was part of a wider two-pronged campaign focusing on the expansion of Christianity and the eradication of "traditional" practices. Historian Jehu Hanciles explains that "with hardly any exception," the CMS "regarded the practices and customs . . . of the African's pre-Christian past with undisguised suspicion and were convinced that these had to be uprooted." Christian recruits were acquired from two groups — modern forward-looking adults, including those taken from captured slave ships, and orphaned and "rescued" children (again, including the so-called recaptives). Indeed, since the early days of Sierra Leone's settlement colonial administrators had emphasized the value of children to the larger Christian enterprise. In 1798, Governor Zachary Macaulay had written to Scottish philanthropist John Campbell about the ideal age of children for education. Macaulay considered the age of twelve or thirteen to be a "tolerably good" age for conversion to "free men of Christ." And he believed that "education should be continued at least 5 or 6 years." Macaulay's activities paved the way for the Christian Institution. Earlier setbacks had forced the CMS to recalibrate its proselytization activities. Captured slave ships were identified as an important repository of vulnerable, kinless individuals. Formed in 1814, for the education of "*receptive* children," the institution evolved into a seminary. By 1827 the Christian Institution drew far and wide for suitable pupils, and it was in an experimental Mountain District feeder school oriented toward Fourah Bay that Covey—now known as James—found himself in 1833.[16]

The nature and content of Covey's education in the Bathurst CMS feeder school is examined in more detail in Chapter 6. But the interwoven relationship between education and apprenticeship in the context of recapture and liberation merits consideration here. Weeks arrived in 1824 and worked as "a mechanic and evangelist" before becoming the head teacher. Historian Christopher Fyfe described Weeks as a "former carpenter." Weeks's education was of a practical kind: he "taught his schoolboys to use a lathe, while his wife taught the girls to spin." He was only one of several catechist/teachers at the school during the period, and like all lay preachers, his rank was subordinate to clergy. The Freetown Christian Institution "suffered many setbacks and struggled" to achieve its "intended impact" according to Hanicles, which, from Weeks's own words appears to have been graduating boys who would "prove useful assistance in our Schools." Data from the CMS archives suggest that enrollment in the Christian Institution did not surpass twenty during the 1830s, and fewer than half a dozen of Covey's Bathurst peers were selected to join this elite group in Freetown. Yet in spite of its limited resources, it furnished numerous schoolmasters and clerks over many decades. Samuel Crowther, the future first African Anglican bishop, was among its most distinguished graduates. He taught Covey in Bathurst from September 1833 until February 1834. Yet in spite of success stories like Crowther, the CMS was unable to prevent students and apprentices leaving for "more lucrative posts" in the "thriving merchant class," at least in the late 1820s and early 1830s. It is a matter of speculation how Covey's schooling and apprenticeship altered his worldview.[17]

Covey's apprenticeship experience was, however, qualitatively different from that of the majority of recaptives settled around the colony because he was part of a special and experimental pact with education and training at the core. Covey was one of 103 boys whose education and apprenticeship was contracted by the colonial government to the CMS. It was thus considerably at odds with the experiences of many apprenticed children, including the semi-fictional "Dazee" narrated by Sherwood. More commonly, men, women, and children were apprenticed through a public system akin to auctioning. Individuals desirous of acquiring cheap, coercible labor had only to come to the public reception compound for liberated slaves, called the King's Yard, to select whomsoever pleased them and pay a nominal fee for the apprenticeship contract. Many former slaves viewed apprenticeship with derision, and Harrison Rankin recorded that the freed "blacks uniformly term" the apprentice "a slave." Few obtained anything like the education of Covey. The apprenticeship varied in length and occupation, and age and gender were factors in specific assignments. Adult male recaptives were conscripted to serve in the Freetown Royal African Corps garrison. Other males performed public works, such as constructing roads and government buildings, alongside prisoners "driven as galley-slaves." Adult women often ended up as servants, housekeepers, governesses, and mistresses. Rankin described how women forcibly taken as sexual slaves broke down under pressure. There were no mandatory follow-up visits on apprentices. And unemployed liberated slaves were easy candidates for subterfuge and re-enslavement, as Peter Leonard observed in 1830. He calculated that by that year the liberated population of Freetown should have been 33,000, and attributed the actual number of 17,000 to 18,000 settlers to "nothing else" but the "cupidity" of "infamous wretches."[18]

In many ways, "liberated" children fared the worst of all. Many of them were sold as apprentices and never seen again. Many thousands were funneled back into the Atlantic trade and liberated a second time, such as the children and adults aboard the *Rosa*, liberated in the Bahamas in 1832, or the fifty-one slaves, including two kidnapped from Regent's Town, on the Freetown peninsula, aboard a French schooner observed by Leonard. Major Henry J. Ricketts, who visited Sierra Leone in 1830, explained that many are "enticed from the colony" and "kidnapped by vagabonds." They were "resold as slaves" only a "few months" after they had been "recaptured in slave vessels." The "numerous creeks" around Freetown "afforded great facility for carrying" off children. Children in Freetown were "entrapped" during daylight, taken across the river, and "immediately sold." In Freetown, the going rate in 1831–35 was apparently £5 per child, but the same youth could fetch $150 to $200 dollars in Cuba.[19]

What Rankin identified as the "transference from master to master" speaks to the role of illicit child smuggling in sustaining the trade specifically and to the value of children in the illicit trade more broadly. It was well known that the "portion of each captured cargo which consists of children under fourteen years" was "distributed among the negro population" and "liable to a second exportation." Rankin spent nine months in Freetown during 1834–35, when Covey was in school in nearby Bathurst. He noted, "As long as any negro whatever may buy a boy from the King's Yard on payment of ten shillings, and hold possession of him without at any time being called upon to account for the child, or even to produce him, so long will many be induced to transfer their young wards . . . to the Mandingo merchant. The whites call the child so purchased . . . an apprentice . . . I cannot conceive a system better adapted to favor the slave-trade than that of apprenticeship at Sierra Leone."[20]

Generally speaking, a liberated adult would likely have some sense of his or her new legal status, and possibly some awareness of the protections envisioned by the apprenticeship contract. Even so, they remained at risk, and at least one of the liberated Amistad survivors, upon return to Sierra Leone, was likely enslaved and sold again. Children, however, had little capacity to exert any control over their future. As the naval officer James Edward Alexander, noted, "on the payment of ten shillings" white and colored inhabitants made servants of the children for seven years. "Liberated" children simply disappeared into Freetown and its environs, and others were transported into neighboring Bulom-speaking communities and sold farther north into Guiné, Bissau, Cacheu, and Cabo Verde.[21]

The kidnapping of "liberated" children is brought into stark relief by Rankin's observations. After only a short period in the colony, he observed a "trial by a jury of negroes," which featured many parties speaking different languages, mediated "with laudable impartiality" by an interpreter with extraordinary "polyglot proficiency." The case concerned the attempted "stealing" of a "free boy, a liberated slave or 'King's boy,'" and a further attempt to "carry him across the river to be sold as a slave to the Bulloms." The phrase "King's boy" refers to the fact that the boy had been subjected to an apprenticeship contract in the aforementioned King's Yard. A succession of witnesses testified, and the boy also addressed the court and "enumerated the many cruelties practiced upon him to secure his concealment, such as compelling him to lie at the bottom of the canoe, and covering him with sail-cloths loaded with stones." The indicted, one Mandingo by the name of Banna, was detained with the boy "in his possession." Several witnesses were unable to be understood because they spoke unknown languages, and Rankin painted a rather farcical portrait of the court. By the end of the trial, however, Banna realized he was facing the death penalty. His final urgent plea was rejected, and he was hanged for his offense.[22]

The fate almost befalling the anonymous "King's boy" in Rankin's narrative highlights the dependency of the wider colonial economy on "liberated" child labor, of which Covey and all apprentices were examples. An 1828 decision by the preceding governor, Neil Campbell, to close the government schools and give "out the children to whoever would take them, without indentures," had resulted in extreme examples of exploitation. Indeed, when Leonard visited

Freetown in 1832–33, there were twenty-eight persons in jail awaiting trial for "decoying the recently liberated Africans" and selling them into the slave trade. But by the time Covey was in the Bathurst CMS school, the rules for apprenticeship had been tightened significantly because of anxieties about the "second slavery" caused by apprentice exploitation. To be sure, being in a mountain community many hours walk from the main smuggling conduit of Freetown provided some additional protection.[23]

Exactly when Covey became an apprentice to the navy is unclear, but it may be that there were few other options in the late 1830s. He may have served in Freetown in the docks before being selected by Fitzgerald as one of twenty to join the *Buzzard*. Weeks explained that whereas when the boys "first arrived here, there was no difficulty for such boys as could read and write tolerably well, finding employment as shop-boys, clerks, etc., among the Merchants in Freetown," it was now "quite the reverse, and a difficulty is felt in obtaining such situations." He continued, "The cause is obvious; the large number of boys, who are leaving the Freetown School yearly and now the Village Schools also who are desirous of obtaining their living in a more easy manner than their parents have been accustomed to." From Covey's story and other evidence the extent of the Royal Navy's dependence on liberated African apprentices is abundantly clear.[24]

Although Covey was not re-enslaved by duplicity, after five or six years, his apprenticeship abruptly shifted in 1838 as he was put aboard the *Buzzard*. Over the next year, the *Buzzard* boarded and seized several ships, including the U.S.-flagged *Clara* and *Eagle*, and liberated hundreds of illegal slaves. He was thus returned to the center of the Atlantic drama from which he had been liberated barely half a decade earlier. And when Gibbs met Covey in New York, he had just survived a very tumultuous Atlantic crossing.

COMMISSIONS, COURTS, AND CHILD DETENTION

Commissions and courts featured significantly in the liberation experiences of Amistad's orphans. They operated as contradictory spaces effecting the expansion and contraction of child autonomy. A Mixed Commission "liberated" Covey in Freetown, but a court in New York sustained Lewis Tappan's claim that Covey was a material witness to the Amistad trial. A federal court in Connecticut dismissed a writ of habeas corpus seeking the release of the three girls, and eighteen months later a New Haven County court sustained a new writ and placed them under the guardianship of members of the Amistad Committee. Ka'le's experience in the courts was muddled by the fact that sometimes he was considered one of the children but at other times he was lumped together with the adult males. And Antonio's encounters with courts were particularly complicated because his allegiances to different parties in the suits changed over time.

Detention comprises a series of ancillary forms of child dependency. Courts enacted control over children and shifted them into various subordinate statuses, because as minors, children lacked the legal capacity to understand and achieve their freedom. Detention includes imprisonment, domestic service, guardianship, and being a ward of the state. Children had a limited capacity to contest these statuses. As a term, "detention" resonates with the universal experiences of children, whose liberty is constantly checked by adults, kin or otherwise. The federal courts in Connecticut recognized the existence of such a distinction when it separated the children from the adults (who were under investigation for possible crimes) and placed them at various points under the custody of different individuals. The liminal status of the children is underscored in records from the 1840 census, which noted the presence of child slaves as property in New Haven. Detention employed broadly includes social, cultural, and legal apparatuses residing at the interstices of slavery and freedom as experienced by children.

Covey's first court experience would have likely taken place in the Liberated African Yard, or King's Yard, where he, with the other children, would have been separated from the adults. Bouët-Willaumez's lithograph of Freetown offers a glimpse of the structure from the ocean, as Covey perhaps saw it for the first time (figure 5.5). Leonard provides one of the earliest accounts of the space. It consisted of a "square piece of ground of considerable size," with long buildings on two sides and a "high wall" enclosing the area. Slaves slept in the building, and there was a house to prepare "their unseemly food," a well, and several water tanks. In the center of the yard were a smithy and a two-level residence for the blacksmith and his family. Covey would have entered the facility, perhaps through the portico (figure 5.6), only after it was "ascertained beyond doubt" that the *Segunda Socorro* had been captured legally. Leonard noted that sometimes the slaves were "cooped up in their wretched and filthy" hulk until "the tedious paltry ceremonies of the law" were complete, unless there was an epidemic onboard. Colonial correspondence preserved in the Sierra Leone National Archives suggests that in the mid-1830s plans were afoot to expand the accommodation space because overcrowding was becoming such a problem. It is difficult to assess this today, as all that remains is the original gate, or portico, embedded in a newer hospital structure (figure 5.7). Sometimes as many as eight hundred to nine hundred were kept in the yard if several seized ships arrived at one time.[25]

Fig. 5.5. View of Freetown with Liberated African Yard (water's edge, left of flagpole), c. 1840 (Édouard de Bouët-Willaumez, *Description nautique des côtes de l'Afrique occidentale* [Paris: Robiquet, 1848]; © The British Library Board)

Fig. 5.6. Streetside view of Liberated African Yard, Freetown, c. 1870 (British National Archives, CO 1069/88 [19]; reproduced with permission from the Image Library, The National Archives, Kew, Surrey, U.K.; photographer possibly J. P. Decker: see Fyfe, *History*, 362)

Leonard's account of the 1831 liberation of the slaves aboard the *Primeira* indicates the bewildering nature of the liberation process. "The men and women, after they reached the yard, when the momentary gratification of setting foot on land once more had passed away, look sullen and dissatisfied. . . . It struck me that on landing they expected to be allowed to go wherever they pleased, and

Fig. 5.7. The gateway to the Old King's Yard (Liberated African Yard),
today in the Connaught Hospital, corner of Percival and Wallace Johnson Streets,
Freetown, 2012. Inscription on the slab above the arch reads: "Royal Hospital and
Asylum for Africans Rescued from Slavery by British Valour and Philanthropy,
Erected A.D. MDCCCXVII, His Excellency Lieut. Col. MacCarthy."

were consequently disappointed and angry when they found themselves still
under control." Sadly, Leonard omitted mention of the specific legal mechanism whereby liberated slaves actually learned of their "freedom." It is likely
British naval officers informed the Africans informally they were liberated at the
point of capture, but formally, they would have had to deliver news of emancipation by mass declarations via several polyglot interpreters, not unlike the experiences of emancipation throughout the Americas in the nineteenth century.
It must have been a puzzling and confusing ordeal for children like Covey, with
no knowledge of English. After the "adjudication," adults were accorded "a
portion of ground" in one of the outlying towns or villages, "marked out by the
government." Leonard estimated that the entire cost over six months, including
a two-pence per diem, for an adult liberated slave was £3, but a female received

only three months' support. By contrast, Covey and "as many of the children as possible above a certain age, on condemnation of the vessel, are apprenticed out . . . to persons of respectable appearance."[26]

Courts continued to feature in Covey's experience as he moved across the Atlantic. Although apprenticeship was a formal and legal arrangement, apprenticeship contracts were rarely subject to court review. There is no record of Covey's personal contract, however. Covey's apprenticeship differed from that of the majority of recaptives, because he was part of a mass arrangement between the Freetown administration and the CMS. After entering the CMS school in Bathurst, Covey began to acquire a practical and scholarly education. In October 1838, his apprenticeship contract was transferred to the Royal Navy, which is how he found himself in New York in September 1839. After Gibbs met him in late 1839, he was permitted temporarily to travel with Gibbs and Tappan to New Haven and on to Hartford. During this period, Covey remained unclear about his status. Before the district court he claimed, "I have been in this country six months; came in a British man-of-war; have been in this town (New Haven) four months with Mr. Bishop; he calls on me for no money, and [I] do not know who pays my board." Timothy Bishop, a banker and business partner of Baldwin and Townsend, was a member of the "Friends of the Africans," or "Amistad Committee," founded by Tappan and active in the United Church of New Haven. Covey met various abolitionists soon after his New Haven arrival. He resided with Bishop for four months until the January 1840 trial.[27]

As the court case dragged on, Covey's indispensability became more apparent. Seemingly unfamiliar with the terms of Covey's apprenticeship, the Amistad Committee doubted whether James would "be willing to remain unless compelled" and laid plans for a subpoena and even incarceration. By October 31, 1839, Covey consented to remain, provided that the committee secured the permission of Fitzgerald. Townsend wrote, "I have seen James and he consents to remain if Capt Fitzgerald will consent. Charles [the *Buzzard*'s cook] is very reluctant to leave him as the Capt gave him a charge not to come back without him. To quiet Charles I have promised him that he shall not be blamed and that the Capt's consent shall be obtained or James shall return on Saturday." It appears, however, that Fitzgerald was unwilling to relinquish him, probably because it would violate the terms of the apprenticeship.[28]

But another factor giving Fitzgerald pause was that he was under serious pressure to leave New York and sail for British territory. The capture of two American vessels had ruffled diplomatic feathers. The owners had filed suit in U.S. courts, and the owner of the *Eagle* sought to recover £1,200 for repairs. Royal Navy logs indicated that Fitzgerald was "having problems finding the money and has had to retain a lawyer to defend himself," and the British Embassy at Washington when "approached for advice" suggested that he contact the frigate *Andromache*, which had just arrived at New York. Thus Covey's autonomy was once again subject to court intervention. Precisely how he was granted leave from his apprenticeship is unclear, but it would appear that a combination of legal threats from both the Amistad Committee and U.S. merchants compelled Fitzgerald to effectively abandon Covey. The *Buzzard* left New York in early November with the *Clara* and *Eagle*, and James was "detained by a subpoena," with an understanding that he would be "sent to Sierra Leone . . . one of these days."[29]

Covey's abandonment would likely have involved some formal transference of guardianship to the Amistad Committee or to a New York–based individual, such as Tappan, but nothing has yet surfaced to substantiate his precise legal status. As the case unfolded Covey wondered about his involuntarily status. Covey's "presence at the court" was "indispensible [*sic*] to a fair hearing of the case," yet he expressed anxiety about his future. Tappan had "promise[d] him some compensation" and to "see that his wants are supplied," but Covey appears unaware of any arrangements. After the January 1840 trial, Covey studied with "the young men in [Yale] college," but again his status was unclear. The Amistad Committee made "no bargain with James as to wages," not "know[ing] what would be proper." Townsend was at a loss, knowing of no "employment to which I can put him in this time of stagnation" but aware that he was "needed again" for the April trial, as "Mr. Baldwin says that the testimony will all have to be gave over again." Detained by some legal act or threat, the obscurity of Covey's legal status mirrors the complexity of the very public court processes over the other five.[30]

As they did for Covey, courts featured prominently in determining the changing status, the degree of autonomy, and the grounds of liberty for Te'me, Kag'ne, Mar'gru, Ka'le, and Antonio. Over the course of several months the grounds for detaining the children shifted rapidly—from that of cargo to be returned to its erstwhile owners or alternatively to the libel claimants for salvage, via witnesses for a criminal prosecution, to prisoners, and finally to wards of the state. Similarly, six different courts were involved, namely the U.S. District Court for the District of Connecticut, the U.S. Circuit Court for the District of Connecticut, the U.S. Court of the Admiralty, the U.S. Supreme Court, the New Haven County Court, and the New Haven Probate Court.

Struggles over the three girls formed the core of these legal tussles, and colorful descriptions highlight the terrifying nature of their ordeal. The girls were subject to a habeas corpus writ seeking their release in September 1839. Attorneys Sedgwick and Staples moved the habeas corpus writ to release the girls because they were "imprisoned without any charge." Hungerford, the opposing counsel, replied that they were detained because they formed part of a pending libel action. The next day, September 19, the three girls were brought into the court "evidently in great fear" as "all of them" were "weeping" and "clasping with a determined clasp the hand of the jailor." The jailer "endeavored to pacify them, with the offer of some fruit; they refused it." After the writ was read, four grounds for their further detention were enumerated, namely, a warrant that they appear as witness to "murder and piracy"; the libel claim of salvage of Lieutenant Gedney; the libel of Montes, "claiming these girls as his slaves," valued at $1,300; and finally a libel from the ambassador of the queen of Spain demanding the "proper restoration of these persons as the property of Spanish subjects."[31]

The habeas corpus hearing resumed on September 20, 1839, and Sedgwick moved that the girls were not enslaved legally. Because they were taken illegally from Africa to Cuba, the "allegations" made by the marshal were "insufficient in law to warrant their detention in custody." Instead, Sedgwick stated they would "answer and reply to the Marshal's return, by their proper guardian appointed by the court." Representatives for the libels disputed this assertion, but Baldwin reframed the case, thus "the grounds on which this writ is brought are, that they are illegally held under the process of the Court of the United States, which has no jurisdiction over them; and that they are held in custody not as persons, but as property—as mere chattels, to be kept in custody till other parties, litigating questions in which they have no interest, can come to a conclusion of their case." Baldwin observed that by such a measure, the girls could be imprisoned for one year or even five years. He forcefully disputed the logic for detaining the girls: "Every presumption is, that all beings, who have the form of our nature, are free." But he tied himself in legal knots when he argued that for the U.S. District Court for the District of Connecticut to be the correct legal venue, the property claim must first be decided. His colleague, Staples, argued that the correct legal status was "foreign paupers," and that the "State of Connecticut is bound to take care of them" but they "not to be holden by the laws." And on this basis, Judge Thompson dismissed the habeas corpus writ.[32]

Precisely how and under what legal basis the children could be detained was confusing, even to the federal executive in Washington, D.C. The three girls and Antonio were initially considered "as witnesses to testify to the charge" of murder leveled against the adults. At one point a surety of one hundred dollars was offered for "Joanna, Frances Ann, Josephine, and Anthony," as "witnesses for the United States in said information and complaint," but after the murder charges were dismissed, they were again subject to a form of detention. At some point Ka'le was added to this group. The U.S. marshal for Connecticut,

Norris Wilcox, informed Judge Judson that in his "custody" he had "the within named persons answering to the following names, to wit: Antonio, Time, Kine, Mahgra, and Carrii" and "committed them in to the custody and keeping of the keeper of the jail in New Haven." The circuit court "refused to admit these children . . . to bail, after ample security was offered" and continued their imprisonment. But the five children, and the adults, were actually detained by a warrant from the district court and not the circuit court. The significance of this distinction was not lost on the executive. The U.S. district attorney, W. S. Holabird, wrote to Secretary of State John Forsyth in January 1840 to point out that President Martin Van Buren's preemptive executive order of January 7, 1840, to take the Africans to the *Grampus* for removal to Cuba, referred to the incorrect court, and if this was not corrected, "should the pretended friends of the negroes obtain a writ of habeas corpus, the marshal could not justify" their further detention under an incorrectly composed warrant.[33]

By 1840–41 concerns about the basis for holding the children had waned and given way to a focus on the adult males' claims to freedom. While the case wound its way through the court system, the children remained in the Westville home of Pendleton, the jailer. The girls and Antonio resided solely in the Pendletons' home, but because of Ka'le's rapid acquisition of English, he moved frequently between the home in Westville and the purpose-built New Haven jail where the adult men were imprisoned. We hear very little about the children's precise status during this period, with one important and curious exception: the census. In 1840, the census data collectors included numbers of slaves held by adults. This question was usually left unanswered in the free state of Connecticut, but records from Pendleton, in New Haven, show that he listed more than thirty slaves, including three girls and two boys. Precisely why Pendleton recorded the Africans under his control as his slaves is unclear. He was responsible for managing their welfare, but food and clothing and other aspects of care for the girls and Ka'le were largely in the hands of the Amistad Committee. Furthermore, no evidence has come to light to suggest Pendleton derived a stipend to support the children in his home, with the exception of Antonio for whom he received $2.50 per week for his maintenance from the federal government. But his decision to house the children, and, in particular, to confine the girls and Antonio to his family home throughout the duration of the trial, set the stage for a final battle in the courts.[34]

The Supreme Court decision resulted in the freedom of Ka'le, but the status of Antonio, Kag'ne, Mar'gru, and Te'me appeared unclear to some observers. The "glorious result" of freedom for the adult captives was not unequivocal. The Amistad Committee was certainly enthused. By April 1841, the committee had acquired a barn with a classroom in Farmington that was ready to accommodate them, and prepared a proprietary claim on the property and contents of the seized vessel and a writ of libel for unlawful arrest and false imprisonment, all with the objective of providing for the Africans' welfare. But in spite of the ensuing fanfare, the Supreme Court's ruling did not extend equally to the children. The adult Africans could indeed now choose to remain in the United States or return to Africa, and their freedom was decoupled from Judson's earlier order of deportation. And whereas the liberty of Ka'le was no longer in question in the view of members of the Amistad Committee, Antonio, who was "also . . . entitled to his freedom," and the three girls, were the focus of one last legal tussle.[35]

During their Westville sojourn, the girls, Ka'le, and Antonio had effectively been detained as house servants. Mrs. Pendleton purportedly refused to teach the girls to sew because they would have no use for clothes upon their return to Africa where they would go "naked." Over time they were treated increasingly badly. Ka'le wrote to Tappan on February 9, 1841, to complain that Pendleton "wants to make all black people work for him, and he tell lies. He says all black people no good; he whip them; he is wicked—very bad. . . . Pendleton, and his wife and his children I think all bad—do not love God." Ka'le wrote, "I do no like him at all" and suggested that it would be "better for Mendi people to go into Mr. Townend's house," where Covey resided. Baldwin and Tappan had received multiple complaints over many months about the deprivations of the jail, but the brutal treatment of the children in the Westville home came as somewhat of a surprise. Townsend claimed that Pendleton was "determined to secure the girls, and had laid an anchor to the windward to get them bound out to him by the selectmen of the town and others" who "will care little for them except to make money out of them." Tappan wrote to Baldwin in March 1841 that a witness had seen "Mrs. P[endleton] whip Antonio, severely, Sunday before last for not brushing her child's shoes." After the Supreme Court decision, the Pendletons refused to relinquish control of their quasi-legal wards. Indeed, Tappan claimed that Pendleton "promised one the girls to a relative of his" in New York City. The Amistad Committee was forced to pursue the freedom of the girls in court.[36]

Tappan filed a suit of habeas corpus in the New Haven County Court with the goal of legally liberating the three girls. There was also discussion between Tappan and Baldwin about an appeal to Judson and a writ to liberate Antonio. The objective of the Amistad Committee was to remove the four from the Pendletons and place the girls under Townsend's guardianship and Ka'le under Tappan's by filing suit before the New Haven Probate Court. In filings before Judge Nathaniel Clark of the New Haven court, "Tame" is described as "being about eleven years of age, "Margru," a "female African" was "of about the age of thirteen," "Kale" was described as "being about twelve years," and "Kenye" or "Kaiee" was described as "being about twelve years." Judge Clark ultimately awarded the guardianship of all three girls to Townsend and Ka'le to Tappan, with a bond of one hundred dollars each, but "without surety" as each of them was listed as having "no property."[37]

Importantly, James Covey, described as "an African and Countryman of" Kag'ne, reappeared in the historical record accompanying the guardianship of "Margru" and "Kenye." Covey, "an African, man of New Haven," was described as "appearing in Court as her [Kag'ne's] next friend and making choice of said guardian in [*sic*] her behalf." He was also described as Mar'gru's "nextfriend" [*sic*]. The use of "next friend" adds a fascinating dimension to the legal history of the Amistad captives. Traditionally, the phrase referred to a person who represented another under disability or otherwise incapacitated and thus incapable of maintaining a suit on her own and, importantly, someone without a legal guardian. In the nineteenth century, the type of "disability" requiring a "next friend" often arose from minority, mental incapacity, gender, race, or lack of access to counsel. Before 1860 even married women who owned property separately from their husbands had to obtain a "next friend" to represent them in court before suing to foreclose. Every application to a court on behalf of a minor or a person detained without access to an attorney, who did not have a legal guardian or someone authorized to act on their behalf with a power of attorney, was made through a next friend.[38]

The deployment of Covey as "next friend" raises some important questions about the path to liberty of two of the girls. It is the only instance where Covey is described as a "man" and the only instance where a majority status is inferred. Equally important is Covey's objective. Joseph Yannielli argues that Tappan brought Covey to court to swear that the two older children wanted to go with Townsend. He claims the girls were "reluctant to leave the familiar surroundings of their new home." Covey's presence was crucial because under Connecticut law, individuals over twelve years had the legal right to choose their guardian. By some measure, however, Pendleton had already assumed the status of guardian or bailer for the children, insofar as they were part of a collective who were detained by the marshal and jailed. Although no probate court had awarded him guardianship, the children had resided with him and his wife and children for almost eighteen months. At the same time, however, by not relinquishing them to rejoin the adults, Pendleton was positioning himself in violation of the Supreme Court mandate.[39]

What precisely occurred in the court remains unclear, but a closer analysis suggests the court reached a correct legal decision albeit by an illegal path. The children were subject to the Supreme Court decision that applied to the

"Amistad Africans," but as children and minors, they were never free or autonomous individuals. With this foremost in mind, Tappan and Townsend sought to become their legal guardians. Pendleton, however, insisted that the girls had the legal right to choose their own guardian. The court did not recognize Pendleton as guardian, so he retained counsel to contest the case, and his attorney argued that the girls were "young women" who were "old enough" to choose their own guardian. To short-circuit this argument, Covey was presented as an individual—a next friend—who could speak for the children, without having to be accorded the legal right to do so by a court. Judge Clark could have appointed a guardian *ad litem* to investigate the conflicting claims and make representations on behalf of the girls, but he did not. It would appear that introducing Covey into the court was a ruse that successfully disestablished any basis for the girls' autonomy or independent decision-making capacity.[40]

This final court case, lasting three days, was as tumultuous as the first habeas corpus hearing and full of drama and hysterics. Tappan described it as replete with "violence and perversion of facts" and "false charges." Pendleton accused Tappan and others of insulting and abusing his family, and conspiring with Covey to remove the girls. Tappan described him as a "wild beast." The case involved many witnesses, including Pendleton "and his whole family, male and female." On the second day Cinquez conversed with the girls "in Mendi" and explained to them that they were to go to Farmington. Kinna gave his testimony about Pendleton's behavior in English. The girls were also examined as witnesses, and Pendleton attempted to give the "impression that they had been exceedingly well taught, and love his family very much."

Pendleton's attorney was hampered in making his case by the fact that his client was cast in the role of slave trader. Cinque testified that Pendleton's objective was to sell the children to southern slave dealers. Furthermore, Tappan claimed he was concerned that the "morals" of the girls had been "injured" in Pendleton's house, in what was a crudely vague allegation of indecency. Yannielli, drawing on the eyewitness account of law student Aaron Olmstead, shows that all manner of argument and language was used to adjudicate the wishes and desires of the children, including sign language and "baby talk." The Amistad Committee introduced witnesses to attest to their infantile minds and incapacity to identify choice. Leonard Bacon, a clergyman, argued "that the girls knew no better what was for their own good than a dog." In Olmstead's view the girls "appeared to be quite as intelligent as ordinary girls of 10 or 12 and could speak English with a good deal of facility," but as Yannielli observes, "the Africans' juvenile status rendered them legally mute." After three days of testimony, the judge awarded custody to the abolitionists, and the children were "pulled and dragged from the side of Mrs. Pendleton, shrieking and crying."[41]

Yannielli's vivid reconstruction of the final day of the hearing draws on news reports and eyewitness accounts. As they exited the courthouse, Te'me, the youngest of the group, "ran out of the building and across the New Haven Green in a final bid for her freedom." Capturing the omnipresent racism of the epoch, one local witness described her as "like a hunted deer." An unnamed abolitionist finally seized and carried her back across the green as "a crowd of law students and other sons of Belial" surrounded them. Another observer, the cleric Bacon, wrote, "Like the slavers on the coast of Africa, a vessel (or carriage) stood ready, in which to stow them," willing or not, "as soon as kidnapped." Yannielli explains that the terrified and exhausted young women found themselves on the cusp of yet another relocation to yet another home not of their choosing.[42]

This remarkable scene underscores the trauma experienced by children in slavery and liberty. The girls were likely confused, distressed, and exhausted, and they may have felt betrayed by Covey. Whereas the objective of the county court proceedings was ostensibly to effect the liberation of the children in accordance with the Supreme Court's ruling, the method must surely have had resonance with Te'me's first experience of enslavement by kidnapping only a few years earlier.

SHIPBOARD REVOLT, THE UNDERGROUND RAILROAD, AND CHILD MIGRATION

Each of the children attained a degree of liberty through courts and tribunals, but all of Amistad's orphans also participated in various ways in unequivocal attempts at liberty that more closely resemble the classic stories of slave resistance. Physical resistance to enslavement is usually associated with adult slaves, but children participated in actions in pursuit of liberty, including the shipboard revolt in mid-1839, passage along the Underground Railroad, and intentional migration. These important contexts for child liberation and migration operate on several levels. Building on the observations about the discrete spaces of child mobility in Chapter 4, this final section examines sites of contestation involving mobility that further muddy the context of child liberty.

The revolt provides one important context for understanding the liberation experiences of five members of the imagined slave ship family. It constituted a physical, legal, and psychological event for all the Africans aboard the vessel, but for the girls and boys it must have been equal parts excitement and trauma. Physical liberation was one of the objectives of the adult males, but several accounts from the period indicate that the children were not imprisoned or enchained on the ship. The actual rebellion took place "on the fifth day out, when about seven leagues" from Havana. In court, when asked how they managed to escape from the chains with which they were imprisoned, Cinquez conveyed that "the chain which connected the iron collars about their necks, was fastened at the end by a padlock, and that this was first broken and afterwards the other irons. Their object, he said, in the affray was to make themselves free."[43]

From the perspective of the young girls, the revolt may have been a welcome surprise. One account inferred that the girls assisted the revolt insofar as they may have helped the adults locate the machetes and cane knives. A letter from Madden suggests that the "female negroes . . . true to their sex, indulged their curiosity in examining the contents" of the cargo, and "faithful also to the communicative character of the fair part of humanity" conveyed information about their discovery to the others. Another account suggests that Kag'ne sought physical protection from Cinquez during the tumult, and a newspaper identified her as his principal "companion." Whether the girls were afraid or excited would likely have depended on the rapidly evolving conditions on the boat. As food and water became scarcer, their emotional state would surely have become more precarious. But certainly, having only recently witnessed the brutal whipping of at least five of their kinsmen and then seeing salt rubbed into the gaping wounds, it is not difficult to imagine the girls experiencing a sense of relief and possibly even the view that justice had been served.[44]

By contrast, Antonio's physical and emotional state during the revolt was complicated by his service in the crew. Celestino, another of Ferrer's African slaves, was the first to be murdered. Cinquez likely clubbed him to death with a "billet of wood." Antonio immediately fled aloft and hid in the rigging. After coming down from his initial refuge in the mainstays, Antonio clearly faced imminent death, but Burnah averted his summary execution. Antonio was tied up on deck with the surviving slave traders and liberated only later when the ship entered U.S. waters.[45]

Although surely traumatic for the children, the physical liberation was equally a result of serendipity and happenstance, "for had they rose on their Captain and his crew two weeks before or been driven into Halifax or Bermuda, they would now have been free as the winds of Heaven." Their physical liberation, however, was short-lived. When officers from the USS *Washington* boarded the ship in August, "leaping on deck with their arms in their hands," the men "immediately drove the negroes below" and back into the slave hold. Newspaper reports suggest several of the Africans jumped overboard and attempted to swim to shore, but the children made no sudden moves of desperation. On land they were transferred to various detention facilities, where they resided for over eighteen months.[46]

Quasi-legal liberation was also effected by revolt. At the moment the vessel's stewardship changed hands, all the children were liberated from slavery. What liberation meant at this point, however, is unclear. The Africans would have to wait almost eighteen months for the Supreme Court to validate a liberty regained at sea. News reports from the period repeatedly referred to the adults as "pirates and murderers," although there was considerable disagreement as to efficacy of instigating a trial for such crimes. Other journalists referred to the Africans as criminals and affirmed that they were captured and arrested for crimes. Proslavery accounts were littered with pejorative descriptions of the liberated Africans as "fat and lazy," for "after the murders, they did little else but eat and steal." The leading New York newspapers, including the proslavery *New York Morning Herald* and the abolitionist *New York Journal of Commerce* and *New York Post* generally exempted the children from these dueling and contradictory caricatures.[47]

Psychologically, the act of liberation was also important because the children were liberated from their temporary slave names and the cultural impositions accompanying enslavement. One vignette illustrating the emotional and psychological impact of liberation comes from Tappan's observations, published in his *New York Journal of Commerce*. When visiting the Africans in New Haven, he noticed that the girls had "made the little shawls that were given them into turbans." By replacing the rags of slavery with attire resembling that of young girls and women in West Africa, Te'me, Mar'gru, and Kag'ne made a deliberate move to reconfigure their experience. Naming and renaming practices also illustrate this psychological transformation. Several Spanish girls' names appear in the record, including Juana, Francisca, Frances Ann, Josephina, and Josefa. Precisely which name applied to Ka'le is unclear because several males had the same or a similar name (Ka'le was a very common Mende name). There is no record that the girls or Ka'le ever answered to the Spanish names appearing in the slave bills of sale. Irrespective of Ka'le's erstwhile Spanish moniker, the revolt resulted in his and the girls' liberations from their slave names. Only Antonio retained his slave name as he transitioned into liberty.[48]

And the psychological liberation that unfolded for Amistad's orphans continued as the girls and Ka'le, and later Covey, moved to Farmington in May 1841. There the children were exposed to new ideas and values that transformed their worldview (Chapter 6). Shortly after their arrival in Farmington, one of their hosts, Charlotte Cowles, noted Kag'ne appeared "very contented," at least based on her "happy looks and cheerful words." The children developed personal friendships with other young people in the village. Indeed, she noted, she had never seen "anything like their affection and generosity." Cowles provided a fascinating description of gift-giving between Ka'le, Kag'ne, Te'me, and Kinna, wherein, she claimed, they seem "to find no pleasure in keeping, but in giving." Rather, they had "less of the spirit of *meum et tuum* about them than any people I ever heard of." This suggests that, at least perhaps on some level, some memories of the communitarian economies and practices of reciprocity they experienced as children endured their passage through slavery to liberty.[49]

To be sure, the children's psychological liberation was counterbalanced by religious indoctrination. In Farmington, they were the "principal topic" of conversation for many months and were quickly integrated into the prevailing religious ideology of the tight-knit community. They attended church, and Cowles remarked to her brother that "they looked very neat and orderly, and behaved as if they had been to church their entire lives." They absorbed the "words of life," although they may have understood very little. Their emotional transformation may also have been outwardly visible. Within weeks of their arrival, they appeared "so changed" in "their whole appearance, in complexion, manners." Cowles observed, that whereas they once "looked" rather "a dusky yellow, like some of our mullatoes," they are now "so black and some of them so handsome that I can hardly believe I saw them before." They engaged with abolitionists, temperance reformers, and preeminent African American orators, such as Henry Highland Garnett and James Pennington. And while it is difficult to imagine the psychological processes attendant to the child experience of liberation, the teacher John Pitkin Norton captured elements of it in his private diary. In November 1841, shortly before the Africans left for Sierra Leone, he observed how they appeared to be able to imagine a new world for themselves. Norton described Kag'ne as "one who lives and moves and thinks somewhat above the level of this our world to whose matter of fact common places so many are chained from the mere want of ability or inclination to rise higher."[50]

Like the revolt at sea, the Underground Railroad connecting New York and New England with Canada is an important site for the exploration of child liberty. Antonio and Covey both encountered the Underground Railroad. Antonio fled to Montreal, Canada, and Covey appears to have at least considered fleeing in 1841. The illicit migration network had yet to gain the importance it was to occupy in the wake of the Compromise of 1850. By the mid-1850s, the path to Montreal was "the most important terminal in Canada East" with connections in New York and Boston. Adult narratives, such as those of Shadrach Minkins and Lavinia Bell, loom large in stories of slave flight to Montreal. The participation of Amistad's orphans provides a unique children's perspective on the earlier workings of the Underground Railroad before it assumed its later prominence.[51]

Antonio appears to have been spirited away by the "Committee of Vigilance" just days before the Boston's Spanish consul, Señor Vega, directed Judson to send Antonio "to Havana, to his mistress." It is unclear who precisely conducted the passenger, but several fragments of information provide some context for interpretation. It is instructive to note that Dwight P. Janes, a New London grocer, abolitionist, and contributor to the Amistad Committee, relocated to Montreal prior to Antonio's departure to work on the railways. Also of interest is a letter from an otherwise obscure Alphonse Bigelow, from March 24, indicating that the "Committee" had "taken measures for the liberation from confinement of the boy Antonio." It may also be important that Covey was visited by a "Thomas Van" in June 1841 in Brooklyn, New York, and received some money by way of Tappan. Thomas Van is very likely a reference to Thomas Van Rensselaer, a leading black abolitionist in New York City. A former slave from New York's Mohawk Valley, Van Rensselaer ran away from his master in 1819 and later operated a New York City restaurant called the Temperance House. He was active in the New York Committee of Vigilance and in campaigns for equal educational and political rights for blacks, and he served on the executive committee of the American Anti-Slavery Society (1840–43).[52]

The committee to which Bigelow referred may have been either the Amistad Committee or the Committee of Vigilance. It is quite plausible that Van Rensselaer himself was responsible for aiding in the spiriting away of Antonio. In early March, Antonio's expressed desires were still unclear, but by March 24, he had made it clear to Tappan that he was being held "against his will." A letter from Townsend to Tappan on March 27 indicates that plans were afoot. He stated, "you would pay Antonio's expense to New York and look out for him if he would come" and suggested that another of the Amistad Committee, Simeon Jocelyn, escort him. From the scant details of his exit from New Haven at the end of March 1841, it is thus possible to discern the hand of Tappan in the planning, subterfuge, and intentional misdirection during the tense period in the wake of the Supreme Court decision.[53]

Indeed Tappan was the "the author of the mischief," as he left Townsend in New Haven, scrambling to explain to the U.S. marshal what had happened. Townsend wrote to Tappan, "I told the marshall that I had advised Antonio to clear out under the impression that I received from Mr. Baldwin that the only claim in Antonio [is] now from his owner in Havanna, and that the marshall was not liable." Tappan explained to Baldwin that after Antonio disappeared, Wilcox came to New York City looking for him and appealed to Tappan as a "conscientious and Christian man." To Baldwin Tappan explained, "When at New Haven, Antonio told me he did not wish to return to Havana, but desired to go to New York and get work. I advised him to leave and go where he pleased. And further, told him that if he would be on board the steamboat Saturday morning I would . . . befriend him to New York. . . . He did not come, and I made no other suggestion, directly or indirectly." Tappan and Antonio were waiting to hear from Judson about his status.[54]

Antonio seems to have disappeared from New Haven on March 30, 1841, aboard a steamboat, the *Bunker Hill*, for New York (figure 5.8). Tappan wrote that the "day before yesterday some one (I know not whom) left word at the store in my absence, that Antonio was on board the Bunker Hill. I started to go see him. Seeing a colored friend I mentioned the case to him—he promised to go on board next morning and bring Antonio to his house. He did so." The anonymous "colored friend" may have been Van Rensselaer, who was an active conductor, but it will likely remain a mystery. Tappan was obviously connected with the Underground Railroad, as he added that he "gave information to the Committee of Vigilance" because it was their "duty" to "befriend fugitive slaves."[55]

Tappan's tantalizing description of the events suggests he relished the intrigue. Tappan explained that the Committee of Vigilance "took charge of

Fig. 5.8. The steamboat *Bunker Hill*, which carried Antonio from New Haven to New York, lithograph by Jurgan Frederick Huge, 1838

Antonio and have conveyed him away. When he left the city and where he went I know not." He admitted that he did know "the place they expected to take him ultimately." But he was economical with the details he conveyed to the marshal. Tappan told him "all the essential facts" but specifically "declined altogether" putting him "upon the scent to find the lad." Importantly, he explained that to assure the marshal that he, Tappan, himself was not obliged to assist, the two visited several friends "to take their views as to my obligations in the case." He added, "I thought also that the delay—thus made—might be beneficial to Antonio."[56]

After New York, Antonio fled to Montreal because his precise legal status remained contested months after the Supreme Court decision. When the district court ruled for the liberty of the Africans, Judson carved out an exception for Antonio. Secretary Forsyth, himself a Georgia slaveholder, sought to appeal Judson's decision but stated "that part which concerns the slave Antonio is not to be disturbed." But the basis for Judson's exception and the confusion about Antonio's status was also partly of his own causing. During the initial court hearings Antonio appeared to have sided with the narratives of Ruiz and Montes in their proprietary claims against the Africans, but over several months he had provided conflicting and contradictory accounts. In records of the trial he is described as having attempted to defend his former owner, Ferrer, and possibly others on *La Amistad*, and then the Africans subsequently bound him.[57]

Antonio also made several statements suggesting that at one time he at least wished to return to Cuba. Whereas the Amistad Committee insisted that "Antonio is also entitled to his freedom" and to "discharge from duress," Baldwin was of the view that Antonio was not eligible for a writ of habeas corpus, because he had not claimed imprisonment. As late as March 12, 1841, he observed, "I understand he desires to return to Havana, and does not wish to [be] liberated. Unless *he desires* it no Court would issue a habeas corpus for his liberation. He is not in fact kept as a prisoner but goes about the streets without restraint." Baldwin urged the Amistad Committee to seek Antonio's "consent" before initiating any proceedings on his behalf.[58]

Indeed, it appears that neither the Amistad Committee nor the defense team of Sedgwick, Baldwin, and former president Adams had dwelled on Antonio's "exceptional" status until the Supreme Court's resolution of the case. Adams wrote, after Antonio's flight, "It is much more congenial to our own principles that he should be at liberty to return to Cuba, or to stay here at his own option, than that he should be delivered up to a Spanish consul as merchandise." Why Antonio "reconsidered his own inclination" is a fascinating question that confounded even the defenders of the Africans. It may be that the record of the court proceedings does not accurately represent his "desire"; the documentary record was surely affected by the fact that an unnamed Brazilian translated Antonio's testimony from Spanish. Moreover, he may have sided with the Spaniards initially because he knew the death penalty awaited convicted slave rebels returned to Cuba. As a slave himself, perhaps he feared guilt by association. At the time of seizure he personally knew none of the living, as he was "new in the schooner," and his only associates, the cook and the captain, his former master, were dead.[59]

But also it is likely that a year and half of captivity with the other Africans provided Antonio with an opportunity for a cultural realignment, in a manner described by Hawthorne with regard to the survivors of the *Emilia*. Over time he began to sympathize with their perspective, and with this sympathy the allure of liberty grew. Even still, Antonio fled north rather than return to Africa with the others. Tappan would have made it clear to Antonio that by remaining in the United States, as a former legal slave he would be exposed to the risk of kidnapping and sale to the South, as befell other young boys, such as Sidney O. Francis from Worcester, Massachusetts, who was kidnapped and sold in Virginia, and adults, most famously Solomon Northrup. Whatever the circumstances leading to his apparent change of heart, the complexity of his legal status was significant. Even after the Supreme Court's decision, the Spanish consul in Boston believed Antonio could be legally removed to Cuba. The "most exceptional" legal status of Antonio also continued to cause Adams great vexation long after the boy had disappeared from the United States.[60]

The Underground Railroad to Montreal was usually overland by foot, carriage, and train and across water by boat. After reaching New York City, Antonio would likely have traveled up the Hudson River via Troy and Albany, where he had a choice of the "Vermont Line" or the "Champlain Line." The Champlain Line was the principal passageway to Montreal in the 1840s and 1850s. It was the final stage in a series of links culminating on the border. At Rouses Point, fugitives boarded trains for Ogdensburg or Montreal, and steamboats took them up the St. Lawrence's River. A remarkable personal narrative suggests that after Albany Antonio took a variation of the Vermont Line via Enosburg, Vermont. After reading Roger Baldwin Jr.'s story about the Amistad captives in 1888, Elias Sherman wrote him a letter. He stated:

> When I was about seven years of age, my father, Elias H. Sherman, resided in Enosburg, Vermont. He was one of the original abolitionists and was a "conductor" and "station agent" of "the Underground Railroad." One morning I found that a handsome young negro had mysteriously arrived during the

preceding night; it was Antonio, the cook of the Amistad, who had escaped. He was jolly and good natured and helped about the cooking. . . . A night or two afterward, he disappeared as mysteriously as he had come—my father had taken him to Canada, about fifteen miles distant. Antonio told me all the circumstances connected with the capture of the Amistad, and his escape through the kindness of friends . . . and I recall all the circumstances, as though but yesterday.

Although some details are incorrect (Antonio was never cook, for example), the account suggests that different people conveyed Antonio in stages, with the final U.S. stage to the Quebec border undertaken by Elias Sherman, who is buried in Fairfield, Vermont, about twelve miles from St. Albans. Although few records attest to the specific locations of crossing into Quebec, Farnham, Philipsburg, Pigeon Hill, and Saint-Armand-Ouest all feature in oral traditions about the Underground Railroad. The stone marking the only confirmed burial site of former Africans slaves in Canada today still holds the unsavory epithet "Nigger Rock."[61]

Where in Montreal Antonio concealed himself is unclear, but in 1841 it was not so large a city that fugitive slaves went unnoticed (figure 5.9). Upon arrival, he lodged with John Dougall, a merchant, abolitionist, and the future publisher of the *Montreal Witness*. Dougall wrote to another of the Amistad Committee, Joshua Leavitt, in April 1841. "I am happy to inform you that the boy Antonio of the Amistad celebrity came in here safely two or three days ago and is consequently beyond the reach of all the slave holders in the world. He is for the present in my employment and I will endeavor to give him some education as he says the Spanish Consul forbad him to be educated with the other captives.

Fig. 5.9. View of Montreal, c. 1845 (Reproduced with kind permission of Special Collections, Benjamin F. Feinberg Library, State University of New York, Plattsburg)

Although a pleasant and good natured lad his ideas are very limited, for instance he asks if England be going to war with New Haven and which is strongest." Tappan read the letter in May aloud to great applause. Correspondence from 1841 attests to Dougall's consolidation of his ties with the fugitive black community. But Dougall was only one of several supporters of fugitive slaves. Dwight P. Janes, who had relocated permanently in 1840, may have assisted Antonio. Janes, who first encountered Antonio in August 1839 in New London, became a permanent fixture of the Underground Railroad in Canada, as well as the actual Montreal railways. He was a founding member of the Canadian Anti-Slavery Society and of the first black newspaper in Canada, the *Voice of the Fugitive*. Members of the free black community awarded him the nickname the "African Consul," indicating his home was the first port-of-call upon arrival.[62]

After his arrival, it is likely Antonio sought out black and African persons rather than English-speaking, Cuban, or Spanish-speaking individuals; the latter at least may have had ties with merchants in Havana, thus jeopardizing his camouflage. Before his arrival, Montreal's black community was experiencing a period of transition. In 1804 there were 142 slaves in the city, and approximately 350 in the province of Quebec, but the numbers had dropped precipitously by the 1830s. After the abolition of slavery in the British territories in 1834, the black population of Montreal also declined significantly. Indeed, whether the small number constituted a "community" in the sense that it could be identified, and exhibited group cohesion characteristics, is itself a matter of debate. It is possible that many free blacks moved westward to Ontario or east to the Maritime Provinces in pursuit of economic opportunities and to escape prejudice. Some have argued that the only mechanism of survival in Montreal during this period was assimilation and integration by marriage. The free black community in 1841 was small, and it would have been difficult for a young man to disappear. The community resided mainly in three *quartiers*, namely Sainte-Marie, Saint-Antoine, and Saint-Laurent. Precisely how many fugitive slaves from the United States lived in Montreal in the 1840s is unclear, but the 1844 census records 40 "coloured race" males in a city of about 64,500.[63]

Antonio's decision to flee north provides rare insight into child decision making, migratory choices, and resistance strategies. Covey may also have considered a journey northward to liberty, but for reasons possibly tied to finances and necessity he remained close to the Amistad survivors and Townsend. Whereas Antonio had to escape north to safeguard his very liberty, Covey may not have lived in quite the same fear of kidnapping, as his status as free was never in question and he was the specific responsibility of Tappan and Townsend. From January 1840 until March 1841 he lived under the protection of the Amistad

Committee, including Townsend and Tappan. When Tappan sought Covey's release from his apprenticeship to Fitzgerald to serve as interpreter to the Africans, he indicated to Fitzgerald that Covey would "be with them constantly." After the case concluded, Covey indicated the feeling was mutual. In a letter to Tappan he wrote: "Sir[,] I see [in] the papers in New Haven [a]bout my going home. If I am going or [n]o please to tell me[.] I wish you may send me a letter. Our African friends love to read and they want to know if I am going home[.] I dont [sic] want to go home and leave those Africans[.] If I am to go home I is [sic] sorry to go home to leave Kanna and Kila Cinque for Ma and all the others. If you please to let me know if I stay here till next January." Covey situated himself among New Haven's Christian community, and Townsend observed he "benefitted and improved by his residence" there.[64]

In an attempt to solidify his otherwise precarious position Covey foregrounded his faith. "I tell you I love Jesus the blessed Saviour and so I love all the Africans[.] I like to go home very well but I remember if I go home it is bad for them. Some of the ~~white~~ men say that the Africans never read[.] It is a sin for them to speak so they do not know how to pray to God who say the African[s] never learn." And he further cemented his claim to remain in New Haven by underscoring his pedagogical role. He explained: "But I will say the African[s] love me and you and all the good friends[.] They love to pray. They read. They love there [sic] teacher and if you sent Book [sic] for them they glad to see it[.]" This letter, and all subsequent ones, were signed "James B. Covey." From a single source, it would appear his adopted middle name was "Benjamin." We can only speculate about his reasons for adopting a middle name, but it may not be inconsequential that the young recaptive "Covie" was branded with the letter B.[65]

After the Supreme Court decision and the release of the children from imprisonment by the Pendletons, Kinna displaced Covey in the role as "principal interpreter." When the men and Ka'le moved to Farmington, Covey appears to have had little further contact with them. In March, Townsend wrote to Tappan asking for assistance, stating that Covey "would be glad for a place for a few months" before returning to Sierra Leone. Townsend had "not yet been able to secure any place for him" but hoped that Tappan would identify somewhere in New York or Farmington, as Covey was "now an expense." Covey was anxious to know his future and was "quite unwilling to remain" in the United States "any length of time." Townsend estimated he had dispersed about $403 to Covey as well as clothes, and he (Covey) did "not expect anything more except" perhaps "one or two articles of clothing." He suggested that "it would be well to give him, either as a matter of debt, for his faithfulness; or as a matter of bounty out

of kindness and goodwill and take a receipt in full for his time and services."
In April, Townsend sent Covey to New York with the hope of finding a job and
some means of maintaining himself. Around the same time, one of the now free
Africans in Farmington asked Tappan of Covey's whereabouts.[66]

Covey resided in Brooklyn, but his employment status and even the identity
of his landlord is unclear. But Covey never appears to have been content to
remain in the United States. Tappan clearly did not concur with the bargain
struck by Townsend, as Covey wrote to Townsend "applying for aid" in early
May. Although he did not "feel" Covey had "any claim" on "wages," as he was
"liberally dealt with," Townsend appeared bothered by Tappan's recalcitrance.
In his opinion, if Covey was "in want" and had "no means of earning his living"
while "kept in this country" although "desirous of returning to Sierra Leone,"
he indeed had a "claim on a kindness to some oversight of his wants." Covey
appears to have had little capacity for economy or trade and had been exploited.
Perhaps a bereavement in the family distracted Tappan from his obligations.[67]

When we next hear from Covey, he is destitute in New York. Three letters to
Tappan exist from this period. In early June 1841, Covey wrote in a short letter, "I
am sick bed I could not able to walk sir." He recalls how a third party gave him
one dollar, but he "want $5.50." His handwriting is shaky, but Covey seems to
indicate that he "began to work the 6 month" and asks Tappan to give a "young
man" some money to "bring to me." He claimed he was "so sick Sir I want pay
Doctor." A second undated longer letter, more carefully composed, expressed a
desire to return to Africa. He declared, "I am unhappy" and observed, "I know
that I love God in my Soul but I have father and mother sister and brother never
heard about God and Jesus Christ[.] will you please to sent me back to Si[e]rra
Leone before I die[?]" He refers three times to "Cinque" and expresses a desire
to return with the Africans. As with the previous letter, he refers to himself as
"your poor boy no father no mother." But the letter differs from the earlier one
in that it reminds his erstwhile employer that "I think on you answer my letter if
you please[.] You see I teach Cinque them and I pray for them[.] You dont pay
me for it[.] But God will pay pay [*sic*] me if you let me go home you ought to
give me $100 or $20[0?]."[68]

After a final epistle from Covey, and the intervention of the Amistad survivors, Tappan appears to have given fuller consideration to Covey's desire to voluntarily re-migrate to Sierra Leone. Covey complained that he was "not well"
and "now I am sick." He received money in response to his earlier letter but not
enough to "look doctor." This final letter provides the context for the relationship with Thomas Van Renssaeler, which suggests that Tappan may have considered relocating Covey outside the United States. Covey's letter continued

on the subject of money. "I have none sir I believe the money what they give to give for the African[s] I belie[v]e some is my too." This letter deployed a curious form of reportage. "Becaus[e] some people ask for money[,] money Mr. Tappan give to you none[.] Did he pay you[?] I say not yet and Mr. Tappan if you dont give me no money sent me home. I am willing to go home." In this letter he criticizes Tappan for collecting funds for the Amistad Committee but giving little to Covey himself. He observed that the other translators, Pratt and Ferry, were remunerated, but that he, Covey, had received nothing and was now abandoned. His letter concluded with a striking biblical invocation from the book of Jeremiah.[69]

These epistolary appeals did not go unheeded. Although no more letters from Covey in this period have come to light, others lobbied on his behalf. In August, a "Committee for the Mendians" convened in Farmington, and Grabeau, Kinna, and Banna petitioned to include Covey in a fundraising trip to Boston and on their possible return voyage. By then Kinna had established himself "as the head of affairs next to Cinque." One of the local residents, John Pitkin Norton, agreed that Covey would "undoubtedly render important assistance" and encouraged Tappan to bring him back into the group. In a letter to "James Benjamin Covey," "Foole Woola" indicated he was "very much glad to have" Covey accompanying them to Mende. Foole stated that he knew that Covey "want[ed] go to mende to go see you[r] father and you[r] mother and your brother and your sister and all your people," for "we all want to go see our fathers and our mothers and our brother and our sister."[70]

If the Amistad survivors' intervention was not the deciding factor, it certainly cemented a plan already afoot. A second letter, from "Carly," further highlighted a form of shipmate bond with *La Amistad*'s survivors, and particularly the children. Ka'le describes how he loved James "very much" and that he "wish[ed] I shall rather have you go with us to Menda." Perhaps because some of the abolitionists were unsure of Covey's conversion to Christianity, the final decision was made only three days before embarkation. Covey was able to join four other Amistad's orphans in their continued quest for liberty as they remigrated to Sierra Leone.[71]

CONCLUSION

The mythology of blanket freedom, enshrined by the landmark ruling of the Supreme Court, is a powerful narrative and one that erases the complexity of Amistad's orphans' encounters with liberation and autonomy. The Supreme

Court did not free the six children, and in any case, the concept of freedom likely made little sense to them. Amistad's orphans force us to rethink the meaning of freedom that informed the arguments before the Supreme Court and writing about the Amistad case ever since. The experience of Amistad's orphans suggests that many former slave children were rarely, if ever, free; instead they remained bound, checked, controlled, monitored, and dependent throughout their minority. To what extent Amistad's orphans' dynamic experiences may serve as a template for understanding the broader contours of the nineteenth-century child experience is beyond the scope of this book. Nevertheless, their experiences indicate that the processes and contexts attendant to the acquisition of autonomy and liberty merit further scrutiny. Whereas adult slaves, when granted, awarded, or winning freedom, had a variety of means at their disposal to operationalize the experience of freedom, children were constrained by a variety of social, cultural, legal, and spatial contexts.

The life of Covey reveals the role of the antislavery squadron in the liberation of child slaves from illicit slavers operating in the Atlantic in the 1830s. But whereas adults liberated from the *Segunda Socorro* may have been settled in a variety of new townships on the periphery of Freetown, children were apprenticed to all and sundry. The experience of apprenticeship often resulted in further exploitation. Apprentices were bought and sold like chattel, and many found themselves a second time on slave ships bound for the Americas. Covey had an unusual Atlantic itinerary and was fortunate to have been selected to join a mission school as part of a large group of boys. But his education was cut short when he, too, was pressed into service aboard the squadron that had rescued him only five years earlier. And when Covey found himself in New York, his liberty was further subordinated to Tappan and the Amistad Committee and court-ordered subpoena. Only in 1841–42, when he threw his lot in with the Amistad survivors and returned to Sierra Leone, was he able to shape his future and expand his autonomy.

By contrast, Antonio's status from the outset of the revolt in 1839 was the basis for his future problems. When he arrived in the United States he was accorded the status of slave, and he appears to have done little to challenge this. He seems to have considered aligning himself with the Cuban-Spanish slave owners as the best safeguard of his future. But as the case wore on, and the realities of the Supreme Court decision filtered through the community of Africans, he revisited his allegiances. After the final word from Washington, D.C., there was still disagreement among the litigants as to the status of Antonio and the obligations of the United States to return him to Cuba. Antonio took matters into his own hands in March 1841 and fled to Canada via the Underground Railroad, with the assistance of the Amistad Committee and the New York Committee on Vigilance.

The remaining four children—Ka'le, Te'me, Kag'ne, and Mar'gru—had equally noncontiguous and interrupted encounters with liberty and autonomy. Whereas the revolt aboard *La Amistad* effectively liberated them, the freedom won was short-lived. In the United States they immediately became a central object of contestation between the litigating parties. The children were fought over because they were not accomplices to crimes and could conceivably be witnesses to events. Although they were detained, they did not languish in prison with the adults. Instead, the New Haven jailer welcomed them into his family home, only to impress them into domestic service. And even after the Supreme Court granted freedom to the Amistad Africans, several months of additional legal tussles and questionable legal arguments were necessary before they were liberated from Pendleton and his family. The liberation, won on their behalf by the Amistad Committee, was a rather Pyrrhic victory. The ghastly scene on the New Haven Green, whereby Te'me was chased, seized, and carried off to Townsend's home, may well have seemed to the girls just another episode of enslavement, against which resistance was futile.

The path to liberty for Amistad's orphans was irregular and nonlinear. Incremental moments of liberty were short-lived and frequently followed by the recurtailment of hard-won autonomy. Antonio's flight north was an aberration. In general, liberty and autonomy for children involved two steps forward and one step back. The last step, however, was the return voyage to Sierra Leone and the quest for families and communities.

6

THE RETURN OF AMISTAD'S ORPHANS

If anything substantive emerged from the first difficult, stilted conversations with Cinquez and the other survivors of *La Amistad*, it was that their seizure of the ship was motivated above all else by a desire to return to Africa and to reestablish contact with their families. After the ship was captured off Long Island and the survivors interviewed, it became clear that the Africans had been attempting to return to Africa. Grabeau, one of the adults who with Cinquez had assumed a degree of leadership, indicated that the Africans surrendered thinking they would be aided in this goal. He stated, "The white men ran after their arms. The black men sat down and gave up their arms. They wanted Capt. Green to take them to Sierra Leone—not not [*sic*] that day—wanted more water. Did not mean to go to sea that day. White man told them ship of war. Wanted to go to sea to Sierra Leone." In court in January 1840 Cinquez, via Covey, stated, "We were going to Sierra Leone. Told Capt. Green we wanted to go to Sierra Leone." A "great anxiety to regain their liberty and return to their native land" was indeed at the forefront of the minds of the adult males during repeated interviews, from August 1839 until the end of the court case. Their return voyage was disrupted by their seizure by the USS *Washington*.[1]

Fueling this narrative of disrupted return was an equally compelling narrative of abduction from family and homeland, "torn from home, kindred, and country, by slavery." Cinquez explained that he was taken from his wife and children. Accounts printed in newspapers, such as Hartford's *Charter Oak*, echoed his and others' stories of being "torn from their homes, and parents, and wives, and children, and country, and doomed to hopeless bondage in a land of strangers." In Gibbs's notes about the Africans, many are described as members of families, as husbands, as fathers, and even grandfathers. Membership in a family and the context of kith and kin were interpreted by the Supreme

Court, and by the defenders of the Africans generally, as fundamental indices of identity. Instead of dispossessed, kinless chattels, the Amistad Africans were key members of networks, families, and lineages; many had established roles in existing social structures. Their status was thus irreconcilable with antebellum slavery ideology denying the existence of autonomous slave family life. Reunification with their families became a legal and humanitarian project anchored by the assumption that their families still existed, that they could be relocated, and that the survivors were ready for return and resettlement.[2]

This final chapter examines the disjuncture between ideas of community and family informing the adults' return migration and the lived experience of the return of Amistad's orphans. The children's return to West Africa was not a seamless process of rediscovery and reconnection but yet another cycle of upheaval and disruption. Their experiences have been obscured by the myth of family reunification. Although likely similarly desirous of a reunification with their families as the adult males, the five returning children faced many and greater obstacles—and much narrower options for resettlement and reintegration— upon return. This final ordeal was a direct product of countervailing forces, specifically the expectations created by the Amistad Committee and the absence of appropriate social and cultural preparation for the children. As we have seen in the previous chapter, child slaves experienced the stages of liberation quite differently from adults. Most important, they were never legally freed but rather remained in check as wards, minors, apprentices, and domestic servants. Moreover, the traumas and the stresses encumbered by the return journey to Sierra Leone were compounded by several additional factors, including their education and training and their forgoing of traditional initiation ceremonies whereby their social role in their respective communities would have been established.

Disassembling the myth of family reunification provides the context for examining how Gibbs and the Amistad Committee constructed narratives of family that bore little relation to reality on the ground in the children's former Galinhas homeland or their new residences in Freetown, on the peninsula at York, and later in Kaw-Mendi. Whereas the adult males had longer memories of their respective family contexts, enabling them to resist the imposition of a Western nuclear family narrative, the children had less capacity to challenge a fabrication imposed by the Amistad Committee. Those who advocated for the Africans' return unwittingly thrust the children into an incoherent imagined domestic context. Furthermore, the training and education afforded the children, at the hands of missionaries, clergy, community volunteers, and university affiliates, narrowed their options upon return. The children's limited formal training and education was irreconcilable with the sociocultural *rites de pas-*

sage experienced by all children raised in the region. When what was gained formally through Western education is weighed against what was lost as a consequence of enslavement and transportation, the incommensurability of the children's return experience is revealed. Compared with adults, former child slaves faced much greater obstacles upon return. And they were bereft of the sociocultural knowledge required for reintegration into a home or family they never knew as adults. Examples of the cultural clashes erupting in the mission stations and in neighboring African villages and communities underscore how their uninitiated status meant Ka'le, Covey, Mar'gru, Te'me, and Kag'ne were likely, in the eyes of many, permanently children.[3]

THE MYTH OF FAMILY REUNIFICATION

A tender and romantic narrative of family relationships and community connectedness furnished the advocates of the Amistad Africans with a powerful rhetorical device, namely, the mechanism to couch the quest for liberty within the framework of a desire to return home with the specific goal of reconnecting with family members. The objective of family reunification was a laudable goal with a multivalent purpose. On one hand, it nurtured the humanitarian impulses of liberal abolitionists and missionaries eager to extend their influence into West Africa, values that were to give rise to the Union Missionary Society in 1841, the American Missionary Association in 1845, and other entities sharing a common purpose. The first issue of the *Union Missionary Herald* announced its plan to establish a "missionary station in Mendi" because "Cinquez and his companions" were "anxious to return to their native country" and "desirous of having a station established there." Indeed, Cinquez and four others were founding members of the Union Missionary Society led by Reverend James W. C. Pennington. On the other hand, it appealed to the colonization constituency, a puzzling mixed bag of missionaries and pro- and antislavery forces, united in the racist aim of a nation freed of the black presence.[4]

As a rhetorical device, family reunification provided the Supreme Court with intellectual coverage from pro- and antislavery partisans, insofar as the court affirmed the legitimacy and legality of slavery within the United States while simultaneously asserting the fundamental immorality of human transportation from Africa. The final judgment of the Supreme Court drew forcefully on a humanitarian sentiment emerging from the idea of abduction from one's homeland. Justice Story wrote "that these victims of fraud and piracy—husbands torn from their wives and families—children from their parents and kindred—neither intended to abandon the land of their nativity, nor had lost all hope of recovering it, sufficiently appears from the facts on this record." After the court's ruling, additional "facts" suggesting the "feasibility" of "reaching their kindred and homes" formed the basis for a new public appeal by the Amistad Committee in the summer and fall of 1841. Newspapers declared that the Amistad survivors "have now a fair prospect of soon being restored to their families and friends in the interior of Africa, from whom and from which they were torn by the merciless slave trade." And a widely circulated letter from by Ka'le and others announced, "We are about to go home to Africa. We go to Sierra Leone first, and then we reach Mendi very quick. When we get to Mendi we will tell the people of your great kindness." Furthermore, once the Africans returned, accounts of their experience in "their native shores" regularly interwove the purposes of "the advancement of liberty & pure christianity" with the desire of locating "relatives."[5]

Evidence from the adults suggests, however, that they were initially more equivocal about returning to West Africa after learning of the Supreme Court victory. Although Tappan and others may have assumed that their desire to return had sustained them during their eighteen-month imprisonment, after Townsend conveyed the news to the adults, he was less sure. He wrote to inquire "whether they wish[ed] to remain in America or return to Africa," to which "they replied ask Cinquez. Cinquez says, 'I think,' 'can't tell now, I think,' 'we talk together and think, then I tell.' So that they will hold a council among themselves and decide." Townsend expressed the view that it was "very probable that many of them would prefer to remain in America." Despite what they had endured, "they say 'America country, good country—America people good people, set us free.'" Furthermore, on several occasions, the three girls indicated that they were still "undecided about returning."[6]

While there is no disputing the success of the rhetoric of family and homeland in establishing the moral legitimacy of the Africans' shipboard revolt, it had other unintended consequences. The rhetoric of family and homeland gave rise to the myth of successful family reunification. For several reasons contemporary narratives of the Amistad story uncritically assert that the survivors rediscovered their homes and families. And whereas this powerful fifth myth, like the previous four examined, emerged from the court process, it continues to gain traction in the present, to the effect that the Africans returned home and were reunited with their families in freedom. Making sense of the experiences of the five of Amistad's orphans who returned to Sierra Leone necessitates an investigation of the persistence of myths of family and homeland that continue to obfuscate the divergent experiences of adults and children in the Atlantic world.[7]

One possible origin for this strand of thought is the intellectual underbelly of contemporary Afrocentrism. With the rise of Afrocentric thought from the 1970s onward, myths of Atlantic return have also gained popularity in particular social and academic circles. Whereas Afrocentrism—as articulated by cultural theorists Molefi Kete Asante, Ron Maulana Karenga, and others—does not essentialize a return to continental Africa per se, it does romanticize the capacity of individuals to excavate the African past and assert connections across the Atlantic. Various strands of what historian Clarence Walker has described as a "therapeutic mythology" encourage black Americans to discard fraught recent history, with its inexorable white authority, and to embrace an empowering vision of African (often Egyptian) heritage and ancestry. Although for historian Steven Howe, Afrocentrism consists of "a mass of invented traditions" informed by "racial pseudoscience," what it lacks in tangibility, it makes up for in emotional and psychological approbation. New holidays and conspicuous consumption of arts and crafts of African origin go only so far to nurture deepening desires to understand origins of self. Framed thus, Afrocentrism has a powerful cultural appeal, albeit to a very narrow constituency.[8]

Perhaps the vibrancy of the family reunification myth has less to do with the scholarship of Afrocentrism and more with the absence of accounts about what actually happened to the African returnees. The missionary endeavor undergirding the return received little scholarly attention until recently. Other parallel tales—real and romantic—have filled this void. The enduring appeal of Alex Haley's *Roots*, the popularity of Edward Ball's *Slaves in the Family*, the emergence of family reunion movements in the 1970s and 1980s, and even press coverage of Sierra Leonean iterations of the rediscovery of Atlantic connectedness uncovered by the historical anthropologist Joseph Opala show that the constituency receptive to variations on this African-Atlantic romance is large. The emergence of a large mobile middle class of African descent in North America—a group increasingly motivated to travel and retrace ancestral paths of forced migration—provides a new vitality to this mythology. In contrast with populist Afrocentric traditions, such as Kwanzaa, myths of return and familial reunification operate as unusually empirical and positivist complements to an otherwise esteem- and self-centered historical consciousness. The mythology drawing together homeland return and family reunification is further strengthened by a Pan-African nostalgia of an imagined sameness and a teleological historiography celebrating African resistance and survival that extends from the colonial period backward into the era of the slave trade. In this light, then, the attraction today of an uncomplicated narrative of return and reunification is understandable. The homecoming of the Amistad Africans to Sierra Leone—

made possible by their own successful physical and legal struggle—accompanied by the possibility that some may have rediscovered their communities and families, operates as a powerful and tangible story fulfilling the imaginary opportunities born of Haley and others.[9]

Family reunification was not purely romance, however. While the sparse evidence about the children's sentiments is ambiguous, it should not be overlooked that several of the Africans did indeed *believe* that they could find their families. By the summer of 1841, several were firmly set on returning. Cinquez said to one of the Farmington volunteer schoolteachers that he wanted to "go and find his wife." And by September one of the reasons why he likely considered reunification possible was revealed. In an interview he explained that his brother had been enslaved and shipped away, but his ship was captured and he had returned to their village after about one year in Freetown. He had brought their mother a ring as a memento of his ordeal! Cinquez believed, and indeed knew, that family reunification was possible. Family reunification also extended to the deceased. Echoing Mende spirituality, which threatens evil if a man does not receive a proper funeral in his natal village, Kinna explained that he wanted to "dig up graves" of the eight Africans who had died and take them back to Mende territory for reburial.[10]

Evidence from interviews indicates that the Africans believed, for reasons unclear, that their American hosts were obstructing their return. One of their Farmington hosts, Charlotte Cowles explained that they have "sad, sad days, when it is difficult for them to think of anything but Mendi." Depression set in. In August, Foone (Foule) drowned himself in a river. Ceci threatened to "cut his throat" and told Banna "if he go home," he should "take care of his child." Their volunteer teacher, Austin Williams, wrote to Tappan urging some resolution of their ordeal: "They entertain the belief that they shall never see their fathers and mothers, brothers, and sisters or their dear children and that they will all die in America. They believe that when they die they will go immediately to mendi and some of them think the sooner the better." Perhaps jolted into action after one such conversation, another volunteer, John Booth, declared, "I find more and more proof that it is quite practicable to get these Mendians home." By October plans had been laid for a return voyage. Their "anxiety" dissipated, and letters and interviews attest to the excitement among the African adults about their return to "their fathers and their mothers—their brothers and sisters—their wives and their children—their homes—their native palm trees."[11]

Notwithstanding the pervasiveness of the myth of family reunification, the reality on the ground was somewhat different. Tappan and others firmly believed all the Africans had "parents or wives, or brothers and sisters" with whom they would be reunited, and that as they had been "hopefully converted," reunification would aid the spread of Christianity. Williams envisioned the adult males undergoing "a course of education" and qualifying "as missionaries and teachers" and then going "to benighted Africa" to spread "civilization and christianity into that long neglected and darkened land." But when they returned to the "father-land by way of Sierra Leone," the adults "scattered" in different directions after a short time in Freetown, "some in one place, some in another." Approximately half the group chose to collaborate initially with the missionary endeavor bankrolled by the Union Missionary Society, Tappan, and many other patrons of lesser and greater means, but there was disagreement about the location of the proposed station, possibly partly along fractured ethnic loyalties. The remainder drifted in various directions, sometimes in search of family members and at other times returning temporarily to the religious endeavor embodied in the missionary compounds. Some purportedly "rushed into" their former "licentious habits," perhaps slave trading, paganism, and polygyny.[12]

Although desirous for family reunification, the Africans and their supporters may have also understood the obstacles they faced in locating immediate kin. Whereas Cinquez and Kinna before their enslavement personally knew individuals who had been liberated and subsequently returned home, Leonard, writing in 1833, noted that among the recaptives taken from territories immediately beyond the colony of Sierra Leone only a "very trifling proportion" got "back to their own country," let alone located actual family. The missionary Leighton Wilson wrote to Townsend and Griswold from Cape Palmas in December 1840 to warn the Amistad Committee that because of "perpetual changes" their land may have "been supplanted by a different and hostile tribe" and thus to "locate themselves at their former homes" would be "extremely doubtful." But evidence supports the view that several individuals successfully reconnected with isolated family members. To accomplish this, they may either have located their villages of origin or natal communities, or learned of the possible survival or demise of their families from survivors in passing in the multiethnic melting pot of Freetown, and particularly the satellite village of Gloucester, where many liberated Mende resettled. Quests for family members contributed to the retraction of the missionaries' plan. When the number of adult males working on the mission farm had dwindled to ten, Raymond wrote that "hardly a day passes but word comes to me that some of 'my people' are in such a place, and such a place."[13]

For Amistad's orphans, however, stories about a homeland remembered and the hopeful imagination of family reunification were almost chimeras. The return to Sierra Leone for five of Amistad's orphans did not emulate the romantic imagination of Opala and others. The circumstances of return and resettlement for the children were narrower as a result of countervailing forces and expectations. And thus child notions of family, community, and homeland are similarly more complicated. Covey echoed the adult males' strong desires to return to Africa, with the hope of recovering vestiges of family and community, but the evidence for the others is equivocal. An observer in May 1841 wrote that Mar'gru was "very anxious to return to her affectionate parent." But Raymond wrote that the girls, especially Mar'gru and Te'me, "left America entirely against their will." Irrespective of these tensions, the nature of the course pursued upon arrival was deeply shaped by the adult male experience in the United States.[14]

Before departure from the United States, Tappan, Baldwin, and their associates had considerable anxieties about what might befall the children on their return. Baldwin expressed the view that without the necessary preparations, the Amistad Africans were in "great danger of becoming vagabonds." In addition to the basic schooling undertaken by all with varying degrees of success, and cultivation of Western domestic skills on the part of the three girls, considerable care was taken to document the familial context of the Amistad Africans. These two forces—education and the "civilizing" Christian ideology of the nuclear family—formed the core components of the missionary impulse informing the sponsors of the return voyage.[15]

But the five children were ill-prepared for the struggles over their roles, responsibilities, and even bodies that would mark their first years with the missionary community upon return. Instead of a warm reunion with the homeland and families from which they were brutally stripped only a few years earlier, they were thrust into cultural contestation for which they were woefully unprepared. Because they left Africa as children, they had missed key moments and events marking the passage to adulthood and establishing social identities. The boys had missed fundamental ceremonies whereby they would have entered manhood and only after which they could then proceed to marriage and familial and village responsibilities. They returned to Sierra Leone uninitiated and thus lacked much of the requisite ethnic, religious, and cultural mores, values, and knowledge. Ka'le and Covey left West Africa as young children, but they returned as awkward old children. Their respective village age sets and *poro* societies—the boys of their respective communities with whom they would have advanced in life, had they remained—were unknown to them. It is hard to imagine how a boy could resume social life in a Sierra Leone village setting without undergoing the ceremonies preparing him for manhood, whereby esoteric and supernatural knowledge was passed from generation to generation and a boy was "eaten" and "reborn" as a man. But because *poro* initiation—in the words of the amateur linguist Frederick William Hugh Migeod, "virtually a system of education"—was traditionally part of an age set practice tied to kinship, village, and lineage, it was not something that could easily be revisited in Freetown, York, or Kaw-Mendi. Betrothal, marriage, and children were effectively out of reach of the uninitiated.[16]

The girls were similarly returning to West Africa uninitiated and thus as displaced elderly children. Te'me, Kag'ne, and Mar'gru had been severed from their respective age sets of their village *bondo* chapters, where the social and cultural guardians of knowledge, wisdom, and feminine experience and power would have initiated them. Without entering the "*bondo* bush" during the post-harvest dry season, the girls would not, according to their communities, have reached womanhood or been granted adult names. There are examples of older liberated African slave women joining *bondo* chapters in urban and rural settings, but this did not necessarily mean the girls could easily join a chapter. Older women—whether they originated locally or came from Yoruba communities or elsewhere—were often familiar with the rituals, responsibilities, and hierarchies of secret societies. By contrast, the girls had been separated from their age sets, lineage, kin, and village since early childhood. Enduring the long sojourn in the *bondo* bush and the physical practices, such as cliterodectomy, was made possible by the presence of childhood friends and older kinswomen. It is difficult to explain what the absence of initiation meant to the girls, but some guidance is provide by Ferme, who explained that among the Mende, the term for uninitiated, *kpowanga*, also means "mad" or "mentally deficient." For many in Freetown and in Galinhas and its hinterland in the mid–nineteenth century, marriage and childrearing were unthinkable in such a context.[17]

To be sure, the Amistad Committee and the Union Missionary Society imagined an altogether different upbringing for the rescued children and for the mission as a whole. The setup was steeped in perceived racial hierarchies from the outset. Members of the executive committee of the Union Missionary Society naively instructed the Afro-Barbadians, Mr. Henry and Mrs. Tamar Wilson, how to conduct themselves in the Mende territory, and they made them subordinate to the white missionaries. Because African children were at the bottom of a metaphorical racial ladder the potential irreconcilability of their cultural identity vis-à-vis traditional West African village life was a distant if not nonexistent concern. The mission society imagined that local Mende would be "touched" by the "kind reception" the Africans had received in the United States and be "predisposed to listen" and would "welcome truth."[18]

Fig. 6.1. Kaw-Mendi mission, c. 1850 (George Thompson, *The Palm Land;*
or, West Africa, Illustrated [Cincinnati: Moore, Wilstach, Keys, 1859])

Furthermore, the leaders of the Kaw-Mendi (Komende) mission (figure 6.1),
at the outset the Raymonds, had no children of their own and thus turned to
the children to create their own family. As the experiences explored below took
a heavy toll on the girls in particular, the Raymonds "watched over them continually with parents' care." As the travails encountered in the initial months
of settlement continued, the Raymonds imagined for themselves an expanded
role. William Raymond wrote, "They look to us as children do to their parents,
and I am happy to say they are dutiful and obedient children." He embraced
many of the prevailing ideologies of contemporary missionaries when he said,
"We are indeed a happy family." Later letters from Mar'gru certainly attest to
the intense bond between the missionaries and the three girls, but the ostensible Christian identities and Western education of the five children insulated
them only somewhat from cultural expectations that neither they nor their U.S.
patrons could have imagined. And nothing prepared them for the upheavals
they were to experience upon return.[19]

THE "AFRICAN FAMILY" IMAGINED

When the Amistad Africans departed North America in November 1841, the
Western nuclear family narrative that emerged in the contexts of the trial unin-
tentionally framed their homeward journey. Whereas many of the adults carried

with them specific, private, and personal remembrances of wives, children, and parents revealed during the course of the trials, interviews conducted by Gibbs, Day, Griswold, and others resulted in the crafting of a family context for them that likely bore little relation to their previous lived experiences. Family stories provided an empirical basis informing the persuasive rhetoric of Baldwin and others before the Supreme Court. A narrative of disrupted family life resonated with antislavery and proslavery forces alike. On some level the manufacture of a nuclear family was of no consequence to the adults, many of whom had much earlier determined their intended course of action once they set foot on West African soil. There is no evidence the adults cared about the representations by Gibbs and others or subscribed to its content. But for the five children, this family narrative embedded at the core of the mythology of reunification, was to have a profound impact on their capacity to rebuild their lives in rural Sierra Leone.

The nuclear structure imagined by the Amistad Committee was born partly of the distorted context of the "family" in the grip of the illicit slave trade, circa 1820–40, elicited through interviews during the Africans' imprisonment in New Haven. The majority of captives spoke related regional languages, and they were enslaved in similar contexts. As such, with the benefit of hindsight, the stories can be not only interpreted as representing a collective voice but also explored on an individual basis. These brief stories provide important information about families in the hinterland funneled into the Galinhas slave barracoons and shed light on the role of slavery within the family and its effects on family structure. But this outline of the family, based on interviews conducted by Americans, identifies specific family affiliations that both the interviewers and the adult male interviewees considered important. Thus several significant caveats underscore the problematic nature of this data. First, Gibbs's own understanding of "family" and what might be considered kinship relations would have informed his views and those of other Anglo-Americans conducting interviews. First, examples of biases founded on ignorance, chauvinism, and prejudice include an emphasis on monogamous households, a Christian disdain for polygyny, and the dismissal of multigenerational households. Second, the African interlocutors would likely have conveyed the kinship affiliations they considered most important in the circumstances, including affiliations of occupation, social status, religion, and age rank, hence the repeated references to hunting prowess. Details of the domestic sphere, including precise descriptions of marital relations and housing arrangements, would likely have been marginal considerations. And third, the translators, including Covey, would have influenced the nature of the information elicited. For example, by reframing questions about kin structure and family using formulaic vernacular phrases and epithets that made sense to both parties in specific conversations, the translators may have flattened or erased important distinctions pertaining to kinship proximity, resulting in the irrecoverable loss of valuable facets.

Among the details recorded by Gibbs and his team (including Covey) are demographic and familial context of thirty-six individuals. The individuals can be grouped into several categories based on Gibbs's presentation of their familial claims. Of the thirty-six individuals, at least fourteen (38 percent) had a father living when they were enslaved and at least fourteen (38 percent) also had a mother living. Of these same individuals, ten (27 percent of the total) claimed both parents were alive when they were enslaved. Only one individual referred to living grandparents. Seventeen (51 percent) of the males were married, and one was wealthy enough to have two wives. Thirteen (39 percent) of the males had children: seven men admitted to one child; one man claimed two; three men claimed three; and one individual claimed four children. Seventeen individuals claimed multiple siblings, one claimed to have one, and Sa identified himself as an "only child." Five claimed at least two siblings, three claimed at least three, and eight (22 percent) claimed five or more siblings. Eight was the largest number of siblings, and two (5 percent) individuals claimed to have eight brothers and sisters, thus nine surviving offspring in total.

This numerical data about the demographic context of those enslaved provided the basis for a tentative sketch of the family, as least insofar as it was imagined by the Amistad Committee. Although it is unlikely emblematic of all families, circa 1820–40, because of the preferences of slavers for particular demographic groups, it does offer a sense of aspects of structure deemed important by both Gibbs and the Africans themselves in the context of a struggle to return home. It is noteworthy, for example, that all but four of the individuals described a familial context of some sort or another from which they were stripped, or of which they claimed to be bereft. The spectrum of family descriptions is expansive to be sure, ranging from noting the death of parents or grandparents to the presence of new children. But a situational or relational context is omnipresent, and it cemented the claim they were African-born and illegally removed from Africa. In terms of establishing a familial context, references to parents, living or deceased, or wives outnumbered descriptions of children or siblings. Nineteen adult men mentioned parents, fourteen revealed wives, and there are twelve references each to siblings and to children. Larger families were common, insofar as 47 percent of individuals described having multiple siblings. Instructively, only one claimed to have been raised alone.[20]

What is particularly striking, however, is the almost complete absence of any reference to non-nuclear key kinship actors and lineage relations. The sole "foster" family member noted was not uncovered until Raymond accompanied Fuliwa to his hometown of Mperri upon return to Sierra Leone. To be sure, there were multiple ethnicities represented among the adult male group. Gibbs concluded most were Mende, but the "Mendi" identity myth erased linguistic and ethnic complexity. Adam Jones was among the first to observe that the Amistad survivors themselves indicated Mende, Temne, Bandi, Gola, Balu (possibly Loma?), Tuma (likely Loma), Kono, and Sando origins. It is beyond the scope of this book to delineate important lineage ties in all of these ethnic groups, notwithstanding navigating the changes from the early nineteenth century to the present day. But it is nonetheless important to note that within lineages—whether the patrilineal, patrilocal Temne, the bilateral, patrilocal Mende, or the obscure lineage structures of the Sando (a chieftaincy between Mende and Kono territory) and Bandi (who have more or less disappeared and been absorbed into Mende)—certain relations loom large and particular individuals have powerful roles. Allowing for a generous average generation of twenty years, irrespective of patrilocality or matrilocality, most of the Amistad adults would have lived with grandparents in their enclosures. Paternal grandparents, for example, may have played key roles in negotiating access to land. Senior-ranked uncles within female lineages (that is, a mother's oldest brother, regardless of relative age) may have occupied central positions in negotiating brideprice contracts and facilitating bridewealth payments. Despite the centrality of such non-nuclear individuals, there were only two references to uncles, one maternal and the other possibly paternal. Even more oddly, there is only one reference to living grandparents, that of Kinna. In spite of the obvious fact that because of their age the children were most likely to have been living with one or both of their respective fathers' parents, none of Amistad's orphans mention grandparents.[21]

Competing for attention among the data about families is information about political organization, hierarchy, and social order. References to parents and wives exist in the greatest frequency, and they are followed in third place by remarks about kings or chiefs. Detailed references to leadership would certainly have resonated with the U.S. courts adjudicating the case, but they played an equally important role in portraying the social order of Gibbs's "Mendi Country" (Galinhas and its hinterland) as a hierarchical, centralized, and patriarchal culture. Thirteen of the adults reference a village or town chief or "king." Cinquez lists Ka-lum-bo as king of "Kaw-men-di." Grabeau mentioned

"Baw-baw" as king of Fu-lu. Bartu identified "Da-be" as the king of the town of "Tu-ma." Bartu's king, "Ti-kba," ruled "Fu-li-wa," in Mano. Sessi was born in "Mas-sa-kum," ruled by "Pa-ma-sa." Kinna's town of "Si-ma-bu" was ruled by "Sa-mang." Fakinna claims his father, "Baw-nge," was "chief or king" of his town "Dzho-po-a-hu." Yaboi was born in "Kon-do-wa-lu," and his king was "Ka-kbe-ni," which was translated as "lazy." Tsukama and his king, "Gnam-be," resided in "Sun-ga-ru." "Ge-le-wa" was king of "Fang-te," a fortified Gola town, and the home of Berri. Foni, from "Bum-be," was ruled by "Ka-ban-du." Other references to kings include the infamous Shaka or Siaka of Gendema, a central figure in the slave trade of the 1820s and 1830s, described in depth by Jones.[22]

Centralized, hereditary chieftaincies certainly existed during this period, and chiefs played important roles, not only in trade, warfare, and slave selling but also in the distribution of political power.[23] But equally critical is what is erased by the simplistic survey in Gibbs's interview data. In the ethnographic description there is no acknowledgment of male secret associations and female mask societies, the communal ties to the world of gods and spirits, which Ferme and historian Stephen Ellis argue constitute the "most important social bonds," and continue to impact Sierra Leone society today.[24] The "diamond shaped figure" of the forehead of the Kono man (Nazhaulu or Konoma) was very likely a *poro* initiation scar. The "breast" tattoos of Fabanna, Grabeau, Pungwuni, and Bartu remained unexplained. The nearest thing to an explanation of the extensive body art came from Griswold's description: "Many submit to the painful process of tattooing. The breasts and arms of some of the captives display in every part the incision of the knife; both sexes practice this custom in Mendi. We inquired the reason, and received for reply, 'to make them proud,' i.e. to make them beautiful." Perhaps this was supposed to infer premarital preparatory acts, but it is unclear.[25]

Poro and *bondo* (the female equivalent, also *bundu* or *sande*) operated as counterweights to hierarchically organized lineage, ward, town, or clan. But the complementarity of the sexes and the separate spheres of responsibility, analyzed by historian Lynda Day, are nowhere to be found in the narratives collected by Gibbs and others. These "religious sodalities" adjudicated succession to ritual, intrafamilial dispute, and political power. Although a physician's examination affirmed of the males "nearly all been circumcised," Gibbs did not draw this out to explore the role of initiation ceremonies. Nor was there recognition of age sets or other aspects of political, social, and judicial authority, all of which were fundamental to countervail the centralizing tendencies of chief-based leadership and the influence of Islam. The gender of power is represented as exclusively masculine in spite of the fact that many societies incorporated important roles of women, and some Mende communities en-throned women as chiefs.[26]

A silencing of earlier references to Islam and religious pluralism reverberates with the masculine homogenization of political power. Many of the Mende, Temne, and Bulom communities were undergoing the preliminary stages of Islamicization during this period, and Muslim doctors and imams were settling throughout the region's chiefdoms by the 1830s and 1840s. Jones cites a Mon-rovia missionary journal, *Africa's Luminary*, for the presence of Muslim clerics in Gendema, Siaka's town, during this period. Earlier newspaper stories men-tioned knowledge of Islam, spoken Arabic, and even writing systems. Madden's statement provides the richest evidence of Islamic knowledge, if not practice. He wrote, "To one of them I spoke and repeated a Mahamedan form of prayer in the Arabic language the man immediately recognized the language and re-peated a few words of it after me and appeared to understand it, particularly the words Allah Akbar (or God is great). The man who was beside the negro I also addressed in Arabic saying Salaam Ailkoun or peace be to you he immediately in the customary Oriental salutation replied Aleckom Salaam or peace be on you." A familiarity with Arabic is also inferred from Grabeau's reference to the way "people write" in "his country," namely, "from right to left." And yet in Gibbs's account, Islam merits no mention.[27]

Tappan's earlier accounts of interviews also indicated he was cognizant of the presence of differing religious persuasions. He wrote that they were "partly Mahomedans and partly Pagans." Again, he noted the men were "circumcised," a male genital cutting practice prevalent among Muslims and members of *poro* societies. Gibbs and Griswold provided only passing reference to animist spiri-tuality, such as Kimbo's observation that "when people die in his country, they suppose the spirit lives, but where, they cannot tell." Prior to their departure Gibbs again revisited the perceived ambiguity of their religious outlook: "They have more just views of the unity of God, than would be natural as mere pagans. But the Mohammedan influence on them has not been great." Rather than attempting to ascribe the spiritual beliefs any particular identity or character, Gibbs's assumption of spiritual emptiness echoes formulaic accounts of individ-uals on the verge of a religious quest and therefore ripe for proselytization. And indeed, Tappan and his colleagues were firmly of the belief that the Amistad Africans were "brought by the providence of God to their very doors" to "impart instruction." And the children, especially, were spiritually empty vessels.[28]

The descriptions of marriage recorded in the interviews also indicate a ten-dency to reshape unchristian alternatives into formulae more reflective of West-ernizing, Christianizing missionary objectives. Marital status was a particular focus of the interview data, but scrutinized with hindsight it exhibits curious crosscurrents to available ethnographic evidence. The precise ages of the men were impossible to establish, but data suggest that the first marriage of males took place in the late teens or early twenties. About half of the men indicated they had a wife or wives when enslaved. One, Burna, described his brother's marriage as taking place after the death of his father. There are hints of the bride-price and bride-service contracts undertaken. Married and with three children, Bau stated that "in his country all have to pay for their wives; for his, he had to pay 10 clothes, 1 goat, 1 gun, and plenty of mats." Importantly, he also noted that "his mother made the cloth for him," which is suggestive of the lineage and gender responsibilities "of a small party of friends" for bride-service, described by British colonial officer Thomas Joshua Alldridge at the end of the nineteenth century, wherein "one of whom must be a woman." Another, Ndzhangwawni, gave "twenty clothes and one shawl for his wife." Acquiring wives was expensive.[29]

In general, during this period multiple marriages were likely restricted to those individuals with disposable wealth. Eighteenth-century Swedish botantist Adam Afzelius observed that "the rich men or head men" may have "from 20 to 40 or 50." And yet this alerts us to yet another possible bias in the data, insofar as even those listed as "gentlemen" or presumably of high status, such Fang, "son of a king," record only one wife. The prevalence of polygyny during the period is difficult to discern, but it was likely relatively widespread. Matthews observed that, the "common people are content with one, or at most two wives," yet Afzelius clarified that "every body is allowed to take as many wifes [sic] as he can maintain." Information from some of the adults upon return undercuts the interview data. Raymond reported that Burna had said "he had no wife"; "instead" he had "seven, and several children." Could it be that polygynous narratives were marginalized in the interview process? Were some of the adult males—unclear about their future in the United States and increasingly cognizant of the Christian requirement of monogamy—reshaping their life histories in contemplation of the possibility of settling and marrying in the United States?[30]

Even more curiously, the only individual identified as having two wives (Fabanna) lived with his only child and wives in one house. Cohabitation of co-wives in one house was highly unlikely, as homes usually consisted of one round or square room of one story. It is more likely that when the interviewees recorded the word "house," as in Burna's narrative, the more appropriate phrase would have been "household" or "family unit." In all the records, there are few accounts of the living situation of the Africans and only one from the

Fig. 6.2. Bulom roundhouse, c. 1890 ("Boulam—
Sierra Leone"; photographer unknown)

children. Julia Brown, who hosted Te'me in Farmington in 1841, recalled the
girl describing her village. She stated, "She liked to talk of their simple life
in the village from which she was so rudely taken. Their houses must have
been bee-hive looking structures, wrough[t] from grasses and twigs and placed
near together, I think for safety." Although the structure appears consistent with
early accounts in Griswold's narrative, and with drawings and photographs of
roundhouses from the region (figure 6.2), the bucolic fable is stripped of ethnographic context. It would thus appear that just as political analytics were
univocal, the data suggests a parallel reluctance to address the polygynous dimensions of family life.[31]

    Irrespective of the biases inherent in the data sample, marriages and families
operated as units of labor organization and mobilization, and they continue to
operate so today. Noteworthy, and embedded in the data about the Amistad
Africans, were records about other family contexts and relationships. In Gibbs's
interview data the largest family unit mentioned was that of Margoná, the first
slave master of the Amistad survivor Moru, who had "ten wives and many
houses." A second slave owner, Garlobá, had "four wives" when he acquired
Pungwuni. These vignettes support the prevailing wisdom that wealth in the

region was measured in people and in one's capacity to operationalize rights-in-persons, particularly through agricultural labor or the manufacture of salt. Further sustaining the consensus in the secondary literature about the prevalence of upland rice cultivation as a primary source of nourishment, a plurality of the Amistad individuals worked in rice production.[32]

But the data on rice cultivation are compromised by what might be best characterized as a latent preference for the possessive individualism of the noble republican frontier yeoman farmer. Eleven of the captives mention rice cultivation, ranging from the context of their own labor to their experience of enslavement. The upland rice paddies worked by the Amistad Africans were likely similar to those existing in the Kenema district today. But instead of using terminology identifying the gendered and age grade complexity of tasks—for example, clearing, hoeing, dyke construction, weeding, and harvesting—several individuals are described as a "planter of rice." The adoption of the term "planter," as opposed to "rice farmer" or "peasant," is suggestive of a republican ideology of the yeoman, tilling the soil and providing for his family. Other references were more oblique: Gbatu mentions that in the "high mountains" in his country "rice is cultivated"; another was captured while "going to a town to buy rice." But a subtle tendency toward possessive individualism and rights-bearing autonomy is buttressed by references to other professions, such as "blacksmith," gentlemanly activities, such as "hunting," or the inactivity made possible by being a "gentleman." Only one individual provides a more plausible correlation between kinship relations, marriage, and rice cultivation. Like Covey, Pungwuni worked as a slave in a rice plantation for two years prior to being resold to European slave traders. His experience speaks directly to a powerful kinship relationship in Mende—even today—that of the role of the mother's senior brother. His mother's brother sold him "for a coat." Perhaps because of his status as slave he was described as "employed in cultivating rice" rather than as a planter. He worked with his "master's" four wives and many children in paddies. But this reference also contained a curious coda, to the effect they worked together with "no distinction made in regard to labor."[33]

Large multigenerational family units working together as production units were also normative during this period. But information gleaned from the Amistad captives' interviews jars with expectations of household unit organization and family size. Advocates of the survivors, such as the teacher Booth, celebrated the imagined nuclear unit thus: "the people live in small houses" and "the children always live with their parents." But the data curiously suggest that the presence of two generations in a household enclosure vastly outweighed three generations, by a ratio of almost one to five. Of the thirty-four who provided longitudinal generational data, twenty-eight individuals mention two generations, but only six affirm the existence of three. Nine of the men describe living with one parent or both. Accounts of siblings sit in tension with reference to children. Many individuals describe living with numerous siblings in the same house or village. And indeed, if captured or seized from their home, farm, or village, age peers or siblings were likely the last family members they saw, or they were possibly captured together. Oddly though, the number of children born of captive men is quite low. For the thirteen men who claimed to have children the total number of progeny was twenty-four. So whereas most men had brothers and sisters, only a few at the time of their enslavement had produced as many children as their parents or had children who had survived infancy.[34]

The relatively small numbers of children must thus be viewed in the context of the likelihood that most of these men were captured in the prime of their productive and reproductive adult lives. Many were likely captured in their late teens and very early twenties, at the peak of their child-producing activities. As Madden, witness for the defense with extensive expertise examining "recaptives" in Cuba, stated, "Most of the negroes shipped, as aforesaid, . . . are under twenty years of age." It is thus difficult to establish an overall median family size because data from the adults reside uncomfortably with the two of Amistad's orphans who began their Atlantic passage as pawns, both girls from large families. Kag'ne's parents were still living and had eight other children—four girls and four boys. Both of Mar'gru's parents were also alive, and she had six siblings, among them four sisters. It is noteworthy that the two who began their journey into slavery as pawns were from two of the largest families described in the data. So while the larger data pool misrepresents the dimensions of family units, hints about the possible families of two children provide a more realistic index.[35]

A picture of the Amistad nuclear family emerges from this data. Although no members of the Amistad Committee advocated overtly for a reconfiguration of the domestic setting as a criterion for funding a new missionary endeavor, the presence of preferences informed by classic Western tropes and Christian "civilizing" ideologies are indisputable. The idealized Amistad nuclear family involved two generations, not three. It consisted of a core male (the returning survivor) reunited with a single wife, and either several children or one or two parents. Other familial relatives were peripheral and less consequential. The imagined Amistad nuclear family resided in one common residence, in a village that included other households of siblings in similar monogamous spousal arrangements. The head of the imagined family was a yeoman farmer, a noble freeholder, whose occupation was tilling the soil. He was part of a village or

community, with hierarchical, centralized power structures, such as chiefs, and
the alternative lateral power dispersion rendered by *poro* and *bondo*. In the
patriarchic Amistad household "the wife attends to the concerns of the house."
The family had no strong allegiance to Islamic or animist beliefs, but rather was
a ready vessel for the transference of Christian values and Western, civilizing
ideologies. This reconstruction, although based on the accounts of adult male
survivors, was most powerful in shaping the context into which the impression-
able, vulnerable children were thrust.[36]

This brief analysis of the African captives' interview data is instructive with
respect to the context of the resettlement experiences of five of Amistad's orphans. As the children had been removed well before important ceremonies
and events marking their progression through adolescence to maturity, they had
little sense of what to expect in terms of family and homecoming. The Amistad
Committee, however, had transparent objectives in assisting the passage of the
African survivors. Their return would be the catalyst for a new missionary enterprise, itself an extension of a radical realignment of evangelical abolitionism
underway in the United States in the 1840s. The adult males were under no obligation to participate in the missionary activities, but the Amistad Committee
considered the children a crucial component of the new compound. The Amistad Committee hastily put together a missionary team shortly before November
1841, but irrespective of the leadership, the children were presumed to be part of
the settlement and, as Raymond's letter suggests, part of a new "family." As the
interview data reveal a number of significant biases and preferences in accounts
of the domestic setting, it is reasonable to infer that these conceptions of family
and household informed the Amistad Committee's expectations and that these
were projected onto the children. And indeed, the projection of specific roles
and expectations had begun long before departure.

THE EDUCATION OF AMISTAD'S ORPHANS

The five children, who disembarked the *Gentleman* in Freetown, Sierra Leone, in January 1842, were embodied with elements of a formal Western education. By contemporary standards, their experiences would be considered a blend
of informal traditional cultural education and formal schooling. At its broadest,
their comprehensive knowledge comprised elements elicited as small children
in the Galinhas region before their forced removal, knowledge acquired during
their experiences of enslavement and liberation, and schooling specifically tailored to the expectations of their protectors. The respective differences in their
education reflected their different itineraries: Covey spent considerably longer

in a formal schooling environment before arriving in New York than Mar'gru, Te'me, Kag'ne, and Ka'le experienced during detention in the United States. And the nature of each of their educational experiences was deeply shaped by gender biases and assumptions. The missionaries accompanying the Amistad Africans to Freetown also assumed that the knowledge the five children had acquired in the context of their ordeals would hold them in good stead for the anticipated rigors of a frontier missionary settlement.

As Christian-educated children living in rural Kaw-Mendi, they were likely viewed as strange by neighboring villagers. To be sure, the girls were briefly shaped by their experiences as small children in Galinhas before their forced removal. Although there exists little by way of remembrances of their pre-removal childhood, historical accounts provide a sense of the type of training and education very young children may have received in their natal villages before enslavement. European visitors in the late eighteenth century "complain[ed]" about "the native children not being well treated here" because they were "obliged to beat [r]ice, carry home water, and do other menial services which was not usual or permitted in the English Schools." But defenders of practices described the children as "accustomed" to such "services." There was no specific age when such tasks and knowledge acquisition began. As anthropologist Caroline Bledsoe demonstrates, girls are drafted into household work—like sweeping—or child-care duties "as soon as they are physically capable." Girls learned cooking by observation at home, but simple medicine and the art of poisoning food to keep their future husbands in line were acquired in the context of *bondo* "bush schools," discussed below. Upon their return the three girls perhaps recalled small details about community and ethnic protocols, although they would have been largely unfamiliar with social conventions passed on from grandmother and mother to daughter.[37]

Removal from the region similarly deprived the boys of farming knowledge and social skills, such as how to interact with elders and authorities. As young boys usually resided with their mothers until at least the age of seven or eight, Ka'le would likely have had to fetch and carry water and assist with home chores, such as keeping the hearth alight, gathering firewood and thatching materials, and tending to chickens, ducks, and goats. From Covey's perspective it is possible to extrapolate a little more about the learning experience, specifically that acquired in the context of enslavement. As a child slave to a Bulom family, Covey would have learned basic agricultural skills, environmental knowledge, the role of the seasons, and specific tasks associated with risiculture, for example, chasing away birds and monkeys. Had Covey or Ka'le not been kidnapped and enslaved, they would have been increasingly exposed to village men and to the authority of their father and uncles and, in their teenage years, would have accompanied men on hunting trips and trading meetings. It is conceivable itinerant imams operating in the Mende area might have exposed them to a form of Islamic education and medicine.[38]

In contrast with what they gained and lost as a consequence of their enslavement, all five children acquired significant formal education in the context of their experiences of liberation. And importantly, their education can be linked to specific individuals with identifiable philosophies, pedagogies, and objectives. Formal education for Covey and Ka'le consisted of reading and writing English, basic arithmetic, and geography and history, all within the context of a formal program of Christian teaching focused on conversion and proselytization. By the time Covey joined the Royal Navy he could read and write English at a level approximating a present-day eighth-grade standard. When Ka'le returned to Freetown his English was a little more advanced that Covey's and his script neater and more confident. Ka'le also likely worked the fifteen-acre vegetable garden in Farmington with the adult males. Education for the three girls consisted of English reading and writing, but during their time in Westville and later Farmington they focused their energies on domestic training and home economics.[39]

By way of detour, the experience of Covey in an unusual experimental school in the Mountain District behind Freetown, from September 1833, merits consideration because of the rich archival record. As a liberated African boy, Covey's education was somewhat anomalous in the context of the apprenticeship system imposed on all recaptive former slaves, as outlined in Chapter 5. In New Haven Covey declared, "I learned to speak the English language in Sierra Leone and have been taught to read and write," and before the district court he made a similar, narrower claim, "I learned to speak English at Sierra Leone," but his laconicism hardly does justice to the unique opportunities afforded him at the hands of the Church Missionary Society (CMS). Covey arrived in Freetown in early July 1833 and was likely housed temporarily with the many other boys liberated, in the King's Yard. In August, the acting governor approached the CMS regarding the possibility of placing "under their charge" 103 "Cossoo" boys and "to have them educated at Bathurst as the place most suitable for this residence and accommodation." The executive committee of the CMS met shortly thereafter in Kissy and resolved to express that they were "highly interested in contributing both to the temporal and spiritual welfare of these poor and injured orphans."[40]

The CMS drew up "regulations and conditions" for its schools for submission to the governor. The terms under which Covey and 102 others were admitted to Bathurst provide fascinating insight into the pedagogical philosophy of the CMS. They also suggest that previous collaborative efforts with the government's Liberated African Department were not entirely to the liking of the missionaries. The "Regulations for the guidance and management for the Cossoo boys school at Bathurst" submitted to Acting Governor Melville, comprising eight articles, required "that these children be received under the sole management of the Clergymen of the Church missionary Society." The hours of schooling following the pattern of "all the society's schools," from "9 to 2 o'clock," and the CMS staff guaranteed that they would ensure all the boys were "suitably employed before and after school hours with a view to initiate them to habits of industry." In case of "sleight sickness," the CMS sought access to "a few common medicines" from government supplies, and in "extreme cases," sought permission "to send them to the Hospital."[41]

Christian proselytization formed the backbone of the program, but on a practical level the CMS mission schools sought to instill self-reliance. The governing document for Bathurst drew on those for earlier Liberated African schools the Christian Institution had developed in collaboration with the colonial administration, including at Bathurst, Regent Town, Gloucester, York, and Kissy. The document regulated "the hours for instruction on week-days" only; Saturdays were set aside for "washing and ironing" clothes. Reverend Charles Lewis Haensel explained the rationale thus, "With the exception of beating the rice and cooking that and their other victual, which is done by my cook, the youths are in every respect their own servants. They sweep and scrub the schoolroom and sleeping room, clean the table, pans, spoons, knives, and forks, wash their clothes and clean their shoes. They clean the yard and work in the farm, whenever they are required to do so. I send, occasionally, one or other to fetch something from Freetown, just to remind them that they are not above carrying a basket full of rice or books, or anything else, on their heads."[42]

The dual purpose embedded in the CMS's acceptance of so many "Cossoo" boys thus becomes clearer. With "pleasing surprise" a contemporary visitor to the Bathurst school in 1833–34, Mary Church, noted "six intelligent looking neatly dressed girls . . . busily engaged with spinning wheels" under the care of Mrs. Weeks, and eighty Liberated African boys "cultivating a farm" and learning "the best manner of raising cotton, arrow root, ginger, &c." This account resonates with the earlier "regulations," which stipulated that the "Liberated African Schoolboys" use after school hours to "cultivate farms, their labour being directed by the Teachers." The purpose of "the produce of such farms" was "to be devoted to the feeding of the children."[43]

Precisely what Covey learned in the school may be extrapolated from CMS records about other schools operating during the same period and contemporary

Fig. 6.3. Day lesson plan for Church Missionary Society boys' school, by Reverend Charles Haensel (Haensel, "Quarterly Report of the Christian Institution," June 24, 1829, CMS/C A1 O108/82, CMS Archive, Cadbury Research Library: Special Collections, Academic Services, University of Birmingham)

correspondence. A lesson plan developed by Reverend Charles Haensel provides an indication of the organization and content (figure 6.3). The CMS offered to take responsibility of "the charge and education moral and religious." The boys were instructed in English in what Weeks considered "an experiment" to test "the capacities of the Africans." In his first report to the mission headquarters he explained that "two days after they arrived at Bathurst, I divided them into three classes, and gave them the first four letters in the alphabet to learn, in two hours 15 boys had learnt them perfectly, I then made a fourth class of these 15 and gave them another board, on which I had pasted the first eight letters, in this manner I continued to promote them until they had acquired the whole of the alphabet, and though it is not yet three weeks since they commenced attending school, we have 18 now learning monosyllables." By December 1833 eighteen were reading the "Sunday School Primer," and the remainder the "steps to reading"; only one remained in "the alphabet class." He observed that when they arrived in Bathurst "not one of them as yet knew a single word of the English language," but when he left Bathurst approximately a year later "13 of them could read their bibles and 36 the Parables and Miracles of our Saviour and other elementary books." In 1834 Weeks introduced "the spinning of cotton, which the boys are taught to weave into cloth so that by these means habits of industry and usefulness are early inculcated." In June 1834 half were advancing well and using "Sunday School Union Spelling book" and the "Central School Book No. 2." Reverend Haensel's lesson plans were adapted for different levels.[44]

Whereas the CMS took charge of the boys, including Covey, the maintenance was borne by the colonial government's Liberated African Department. An earlier arrangement provided that each child receive "1 1/2 yards cotton cloth, to each, one blanket, one mat, one iron spoon, one tin pot, one tin dish." In addition, from 1833, the CMS required one and a half shillings per diem for each boy and "a sufficient quantity of check and duck [a rough cloth] for the purpose of making each boy a suit of clothes every six months, which will be made by the colony born girls in the society's schools." Each month the costs of food and the wages of the teachers were paid in advance to the CMS. But the boys were not guaranteed a place in school indefinitely. The terms and conditions included "half-yearly examination of the general progress of the scholars." After each exam a "selection" took place and those children "as give no promise of being benefitted by continuing at school" were sent off into an apprenticeship arranged by the clergymen of the respective districts. The Bathurst community "hoped, however, that the number answering to his description will be very small."[45]

In June 1834 Weeks identified fifteen to twenty for whom he entertained "very faint hopes of their ever learning to read," and in September 1834 the decision was taken to remove twenty underperformers and "one boy for his general bad conduct."[46] In December 1834 a further five "backward and dull" boys were "apprenticed out." The CMS missionaries were leery of abuses in the apprenticeship system, having "often witness[ed] how cruelly such apprentices are treated, and how badly they are provided for." Private correspondence suggests that the missionaries viewed it as a "second slavery." The CMS missionaries thus took full charge of the selection of "applicants" seeking apprentices and the entire apprenticeship placement process. They also maintained a record of the "indentures made out by the Manager" of the boys; boys were apprenticed only to those individuals whom the missionaries considered "fit to be entrusted" with their erstwhile pupils.[47]

A picture thus emerges of Covey's education at the hands of the Reverend and Mrs. Weeks and other missionaries. Covey likely survived the first several examinations and "apprenticing out" of poor learners, but he was not one of the few named boys who achieved such distinction that they gained admittance as "initiatory scholars" to the Christian Institution. Records suggest that of the original 103, only 6 went on to Fourah Bay to train to become teachers and catechists. At some point Covey's formal Western education came to an end, and it is likely he had an apprenticeship in Freetown or another village prior to joining the Royal Navy. Covey was thus part of an unusual experiment, but one that was deemed successful enough to be repeated in other CMS schools in the 1837.[48]

The formal Western education of Ka'le and the three girls followed a different course. It took place in detention in New Haven and Hartford, to a lesser extent in the Pendletons' Westville home, and in Farmington, inconsistently between August 1839 and November 1841. The earliest discussions of attempts to communicate with the Africans, including the children, provide insight into their first encounter with U.S.-style instruction. In early September 1839 Tappan was already making some headway with the children. He wrote, "I distributed some religious tracts, . . . and attempted to instruct the African prisoners, especially the children. They pronounce words in English very distinctly, and have already nearly the numerals. In showing them some books containing pictures of tropical animals, birds, &c., they seemed much pleased to recognize those with whose appearance they were acquainted, endeavoring to imitate their voices and actions. With suitable instruction these intelligent and docile Africans would soon learn to read and speak our language." He indicated that "the opportunity to impart instruction to these pagans" was a collaborative charitable project "of the benevolent inhabitants" of New Haven.[49]

Rather than formal education, however, their first months were taken up primarily with "examination," in order to ascertain their origin and personal stories. Griswold explained, "From two to five hours each day have been spent in imparting instruction. At first their progress was slow and attended with some difficulties. They had been accustomed neither to the requisite effort of mind nor fixedness of attention." Subsequently, "in accordance with the advice of Mr. Gallaudet," Day acquired "pictures of simple objects" and commenced teaching. In order to grapple with the linguistic challenge, "grammars and spelling books and primers without number, in all sorts of unknown tongues, [we]re sought for and secured." A letter printed in Tappan's newspaper indicates "the first lessons" treated the Africans as if they had a disability, and utilized a "black board and slates" and adapted "Mr. Gallaudet's Elementary work for Deaf and Dumb." The first lessons were more a form of "preaching" on "the subject of the religion of the white men," because the teachers, such as Griswold, struggled to grasp how to instruct "those so old and yet so young." When Covey and the other translators appeared, efforts were made for a more "systematic instruction." But evidence also suggests Cinquez and others resisted these efforts, and they mocked their teachers for their inability to "do nothing" athletic.[50]

During their early detention, the three girls and Ka'le were schooled in a separate "division" but slept in "one bed" in a room apart from the men. After a brief period of formal imprisonment, the girls, Ka'le, and Antonio were physically separated from the adults and placed with the Pendletons in Westville. In the Pendletons' home they continued their instruction "in the primary branches of an English education," and students from Yale regularly visited them. They continued to study English, took Bible lessons, and attended church regularly. Antonio appears to have been prohibited from studying, however. Indeed, the scant details on the type of schooling rarely distinguish between that provided for the children and instruction for the adults still imprisoned.[51]

During this period Ka'le wrote several letters demonstrating a steady hand. Ka'le penned a widely circulated letter to John Quincy Adams, for, according to a later account, he "had picked up more English than the older ones." This letter provides a sense of the methods employed, namely, rote learning blended with religious training. Ka'le wrote, "we write every day; we write plenty letters; we read most all of the time; we read all Matthew, and Mark, and Luke, and John, and plenty of little books." But other accounts suggest they were treated as servants. Mrs. Pendleton considered it useless to teach the girls to sew. Tappan alleged that Colonel Pendleton had "promised one the girls to a relative of his" in New York City. Tappan also learned that a witness had seen Mrs. Pendleton "whip Antonio, severely." After the Supreme Court decision, the Pendletons refused to relinquish control of the five children. Thus while the specific content of their children's lessons remains unclear, it appears the education they acquired was closer to home economics and a future in domestic service.[52]

As the trials wore on, the Amistad Committee raised public funds to pay for more regular instruction. The adult males resided in prison until the Supreme Court ordered their release in March 1841, but they had a regular teacher from October 1840. After a writ of habeas corpus finally wrested the children from the Pendletons' home, they were relocated to Farmington, with the exception of Antonio who had fled north to Montreal. The Amistad Committee raised funds to build "one or more small buildings for their use and comfort" in Farmington. Elijah Lewis, an active conductor on the Underground Railroad, interviewed by Julie Brandegee in 1898, remembered seeing the Africans attend school over Edward Deming's store. Indeed all the Africans, children and adults, attended school five hours a day, six days a week.[53]

Although the children's removal from the Pendletons' home in Westville was no doubt disruptive, they flourished in Farmington. Ka'le lived with the adult males in a purpose-built barrack, which the children called "Cinque's house." The three "little African" girls were billeted with prominent abolitionist families and moved around. Te'me lived with the Reverend Noah Porter and his wife. Mar'gru resided with Timothy Cowles. And Kag'ne lived first briefly with Charlotte Cowles and then with her sister Elizabeth. In letters to her brother Samuel, editor of the *Charter Oak*, Charlotte describes her encounters with "Tenyeh," the "one who lives with us." She wrote "Tenyeh, (Te-meh) as we have at last learned to spell her name is very happy with us and we have become acquainted with the greater part of them [the adult males] from their coming here to see (her)." In April she describes a particular complex interaction thus, "One evening, Henyeh [*sic*] told us a great deal about her adventures, all the way from Mendi to Farmington. She said that at Lomboko she was burnt upon her shoulder with a red-hot pipe. I asked her to let me see the spot, not at all doubting her word. She looked up at me and said 'you think me tell lie? You look there.'" Te'me then resided with Dr. Chauncey Brown and his wife Julia. Late in life Julia Brown wrote down her memories of "Tamie"; she was "rather serious" and "uniformly cheerful." Brown considered it "remarkable how easily Tamie learned to speak our language and she could read quite well." Te'me went "to and from her school daily." In addition to reading the Bible, Te'me "tended carefully" to her "little garden" and grew pineapples. Brown also recalled how the aurora borealis caused her "despair" because she thought the world was ending.[54]

School instruction continued in Farmington under the volunteers John Pitkin Norton and James Booth. Although the children's aptitude for learning was noted, Norton complained that they had had "very little regular instruction" since their residence.[55] Booth thus endorsed using the spelling books of Samuel Griswold Goodrich, such as the Peter Parley series, which were recommended also by the Connecticut Board of Common Schools. By July, the two classes had been reorganized into four classes "of the elementary kind," and Booth wanted to hire another teacher. Ka'le and the girls excelled, along with Kinna and Fuliwa, and they were in the most advanced class. Cowles noted that Ka'le was "very bright" and attended school with the adults in the morning, and again from two in the afternoon until nine in the evening. Kag'ne attracted the attention of Norton, who noted her "mind" was a "concentration of good taste, pure and imaginative feeling."[56]

The children continued to study in Farmington, but they also attended abolitionist meetings, witnessed famous African-American orators, and participated in fundraising activities in Hartford and elsewhere. They traveled to New York and elsewhere and met foreign guests, including Joseph Sturge, who observed that Ka'le "could speak our language with great facility." They visited a "Deaf and Dumb Asylum," where Mar'gru was shown and "repeated" the "deaf and dumb alphabet." In May they "performed" publicly to some of their benefactors. An observer noted, "The Africans next read twice round from the New Testament, by which they showed the success with which they had mastered our language, as well as the proficiency they had made in learning to read. While some had done better than others, they had all succeeded beyond all human expectation. Only reflect, they had first to learn the language of the country, before they could understand, so as to receive instruction." Covey was also present, and he "made an admirable address, which drew tears from nearly every eye, and the manner in which he quoted and illustrated Scripture was amazing, and would serve as quite a lesson to a learned divine." Another journalist noted that Ka'le spelled "husbandman" and "commandments" correctly "and with readiness," but he generally portrayed the adult males in a more unflattering light.[57]

But like Covey's experience in Bathurst, the children's schooling during their long sojourn in Connecticut was specifically tailored to the expectations of their protectors. Gender biases, racial prejudices, patriarchy, and assumptions about future prospects riddled the education of Ka'le and the three girls, insofar as they were expected to be "scrupulously obedient to their teacher," and indeed to all their self-appointed guardians, protectors, and supervisors, ideologies that were also embodied in the CMS missionaries' larger project of proselytization. One of the last published accounts of their demonstration of newly acquired knowledge in Tappan's newspaper underscores the two interwoven purposes. "The audience were surprised and delighted with their accurate spelling, correct pronounciation [sic], fluency in reading, and quickness of perception. In some cases an elevated tone of religious feeling was manifested in the answers which they gave." As the survivors prepared to leave for Sierra Leone, soon-to-be missionary Raymond heaped praise on Ka'le and Mar'gru for their reading skills. And he took a personal shine to Mar'gru as a potential nanny to "assist in taking care of" the Raymonds' infant.[58]

Whereas spelling and reading were important, they were inseparable from the moral elevation of religious indoctrination and the gendered contours of a Christian education. The objective of a formal education for the children was thus to create malleable and resilient missionary vessels, who could operate effectively on the bold new frontier of the missionary enterprise. But by educating the children, Tappan and the Amistad Committee unwittingly further narrowed their opportunities in resettlement. What they gained in a formal schooling environment did not fill the vacuum of a lost African childhood.

THE PERMANENCY OF CHILDHOOD

Ka'le, Mar'gru, Kag'ne, Te'me, and Covey left the Galinhas coast in the 1830s as uninitiated children, and they returned to Freetown in 1842, still uninitiated children. It is difficult to imagine what the experience of return would have been for the children, but several stories speak to the dangers. Anecdotal information about the lives of the five once they returned demonstrates the difficulties they encountered reintegrating into Freetown's and wider Sierra Leonean culture and society. The girls openly defied attempts to remake them into African women and potential wives. And the boys, perhaps acknowledging the anomie resulting from their permanent uninitiated state, rejected any notions of cultural reintegration and instead threw their lot in with the missionary endeavor. Furthermore, these vignettes from their troubling resettlement suggest that in the eyes of many local Africans, five of Amistad's orphans were likely forever trapped in permanent state of childhood.

From the outset the children's return journeys were qualitatively different from the adult passage. In the words of Raymond, when they "left America they wept much" on "account of what they feared would befall them." The children were unprepared for what was to come, and the adults accompanying them had likely as little appreciation for the possible complications. Before their departure for Freetown, the Sierra Leone lieutenant governor John Ferguson wrote to Tappan to welcome the return of the Amistad survivors. He did not anticipate any problems with their resettlement, "It is not likely that a two years' residence in America will have effected such changes in the constitution of those Africans, as to render their arrival here, at any season, hazardous." But Ferguson's statement alluded to physical and environmental effects of a long stay in North America. His narrow experience resettling African recaptives from seized slave ships left him ill-prepared to counsel the missionaries about the specific complication of their undertaking. He appeared unaware that the returnees included several children, and he could not have been very familiar with the initiation rituals to which all boys and girls were exposed in order to enter adulthood.[59]

Upon arrival in Freetown, the three girls were immediately subject to overtures to remake them in the mold of local women and potential brides through female genital cutting in the context of the *bondo* initiation rites. Accounts of the specific events are sparse in detail, but letters from Raymond provide some sense of the "trying circumstances." He explained that in Freetown, the three girls were "not unfrequently" found "crying," although it was difficult to ascertain the cause. Once the smaller group had relocated to the town of York, Mrs. Raymond "succeeded in gaining their confidence to such a degree" that they began to confide in her. According to Raymond's account, while in Freetown, Cinquez and "Ta-fe" had tried "all they could to make them go through *Bun-du*," which he explains as "the rite of circumcision." The account is curious from a number of angles. First, it implies *bondo* membership was an urban phenomenon, which the girls were no longer threatened by in a rural location, such as York. Second, and against most accounts of *bondo* activity and regulations, it suggests that males—and not women in Freetown—were recruiting the girls as brides or pressuring them to submit to the norms of womanhood. And third, it adopts a masculinist analytical framework, highlighting the circumcision process as the core element and ignoring the role of circumcision as a rite preceding what today would be considered a "forced marriage."[60]

Bondo was widespread in Freetown and the many peninsula towns where liberated Africans were settled. Historian Frances White explains that *bondo* provided Krio market women with an entrée into the societies of the hinterland communities with which they traded and thereby brought rural forms of secret societies into the urban setting. White describes settler women as "cultural brokers," for whom *bondo* represented "both female solidarity and intragroup antagonism." It was particularly important for liberated women as they attempted to "cement ties" with indigenous communities. Although information from the 1840s is scarce, by the 1850s, *bondo* "played a major role" in settler women's lives. White notes that epidemics of disease in the liberated African settlements were a basis for its popularity, particularly among Muslim Krio women traders. *Bondo* provides connection to families, connected girls and women to other women in similar positions, and modified the isolation young women might feel as they relocated in the context of marriage. And, indeed, many Muslim Krio men insisted their potential wives graduate first from the "bundu bush."[61]

Raymond's account of the "*Bun-du*" from which the girls sought refuge is a fascinating narrative. He explained, "This rite is performed in a house made on purpose, somewhere on the outskirts of the town, after which the females circumcised, generally girls about the age of puberty, stripped naked—except a cloth about the loins—their bodies shining with oil—march through the streets accompanied by fifteen or twenty women drumming, singing and dancing, as much resembling Bedlam let loose as anything our minds can conceive." Notwithstanding the erotic and voyeuristic exoticism permeating this narrative, his strikingly visual account suggests Raymond had witnessed the public aspects of the performance of the *bondo*—the public call by drum for initiates to come forth. Raymond identified the *bondo* house, into which the initiates retreat, and the public physical display, including absence of all but rudimentary clothing, drumming, dancing, and singing. But Raymond left the reader guessing whether or not it was in the context of such a public call that the girls were pressured, or whether the pressure took another form.[62]

By describing *bondo* as "Bedlam," however, Raymond identified as disorderly and chaotic a ceremony that was anything but. *Bondo* societies were then, and are still today, entities and rituals structuring order and power. *Bondo* societies consist of women of all ages, organized in age sets according to the year of entrance or initiation. The elders of *bondo*, spearheading the call and drumming, act as intermediaries between ancestors and the living. Long before the return of Amistad's orphans and the observations of Raymond, European visitors documented the existence of *bondo* and the male equivalent, *poro*. Jones suggests that the ritual of such societies underwent little change during the slave trade. But there is no reason to believe the societies' rituals were static; they were dynamic social environments, and to young girls unprepared or unsuspecting, possibly frightening or traumatic.[63]

The processes of the ceremonies may be separated into several critical themes. Societal gender division and the gendered realms of power are one important aspect for understanding *bondo*. A second component concerns the transmission of knowledge, cultural practice, and spiritual belief as a preparation for marriage, authority, and motherhood. A third aspect of *bondo* is the value of secrecy, consisting of the known, unknown, and rumored or imagined. These are not exclusive themes but rather overlapping and mutually informing.[64]

The concepts of a gendered division of power, hierarchy of gender, and of a temporary reign of female power would have been puzzling to the young girls, who for some time had been living in a Western Christian domestic setting, where they operated as maids, servants, nannies, and housekeepers and were trained for a similar subordinate role in the context of a monogamous marriage. Here they learned the gendered division of labor, but also the omnipresence of patriarchy. *Bondo* societies envision an entirely irreconcilable view of the gender of power. Anthropologist Carol Hoffer MacCormack noted that the "tendency in Western culture to define women as weak and needing protection, since they bear children," sits in opposition to Mende attitudes. In West Africa "the same biological facts are given a different cultural interpretation. The bearing of children demonstrates that women are strong and active agents in a society, capable of holding political office." *Bondo* also conveys the significance of gender hierarchies, although respect and obeisance to elder women would likely have been less puzzling. Moreover, the female ceremonies of *bondo* and male ceremonies of *poro* alternate over different years. In some communities *poro* societies control a community for three years, followed by *bondo* for two, forming a five-year cycle. Thus, when the girls were pressured to submit to *bondo*, it may have been the second of a two-year reign. That male *poro* would "always give way" to *bondo* was viewed by Alldridge as "an opening for women's rights." When in operation, *bondo* societies have charge of the land, women induct new initiates, they mitigate co-wife rivalry and enhance female solidarity, but they are time sensitive too. The pressure to join was thus both political and temporal in nature.[65]

Secret societies were and are gender-based above all else, which provides a basis for speculation about the motivations behind the traumatic incident. *Bondo* was a highly ethnicized and local practice then as it is now, and, in the words of anthropologist Jacqueline Knörr, it plays a "major role in ethnic identification and authenticity." The girls could have been pressured to join a local Temne lodge, or possibly a Mende lodge made up of urban migrants and liberated Mende-speaking recaptives. But contra Jones's claim that the societies did not change considerably in the eighteenth and nineteenth centuries, *bondo* underwent significant change in the creolized environment of Freetown. In the 1840s Freetown was still a relatively small city, with a population of twenty thousand and many peripheral towns and villages (figure 6.4). It would have been difficult to remain unnoticed, and the young girls would have come into contact with many Sierra Leone women. Knörr argues that against the tensions of creolization, female participation increased and new societies flourished, and it is equally likely the girls were to become part of a nascent Krio or more accurately *proto*-Krio secret society. By inference, then, following Knörr's analysis, the resistance on the part of the three may have been an unequivocal indication that they intended to identify as recaptives and marry only recaptive (Krio) men, for to marry a native man would likely necessitate initiation. By contrast, the men (and surely unnamed women) who pressured Te'me, Kag'ne, and Mar'gru may have wanted the girls to join *bondo* in order to "mediate" ties between the city and the rural community in which they would eventually settle. Local Freetown women may have asserted the necessity of initiation if the girls hoped to become traders and hold market stalls in their future home in Mende territory, because *bondo* societies negotiate and ascribe social position and economic rights. And it is possible that because the girls were orphans, older women in Freetown stepped up to the role that would have been occupied by their mothers, aunts, and sisters in their original village.[66]

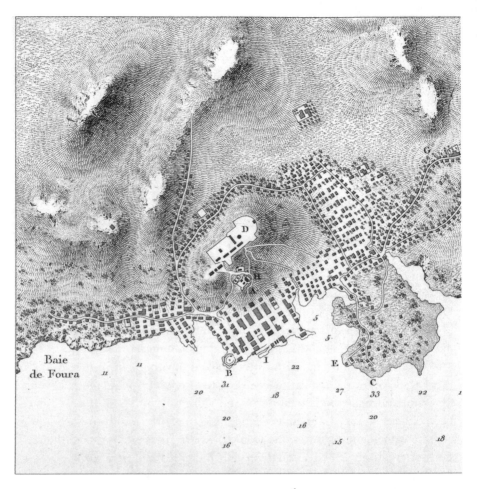

Fig. 6.4. Sketch of aerial view of Freetown, c. 1845 (Édouard de Bouët-Willaumez, *Description nautique des côtes de l'Afrique occidentale* [Paris: Robiquet, 1848]; © The British Library Board)

Aside from the obvious social, political and temporal pressures, it is likely that African women in Freetown and elsewhere viewed the three girls as bereft of knowledge and incapable of a fulfilled womanhood and marriage. *Bondo* was a necessary prerequisite to marriage. Initiation resolved this tension. A tendency in some accounts to view *bondo* societies narrowly, as "merely a means of teaching girls to be good wives and mothers," belies a more complex reality. Matthews noted that it is in the *bondo* bush that the girls "are taugh[t] the religious customs and superstitions of their country; for, till that period they are

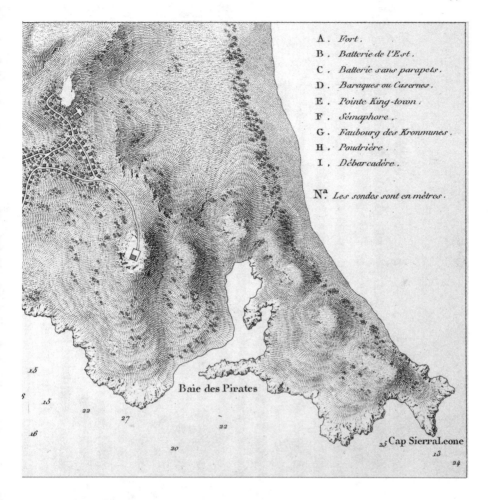

A . *Fort .*

B . *Batterie de l'Est .*

C . *Batterie sans parapets .*

D . *Baraques ou Casernes .*

E . *Pointe King-town .*

F . *Sémaphore ,*

G . *Faubourg des Kroumanes .*

H . *Poudrière .*

I . *Débarcadère .*

N.ª *Les sondes sont en mètres .*

Baie des Pirates

Cap SierraLeone

not thought capable of understanding or practising them." Participants were those "who are judged marriageable," and after the conclusion of the whole process, more than a month, the "released" girls were "immediately given to the men destined for their husbands." Writing during the same period, Afzelius noted that girls are selected as wives "before the operation" and "given away to be married" about "a fortnight after." *Bondo* instilled a sense of social order. A photograph of new *bondo* initiates and two pairs of adult chaperones on either side, taken near the beginning of the twentieth century by the Freetown photographer Alphonso Lisk-Carew, shows young girls generally averting their eyes (figure 6.5). Alldridge described the "bundu" as a "great order" for knowledge

Fig. 6.5. "Dancing Girls and Bondu Devils, Sierra Leone Protectorate," c. 1915 (photograph by Alphonse Lisk-Carew, Freetown, Sierra Leone)

transfer but noted that "not all of the maidens had been asked in marriage, some being too young."[67]

Betrothed or otherwise, *bondo* instructs girls in domesticity, farming, sexual matters, dancing, and medicine. In certain cases, such as special aptitude or membership of a high-ranking lineage, girls may be taught specialized skills. Bledsoe contends that girls "learn little more than they already knew before they entered the bush" or "if they did not become secret society members," but what cannot be dismissed is the absence of such knowledge on the part of Amistad's orphans. As MacCormack notes, "the emphasis is not on learning new skills so much as on learning new attitudes toward their work." In this way, Kag'ne, Marg'ru and Te'me, who forwent the knowledge acquired in the role of a daughter, would have been trained to "anticipate the role of wife" and the ways in which she "must work cooperatively with her co-wives and her husband's female kin." Because the girls were removed from their homes as young children, deprived of the knowledge acquired as daughters and not prepared for a life of polygyny, the event must have been confusing. Perhaps the girls interpreted participation in *bondo* as an attempt to compel them into marriage.[68]

Perhaps equally confusing, from the perspective of Westernized, ostensibly Christian, girls would have been the notion of secrecy accompanying *bondo*. In scholarly literature *bondo* is generally referred to as a secret society, but in contemporary writing secrecy is more implied that asserted. The term "secrecy" applies more to the rituals undertaken and knowledge imparted than the entire ceremony itself, much of which is very public at the outset and conclusion. Matthews's account of the "very curious" ceremonies suggests direct personal observation or a conversation with an initiate. He wrote, "Every year during the dry season, and on the first appearance of a new moon, the girls of each town" are "collected together" and, "in the night preceding the day on which the ceremony takes place, are conducted by the women of the village into the inmost recesses of a wood." Although he could not enter the "consecrated spot," like Raymond, he doubtless observed the concluding portion wherein the girls were "conducted in person, with music, and their heads and their bodies covered, to every principal person's house in the town." The girls would surely have been terrified of what took place in the *bondo* bush, but it is unlikely they knew precisely what was to happen there. They may have witnessed other ceremonies involving the *bondo* "devils" in Freetown and possibly also in their natal villages as small children. The *bondo* devil, as seen in the image taken by Alldridge, was an individual dressed in a terrifying wooden mask, who ran around the village for several days and nights ceremonially frightening children and causing "pandemonium" (figure 6.6). For Christian girls, any mention of a devil would likely have provoked a visceral response. But the public aspects

Fig. 6.6. *Bondo* initiates and adherents, Mende, c. 1900 (Thomas Joshua
Alldridge, "The Bundu Devil Attended by Her Satellites, a Country Institution
Common Throughout Mendi Land," RCS Y3046F/024; reproduced by kind
permission of the Syndics of Cambridge University Library)

of the ceremonies were also celebratory. Matthews's and Alldridge's accounts
affirm that the public aspects of the ceremonies, at the end of the "few months"
of "concealment," involved a "trifling present" and "adoration" from the observers. Notwithstanding, Raymond indicated that Mar'gru "knew what was done
there" and "would not go."[69]

The central violence in Raymond's phallocentric narrative of *bondo*, however, is the practice referred to problematically as "circumcision." Raymond
implied that a fear of circumcision resided at the heart of the unhappiness of
the girls while in Freetown. And Mar'gru, the eldest and thus most marriage-

able, noted that the men in Freetown "continually annoyed her," suggesting that genital cutting was an expectation for marriage. Whether or not the specific *bondo* society for which Mar'gru, Kag'ne, and Te'me were being groomed practiced a form of genital cutting will never be known. There is considerable disagreement in sources from the eighteenth and nineteenth century about the prevalence of cutting. Matthews describing the "Suzeés and Mandingoes," wrote that "both sexes undergo the operation when they arrive at puberty." With respect to girls, he elaborated further, "The performance of this singular rite on the females is by cutting off the exterior point of the *clitoris*. . . . They are seen by no person but the old woman who performed the operation, and who brings them their provisions daily." With the "body" thus "subdued with pain" and the "mind soften by the gloomy stillness," Matthews asserted, initiates become receptive to inculcation. Afzelius provided conflicting accounts depending on the ethnic group. He noted that several informants stated that girls "undergo" a "kind of operation both young and aged," and that the Susoos and Mandingoes cut the "labia vulvae" (*labia minora* and *majora*). The "operation," he explained, rendered them "fit for a man." But with regard to the Bulom he stated, "It is wrong what Matthews says, that the women cut off their clitoris, it is never done nor can it be." Notwithstanding the fact that Afzelius misquoted Matthews, there is substantive evidence to show that the practices varied among the region's ethnic groups.[70]

It is difficult to grasp the emotional experience of the girls at the prospect of being forcibly taken into a bush and mutilated as a necessity for achieving true womanhood. But Raymond's account suggests they were highly distressed. Rather than a male expectation for marriage, Matthews stated that "the women hold it in such high veneration, that to be reproached with the want of it, is the most villifying [*sic*]" insult "they can possibly use," to the degree that even outsiders were reproached if they relocated to an area where the practice was prevalent. But it is unclear how relocating the group from Freetown to York prevented further attempts to compel them to join a *bondo* chapter. The pressure to conform would likely have been high. MacCormack suggests that the idea that girls are transformed into women through the intervention of *bondo*, rather than leaving matters to nature, provides a rationale for operations on the genitals. She wrote, "By excising the clitoris, a rudiment of maleness, all sexual ambiguity is removed from the incipient woman. She then fits 'purely' and 'safely' into the social structure, free from the 'impurity' and 'danger' of categorical ambiguity." Women informants also told her that the ritual "made them clean." Sociologist Richard Fanthorpe put it more crudely when he stated that young Sierra Leonean women say that, if a clitoris is left uncut, it might grow "uncontrollably" into a penis. To be sure, a physical representation of moral control and moral transformation resides at the heart of the *bondo* ceremony. According to anthropologist Chuck Jedrej, the initiate's "moral transformation" from child to adult occurs via three phases—from novice, to virgin, to bride— each marked by public appearances. Ferme similarly argues that a cultural aesthetic of concealment is fundamental, insofar as overt displays of emotion are morally distasteful and court spiritual danger.[71]

The specific *bondo* chapter to which the girls were to be initiated was also a likely factor, insofar as pain inflicted depended on the specific *sowei* performing the act. Today the practice described as "circumcision" is generally referred to as female genital cutting. MacCormack's interviews of *bondo* participants in the 1970s reveal how a capacity for the "surgery" garnered attention by initiates prior to induction. She observed, "Shortly after entering the Bundu bush, girls experience the surgery distinctive of a Bundu woman in which the clitoris and part of the labia are excised. . . . [A] Bundu woman told me that excision helps women to become prolific bearers of children. A Majo [a cutter] reputed 'to have a good hand' will attract many initiates to her Bundu bush, increasing her social influence in the process." Viewed in this light, the girls may also have been troubled by accounts of the "circumcision" from other girls and women in Freetown.[72]

Whereas the genital cutting of the young girls may have seemed barbaric to their American protectors, missionaries and colonial officials viewed the practice of male circumcision as inconsequential. Members of all three Abrahamic religions practice circumcision of the male foreskin, and it is perhaps because of the congruity with European and North American practice that there are no records of Covey or Ka'le being taken away for genital cutting. A dismissive cultural relativism, however, belied the deeply troubling status of uncircumcised young men in Galinhas and neighboring territories. Early anthropologists identified the ritual of circumcision as one of the region's three most momentous events in a male life, after birth and death. Notably marriage is not among the three, and sociologist Glenn August Caulker explained that uncircumcised men could not marry. It is more likely than not that the silence in the sources about this matter supports the view that both Covey and Ka'le remained uncircumcised throughout their later lives because the rite is generally performed during the *poro* ceremony.[73]

There are several reasons why the absence of a male circumcision narrative is important. In the 1840s, circumcision took place primarily in the context of the *poro* society initiation ceremony. Initiation of boys into men via *poro* provided the new adults with an age set for life, from which stemmed all significant social, cultural, political, and economic relations. Resisting the puberty ritual of circumcision would have constituted a rejection of manhood. Indeed, shortly after Banfield met Ka'le in Kaw-Mendi in 1917, he described how a missionary teacher "called" a local *poro* lodge head to the compound in Mayoso to construct a "Poro Bush" and conduct the circumcision ceremony. "For if a boys is [*sic*] not circumcised he is open to all kinds of ridicule." Perhaps earlier proselytization failures compelled the Christian and Missionary Alliance to open its boarding school to such cross-cultural syncretism. But regardless of the motivation, by forgoing circumcision in the early nineteenth century, Ka'le and Covey effectively guaranteed their exclusion and confined their social world to the mission compound and the missionary endeavor.[74]

Had the two not been kidnapped from their homes and enslaved as small boys, they would have been circumcised in the context of the *poro* society initiation, a ritual ceremony of puberty that occurred throughout Galinhas and neighboring regions whence they originated. American and European visitors observed that the *poro* ceremony was, like *bondo*, partly held in a secluded bush, into which only initiated may venture. Olfert Dapper, who visited the Guinea coast in the seventeenth century, noted that initiates were youths of several ages united in the exuberance of puberty, and they were taught the "law, war, political authority and everything a counselor need[ed] to know." His contemporary Richard Jobson compared the "musicke, drumming, and dauncing" of public festival of the "cutting of Prickes" to theatrical "fayres" in England. Matthews described the "purrah" as a "wise, political institution" that "disseminated throughout the country for the purpose of putting an end to disputes and wars." On return to their villages the initiated had been "transformed" into adults and "gained new life and understanding." The *poro* ceremonies are routinely referred to as "bush schools," and in this way they operated as the primary educational institutions for the transmission of cultural knowledge.[75]

Initiation of the two boys into the age *grade* for *poro* novitiates would have provided the new adults with an age *set* for life, from which would have stemmed all capacity to enact social, cultural, political, and economic relationships. Like *bondo*, entrance to the *poro* bush began with a public call by singing and drumming and may have taken place only once every several years, depending on the size of the community. In this way, the *poro* age grade was not made up of boys of precisely the same year of birth; more commonly it included those for whom puberty had just begun up to and including those several years older, from eight to eighteen. Male seclusion in the *poro* bush lasted much longer than girls in the *bondo* bush. Accounts vary about the length of time, spanning several months to as many as five years or more. Over several centuries, it is likely that the expectations, like practices and beliefs, changed; certainly the practice differed by region and ethnolinguistic group. By the late nineteenth century, an informant to the commission investigating the Mende rebellion against colonial rule, distinguished four different types of *poro*, including the "one-word Porro" or "secret oath."[76]

Notwithstanding the obsession with circumcision on the part of many Western observers, the key element of the *rite de passage* was the acquisition of a *poro* name by which all one's age set peers would forever call their respective co-initiates. This secret name was known only to the age set, and it sealed the secret corporate connection between the youths, a connection they were to carry throughout their adult lives. Matthews described the inviolable "strictest secrecy" as reminiscent of the freemasons. Participation in the school and ceremonies was led by senior grade, including chiefs and big men, and thus entrance into the *poro* age grade also established relationships between respective age sets, consisting of boys of a similar age with a common background and identity, such as the young men photographed by Alldridge (figure 6.7). During the *poro*

Fig. 6.7. *Poro* initiates, Mende, c. 1900 (Thomas Joshua Alldridge, "Poro Boys in Dancing Costume, Juru, Gaura Country, Upper Mende," WA900275; photograph reproduced with the kind permission of the Royal Pavilion and Museums [Brighton and Hove])

Fig. 6.8. Entrance to a *poro* bush, Kenema district, Sierra Leone, 2012

ceremonies, initiates acquired knowledge of sexuality and sexual performance and learned medicinal dances and treatments for a variety of sexual ailments, including impotence; they carried this knowledge with them throughout their lives, and even across the Atlantic. Gangá communities in central Cuba today still perform medicinal ritual dances in an extinct Mende dialect. Were Covey and Ka'le to have entered *poro*, through its grass archway festooned with leopards or other terrifying beasts (figure 6.8), they would have maintained close ties with their respective age sets over a prolonged period and passed through a series of age-related statuses together with their respective peers.[77]

Unlike the Abrahamic covenant performed during infancy, *poro*-based circumcision in the early to mid–nineteenth century took place during puberty rituals. Precisely when and under what circumstances regional cultures adopted the practice is unknown. Gibbs's observation—that of the adults "nearly all been circumcised"—is thus unhelpful in assessing the implications for Ka'le and Covey. But because the villages of Ka'le and Covey were only moderately Islamicized at the time of their kidnapping, if at all, both boys would likely have been uncircumcised when kidnapped. Leonard, inspecting the ninety-eight boys rescued from the *Primeira* in 1832 observed that half were circumcised, possibly because they "belonged to a different tribe," as "their general appearance" seemed "slightly different." Perhaps the circumcised boys were from further inland where Islam was more prevalent. Because of the link to puberty, Koelle, who traveled in the Galinhas region in the 1850s, considered the *poro* circumcision ceremony to be quite unlike "Muhammadanism" and not "connect[ed]" with "any religious ideas." Even Johann Büttikofer, writing in the 1890s after Islamicization had enveloped the Mende, Vai, and Galinhas regions, noted that many boys undergoing *poro*, Muslim or otherwise, were not circumcised until they entered the "belly" bush school. By the mid–twentieth century, Islamicization meant that almost all boys were circumcised prior to *poro* initiation, and any who were not were hastily cut before the ceremonies began. Universally, resisting circumcision would likely have provoked "disfavour" and have been viewed as resisting elevation to manhood. Early European visitors noted that being uncircumcised marked the individual as immature, unruly, and worse, sterile or infertile.[78]

For Ka'le and Covey, exclusion from *poro* also meant that they were bereft of an intrinsic capacity for "supra-ethnic" dispute resolution, the "peace poro." Matthews explained that *poro* guarded against "jealousy, pride, and irritability" and when two "tribes" or "nations" at war sought to make peace, they routinely appealed to a third party "mediator" to act as "umpire," for the "grand fundamental article of the purrah law is, that no blood shall be shed while it is in force." If *poro* meant "unity," as Davidson and others assert, then exclusion from the lodge was exclusion from the lineage. Rediker draws on *poro* to provide a compelling interpretation of how the initial revolt aboard the Amistad coalesced into a "displaced but reconstituted floating Poro Society." From the 1840s and throughout the nineteenth century, the Mende, Gola, and Galinhas regions were consumed with warfare. Missionaries and colonial officials visiting the region witnessed how the peace *poro* could result in the "immediate cessation of hostilities." Both boys would have witnessed extensive fighting, enslavement, and reprisal actions.[79]

On some level, Raymond and others must have been aware of some dimension of Ka'le's and Covey's social exclusion. Upon arrival in Freetown the adults quickly made their missionary companions aware of the "secret" meaning of facial and bodily scars in relation to *poro*. And whereas *poro* may have provided traditional leaders with hierarchical powers to inculcate values and prevent the encroachment of upstarts, without corporate membership, access to such protections for Ka'le and Covey was impossible. Missionaries' accounts analyzed by Yannielli demonstrate that many of the Amistad survivors were embroiled in these internecine conflicts. Covey participated in some of these conflicts, and he exhibited difficulty in maintaining alliances in the rapidly shifting epoch of abolition in the context of the transition to legitimate commerce. Covey "allied himself with a local warlord and was participating in a slaving expedition" in 1845. Raymond alleged that Covey allied with another Amistad survivor, Kinna (known also as Lewis Johnson), to attack the town of Mperri and battled with other survivors, including Fuliwa, Sa, and Sokoma. Raymond wrote in 1844 that the whole region outside the "speck of land" that was Sierra Leone was "still swept, and scourged, and brutalized, by the horrors of slavery." Ka'le, for his part, lived through the violent insurrection against British colonial rule in the 1890s during which, asserts historian Arthur Abraham, *poro* provided continuity and unity. And even in his senior years, "porro" was viewed as "a power for combining the people."[80]

But perhaps equally important, in forgoing *poro* initiation and circumcision, Ka'le's and Covey's actions, like those of the three girls, sealed their social and cultural exclusion and tied their anomalous fate to the mission compound. *Poro* initiates participated in political councils and passed judgments and sentences, including the death penalty. What missionary August Cole identified as "political" *poro* controlled "the established institution of every country, influencing its government and regulating its laws" over all land and age sets. Throughout the nineteenth century and into the twentieth the *poro* councils played an important legislative function; they could be assembled and dissolved quickly. By remaining outside *poro*, Ka'le and Covey were likely unable to trade with particular people or negotiate with chiefs and town councils for access to land or wives.[81]

The social exclusion likely forced upon Ka'le and Covey by non-initiation meant they forever lacked the standing to contract significant social and cultural ties with their kinsmen. Although it was the case that strangers could, and at times did, seize power and control trade—Davidson provides several late nineteenth-century examples and affirms that initiation and agnatic ties were not the exclusive means of ordering social relations—strangers and nonmembers were considered "upstarts" and "mere" boys, who spoiled the country. Because of this they would have had extreme difficulty negotiating a marriage with anyone but a Christian woman affiliated to the fledgling missionary compound. Covey died in 1850 and Ka'le lived until his nineties, at least until 1917, but nothing suggests either married or had a biological family. Perhaps in celibacy, they further solidified their Christian, foreign identities. Unmarried individuals "astonish[ed]" the adult male population of the region. Koelle suggests being full grown and yet unmarried was accorded the hallowed status of "god-man."

Celibacy and monogamy were associated with Christian missionaries and the uninitiated. It is possible that, by remaining outside *poro*, Covey or Ka'le may have been insulated from some of the most extreme violence. Ka'le certainly lived to an exceptional age. But such a view suggests a greater capacity to choose than was likely at their disposal on return to Freetown and settlement in the missionary compound in Kaw-Mendi. In resisting *poro*, the only alternative strategy for social cohesion was the mission compound and the missionary endeavor.[82]

CONCLUSION

Leonard, reflecting on the ideal outcome of return, remarked in 1833 that only "return" to the "happy home" and from which slaves had been "forcibly separated" could forestall the "doom of everlasting banishment from the place" of "nativity." Only reunification with "every loved attachment" could provide the recaptive African with "perfect freedom" and "genuine liberty." Leonard was speaking about slaves captured off the coast of Sierra Leone and brought quickly back to the mainland, such as the survivors of the *Primeira*, whom he witnessed, or Covey's ship the *Segunda Socorro*. Writing in the nineteenth century, he was concerned with adults, and men in particular. But his further observation—that accomplishing this was "impossible"—speaks directly to the peril experienced by all the Amistad Africans because the "country is almost unknown." "Freedom, with nothing to live for, is but a superficial embellishment to the miseries of a wretched existence."[83]

Notwithstanding Leonard's assertion, the myth of family reunification is powerful and attractive. The idea that the Africans left the United States and returned to their families and villages appealed to abolitionist humanitarians in the nineteenth century—and it continues to appeal to the general public and scholars alike today. The persistence of this myth is at least partly because it resonates with a rich tradition of triumphalist "roots"-centered literature and popular media that cling to the hope that the alienation of slavery and transportation can be undone by Atlantic journeys of rediscovery of kinship and commonality. Although specific instances of continuity and connection have been established in a variety of contexts, the mythology of family reunification obfuscates the experience of the child slave. The presence of child slavery then and today not only disrupts romantic Atlantic "remembrances" of kinship, as anthropologist Bayo Holsey argues, but it muddies attempts to insist on the possibility of the recovery from the trauma of slavery in the form of resettlement and reunification.[84]

It would be a profound oversimplification to conclude that the five of Amistad's orphans who returned to Sierra Leone were as prepared for the experience as were their adult companions. Such an uncritical statement belies the complex impact of ideology, philosophy, pedagogy, and religious purpose. In this final chapter I have argued that the specific attitudes of their guardians and protectors not only ill prepared the children for what they were embarking on, but it very clearly narrowed their options and their capacity to resettle and reintegrate. In the United States, Gibbs and others collected important data about the Africans' origins and background, but it was deeply shaped by their respective understanding of family, community, marriage, and childrearing; it made little sense to the children. Furthermore, the children's experiences of education, while in some ways situationally and temporally sensical, significantly narrowed their opportunities upon return. And finally, the children were removed from their cultural context as children and thus deprived of the traditional initiation ceremonies that mark the passage to adulthood.

On their return, Amistad's orphans resisted attempts to reintegrate them based on gender and marital expectations. But they may also have been oblivious to the dimensions of their misunderstanding. Ferme explains that "until children are taught how to use knowledge so that they might achieve real understanding, they are capable only of imperfectly perceiving the world around them and are unable to operate in it according to codes of prescribed social behavior." In remaining uninitiated, Amistad's orphans may have been unwittingly cemented both as outsiders and permanently as children.[85]

EPILOGUE: AN AGE OF CHILD ENSLAVEMENT

The lives of Amistad's orphans provoke us to think about the survival strategies of children in contexts of conflict and social distress. In many ways the children remained socially segregated; their options for cultural reintegration and social advancement were few. Their experiences of enslavement, transportation, liberty, and resettlement deeply shaped their personal outlook and narrowed their perspective. They were permanently detached from those who would have been their social peers and ethnic kinsmen, and even in Kaw-Mendi they remained marginalized from the social and political life of the indigenous communities into which resettlement thrust them. Their experiences of trauma and distress cast them in the permanent status of child. The six children survived childhood, but whether their survival meant they became adults will surely be debated for a long time to come.

Of our imagined slave ship family, the least is known about Antonio. He moved to Montreal, but records from the abolitionist Dougall family provide little insight into what became of him thereafter. The five who returned to West Africa experienced considerable hardship and deprivation, but they were also the most loyal supporters of the mission. Upon relocating from York to Kaw-Mendi, thirty miles from the coast in the midst of a "very extensive" slave trade run by King Tucker, they lived in rudimentary houses, built of wattle, mats, mud, and sawn wooden boards. Their "mud-walled palace" was surrounded by cleared farmland, and they fought constant battles against "bug-a-bugs" to preserve their houses and clothing. They lived in a land enveloped by—according to Wesleyan superintendent Thomas Raston's poetic mind—"wide wastes of accumulating mire and filth," a "loathsome stench and devastating miasmas." The neighboring communities lived in a "semi-barbarous state," subsisting on "food of the simplest description," without "the slightest preparation or dressing," and clung tenaciously to "their pagan rites and customs." And they remained "bitterly opposed to civilization even in its most incipient forms."[1]

Whereas the "principal part of the Mendians" who had been "rescued from the schooner Amistad" had "proved themselves unworthy of the expense and the trouble engaged," at least according to some of the missionaries, the five returning Amistad's orphans were a source of pride to their advocates in the United States and West Africa. The girls were effectively refashioned as the domestic servants of the Raymonds and renamed following their baptism. In a letter to Tappan in October 1844, Raymond explained, "Sarah I have made my housekeeper; Charlotte is cook, and Maria waits upon my wife and does the housework." Kag'ne (Charlotte) lived in the mission compound with the Raymonds until William Raymond died in 1848. She died one month later.[2]

Covey lived on and off with the Raymonds in the mission and became embroiled in the wars in Sherbro and Mende territory that enveloped the compound in 1845–46. His allegiances shifted constantly; in November 1845 he was transporting slaves for Henry Tucker to Galinhas. In 1846 he joined with Kinna and others and led an assault on the town of Mperri and communities neighboring Kaw-Mendi. Eventually he was permanently expelled from the mission along with the remaining adult males. He attempted to return to the missionary fold in 1848–49 and lived on the periphery of the hundred-acre compound. He never married and had no children. In October 1850 he fell ill and believed he was bewitched, perhaps the victim of a "ritual sanction" from a local *poro* lodge. He refused Western medicine and died shortly afterward in the presence of one of Raymond's replacements, John Brooks.[3]

Te'me also resided with the mission into the 1850s, and several accounts suggest she may have located her father in 1853, although this conflicted with her earlier claim that he had passed away.[4] If she was indeed from Te-Congo, only thirty or forty miles from the mission, it may have been a stepfather, a senior lineage male, or her mother's senior brother, any of which might be represented as "father" to an outsider. She was treated as a house servant, or "girl," by the missionary Ann Harnden. She—"Maria Brown of Amistad memory"—worked under the supervision of George Thompson and married Sierra Leone native Thomas Bennett around 1852. "A truly valuable woman" and "a true Christian," she died in 1857; her last words were communicated to Thompson through her husband.[5]

The most detail exists about the remarkable experiences of Mar'gru. She returned to the United States in the mid-1840s and studied at Oberlin College. She was very likely the first female African scholar in a North American tertiary institution. She returned to Sierra Leone and worked as a "missionary teacher" on the mission after several years. She married the "native teacher" Edward Green in 1852, and they may have had one child, although there is no solid evidence. In 1854, members of her family located her in the Kaw-Mendi mission. Although her husband was an early loyal follower of Raymond, and even an informant on the mischief of the adult Amistad males, he was expelled from the mission for adultery in the 1850s. Mar'gru was expelled as well. Thereafter the trail becomes murky. She may have lived until the 1880s.[6]

Ka'le lived on the mission throughout his life. Although early on his Christianity was in question, he eventually converted. Although he fell under the "bad influence" of some of the "men" and caused a considerable "bill of expense" to Raymond and the mission when he first arrived, he eventually settled into the rhythm of the community and became a teacher. He never married but remained a mission stalwart even after the AMA sold the mission to Church of the United Brethren in Christ. Ka'le lived through very turbulent times, including the "native rising" in the 1890s. In 1898 the mission was destroyed and seven missionaries murdered.[7] He survived the extraordinary violence of 1898 and much more. Banfield claimed to have interviewed him in 1917, and the surviving photograph of him from around that time may well have been taken by Banfield himself.

For more than a decade I have pursued a better understanding of how and why child trafficking has emerged as a central issue of twenty-first-century humanitarianism. Since I first encountered child slave biographies in the *Monatsblatt der Norddeutschen Missions-Gesellschaft* in a New York City library in March 1997, I was drawn to the deployment of first-person accounts of child slave "rescue" and "redemption" as a way of mobilizing support for the missionary enterprise in colonial Africa. And I returned to the historical experience of child slaves after reading a published version of a famous letter from Ka'le to John Quincy Adams at the suggestion of Robert Harms. After examining the original handwritten letter in New Haven, I began to wonder how many other firsthand accounts of African slave experiences existed from children written when they were still children. After some preliminary research, I learned that several of the Amistad children had received some limited scholarly attention. These realizations brought my objective into clearer focus: to reunite the children and reconstruct their imagined family, in order to weave together a fabric about children's experiences of illegal enslavement and their quest for autonomy, liberty, and community. Having completed this book, I am more convinced than ever that a better understanding of contemporary child trafficking networks will emerge from closer attention to the rich history of African child smuggling and child slavery.[8]

I offer this book as a way to invigorate debate about the nature of and the extent of child slavery and child smuggling in the Atlantic nineteenth century. For some time African historians have recognized the role of Atlantic abolitionism and "legitimate" commerce in the expansion of slavery and development of new forms of coercion throughout the continent. Over several decades Cuban historians have similarly recalibrated their understanding of the tractability of the slave-based economy in the nineteenth century, infused not only with fresh European migration but also with a regular and strong supply of new captive African labor. North American historians are increasingly cognizant of the fact that the resilience of the antebellum economies stemmed at least in part from an irregular albeit significant influx of slaves via an expansive and highly orchestrated clandestine maritime enterprise; it is untenable that slavery in the southern states was sustained without new imports from Africa and the Caribbean post-1808. Whereas the arrival of *La Amistad* on the shores of Connecticut may have offered proof to abolitionists of a vast subterfuge of which they were no doubt suspicious, today the existence of slave smuggling networks seems less remarkable. By contrast, shifting the focus to the children on the periphery of the famous narrative draws three discrete regional histories into an important new conversation.

The experiences of Amistad's orphans speak directly to the role of children in the persistence, rearticulation, and innovation of Atlantic connections between Africa and the Americas as prohibitions on slave trading unfolded over several decades. This book demonstrates that children were a critical population in nineteenth-century Atlantic slave-trading networks. Children offered slave traders opportunities to evade abolition. For too long the role of African child slaves in the illegal slave trade has been underestimated, in spite of the now well-established fact that for several decades between 35 and 50 percent of Atlantic slave cargoes were children. Slave traders actively sought children in increasing numbers. Child enslavement offered specific capacities to producers and consumers with which they could avoid detection and continue their clandestine activities. Individual slave traders on both sides of the Atlantic specialized in importing children. And they did this because markets in the Americas wanted young slaves.

La Amistad sailed with a handful of children. But the relatively small number of children aboard this one vessel belied the massive scale of illegal child importation into Cuba during the period, and from Sierra Leone in particular. The voluminous data from the period demonstrate powerfully the expanding role of children in the illicit slave-trading enterprise of the mid–nineteenth century. Whereas the story of *La Amistad* is routinely portrayed as exceptional in many U.S. history circles, the underlying slavery narrative is spectacularly normative for the period. The exceptionality of the story resides largely in the fact that the struggle over the identity of the thirty-five African survivors arriving on the steps of the U.S. Supreme Court resulted in liberty and a return voyage to West Africa.

Previous narratives of the Amistad story have tended to focus on the adult males, and the charismatic nature of some of the individuals makes this understandable. But a focus on the children alters our perspective on slavery and the slave trade in five ways. A focus on children shows that children are not so easily categorized in terms of identities and origins. Attention to how children moved highlights the multidirectional movement of child slave voyaging and the discrete spaces inhabited by child mobilities. Scrutiny of the enslavement narratives of the children demonstrates the narrowness of child-specific enslavement practices. Similarly, the incommensurability of the notion of child freedom is revealed by an analysis of the many stages of liberation endured by the children. And finally, the return to West Africa underscores the trauma and anomie experienced in the processes of return and resettlement and how individuals enslaved as children may be trapped in a permanent state of childhood.

In this book I have reconstructed a brief episode in Atlantic history and reunited an imagined slave family. For too long recovering the experiences of African child slaves has seemed an almost impossible task. But this is no longer the case. Together Amistad's orphans permit me to speak about the identities and origins of child slaves, their paths to enslavement, the discrete locations they inhabit and Atlantic spaces within which they move, their paths to liberation, and their capacity to return, resettle, and reintegrate. My hope is that the dynamic definition of orphan and the broader analytical facility accompanying orphanhood claims will be developed by others to further enrich our knowledge of the child slave experience and the deliberate strategies of survival that build on the spectrum of kinlessness imposed on children by enslavement.

And perhaps the concept of orphanhood and the metaphor of orphaning will provide a useful mechanism for interrogating the contemporary experiences of survivors of slavery and trafficking by focusing our attention on their vulnerability and their specific role within the broader humanitarian category of vulnerable populations. The types of kinship structures available to orphans are those that emerge from the self, from intentional personal strategies for survival. The experiences of Amistad's orphans provides a set of apparatuses with which to investigate changes in African family structure wrought by humanitarian interventions, economic upheavals, political unrest, and social transformations caused by the dramatic rise in trafficking.

A reappraisal of the participation of African slave children challenges several prevailing wisdoms, most significantly the notion that the nineteenth century was first and foremost an epoch of abolitionism. If one thing emerges most clearly from the experience of the imagined slave ship family of Amistad's orphans, it is that the wider context in which they journeyed, struggled, and survived was anything but an "age of abolition." While I appreciate that the dynamics of abolition were fascinating and dramatic, an emphasis on legal paradigms, enforcement, and diplomatic interventions does little historical justice to the lived experience of the millions of Africans enslaved and transported during the nineteenth century. Although the trans-Atlantic slave trade was steadily abolished over many decades, total numbers of enslaved actually increased in continental Africa. The trans-Atlantic trade was only one trajectory of a multi-dimensional economy. Abolition did not abolish slavery; in complicated and still unclear ways it altered the paths of slave traders and the mechanisms of enslavement, and it extended the horrors of slavery for millions of women and children. As the trade across the Atlantic waned, the Indian Ocean trade expanded rapidly. The dramatic increase in child trafficking today can only be comprehended by attention to these historical developments.

At the very least, these children's stories may serve as a rejoinder to those historians who consistently and indiscriminately trumpet the achievements of the abolitionism. The lives of the many millions of African children enslaved in the nineteenth century, and the many tens of millions of children enslaved in the twentieth century as well as up to and beyond the present day, belie the triumphalism of abolitionism. The story of Amistad's orphans demands that we dispense with the misidentification of the epoch as an age of abolition and recognize that the early nineteenth century was but the beginning of a new age of child enslavement.

CHRONOLOGY

1795	Pinckney's Treaty establishes commercial relations between United States and Spain.
1807	Great Britain abolishes slave trade.
1808	United States abolishes slave trade.
1811	Spain abolishes slavery at home and in all colonies except Cuba, Puerto Rico, and Santo Domingo.
1814	United States and Great Britain attempt to end slave trade in Treaty of Ghent.
1815	At the Congress of Vienna, Great Britain pressures Spain, Portugal, France, and the Netherlands to abolish the slave trade.
1817–18	Spain signs a treaty with Great Britain agreeing to end the slave trade north of the equator immediately and south of the equator in 1820; British naval vessels are given the right to search suspected slavers.
1819	U.S. law equates slave trading with piracy, punishable by death; United States and Spain renew commercial agreements in the Adams-Onís Treaty; antislavery squadron officially stationed in Freetown, Sierra Leone; Upper Canada attorney general John Robinson declares all black residents of Canada free.
1820	Spain prohibits transportation of African slaves in North Atlantic; first U.S. joint antislavery patrol with Royal Navy.
1824	Great Britain and the United States negotiate treaty categorizing slave trade as piracy. U.S. Senate undercuts the treaty's force; treaty fails.
1825–26	James Covey and Antonio born.
1826	Covey's parents relocate to Golahun; France officially ends all slave trading.
1828–29	Mar'gru born in Gbandebu and Ka'le born; New York State abolishes slavery.
1830–31	Covey kidnapped and sold to Bayemi at Mani; works on rice farm; Kag'ne born in Gbandebu and Te'me born in Te-Congo.
1833	Great Britain ends slavery in all colonies. May: Covey sold to slave traders on coast.

June: Covey bought by José de Inza; put aboard *Segunda Socorro.*

July: *Trinculo* captures *Segunda Socorro;* Covey liberated and apprenticed.

October: Covey transferred to village of Bathurst, "School for Cossoo Boys," with Reverend James Weeks and Samuel Adjayi Crowther.

1835   June 28: Anglo-Spanish agreement about slave trade renewed and tightened. British cruisers authorized to arrest suspected Spanish slavers and bring them before Mixed Commissions in Sierra Leone and Havana; vessels carrying slave-related equipment declared prima facie slavers; all forms of Atlantic transportation of African slaves completely illegal, including coastal movement.

1835–36   Antonio transported from Sierra Leone to Cuba; purchased by Ramón Ferrer in Havana; Portugal abolishes trans-Atlantic slave trade.

1838   October: Covey joins crew of *Buzzard.*

November: *Buzzard* (with Covey) captures *Empreendedor.*

1839   March: *Buzzard* (with Covey) captures *Clara* and *Eagle.*

April: Mar'gru, Ka'le, Te'me, and Kag'ne moved from Lomboko to Havana.

May: Mar'gru, Ka'le, Te'me, Kag'ne in Martínez and Company barracoon; survivors of *Teçora* imprisoned in La Miseracordia barracoon, Havana.

June 12: *Buzzard* arrives in New York with Covey, escorting two American slavers, *Eagle* and *Clara,* to be tried for piracy.

June 22–26: Montes purchases Mar'gru, Ka'le, Te'me, and Kag'ne from Xiques and Azpilaca; obtains passport to transport *ladinos* (blacks born in the New World) to Puerto Príncipe, Cuba.

June: *La Amistad* leaves Havana for El Guanaja with slaves and owners; revolt aboard vessel; Antonio tied up; Mar'gru, Ka'le, Te'me, and Kag'ne free to move around vessel.

July–August: *La Amistad* steered east by day and northwest by night, toward United States.

August: *La Amistad* captured by USS *Washington* off Long Island, New York; Mar'gru, Kag'ne, Ka'le, Te'me, and Antonio held and taken with *La Amistad* to New London, Connecticut.

August 29: Judge Andrew Judson convened a special session of the U.S. District Court for the District of Connecticut. Libels for a salvage submitted. Africans return to *La Amistad* to recount experience. Children held in prison. Adult males held in custody on charges of murder and piracy pending determination of the salvage claim.

September 9: Gibbs meets Covey and Charles Pratt in New York; Tappan, Leavitt, Jocelyn, and others form Friends of the Amistad Africans Committee.

September 17: U.S. Circuit Court for the District of Connecticut impaneled grand jury to consider the indictment for piracy and murder. Justice Smith Thompson rules that the federal courts have no jurisdiction over an alleged crime on a foreign vessel at sea; all criminal charges dismissed.

September 19: Judge Judson opens the district court session to consider the libels filed. U.S. attorney Holabird asks court to consider the Spanish ambassador's request for the return of all property, including Africans; Staples and Sedgwick file habeas corpus writ to seek release of Mar'gru, Kag'ne, and Te'me.

October: Covey in New Haven; Africans are able to communicate their story; teaching of English language and Christianity begins; girls and Ka'le released into custody of Pendleton, jailer.

October 17: Cinque, Fuliwa, and Tappan bring civil suit against Ruiz and Montes for assault and battery and false imprisonment. The Spaniards are arrested in New York City. Covey translates.

October 22: Hearings in the New York Court of Common Pleas. Within a week, the court frees Montes and reduces Ruiz's bail. Montes and Ruiz flee to Cuba.

November: Judge Judson opens district court trial in Hartford. Baldwin seeks dismissal on jurisdictional grounds; Baldwin introduces evidence that the Africans were not legally enslaved; Covey ill; hearing postponed until January in New Haven.

November 25: Publication of Madden's testimony reinforces popular awareness that the survivors are originally from Africa.

December: Barracoons at Lomboko raided by the Royal Navy.

1840　January 7–8: District court trial resumes in New Haven.

January 13: Judson presiding in district court rules the Africans not slaves and are to be turned over to the president for return to Africa; orders Antonio delivered to the heirs of Ferrer; Holabird appeals decision, except pertaining to Antonio.

April 29: Judge Thompson opens appeal at the circuit court at New Haven. Thompson affirms the decision of the district court; Holabird appeals to Supreme Court; writ of certiorari to Supreme Court accepted.

August: Adult Africans taken to Westville prison.

October: Roger Baldwin engages John Quincy Adams to join in arguing the case for the Africans before the Supreme Court.

1841　February 22: Oral arguments begin before Supreme Court; court suspends arguments after death of Justice Barbour on February 25.

March 1–2: Arguments resume and close.

March 9: Justice Joseph Story delivers opinion affirming Africans' freedom. Justice Thompson, as circuit justice for the District of Connecticut, orders their release.

March 15: Writ of habeas corpus filed in New Haven to seek release of Te'me, Kag'ne, and Mar'gru.

March 29: Antonio leaves New Haven for New York by steamer *Bunker Hill*.

March 31: Antonio leaves New York City for Montreal via Albany and Vermont.

April: Mar'gru, Kag'ne, Te'me, and Ka'le go to Farmington, Connecticut.

May: Antonio arrives in Montreal.

June: Covey writes for assistance from New York.

August: Africans ask for Covey to join them; formation of Union Missionary Society by African American abolitionist James W. C. Pennington; girls meet Pennington.

October: Covey comes to Farmington; funds raised for return to Sierra Leone.

November 27: Mar'gru, Kag'ne, Te'me, Ka'le, and Covey leave with missionaries for Africa aboard *Gentleman*.

1842   January: Arrive in Freetown; attempt to subject Mar'gru, Kag'ne, and Te'me to *bondo* and female genital cutting.

March: Relocate to village of York, outside Freetown.

1844–45   Mission at Kaw-Mendi established; Mar'gru, Kag'ne, Te'me, Ka'le, and Covey live in mission.

1846   Missionary William Raymond dies; replaced by George Thompson; Covey leaves mission; the Amistad Committee merges with the American Missionary Association, assuming financial responsibility for the Mendi mission; Mar'gru returns to United States to attend Oberlin College.

1848   Covey capturing slaves in Galinhas; Mar'gru returns to mission; Kag'ne dies; Connecticut abolishes slavery.

1850   October: Covey dies in Kaw-Mendi.

1852   Te'me marries; Mar'gru marries.

1857   Te'me dies.

1858   Mar'gru expelled from mission.

NOTES

26th Congress	"Africans Taken in the Amistad, Congressional Document, Containing the Correspondence, &c., in Relation to the Captured Africans," (New York: Anti-Slavery Repository, 1840), reprint of 26th Congress, 1st Session, Document no. 185, House of Representatives
ACCHC	Amistad Collection, Connecticut Historical Society
ACS	American Colonization Society, *African Repository and Colonial Journal*
AFASR	*American and Foreign Anti-Slavery Reporter*
AHM	Archivo Histórico Provincial, Matanzas, Cuba
AHN	Archivo Histórico Nacional, Madrid
AM	*American Missionary*
AMA	American Missionary Association, Amistad Research Center, Tulane University
ANC	Archivo Nacional de la República de Cuba
Baldwin	Baldwin Family Papers, MSG box 55, folder I/22, Yale University Library and Manuscripts Archive
Barber	John Warner Barber, *A History of the Amistad Captives* (New Haven: E. L. and J. W. Barber, 1840)
BFBS	British and Foreign Bible Society Archive, Cambridge University Library, BSA/E 3/3/633/File 1/January 1916–October 1917
BNA	British National Archives
Campbell	John Campbell Papers, 1795–1814, Duke University Library Manuscript Collection
CA	*Colored American*
CMS	Archives of the Church Missionary Society, Cadbury Research Library, Special Collections, University of Birmingham, U.K.
CO	*Charter Oak*

Covey I   James Covey's first deposition, with additions by Samuel J. Hitchcock, Baldwin Family Papers, MSG 55/I/21/241 (dated October 4, 1839), Yale University Library and Manuscripts Archive

Covey II   Deposition before District Court in Hartford, reproduced before Circuit Court and Supreme Court. Available in numerous anthologies, e.g., United States Supreme Court, *Reports of Cases Argued and Adjudged in the Supreme Court of the United States*, vol. 40 (John Conrad, 1903), 345–46.

Judson   Andrew T. Judson Papers, Coll 247, box 1/7, Manuscripts Collection, Mystic Seaport Museum

LAC   Library and Archives of Canada

LOC   Library of Congress

Madden I   "Deposition of Dr. Richard R. Madden, November 20, 1839, U.S. District Court, Connecticut," reprinted in NYCA, November 25, 1839

Madden II   Case of the Amistad. Deposition of Dr. Madden, November 7, 1839 (printed copy, no publication information), West India Miscellaneous, 1839; vol.: Removal of the Liberated Africans from Cuba, Superintendent Dr. Madden and Superintendent Mr. Clarke, Foreign Office, Correspondence from Dr. R. R. Madden, Mr. D. R. Clarke, and the Foreign Office relating to the removal of the "Liberated Africans" from Cuba, 1839, BNA, CO/318/146

NARA   National Archives and Records Administration, Northeast Region, Waltham, Mass., Records of the District Courts of the United States, RG 21 USDC-CT Case Files, 1790–1915, terms: September 1839–February 1843.

NHCR   *New Haven Columbian Register*

Norton   John Pitkin Norton Papers, MS 367, series 2, box, 3–4, folder 18–19: Diary of J. P. Norton

NYCA   *New York Commercial Advertiser*

NYH   *New York Herald*

NYHS   New York Historical Society

NYJC   *New York Journal of Commerce*

NYMH   *New York Morning Herald*

NYS   *New York Sun*

PPHC   Great Britain, Parliamentary Papers, House of Commons

Rankin   F. Harrison Rankin, *White Man's Grave: A Visit to Sierra Leone in 1834* (London: Bentley 1836), vols. 1 and 2

RE   *Richmond Enquirer*

SNLA   Sierra Leone National Archives, Freetown, Sierra Leone

TASTD   David Eltis, Stephen D. Behrendt, David Richardson, and Herbert Klein, eds., *The Trans-Atlantic Slave Trade* (Cambridge: Cambridge University Press, 2000), CD-ROM

Trial   *Trial of the Prisoners of the Amistad on the Writ of Habeas Corpus Before the Circuit Court of the United States, for the District of Connecti-*

cut, at Hartford; Judges Thompson and Judson, September Term, 1839
(New York, 1839)

UM	Union Missionary
UMH	Union Missionary Herald
Voyages	David Eltis, Stephen Behrendt, David Richardson, and Manolo Florentino, Voyages: The Trans-Atlantic Slave Trade Database, Emory University (http://www.slavevoyages.org)
YULMA	Yale University Library and Manuscripts Archive

INTRODUCTION

1. For more on Banfield, see Fuller, Banfield.
2. Banfield to Ritson, April 10, 1917. "West African Languages." BFBS, BSA/E3/3/633/ File 1/January 1916–October 1917.
3. Barber. The most recent narration of the Amistad saga is that of Rediker, Amistad.
4. Rediker, Amistad, 34, 185; Adejunmobi, Vernacular, vii; also, Smith, "Peace and Palaver," 599–621. The precise phrase also appears in Thompson, Palm Land, 27, written by a former missionary who knew Ka'le personally. For examples, see Forbes, Six Months, 59; Adams, Remarks, 20; Matthews, Voyage, 82; Spilsbury, Account, 12; Clarke, Inhabitants, 328, 355.
5. The literature on oral history is expansive, but for the particular issues of temporality and internal chronologies, see Vansina, "Use of Oral Tradition," 55–82; Henige, Chronology; Miller, African Past; Tonkin, Narrating; White et al., African Words.
6. For child slaves as variously marginal, insignificant, inaccessible, or exceptional, see King, Stolen; Hofstee, "Great Divide"; Lovejoy, "Children of Slavery"; Smallwood, Saltwater Slavery; Manning, Slavery, 98–99; Meillassoux, Anthropology, 134.
7. For the "Age of Abolition" conceptual apparatus, see Drescher, Econocide; Dorsey, Slave Trade; Lambert, White Creole Culture; Brown, Moral Capital; Hochschild, Bury the Chains; Kaufman and Pape, "Explaining"; Huzzey, Freedom Burning. For abolitionist and humanitarian ideologies and personalities, see Vaughan, Statesman; Metaxas, Amazing Grace; Barclay, Thomas Fowell Buxton; Temperley, British Antislavery; Meier, Thomas Clarkson; Lloyd, Navy.
8. I am particularly indebted to two recent volumes: Campbell, Miers, and Miller, Children; Campbell, Miers, and Miller, Child Slaves.
9. Lovejoy, "Background to Rebellion"; Hawthorne, "Being Now," 53–77; Curtin, Two Jamaicas; see also, Goveia, Slave Society, and Mintz and Price, Birth.
10. Rankin, vol. 2, 10.
11. Scott and Hébrard, Freedom Papers, 4–5.
12. Ferme, Underneath, 198: they are often likened to animals or other living things and may acquire names reflecting this because of their inability to control themselves.
13. E.g., "Poor and injured orphans," in "Special Meeting at Kissy," August 28, 1833, CMS/B/OMS/Q A1/O1–2: Minutes of Sub-Committees. Baldwin stated, "Certain persons thought proper to institute a new process, thinking thereby to deprive these interesting but friendless children of the benefit of this writ of habeas corpus." In "Case of the Africans," in Trial, 10.

14. Brown, "Social Death and Political Life," 1246.
15. Bornstein, "Value of Orphans," 123–48; Murdoch, *Imagined Orphans.*
16. Stephens, "Children," 3–48; Zelizer, *Pricing*; Leinaweaver, "Choosing to Move," 376.
17. Bornstein, "Value of Orphans," 128.
18. Sentimentalist historiography argues, generally, that attitudes to children have changed dramatically over time. Preindustrial communities did not distinguish children from adults in many ways; industrialization refigured children as incapable and separated them from adult life. Adherents to this approach include Philippe Ariès, Hugh Cunningham, Edward Shorter, Laurence Stone, J. H. Plumb, and Marc Kleijwegt. Bernstein, *Racial Innocence*, offers a Butlerian performance formula of "surrogation" that compensates for loss incurred through growth. For adolescence, see Mead, *Coming of Age*, and her primary critic, Freeman, *Margaret Mead*; Shankman, *Trashing*; Stevenson, *Life in Black and White*, 257. Nor does the alternative "continuist" approach have little cogency for the child slave experience; "continuists" claim that their archival research suggests that perspectives on childhood and adolescence have been continuous over time and that the experiences of children have changed little. Adherents include Natalie Zemon Davis, Emiel Eyben, Linda Pollock, Steven Ozment, Barbara Hanawalt.
19. Patterson, *Slavery*, 5–7.
20. King, *Stolen*, xviii–xx; Gomez, *Exchanging*; Chambers, "My Own Nation," 72–97; and Hall, *Slavery.*
21. Chatterjee, "Colority Subalternity"; Chatterjee, "Slave's Search"; Brown, "Social Death and Political Life," 1248; e.g., Bogen, *Luckiest Orphans*; Cmiel, *Home*; Zmora, *Orphanages*; Hacsi, *Second Home*; Brown criticizes Hartman, *Lose Your Mother* for her reliance on Patterson's "totalizing" definition, 1239: "those he has inspired have often conflated his exposition of slaveholding ideology with a description of the actual condition of the enslaved."
22. Hawthorne, "Being Now"; Arendt, *Human Condition*. For recent modern biography of orphan survival, see Mundy-Castle, *Mother's Debt.*
23. Barber. The history of the adult captives has been covered in Jones, *Mutiny*. See also, Finkelman, *Slavery in the Courtroom*; Finkelman, *Slavery, Race*; Martin, *Amistad*; Osagie, *Amistad*; among the Amistad captives in Professor Gibbs's records were an adult called Ka-le and a boy child called Ka-li. In almost all subsequent correspondence, including the famous letter to President Adams and secondary material, the child signs himself and is referred to as Ka-le or Carly; Covey I.
24. Rediker, *Amistad*, 160–61: provides an excellent discussion of the pamphlet's creation.

1. "MOST FAVOURITE CARGOES"

1. King, *Stolen*, xx–xxii; Mintz, *Huck's Raft*; Schwartz, *Born in Bondage*; Dunaway, *Slavery*; Hofstee, "Great Divide," 65–66; Eltis, "Age Categories"; see Lewis, *Central Africa*, 322; Thomas, *Cuba*, 162, refers to Ka'le as a "mulécon" but provides no explanation about how, when, or where this term was used.

2. Hofstee, "Great Divide," 82. Even King, who cited Hofstee in her new edition, describes the purchasing of children in terms that imply they were a lesser alternative. King, *Stolen*, xi: "youngsters were sought after by captains interested in filling their holds quickly with 'affordable' chattel"; Lovejoy, "Children of Slavery," 198: "Children largely entered the transatlantic trade in the absence of more preferred adult slaves." See also Smallwood, *Saltwater Slavery*, 71, 158; King, *Stolen*, xxi.

3. Gronniosaw, *Narrative*; Rediker, *Slave Ship*, 104. Contemporary Africanist sociological literature provides for an interesting discussion of how and why children may consent to participate and under what conditions children seek to show respect to adult caretakers or are constrained by power relations in the community. See Ahsan, "Potential"; Nyambedha, "Ethical"; Clacherty and Donald, "Child Participation"; and, Twum-Danso, "Situating."

4. See Eltis et al., TASTD, 10; Smallwood, *Saltwater Slavery*, 163; "James Jones to Lord Hawksbury" (1788), Add. MSS. 38416, fols. 208–12, reprinted in Donnan, *Documents*, vol. 2, 592; "James Jones to Lord Hawksbury" (1788), Add. MSS. 38416, fol. 216, reprinted in Donnan, vol. 2, 592; Campbell, Miers, and Miller, *Children*, 3; Campbell, Miers, and Miller, *Child Slaves*, 1–2.

5. Thompson, *Thompson in Africa*, 18–20. See also, Rediker, *Amistad*, 52–53; García Rodríguez, *Voices*, 29; Eltis, "Age Categories."

6. Wright, *African Philosophy*, 99.

7. "Libel of Pedro Montez," in "Case of the Africans," in *Trial*, 7, the value of $1,300 is accorded the three girls, excluding the one boy; Bergad, "Slave Prices," 653, lists averages prices in 1840 for females aged one to fourteen, in Colón and Matanzas, at 250 pesos and males at 177. See also appendix of slave prices, Bergad et al., *Cuban Slave Market*. See also, Eltis, *Economic*, 198; "Testimony of Antonio, January 9, 1840, U.S. District Court, Connecticut," NARA; Testimony of Antonio, as recorded in "Case of the Africans," in *Trial*, 29. This is consistent with Hofstee, "Great Divide," 87; Christopher, *Slave Ship Sailors*, 53–70; Rediker, *Slave Ship*, 291–301; Custody Trial, March 15–19, 1841, New Haven County Court Records, Connecticut State Library, Hartford.

8. For "plasticity" of childhood, see Wells, *Childhood*, 2; Hopgood, "Language," 112–19; Swain, "Sweet Childhood," 200; Lewis, "Symposium," 75–84; Chess and Hassibi, *Principles*, 3–15. The expansive and expanding "growing up" literature draws effectively on rich personal archival corpuses that originate with or around children, such as children's letters and diaries, journals and books for children, government pamphlets, propaganda, and official manuals. Prominent members of the "growing up" school include Catriona Kelly, Steven Mintz, and Jon Saari; Hofstee, "Great Divide," 67.

9. Handler, "Survivors," 25–56; King, *Stolen*; Diptee, "African Children," 183–96; Lovejoy, "Children of Slavery," 197–217; Ariès, *L'enfant*; Pollock, *Forgotten Children*; Cunningham, *Children of the Poor*; James and James, *Constructing Childhood*; Stearns, *Growing Up*; Fass, *Children*; Anderson-Levitt, "Schoolyard Gate," 987–1006; King, *Stolen*, xviii–xx; Handler, "Survivors"; Lawrance, "All We Want," 13–36; Manzano, *Life and Poems*.

10. Law, *From Slave Trade*; Lawrance and Roberts, *Trafficking in Slavery's Wake*.

11. Sweet, *Recreating Africa*; Hawthorne, *From Africa*; Carney, *Black Rice*; Stampp, *Peculiar Institution*; Elkins, *Slavery*. The literature on the slavery/freedom binary is immense, and I cannot do it justice in a footnote. But I am particularly drawn to the "joined at the hip" metaphor of Huggins, *Black Odyssey*, xliv. For an excellent model of how to problematize the binary notion of slavery and freedom via an alternative but parallel lens, see Glickman, *Living Wage*; Greene, *West African*; Diptee and Klein, "African Childhoods," 4. See, for example, Reynolds, *Dance Civet Cat*; Grier, *Invisible Hands*; Price, "Changing Value," 411–36; Gottlieb, *Afterlife*; Shadle, "Girl Cases"; Wright, *Strategies*.

12. King, *Stolen*, 26; for Middle Passage tropes see Diedrich et al., *Black Imagination*.

13. Lovejoy, "Children of Slavery," 200; Smallwood, *Saltwater Slavery*, 163–65, 173; Brown, *Reaper's Garden*, 46. See Lovejoy, *Transformations*, 65–66, 143; Manning, *Slavery*, 99. In the "declining years" the trans-Saharan trade was "focused almost exclusively on children." Klein, "Women and Slavery," 76; Hofstee, "Great Divide," 64–106. Between 1831 and 1850, among slaves shipped from the Congo, children constituted 51 percent; see Vos, "Without the Slave Trade," 47; Hofstee tested various hypotheses about the ratio of children to adults, versus tonnage of ships, and the ratio of boys to girls, to evaluate whether merchants were forced to purchase children by the market and not by preference. Mariana Candido cites cases from the 1730s where children were lumped together with people with "physical disabilities" as part of the royal tax of one-fifth as they had "less commercial value," in the port of Benguela (Candido, *African Slaving Port*, 180, 206). Hofstee, "Great Divide," 70; Voyage 18076, *Maria* (1791), cited by Hofstee, "Great Divide," 72, 76.

14. Conrad, *Children of God's Fire*, 31; Ricketts, *Six Months*, 87; Testimony of Jose Cliffe, M.D., before House of Commons of Great Britain, Select Committee, reprinted in Philadelphia Meeting of Friends, *Exposition*, 154; Hofstee, "Great Divide"; *Voyages*, Voyage ID 2071; PPHC, vol. 49 (1845), 593–633; BNA, FO84/383, ADM, 41.03.31; Dalleo, "Africans in the Caribbean," 24. This is certainly an outlier and possibly a novice trader. Dorsey, *Slave Trade*, 145, notes the captain was the only Puerto Rican Creole to sail a vessel from Africa; Ricketts, *Six Months*, 87; Raymond to anon., August 26, 1844, *UM*, vol. 50 (January 1845), 8.

15. Murray, *Odious*, 40–49; *Exposition*, 91. Forbes, *Six Months*, 90–91, stated that a ship's crew could make £250 per 100 slaves disembarked alive in Cuba. In 1838, a "clear voyage" could make a "captain of the flag" £100–200. A "pilot" could "clear a thousand pounds a voyage," and it was "quite possible" to make three voyages a year; Madden, "In Re, Slave Trade," in Madden, *Poems*, 133; Forbes, *Six Months*, 101, describes how "speculators" financed the innovation of large armed steamers capable of carrying 3,000 slaves; Philadelphia, *Exposition*, 41; Raymond to Raston, August 26, 1844, and Raymond to anon., August 26, 1844, *UM*, vol. 50 (January 1845), 6, 8. Comparative data on slave children prices in Sierra Leone is difficult to find. Most prices were presumably for adult slaves. Forbes, *Six Months*, 77, states adults in the 1840s were ten shillings or one musket, but on page 57 he notes that one "domestic slave" was "sixty bars," which was equivalent to sixty shillings "of our money" or six muskets. In

1850, Thompson, *Palm Land*, 181, 186, noted the "full price of a slave" at £5 or $24, and the price in Kittam and Bom as $5 to $20. For Abomey in the 1810s and 1820s, a "prime slave" was £14, according to Adams, *Remarks*, 64. Slaves sold in Rio in the early 1840s went for £55 cash, or £77 in three annual installments, but in 1846 never lower than $320 or £64 (Philadelphia, *Exposition*, 68, 79); Philadelphia, *Exposition*, 154–55.

16. Campbell, Miers, and Miller, *Children*, i, employs the term "malleable." Rankin, vol. 2, 92; Madden, "In Re, Slave Trade," in Madden, *Poems*, 131; Roberts, "End of Slavery," 80.

17. "Narrative of the Africans," *NYJC*, October 10, 1839; also *Trial*, v; Vos, "Without the Slave Trade," 48–49; Eltis and Engerman, "Slave Trade," 238; Eltis and Engerman, "Fluctuations," 318; Hogerzeil and Richardson, "Slave Purchasing," 160–90.

18. Lovejoy and Richardson, "Trust, Pawnship," 335–36; Lovejoy and Richardson, "Business of Slaving," 67–89; Lovejoy and Falola, *Pawnship in Africa*; Ferreira, *Cross-Cultural*, 79–80. For a reassessment, see Lovejoy, "Pawnship, Debt."

19. Matthews, *Voyage*, 156; Ferreira, *Cross-Cultural*, 80; Spilsbury, *Account*, 40. See also Sundstrom, *Trade of Guinea*, 36–45; Howard, "Pawning," 273–78; Hair, "Enslavement," 193–203; Kea, *Settlements*; Miller, "Significance of Drought," 17–61.

20. See also Alagoa and Okorobia, "Pawnship in Nembe," 74, and Ekechi, "Pawnship," 83–104; Diptee, "African Children," 187.

21. Rodney, *History*; Lovejoy, *Transformations*; Candido, *African Slaving Port*, 10; Rediker, *Amistad*, 37–39; Forbes, *Six Months*, 102–3; For sale by family members, see Piot, "Of Slaves," 31–49; Miller, *Way of Death*, 380, 668; Miller, "Significance of Drought," 17–61. For enslavement of children as punishment for parents' actions, see Thornton, "Slave Trade," 41, 44; Candido, *African Slaving Port*, 210; For general information about separation and the middle passage, see Smallwood, *Saltwater Slavery*; Bergad et al., *Cuban Slave Market*; Madden I; Handler, "Survivors," 32.

22. For the "pelagic phase" of abolition, see Lawrance and Andrew, "Neo-Abolitionist Trend," 599–678; Zeuske, "Rethinking," 5; Dorsey, *Slave Trade*; Brown, *Reaper's Garden*.

23. Murray, *Odious*; Ackerson, *African Institution*; Carey, *British Abolitionism*; Brown, *Moral Capital*; Getz, *Slavery*; Klein, *Slavery and Colonial Rule*; Searing, *West African*; Law, *From Slave Trade*; Thomas, *Slave Trade*, 513–36.

24. Falola and Lovejoy, "Pawnship," 9, 22.

25. Raymond to Raston, August 26, 1844, *UM*, vol. 50 (January 1845), 6; see Eltis, *Economic Growth*, 149.

26. Fourth Disclosure in No. 86, Mr. Crawford to Captain General, November 19, 1844, in Great Britain, Immigration Commission, *General Report*, 1845, 108; "Answer of S. Staples, R. Baldwin, and T. Sedgewick, Proctors for the Amistad Africans, to the several libels of Lt. Gedney et al. and Pedro Montes and Jose Ruiz," January 7, 1840, NARA.

27. See Vaughan, *Statesman*; Hochschild, *Bury the Chains*; Metaxas, *Amazing Grace*; Barclay, *Thomas Fowell Buxton*; Temperley, *British Antislavery*; Meier, *Thomas Clarkson*; Lloyd, *Navy*.

28. Thomas, *Slave Trade*, 513–36; Eltis and Engerman, "Was the Slave Trade"; Vos, "Without the Slave Trade."

29. Menschel, "Abolition Without Deliverance," 188, 192–93. Davis, *Inhuman Bondage*, 16 asserts, inaccurately I think, that Lt. Gedney landed *La Amistad* in Connecticut because he knew slavery was still legal and hoped to profit. As Menschel explains, it is a profound oversimplification to assert that slavery was legal. Moreover, the Nonimportation Act explicitly prohibited the delivery of new slaves into the state. Notwithstanding this observation, an examination of the 1840 census data for New Haven reveals a curious and sudden rise in the number of slaves "owned" by its citizenry, indicating that captives were listed as property of the New Haven jailer (U.S. Bureau of the Census, Sixth Census of the United States, 1840, M704). For additional discussion of the Connecticut law of slavery see also, Johnson, "Amistad Case," 21. For the illegality of the imprisonment, see Adams, *Argument*, 4.

30. 40 U.S. 518 (1841) at 588. Pickney's Treaty was also known as the Treaty of San Lorenzo or the Treaty of Madrid. Articles VI, VII, X, and XV pertain to the treatment of vessels, parties, and cargo aboard. Treaty of Friendship, Limits, and Navigation between Spain and the United States, October 27, 1795; Adams, *Argument*, 87. See also Jones, *Mutiny*; Gardiner, *Treatise*, 197–98.

31. Adam Jones first described Lomboko as a corruption of Dumbocoro. See Jones, *From Slaves*, 51. Spielberg's choice of El Morro, San Juan, raised "Lomboko" to inappropriate prominence. See Lemisch, "Black Agency," 68, n.21; Harms, "Transatlantic," 67; Osagie, *Amistad*, 4.

32. Several adult males were captured "on land on the east end of Long Island" (New York State), and additional matters pursuant, including whether the District Court of Connecticut had jurisdiction, were never resolved. Copy of excerpt of letter by Staples to Tappan, April 6, 1841, in Baldwin 252.

33. Hannah Moore to William Harned, October 12, 1852, AMA; Weigold, *Hannah Moore*, 32–80; HMS *Lily*, Commanded by John Reeve, of the Second Division of the West African Station, boarded and seized vessels off the coast of Sierra Leone between 1837 and 1839. This vessel is almost certainly Pedro Blanco's *Cirse*. *Voyages*, Voyage ID 2590; Lawson, *Three Sarahs*, 4, n.4; Kaufmann and Pape, "Explaining," 631–68.

2. THE ORIGINS OF AMISTAD'S ORPHANS

1. *United States v. Amistad*, 40 U.S. 518 (1841), 593. Here "Mendi" is used to denote the historical and textual identification of the period, and "Mende" is used to distinguish contemporary writing and documentation about language and ethnicity.

2. Barber, 27. The problematic words "tribe" and "tribal" appear sporadically in a variety of documents. Often "people" takes the place of "tribe." "Introductory Narrative," in *Trial*, iv.

3. Jones, "Recaptive Nations," 42–57. Ethnic or national origins have been used to support many and varied arguments, ranging from agricultural practices and technology to political outlook and rebelliousness. Records from the period prior to abolition

exist in a variety of archival contexts, ranging from purchase contracts, ship logs, and import-export documents to baptismal records, inquisition trials, and planta-tion journals. With the prohibition of the trans-Atlantic trade, a new source of "pre-orthographic" slave names emerged from Registers of Liberated Africans in Freetown, Havana, and St. Helena, spanning 1808 to 1863. Almost 100,000 individual Africans have been identified by name in the registers of the British and the Sierra Leone na-tional archives. And the Havana and Sierra Leone registers often list country of origin. These voluminous sources are transforming the understanding of the trans-Atlantic trade, and new methodologies have been developed to synthesize the data. Holsoe, "Cassava-Leaf People"; Davidson, "Trade and Politics"; Njoku, "Labor Utilization"; Abraham, *Mende*; Dorjahn and Isaac, *Essays*; Richards, *Indigenous*; Day, *Gender*. To the best of my knowledge, no evidence of the children's country marks has yet come to light. For the significance of such marks generally, but not about children, see Gomez, *Exchanging*.

4. Baldwin, *Argument* (1841), 4–13, 15, 19, 23–32. "Introductory Narrative," in *Trial*, iv. Booth to Tappan, July 27, 1841, AMA, #F1-5038; Gibbs to Tappan, July ?, 1841, AMA, #F1-5042; Norton to Tappan, August 27, 1841, AMA, #F1-5056. See Jones, *From Slaves*, 45–53, for discussion of languages.

5. *Trial*, iv, 24, 27–28. "Plans to Educate the Amistad Africans in English," *NYJC*, Octo-ber 9, 1839; "The Captured Africans of the Amistad," *NYMH*, October 4, 1839; "Ex-traordinary Arrest," *NYMC*, October 18, 1839; "Domestic News—From the N.Y. Star," *RE*, October 25, 1839; Owens, *Black Mutiny*, 313; Edwards, *Abolitionists*, 53; "Trial," *NYMH*, November 22, 1839: "The Amistad case has got the go by, and the parties will have to commence again di novo, on the 7th of January. James Covey, the Buzzard interpreter, has an attack of the gout, or some similar disorder, contracted under the luxurious feed of the New Haven theological students, and the court has adjourned in order to give the savans a chance to nurse up the nigger."

6. "African Testimony," *NYJC*, January 10, 1840; *Trial*, iv; "*Gedney v. Amistad* 1839," box 33 of 183, NARA; "African Testimony," *NYJC*, January 10, 1840.

7. ACS, 1839, 318; Gibbs, "Mendi," "Vai."

8. Gibbs to Tappan, July ?, 1841, AMA, #F1-5042; Booth to Tappan, July 27, 1841, AMA, #F1-5038.

9. Barber, 25–28.

10. Barber, 27.

11. Barber, 29.

12. *Trial* (reprinted in Finkelman, *African Slave Trade*). One theory concerning Cinquez was that he was Kru, or a "Crumen." "The Captured Africans of the Amistad." *NYMH*, October 4, 1839.

13. Winterbottom, *Account*; "*Gedney v. Amistad* 1839," box 33 of 183, NARA; Barber, 9–15. For further discussion of Griswold, see Sale, *Slumbering*, 93–96.

14. Brunton, *Grammar*; Nyländer, *Grammar*; *Trial*, iv.

15. "The Amistad Case," *Evening Star*, January 9, 1840; "*Gedney v. Amistad* 1839," box 33 of 183, NARA; "African Testimony," *NYJC*, January 10, 1840, 2; Weiner, *Black Trials*, 122.

16. "Case of the Africans," in *Trial*, 28: Ferry "was not a native of Gallina . . . came from Gallina to the West Indies." Hungerford, September 20, 1839, in "Case of the Africans," in *Trial*, 34; "Case of the Africans," in *Trial*, 28.

17. Madden I.

18. NYCA, November 25, 1839; Trist, "Case."

19. Eltis, *Economic Growth*, 198, suggests a bribe of approximately 10 percent of the cost of the slave.

20. Bethell, "Mixed Commissions," 70–93; Madden I.

21. Madden I.

22. "*Gedney v. Amistad* 1839," box 33 of 183, NARA; "Testimony of Mr. D. Francis Bacon," reprinted in NYCA January 13, 1839; also in Barber, 21.

23. Yannielli, "Dark Continents"; Barber, 21; "Testimony of Mr. D. Francis Bacon," reprinted in NYCA January 13, 1839.

24. *Twelfth Annual Report of the American Colonization Society* (Washington, D.C.: James Dunn, 1837), 22; Barber, 21: "In the evidence given, I have therefore been careful to make use of no circumstances relating to the traffic of which I was thus informed, and to which are not facts of common notoriety on the coast among those who have never been at Gallinas. To those Spaniards at Gallinas and New Sesters, I can never forget my numerous and weighty obligations."

25. Madden I; "Case of the Amistad," *RE*, September 24, 1839, p. 2; "To the Committee on Behalf of the African Prisoners," *NYJC*, September 10, 1839: "The little girls, and the negro boy, Antonio, are committed as witnesses, 'for neglecting to become recognized to the United States with surety,' and Shinquau and his comrades are bound over 'for murder on the high seas.'"

26. "The Captured Slaves—Their Curious Position," *NYMH*, September 2, 1839; "To the Committee on Behalf of the African Prisoners," *NYJC*, September 10, 1839; "African Captives in Court," *CA*, September 28, 1839; "The Case of the Amistad," *RE*, September 24, 1839.

27. "In the Matter of the Habeas Corpus for the Three African Girls, September 1839 term," NARA; "Case of the Africans," in *Trial*, 27–28; "Deposition of John Ferry," September 7, 1839, NARA; Bahoo is likely "Ba-u" number sixteen in Gibbs's list. Barber, 12; "Case of the Africans," in *Trial*, 8. For signs, see Silva, "Signs."

28. "Deposition of John Ferry, September 7, 1839," NARA; "Deposition of Augustus Hanson," NARA; Fairhead et al., *African-American*, 15.

29. "In the Matter of the Habeas Corpus for the Three African Girls, September 1939 term," NARA; "Case of the Africans," in *Trial*, 24.

30. ACS, 1839, 317–18.

31. ACS, 1839, 317; Barber, 9; a hand-drawn map accompanied a letter from Booth to Tappan, October 4, 1841, AMA, #F1-5075A.

32. Madden I.

33. Davidson, "Trade and Politics," 30; Afzelius, *Journal*, April 17, 1795; Bruun, *Universal Geography*, 231; Corry, *Observations*; Conder, *Modern Traveller*, 236. For other references to "Windward" and "Rice Coast," see Carney, *Black Rice*, 90; Wood, *Black Majority*, 59. For "Kru Coast," see Rankin, vol. 1, 336. For contemporary references to

"Grain Coast," see Bell, *System*, 497, 489; Mitchell, *Accompaniment*, 433: "derived its name from the Guinea-pepper, or grains of Paradise . . . a delicious luxury." Johnson, *Physical*, 386, identifies the name "Grain Coast" as "from the grains of the Meleguetta pepper, which it yields abundantly, and inland to the mountain edge of the plateau." See also figure 3.4 from Bouët-Willaumez, *Description nautique*; Bell, *System*, 492; Barber, 21–26; Mitchell, *General*, 550.

34. Rodney, *History*, 2; Taunton Hydrographic Office, L2534, possibly meaning "cloudiness"; Burton, "Observations," 287; Koelle, "Narrative," 16; Conneau, *Slaver's Log Book*, 246. The 1976 republication of Conneau or Canot is important. See Jones, "Theophile Conneau"; Hall, "Abolition," 33–36.

35. Purdy, *Memoir*, 71; Barber, 14; Murray, *Encyclopædia*, 1229: the Sherbro River is navigable for "twenty leagues up"; Boyle, *Practical*, 302; Murray, *Encyclopaedia*, 1210; Laing, *Travels*, and Caillié, *Travels*, vol. 1. Thirty years later, they were still the primary source of information. See Knight, *English Cyclopaedia*, 113; Bell, *System*, 492–94, 497.

36. Davidson, "Trade and Politics," 48; Matthews, *Voyage*, 106; Pedro Martínez to Angel Jimenez, September 26, 1838. PPHC, vol. 49 (1839), 38–39; Bell, *System*, 494; Brun, *Universal*, 230. Carney, *Black Rice*, 15–16, 21–22, 29, notes that "rice proved so abundant" along the "rain-fed environments" of the Sierra Leone coast, that slavers "routinely purchased it for provisions." Indeed by the late eighteenth and early nineteenth centuries, the "Rice Coast . . . centered on the region around Sierra Leone." Barber, 15. Pungwuni "was employed in cultivating rice" by his slave master. Bahoo was enslaved on his way "to plant rice," and Ngahoni was also "seized" in a "rice field." For Samuel Gamble's description of Baga rice cultivation methods, see Mouser, *Slaving Voyage*; Little, *Mende*, 77; Njoku, "Labor Utilization," 6–11, 20; Karr et al., "Economics"; Njoku, "Economics"; Hawthorne, *Planting Rice*; See also Hawthorne, "From 'Black Rice'"; Fields-Black, *Deep Roots*; Davidson, "Trade and Politics," 19.

37. Njoku, "Labor Utilization," 26–28, 80; Barber, 9–15, 24–27; Little, "Mende Farming Household," 40; Gomez, *Exchanging*, 92–93; Day, *Gender*, 45–93; Davidson, "Trade and Politics," 7–10, 14, 16, citing H. U. Hall, *The Sherbro of Sierra Leone* (Philadelphia, 1938); d'Azevedo, "Setting," 43–125; also d'Azevedo, "Common Principles."

38. Davidson, "Trade and Politics," 9, 44, 48; Koelle, "Narrative," 10, 13, 14; d'Azevedo, "Tribe," 10–29. For debate about the Mende encroachment, invasion, or settlement of the region, see Person, "Les Kissi"; Rodney, "Reconsideration"; Person, "Ethnic Movements"; Davidson, "Trade and Politics," 41; Massing, "Mane," 21–55; Murphy, "Patrimonial," 24–52; d'Azevedo, "Some Historical Problems."

39. Davidson, "Trade and Politics," 73, citing records from the missionary George Brooks from 1852; Jones, *From Slaves*, 4–5, 55–80; Misevich, "On the Frontier," 26; d'Azevedo, "Setting," 55–56; Davidson, "Trade and Politics," 23, 57, 60–61, 66, 70.

40. "Galena" or "Gallinas" was, by some measure, a derogatory term used to describe variously the coast, and also the Vai country and language, after the Portuguese word for guinea fowl. See Jones, *From Slaves*; interview with Tazieff Koroma, April 26, 2012, Freetown, Sierra Leone, by Benjamin N. Lawrance; Despicht, "Short History," 5, 10.

41. E.g., Carney, *Black Rice*; Midlo Hall, *Slavery*; Hawthorne, *Africa to Brazil*; Trotman and Lovejoy, *Transatlantic*; Adderley, "New Negroes"; Barcia, *Great African Slave*

Revolt. Rodney, *History,* 95–113; Misevich, "Origins," 163; Klein and Luna, *Slavery in Brazil,* 214.

42. Jones, "Recaptive Nations," 53.

43. "Introductory Narrative," in *Trial,* iv; Testimony of Don José Ruiz, August 29, 1839, in Barber, 7.

44. Barber, 15; Hair, "Ethnolinguistic Inventory," parts 1 and 2; Hair, "Ethnolinguistic Continuity"; *UM,* vol. 1, no. 2, 71. Konrad Tuchscherer conveyed to me the belief that "the name is an archaic Mende name. 'Magulu' or 'Magalu' translates in Mende as 'Cherish' or 'Love Deeply.'" (Personal communication by email June 8, 2012).

45. "The Captured Slaves—Their Curious Position," *NYMH,* September 2, 1839; "To the Committee on Behalf of the African Prisoners," *NYJC,* September 10, 1839; "African Captives in Court," *CA,* September 28, 1839; "The Case of the Amistad," *RE,* September 24, 1839; Thompson, *Thompson in Africa,* 241–65; Brooks to Thompson, August 25 and October 5, 1850, AMA.

46. John Ferry, as reported in "The Amistad Circuit Court Trial," *NYCA,* September 23, 1839; Barber, 15.

47. Ten of the Amistad survivors adopt European names between January and March 1842, upon arrival in Sierra Leone. See *Anti-Slavery Reporter,* June 20, 1842; "The Mendi Mission," *Cleveland Daily Herald,* July 11, 1842 (both based on a letter by William Raymond). Thanks to Marcus Rediker and Joseph Yannielli for assistance with this matter; Lawson, *Three Sarahs;* Cable, *Black Odyssey;* Osagie, *Amistad;* Owens, *Amistad,* 288; interview with Isabela de Aranzadi, Freetown, Sierra Leone, April 28, 2012, by Benjamin N. Lawrance.

48. Letter from Viscount Greenwich, October 4, 1832, concerning slaves liberated from Portuguese vessel *Rosa,* in Colonial Correspondence, 1833, SLNA; Misevich, "On the Frontier," 181; for English names of Galinhas chiefs, see Despicht, "Short History."

49. Childs, "Language Contact."

50. The "slave wars" usually refers to the "Machete Wars" of the 1870s to 1890s in Mendeland, the prelude to formal British colonization. See Abraham, *Mende;* Jones, *From Slaves;* Day, *Gender.* Interview with El Hadji Moussa Kpombai, May 1, 2012, Gbendebu, Sierra Leone; interview with the paramount chief of Dama, El Hadji Samdi Momoh Fowai, May 1, 2012, Gbendebu, Sierra Leone, by Benjamin N. Lawrance.

51. Williamson and Blench, "Niger–Congo," 11–42; Bendor-Samuel and Hartell, *Niger–Congo;* Grégoire and de Halleux, "Etude lexicostatistique," 53–71. For Mande, see Kastenholz, *Sprachgeschichte;* Koelle, *Polyglotta Africana.*

52. "To the Committee on Behalf of the African Prisoners," *NYJC,* September 10, 1839; d'Azevedo, "Tribe and Chiefdom."

53. Turay, "Language Contact"; see diagram 5 in Jones, "Who Were the Vai?" 172, 174; this article built on the famous articles by Thomas, "Who Were the Manes?" For evidence of Vai as a nineteenth-century trade language, see Anderson, *Narrative,* 39. Jones, "Who Were the Vai?" 176; Barry, *Senegambia,* 20; Barber, 9–15.

54. "To the Committee on Behalf of the African Prisoners" *NYJC,* September 10, 1839; Brenzinger et al., "Language Death"; Batibo, *Language;* Misevich, "Origins," 162–63.

55. Barber, 15. For "Ko-le" and the African Names Project, see Anderson et al., "Using Pre-Orthographic African Names." Interview with paramount chief of Dama, El Hadji Samdi Momoh Fowai, May 1, 2012, Gbendebu, Sierra Leone, by Benjamin N. Lawrance; "Testimony of Fuliwa," January 8, 1840, NARA.

56. Sweet, "Mistaken Identities," 279–306; Rediker, *Amistad*, 65, calls him "Afro-Cuban." Janes to Baldwin, August 31, 1839, AMA, #F1-4594; NYJC, September 12, 1839; "The Captured Africans," *NYMH*, September 18, 1839, p. 2; *Trial*, iii, 29, 34, 42; "The Amistad Circuit Court Trial," *NYCA*, September 23, 1839; "Case of the Africans," in *Trial*, 29; Barber, 24; "Claim of Spanish Vice Consul for Antonio," box 33 of 183, NARA; *NYCA*, January 15, 1840.

57. Janes to Baldwin, August 31, 1839, AMA, #F1-4594.

58. "The Captured Slaves—Their Curious Position," *NYMH*, September 2, 1839; Testimony of Don José Ruiz, August 29, 1839, in Barber, 7; "Testimony of Antonio, January 9, 1840, U.S. District Court, Connecticut," NARA; "Testimony of Henry Green, November 19, 1839, U.S. District Court, Connecticut," NARA; "Herald on Amistad Trial," *NYMH*, November 21, 1839; Barber, 10.

59. Importantly, Cinquez testified that, "The cook could not speak the Mendi language but used some words that they could understand." "African Testimony," *NYJC*, January 10, 1840, 2. "The Captured Slaves—Their Curious Position," *NYMH*, September 2, 1839; "Testimony of Antonio, January 9, 1840, U.S. District Court, Connecticut." On the curious origins of "Gangá" and its appearance in Cuba, see Misevich, "Origins," 163–64; Barcia, *Great African*, 15–16; Barcia, *Seeds*, 20–22; Garcia Rodriguez, *Voices*.

60. NYS, August 31, 1839; NYJC, September 2, 1839.

61. Tappan to Leavitt, "Excursion with the Amistad Africans," in Sturge, *Visit*, xliv; Janes to Baldwin, August 31, 1839, AMA, #F1-4594; For removal of "manacles" or shackles immediately prior to seizure, see Captain Fitzgerald's statement in the *NYCA*, November 15, 1839. Also, Leonard, *Records*; Walsh, *Notices*; and Rankin, *White Man's Grave*.

62. Zeuske and García Martínez, "La Amistad"; "Testimony of Antonio, January 9, 1840, U.S. District Court, Connecticut"; "The Captured Africans," *NYMH*, September 18, 1839, p. 2.

63. Barber, 15.

64. I am grateful to Tucker Childs for clarification about the current scholarly classification of these languages. See Childs, *Grammar of Mani*. Jones, "Who Were the Vai?" 159–78; Childs, *Grammar of Kisi*; Childs, *Dictionary of the Kisi*; Prichard, *Researches*, 75. The best map for this is to be found in Jones, "Who Were the Vai?" 160. For broader discussion of the region, see Hair, "Ethnolinguistic Inventory," part 1, 47–73.

65. Massing, "Segmentary," 1, 9 n.1; see also Person, "Ethnic Movements"; Hawthorne, *Planting Rice*; Childs, *Grammar of Kisi*, 4–5: wives were often given to strangers. Childs, "Mande and Atlantic Groups." For acephalous, see Hawthorne, "Nourishing," and Hubble, "View."

66. For farming practices, see Lovejoy, "Kola." Also, Parsons, *Religion*; Jackson, *Kuranko*. Interview with Esther Mokuwa and Paul Richards, April 27, 2012, Freetown, Sierra

Leone, by Benjamin N. Lawrance. Interview with Tazieff Koroma, April 26, 2012, Freetown, Sierra Leone, by Benjamin N. Lawrance; Shennan, *Archaeological*, 128–29.

67. Barber, 15. See Ferme, *Underneath*, 205; interview with Taziff Koroma, April 26, 2012, Freetown, Sierra Leone, by Benjamin N. Lawrance; interview with the paramount chief of Dama, El Hadji Samdi Momoh Fowai, May 1, 2012, Gbendebu, Sierra Leone, by Benjamin N. Lawrance; interview with Esther Mokuwa and Paul Richards, April 27, 2012, Freetown, Sierra Leone, by Benjamin N. Lawrance.

68. Barber, 15; Covey I; interview with Esther Mokuwa and Paul Richards, April 27, 2012, Freetown, Sierra Leone, by Benjamin N. Lawrance; Gibbs, "Mendi."

69. Gibbs, "Mendi," 48. A much more extended version exists in ACS, 1839, 317–18. Interview with Taziff Koroma, April 26, 2012, Freetown, Sierra Leone, by Benjamin N. Lawrance. Misevich, "Origins," 169. I offer my thanks to Philip Misevich for his assistance with this matter. Interview with El Hadji Moussa Kpombai, May 1, 2012, in Gbendebu, Sierra Leone, by Benjamin N. Lawrance. Gibbs notes that "Kon-no-ma" (no. 4 in his list) "was born in the Konno country; his language is not readily understood by Covey." Barber, 10.

70. Dougan to [Schön?], August 26, 1833, CMS/B/OMS/G C1/13: Committee Minutes, April 12, 1833–November 8, 1834; "Special Meeting at Kissy," Wednesday, August 28, 1833, CMS/B/OMS/Q A1/O1–2: Minutes of Sub-Committees; Doc. 216, Dougan to Schön, August 26, 1833, CMS/B/OMS/C A1/O4: 1828–42; "Report from Bathurst, 26th June 1835," CMS/B/OMSCA1/0232: Reverend William Young.

71. "The Locality of Mendi," *UMH*, vol. 1, no. 6, 125; personal email communication, May 22, 2012; see Misevich, "On the Frontier," 84; Clarke, *Inhabitants*, 357. Rev. James Frederick Schön to the Select Committee on the Slave Trade, April 11, 1848, in the *British Parliamentary Papers on the Slave Trade*, vol. 4 (Shannon: Irish University Press, 1968), 182; Gibbs to Tappan, July ?, 1841, AMA, #F1-5042 (emphasis in original); Norton to Tappan, August 25, 1841, AMA, #F1-5053; see Jones, *From Slaves*, 230 n.53; "The Locality of Mendi," *UMH*, vol. 1, no. 6, 125.

72. Baldwin to Jocelyn, Leavitt, Tappan, March 12, 1841, Baldwin 252; Rediker, *Amistad*, 179–80.

3. THE ENSLAVEMENTS OF AMISTAD'S ORPHANS

1. "The Case of the Amistad," *RE*, September 24, 1839; "African Captives in Court," *CA*, September 28, 1839; "Case of the Africans," in *Trial*, 36; 40 U.S. 518 (1841), 563; Baldwin, *Argument*, 12; 40 U.S. 518 (1841), 551.

2. Morris, *Southern Slavery*, 372; Van Cleve, *Slaveholders' Union.*

3. "Rough draft of Andrew Judson's ruling on the Africans, January 1840," Judson.

4. See Congressional Record, *Congressional Globe*, House of Representatives, 26th Congress, 1st Session, p. 416; also, 26th Congress.

5. "Extraordinary Arrest," *NYMH*, October 24, 1839.

6. *NYMH*, October 24, 1839.

7. *NYCA*, October 26, 1839; *Gardner v. Thomas* 14 Johns (NY 1817), Rep. 135.

8. "Answer of S. Staples, R. Baldwin, and T. Sedgewick . . . January 7, 1840," NARA; "Present State of the Amistad Case," *NYCA*, October 1, 1839: "Carre, about seven years old," to answer "to the crime of murder."

9. "In the Matter of Habeas Corpus of the Three African Girls, September 1939 term," NARA; see 40 U.S. 518 (1841), 593; "African Captives in Court," *CA*, September 28, 1839, parenthetical ellipses in original; *NYCA*, May 2, 1840: "it was desirable that the children at least should be let out on bail."

10. "A Curious Affair," *Long Island Farmer*, February 12, 1842.

11. Miers and Kopytoff, *Slavery*; Campbell et al., *Children*; Campbell et al., *Child Slaves*. See, for example, McMahon, *Slavery*.

12. The literature on this history of the concept of freedom is immense. For example, see Patterson, *Freedom*, vols. 1 and 2, and Davis, *Origins*; DuBois, *Colony*; DuBois, *Avengers*. Children are generally excluded from this literature. One exception is Mundy, "Medieval," 120–22; Lovejoy, *Transformations*, 68; Ricketts, *Six Months*, 62.

13. Manning, *Slavery*, 99; Lovejoy, *Transformations*, 168.

14. See Corry, *Observations*, 71, 74; Hawthorne, *From Africa*, 81–90. John Matthews observed in the 1790s that "witchcraft is slavery inevitable." Matthews, *Voyage*, 81. Raymond to [Tappan], February 1845, *UM*, vol. 2, no. 6 (June 1, 1845), 61; Koelle, "Narrative," 10–11.

15. Manning, *Slavery*, 118. Lovejoy, *Transformations*.

16. Lovejoy, *Transformations*, 26, 120, 169; Austen, *Trans-Saharan*; Lydon, *Trans-Saharan*.

17. MacCormack, "Wono," 187.

18. Lovejoy, *Transformations*, 169; Barry, *Senegambia*, 30; Grace, *Domestic Slavery*, 12; Grace, "Slavery and Emancipation," 421.

19. Holsoe, "Slavery and Economic Response," 287; Jones, *From Slaves*, 55–78; Koelle, "Narrative," 10–11; Rodney, *African Slavery*; Kopytoff and Miers, "African 'Slavery,'" 9.

20. Raymond to McDonald, January 8, 1846, AMA, #F1-5615. One particular way such a debt may be incurred was through an illicit affair, adultery, or what was called at the time "criminal conversation." Although several of the adult Amistad captives were "sold into slavery for making too free with another man's wife," none of the children appear to have been enslaved by punishment. "Mendis Perform," *NYH*, May 15, 1841, identifies "Bur-na" as "Banna." For enslavement of children as punishment for parents' actions, see Thornton, "Slave Trade," 41, 44. Shu-le (no. 18) "was taken for a slave by Ma-ya, for crim. con. with his wife." Momawru then captured both Shu-le and his erstwhile master, who enslaved them and then sold them, and thereafter they were sold again to a Spaniard. Similarly, Fa-gin-na (no. 25) "was made a slave by a Tamu for crim. con. with his wife." Tamu then sold him on to a Mende man, who subsequently sold him to a Spaniard. Barber, 9–15.

21. Holsoe, "Slavery and Economic Response," 289.

22. Forbes, *Six Months*, 16.

23. Caillié, *Travels*, 333; Klein, "Children," 126; Roberts, *Warriors*, 114; Jones, *From Slaves*, 45–47; Lloyd, *Navy*, 93–99; Annual Reports of Her Majesty's Commissioners at Sierra

Leone (Freetown, Sierra Leone, December 31, 1840, and December 31, 1841); Clowes, *Royal Navy*, vol. 6, 306.

24. Matthews, *Voyage*, 175; Prince, *History*, 101: fifteen-year-old Asa-Asa was sold multiple times for cloth, guns, and money. See Barry, *Senegambia*, 160–70, for the coastal oriented trade from Futa Jallon.

25. Great Britain, Foreign and Commonwealth Office, *British and Foreign State Papers*, vol. 11 (Sierra Leone Commissioners), 1823 (H.M.S.O., 1843), 436; Holsoe, "Slavery and Economic Response," 294; Koelle, "Narrative," 11. By the late 1840s, slave raiding in the Galinhas region was possibly in temporary decline. Koelle, "Narrative," 12, reported one informant stating: "They can go to the Gallinas people, but *we* no longer have slave-trade in our country."

26. Klein, *Slavery*, 4; see also, McMahon, "Trafficking," 31, for seizure on beaches. British traders documented armed kidnappings in Sierra Leone, including acts perpetrated by women. "Report of the Directors of the Sierra Leone Company" (1795), in Donnan, *Documents*, vol. 2, 618–19.

27. Barber, 15; for general information about separation and the Middle Passage, see Smallwood, *Saltwater Slavery*.

28. "Report of the Directors of the Sierra Leone Company" (1795), in Donnan, *Documents*, vol. 2, 619; MacCormack, "Wono," 193; letter from Ka-Le to President John Quincy Adams.

29. Rankin, vol. 1, 327–28.

30. Barber, 15; Covey II.

31. Interview with Esther Mokuwa and Paul Richards, April 27, 2012, Freetown, Sierra Leone, by Benjamin N. Lawrance. Barber, 15. In a conversation with Mariane Ferme, she expressed doubt about this translation. See Ferme, *Underneath*, 205: "In Mende the fact that many individuals shared a limited number of names carries with it the potential for confusing . . . instead of distinguishing."

32. Barber, 9–15; Hair, "Enslavement," 195, 201; Handler, "Survivors," 32, 36. For kidnapping, see Nwokeji, *Slave Trade*, 126–43. For Vassa's/Equiano's early life in Africa, see Carretta, "Olaudah Equiano"; Carretta, "Introduction," x–xi; Carretta, *Equiano*. For the subsequent debate, see Lovejoy, "Autobiography"; Carretta, "Response," 115–19; Lovejoy, "Issues of Motivation," 121–25; Byrd, "Eboe"; Byrd, "Olaudah"; Chambers, "Almost an Englishman."

33. Matthews, *Voyage*, 165; Spilbury, *Account*, 33.

34. Spilbury, *Account*, 33; Miller, *Way of Death*, 380.

35. John Hawkins, in Donnan, *Documents*, vol. 1, 48–49; *Maryland Colonization Journal* 9, no. 4 (September 1857): 52.

36. I disagree with Nwokeji's claim in *Slave Trade*, 128, that this practice was likely confined to those who could "get away with" it. For panyarring practices, see Falola and Lovejoy, *Pawnship*, 14–15, 62; Ojo, "Èmú," 31–58; Shumway, *Fante*, 56, 59–61. Zeuske and García Martínez, "La Amistad," 215. Historian Robin Law describes it as a "private-order mechanism" and a practice that could be prohibited in strong centralized states. Law, *Ouidah*, 134, 149. Panyarring was common on the Gold Coast, and Venture Smith's account of an armed attack on a convoy of slaves and goods, which included

himself, raises the possibility that there was an opportunistic component to the raid. Smith, *Narrative*, 13: "improved the favorable opportunity." Lovejoy described the process as "the seizure of goods that were considered to be legitimate compensation for a debt," but it was more than simply seizure as it also included violence. Lovejoy, *African Venture*, 42. In the Gold Coast panyarring appeared to be a collective punishment. Lovejoy's analysis of Smith's narrative suggests that communities could be held collectively responsible for debts but also for "wrongdoing," and anyone and anything could be seized or destroyed.

37. Richards, *Fighting*, 97; Raymond to McDonald, January 8, 1846, AMA, #F1-5615. And indeed among the adult victims aboard *La Amistad*, several accounts may reflect a local variation of such a practice. Fuliwa recounted how "his town was surrounded by soldiers, some were killed, and he with the rest were taken prisoners." Yaboi also stated his "village was surrounded by soldiers." Barber, 11, 14.

38. See Kea, "I Am Here to Plunder," 109–32. Falola and Lovejoy, "Pawnship," 16. For etymology and early use see Law, *English*, xvii, 82–83.

39. For sale by family members, see Piot, "Of Slaves"; Miller, *Way of Death*, 380, 668; Miller, "Significance of Drought," 17–61. Raymond to McDonald, January 8, 1846, AMA, #F1-5615. But elsewhere in Africa, debt pawnship of boys outstripped that of girls by a ratio of two to one. Vos, "Without the Slave Trade," 54. Matson, *Remarks*, 23: 1,033 of 1,683 slaves liberated were children "doubtless . . . sold by their parents." Raymond, April 21, 1845, *UM*, vol. 2, no. 8 (October 1845), 76.

40. Barber, 15.

41. Lovejoy and Richardson, "Trust, Pawnship," 335–36; Lovejoy and Richardson, "Business of Slaving," 67–89; Lovejoy and Falola, *Pawnship*; Lovejoy, "Pawnship, Debt."

42. Spicksley, "Pawns"; Matson, *Remarks*, 23; Lovejoy and Richard, "Business of Slaving."

43. Matthews, *Voyage*, 156, 155.

44. Spilsbury, *Account*, 32. See also Sundstrom, *Trade*, 36–45; Alexander, *Excursions*, vol. 1, 89; Howard, "Pawning," 273–78.

45. Raymond to McDonald, January 8, 1846, AMA, #F1-5615; Alagoa and Okorobia, "Pawnship in Nembe," 74; Ekechi, "Pawnship," 83–104; Matthews, *Voyage*, 119.

46. Diptee, "African Children," 187.

47. Merchants at Old Calabar, for example, had access to the *ekpe* lodge where pawns were being held in the cases of default on debts. Lovejoy and Richardson, "African Agency," 56.

48. "Report of the Directors of the Sierra Leone Company" (1795), in Donnan, *Documents*, vol. 2, 620; Barber, 9–15. Grabeau indicated he was seized on a road and implied that it was with the consent of his uncle, who had "bought two slaves in Bandi, and gave them in payment for a debt; one of them ran away, and he (Grabeau) was taken for him." Matthews, *Voyage*, 81–82.

49. Matthews, *Voyage*, 82, 79, 81; Raymond to McDonald, January 8, 1846, AMA, #F1-5615.

50. Matthews, *Voyage*, 79–80; Lovejoy and Richardson, "Trust, Pawnship," 353.

51. Miller, *Way of Death*, 384–85; Manning, *African Diaspora*; Lovejoy, *Transformations*, 63–64; Klein, *Atlantic Slave Trade*, 46, 85; Rediker, *Slave Ship*, 5–6.

52. Narrative of Samuel Crowther's enslavement, February 22, 1837, CMS/CA 1/O 79. Prince, *History*, 101; Barber, 9–15.
53. Narrative of Samuel Crowther's enslavement, February 22, 1837, CMS/CA 1/O 79.
54. Prince, *History*, 100.
55. Barber, 15; Dalby, "Mel Languages"; Dalby, "Mel Languages in the *Polyglotta Africana*." For descriptions of the "Bullom" shoreline, see Boyle, *Practical*. "Mani" is most likely a remnant name from a former Mani-speaking community, now displaced by Mende. See Thomas, "Who Were the Manes?"; Nyländer, *Grammar*, 154. Interview with Bay Adam of Pepel, Bunce Island, April 25, 2012, by Benjamin N. Lawrance. For a schematic rendition, see Jones, "Who Were the Vai?" 172.
56. Grabeau explained that in the Lomboko "prison" they were given "rice and fish to eat" by the Spaniards. Barber, 9. Raymond, January ?, 1845, *UM*, vol. 2, no. 6 (June 1, 1845), 59.
57. Raymond to Children of the Sabbath School of Rev. Duffield, Detroit, Mich., August 16, 1844, *UM*, vol. 50 (January 1845), 4; Clarke, *Inhabitants*, 331.
58. Spilsbury, *Account*, 14. The precise location of Crawford's Island is unclear, but it is likely one of the three Îles de Los, today part of the Republic of Guinea, off the coast of Conakry. Ricketts, *Narrative*, 213. The navy seized ninety slaves and their captors as they tried to escape from a barracoon to the "mainland." Lloyd, *Navy*, 93–99; Annual Reports of Her Majesty's Commissioners at Sierra Leone (Freetown, Sierra Leone, December 31, 1840, and December 31, 1841); Clowes, *Royal Navy*, vol. 6, 306. Hawthorne, *From Africa*, 108; Forbes, *Six Months*, 83: "after each meal they are obliged to dance for exercise." Bacon, *Wanderings*, 165; "Voyage of John Atkins to Guinea" (1735) in Donnan, *Documents*, vol. 2, 264–65; see Hawthorne, *From Africa*, 101–3; Conneau, *Slaver's Log Book*, 246; Barber, 15. In a private communication, Walter Hawthorne suggested that the slave purchaser may have been a "Luso-African." For the Vai phrase for "I shall redeem it with a slave," see Koelle, *Outlines*, 93. Conneau, *Slaver's Log Book*, 246.
59. Raymond to Children of the Sabbath School of Rev. Duffield, Detroit, Mich., August 16, 1844, *UM*, vol. 50 (January 1845), 4; Spilsbury, *Account*, 14–15; Barber, 14
60. Forbes, *Six Months*, 105; Barber, 10; de Zulueta et al., *Trial of Pedro de Zulueta*, 278; *Maryland Colonization Journal* 9, no. 4 (1857): 52.
61. *Maryland Colonization Journal* 9, no. 4 (1857): 52–54; Conneau, *Slaver's Log Book*, 246–47, 250; Forbes, *Six Months*, 83; Lloyd, *Navy*, 93–99; Annual Reports of Her Majesty's Commissioners at Sierra Leone (December 31, 1840, and December 31, 1841); Clowes, *Royal Navy*, vol. 6, 306; de Zulueta, *Trial*, 278; Bacon, *Wanderings*, 165, for the account of an attack on the barracoon of Don Miguel in Cape Montserrado, circa 1831. Raymond to Commodore Jones, December 23, 1844, *UM*, vol. 2, no. 6 (June 1, 1845), 1.
62. Barber, 13–14; Koelle, "Narrative," 13–14.
63. Koelle, "Narrative," 13–14; *UM*, vol. 50, no. 1 (May 1844), 10; *Maryland Colonization Journal* 9, no. 4 (1857): 52; Report of Lt. Gov. Ferguson, Sierra Leone, October 23, 1841, AMA, #F1-5096; see Jones, *From Slaves*, 69; Jones, *From Slaves*, 51; Huzzey, *Freedom Burning*.

64. Jones, *From Slaves*, 49–51; Personal communication to the author. Charlotte to Samuel Cowles, April 12, 1841, ACCHS. *Maryland Colonization Journal* 9, no. 4 (1857): 51; Paquette, "From History to Hollywood." Spielberg's choice of El Morro, San Juan, raised "Lomboko" to inappropriate prominence; see Lemisch, "Black Agency," 68 n.21; Bickford-Smith and Mendelsohn, *Black and White*, 67; Osagie, *Amistad*, 4; Taunton Hydrographic Office, L2534: latitude 7°1′11″ N and longitude 11°39′0″ W. (This would actually place it in the Atlantic Ocean.) Jones, "Theophile Conneau," 91. Cinquez provides the only concrete reference when he stated, "He had heard of Pedro Blanco, who lived at Te-i-lu, near Lomboko." Barber, 9; Raymond to AMA, December 4, 1844, *UM*, vol. 2, no.5 (April 1, 1845), 49.

65. Raymond to Tappan, July 10, 1844, *UM*, vol. 50 (January 1845), 3; ANC, Tribunal de Comercio, leg. 58, no. 15, *Don Pedro Blanco contra Don Guillermo Salguela para que le cuartos . . .* (1832–1839).

66. Forbes, *Six Months*, 82; Jones, "Theophile Conneau," 102 n.26. Martin Delany and the American Colonization Society were among a coterie of contemporaries imbricated in the mythology of the "swarthy," "wretched proprietor." Blake, *History*, 342; Delany and Levine, *Martin R. Delany*, 84; Ward, *Royal Navy*, 73, 132–33; *Maryland Colonization Journal* 9, no. 4 (1857): 51; see the otherwise unreliable Drake, *Revelations*, 92–93; letter of Captain Charles Bell, of the U.S. brig *Dolphin*, Monrovia, Liberia, April 3, 1840, in ACS, 1840, 296; Raymond to Raston, August 26, 1844, *UM*, vol. 50 (January 1845), 6. Conneau, *Slaver's Log Book*, 246.

67. Bouët-Willaumez, *Description nautique*, 179; also Drake, *Revelations*, 92–93; Zeuske and García Martínez, "La Amistad," 120, 122, 125; Bergad et al., *Cuban Slave Market*, 66; Conneau, *Slaver's Log Book*, 247; for a description of Don Miguel's "open house" from circa 1831, see Bacon, *Wanderings*, 164.

68. Barber, 21; Rankin, vol. 2, 92; Madden, "In Re, Slave Trade," in Madden, *Poems*, 131; Raymond to Children of the Sabbath School of Rev. Duffield, Detroit, Mich., August 16, 1844, *UM*, vol. 50 (January 1845), 4; Bacon, *Wanderings*, 165; Richards, *Fighting*, 97.

69. SLNA, Freetown Register; Walsh, *Notices*, vol.2, 480, provides three examples of the types of brand marks for slave. Charlotte to Samuel Cowles, April 12, 1841, ACCHS; Longo, *Isabel*, 86; *Voyages*, Voyage ID 3598; Walsh, *Notices*, vol. 2, 480; Arnalte, *Los últimos*, 115–16, 126–28; Ortiz, *Los Negros*, 164–65; New slaves arriving in Cuba or Brazil were sometimes branded on arrival. Or they were rebranded by their new owners. See Madden, *Twelvemonths*, 109; Tappan to Leavitt, "Excursion with the Amistad Africans," Sturge, *Visit*, xliv.

70. BNA, FO 315/77/68: "Papers of the Spanish Schooner Segunda Socorro." Macleay to Palmerston, no. 70, February 24, 1834. *Correspondence with the British Commissioners*, 1835, 93; Law, *Ouidah*, 159; BNA, FO84/273, Macaulay, Doherty, 39.12.15, enc.; PPHC, vol. 49 (1845), 593–633.

71. *Voyages: The Trans-Atlantic Slave Trade Database*, Emory University, http://slave voyages.org/tast/database/search.faces?yearFrom=1835&yearTo=1836&mjslptimp =31300; See García Martínez and Zeuske, *La sublevación*, for a discussion of Ferrer's movements and operations.

72. See Zeuske and Martínez, "La Amistad," 207, 215; Clarence-Smith, "Portuguese Contribution"; Madden, "In Re, Slave Trade," in Madden, *Poems*, 131; *Voyages: The Trans-Atlantic Slave Trade Database*, Emory University, http://slavevoyages.org/tast/database/search.faces?yearFrom=1820&yearTo=1866&mjbyptimp=60208&mjslptimp=31300; Madden II; Knight, *Slave Society*, 50, 181. Raymond to Raston, August 26, 1844, *UM*, vol. 50 (January 1845), 6; *Voyages: The Trans-Atlantic Slave Trade Database*, Emory University, http://slavevoyages.org/tast/database/search.faces?yearFrom=1830&yearTo=1839&mjslptimp=31300; *Voyages: The Trans-Atlantic Slave Trade Database*, Emory University, http://slavevoyages.org/tast/database/search.faces?yearFrom=1830&yearTo=1839&mjslptimp=31312.

73. Walsh, *Notices*, vol. 2, 473; Zeuske and Martínez, "La Amistad," 211; Madden II; Bergad et al., *Cuban Slave Market*, 53; "The African Captives," in *Trial*, 27.

74. Madden I; Zeuske and Martínez, "La Amistad"; AHN, Madrid, Estado, Trata de negros, leg. 8024/30, no. 24, letter from William Hervey, British Legation in Spain, Madrid, September 11, 1838. This ship attacked other slave ships operating between Madagascar and Mozambique, robbed them, and sold the slaves in Cuba. Thanks to Michael Zeuske for this information. Riera, Martínez, Blanco, and José Rainon Recur were co-owners of the ill-fated *Cirse*, piloted by Serafín Antônio Spenser (*Voyages*, Voyage ID 2590), which was seized by the *Buzzard* in late 1838. The *Cirse* was the original vessel carrying the majority of the male adults aboard *La Amistad* from Galinhas to Cuba. See Eltis, *Economic Growth*, 148–49; Zeuske and Martínez, "La Amistad," 211; *Diario de la Habana*, Enero 1ro de 1838 [January 1, 1838], 4; ANC, Fondo Tribunal de Comercio (1841), leg. 285, no. 4–5, fol. 39r. See Zeuske and García Martínez, "La Amistad," 122, 136; Madden II.

75. Barber, 19; based on a calculation of a total of 180,000 during the decade (Eltis, *Economic Growth*), and 42 percent below fifteen years (Bergad et al., *Cuban Slave Market*).

76. Aimes, *History*; Phillips, *American*; Fraginals, *El Ingenio*; Barcia, *Burguesía esclavista*; Scott, *Slave Emancipation*; Knight, *Slave Society*, 58; Bergad et al., *Cuban Slave Market*, 44, 53; Eltis, *Economic Growth*, 187; Domingo del Monte wrote José Antonio Saco: "From Havana there leave every year on average 36 ships, and from Matanzas various Catalans send another 15 or 20." Saco, *Historia*, 4, 334, cited by Zeuske and Martínez, "La Amistad," 218; see also Murray, *Odious*, 103–4; Madden, "In Re, Slave Trade" in Madden, *Poems*, 132.

77. Eltis, *Economic Growth*, 245; Klein, *Middle Passage*, 215; Bergard, 26, n.12; *Voyages: The Trans-Atlantic Slave Trade Database*, Emory University, http://slavevoyages.org/tast/database/search.faces?yearFrom=1817&yearTo=1820&mjslptimp=31300; Bergad et al., *Cuban Slave Market*, 26, 29, 57; Eltis, *Economic Growth*, 122–23. *Voyages: The Trans-Atlantic Slave Trade Database*, Emory University, http://slavevoyages.org/tast/database/search.faces?yearFrom=1831&yearTo=1840&mjslptimp=31300; Thomas, *Cuba*, 156; Zeuske and Martínez, "La Amistad," 217; Pedro Martínez to Angel Jimenez, September 26, 1838. PPHC, vol. 49 (1839), 38–39. AHN, Madrid, Estado, Trata de negros, leg. 8024/30, no. 5: carta de Joaquin de Espeleta desde la Habana, 30 May 1838 al primer Secretario de Estado en Madrid; "Second Enclosure, No. 67," Great

Britain, Emigration Commission, *General Reports of the Immigration Commissioners,* 1839–1845, 109. Turnbull, *Travels,* 435–26; Zeuske and Martínez, "La Amistad," 202: Ferrer's nom de guerre was Ramón Roselló. For Trist, see Turnbull, *Travels,* 435–66; PPHC, Correspondence with the British Commissioners, at Sierra Leone, the Havana, Rio de Janeiro, and Surinam: From May 11 to December 31, 1840 [London, 1841], 101.

78. Madden, *Cuba,* 38; Bergad et al., *Cuban Slave Market,* 43–45, 64.

79. Eltis, *Economic Growth,* 122–23; Turnbull, *Travels,* 145; Bergad et al., *Cuban Slave Market,* appendix 22, 26, 54–55, 62, 65, B.I, 168, B.2, 180, and B.II, 228; Two numbers exist—see *Trial,* 8, and NARA, RG 21, Sept. 1839–Feb. 1843.

80. *Voyages: The Trans-Atlantic Slave Trade Database,* Emory University, http://slavevoyages.org/tast/database/search.faces?yearFrom=1819&yearTo=1866&mjslptimp=31300; http://slavevoyages.org/tast/database/search.faces?yearFrom=1819&yearTo=1866&mjslptimp=31312; http://slavevoyages.org/tast/database/search.faces?yearFrom=1820&yearTo=1829&mjslptimp=31312; http://slavevoyages.org/tast/database/search.faces?yearFrom=1830&yearTo=1839&mjslptimp=31312; http://slavevoyages.org/tast/database/search.faces?yearFrom=1830&yearTo=1839&mjslptimp=31301.31302.31303.31304.31305.31306.31307.31308.31309.31311.31313.31314.31315.31316.31318.31319.31320.31321.31322.31323.31324.31399; http://slavevoyages.org/tast/database/search.faces?yearFrom=1835&yearTo=1839&mjslptimp=31312.

81. Zeuske and García Martínez, "La Amistad," 213; Archivo Histórico Provincial de Camagüey (Cuba), Fondo Protocolos, Notario Manuel Martínez Valdés, 1834–35 and 1843; Notario José Rafael Castellanos, 1838, 1839; Notario Manuel Martínez Valdés. Tomo 1834–35; Fondo Protocolos, Notario Luis de Cordova, 1836–37; AHN, Madrid (Spain), Estado, Trata de negros, leg. 8024/30, no. 6: "Testimonio dela sumaria formada á consequencia de queja producida p.r los Com.s de S.M.B contra el barco de vapor Principeño sobre haber introducido en este puerto negros bozales," Havana, May 22, 1838, Juan B. Topete (Reprinted as annex no. 6 in García Martínez and Zeuske, *La sublevatión*); Zeuske and García Martínez, "La Amistad," 215. *Despatches from United States consuls in Havana, Cuba, 1783–1906* (Washington, D.C.: National Archives, National Archives and Records Service, General Services Administration, 1956–61). Edda Fields-Black is conducting research on slave smuggling from Cuba and Puerto Rico into the United States.

82. Murray, *Odious,* 272; Eltis, *Economic Growth,* 191; Barcia, *Great African,* 72; ANC, Fondo Tribunal de Comercio (1841), leg. 285, no. 4, fol. 11r.

83. Massé, *L'île de Cuba,* 352.

84. Bergad, *Cuban Slave Market,* 35, 49–51, 56–57, 64.

85. Turnbull, *Travels,* 61.

86. Knight, *Slave Society,* 50.

4. THE JOURNEYS OF AMISTAD'S ORPHANS

1. Smith, *Political,* vol. 1, 53–60.

2. Zeuske, "Rethinking," 5, on the "Teçora myth."

3. "Private Examination of Cinquez," NYCA, September 13, 1839. I am indebted to Marcus Rediker for sharing this information and other materials cited in this chapter.

4. The phrase "La Forcora" appears in *New York American*, September 16, 1839; extract of a letter dated Saturday evening, October 5, 1839, New Haven, "Plans to Educate the Amistad Africans in English," *NYJC*, October 9, 1839; Tappan to Amistad Committee, September 9, 1839, AMA.

5. The copper-bottomed Baltimore Clipper schooner was purpose-built for the slave trade and measured 70 46/95 tons (Custom House Measurement); Rediker, *Amistad*, 65–68. Zeuske, "Rethinking," has proven it was built in Cuba, not in Baltimore. Other contemporary schooners in this class making a trans-Atlantic voyage from Galinhas to Cuba include the *Constância* (ID 1717) and the *Salomé* (ID 1712). As Rediker observed, many without lower decks made the Middle Passage, and quite a few of them were schooners, like *La Amistad*. Personal communication by email, July 12, 2013. "Case of the Amistad, To the Right Honorable Lord Palmerston, Her Majesty's Principal Secretary for Foreign Affairs, &c &c." (November 9, 1839), FO 1, Memorials and Petitions of the British and Foreign Anti-Slavery Society, 1839–50, E2/19, Rhodes House, Oxford.

6. Zeuske, "Rethinking"; Zeuske and García Martínez, "La Amistad," 202; García Martínez and Zeuske, *La sublevación*, 4; ANC, Tribunal de Comercio, Pedro Blanco; ANC, Fondo Misceláneas de Libros, leg. 11 408; See Zeuske, "Rethinking"; García Martínez and Zeuske, *La sublevación*, 37. Ninety-eight tons was just below the average tonnage of 105 tons for vessels from Galinhas to Cuba, 1830–45. *Voyages: The Trans-Atlantic Slave Trade Database*, Emory University, http://slavevoyages.org/tast/database/search.faces?yearFrom=1830&yearTo=1845&mjbyptimp=60208&mjslptimp=31300. The *Hugh Boyle* was also mastered by Charles Roach; it sailed from Cuba to New Orleans in July 1839 with tobacco, plank, and caboose, then to New Sesters/Bassa on the West African coast to purchase rice, then to Galinhas, where it picked up slaves. It arrived in Cuba on October 21, 1839, with 325 African captives. See, ACS, *The African Repository*, vol. 16 (1840): 121–22.

7. Zeuske, "Names of Slavery," 64; "Slaves Case," Baldwin, R.S. Baldwin Legal Papers Briefs, 1836–39, Baldwin.

8. Christopher et al., *Many Middle Passages*.

9. Williams to Tappan, September 23, 1841, AMA, #F1-5069: "Cinque has a brother in Sierra Leone: he was taken and carried to the coast and put on board a slaver, was taken by a man of war of her B[ritannic] M[ajesty's] squadron and taken into Sierra Leone. He remained their one year and then went home to his father about the time that Cinque was taken he returned to S.L. where C. supposes he is now." September 8, 1841. Norton: "They trade with Sierra Leone by means of emancipated Mendians captured by the British from the slavers." Lovejoy, *Transformations*, 64, described 10 percent as a "guess"; Miller, *Way of Death*, 413, describing Angolan slaves and a six-month journey estimated 40 percent.

10. Manning described the "average" march for slaves in Upper Guinea as less than 200 kilometers. Manning, *Slavery*, 65; Misevich, "Origins," 169; Jones, "Recaptive Nations." *Voyages: The Trans-Atlantic Slave Trade Database*, Emory University, http://

slavevoyages.org/tast/database/search.faces?yearFrom=1819&yearTo=1824&mjbypti
mp=60000&mjslptimp=60200; Jones, "Recaptive Nations," 52; *Voyages: The Trans-
Atlantic Slave Trade Database,* Emory University, http://www.slavevoyages.org/tast/
resources/slaves.faces.

11. Davidson, "Trade and Politics," 110; Thompson, *Palm Land,* 233; Klein, "Children," 126.

12. Davidson, "Trade and Politics," 110; Jones, *From Slaves,* 63, 67–68.

13. Davidson, "Trade and Politics," 120, n.101; Testimony of Augustino, Conrad, *Children
of God's Fire,* 39.

14. Davidson, "Trade and Politics," 68; Forbes, *Six Months,* 72; Koelle, "Narrative," 12;
Thompson, *Palm Land,* 189.

15. Thompson, *Palm Land,* 186–87, 191; Sherwood, *Dazee,* 10.

16. Sherwood, *Dazee,* 9, 11, 14; Testimony of Augustino, Conrad, *Children of God's
Fire,* 39.

17. Thompson, *Thompson in Africa,* 137; Barry, *Senegambia;* Jones, *From Slaves,* 61, 65;
Davidson, "Trade and Politics," 79, 102–3.

18. Charlotte to Samuel Cowles, April 12, 1841, ACCHS; Leavitt to Adams, August 29,
1841, AMA, #F1-5060; Booth to Tappan, October 4, 1841, AMA, #F1-5075A.

19. Conneau, *Slaver's Log Book,* 247; Taunton Hydrographic Office, L2534.

20. Barber, 14: Foni was located in one of Luiz's barracoons, one day's walk inland from
the embarkation point; Ricketts, *Six Months,* 83.

21. Forbes, *Six Months,* 18, 77, 94–95; Bacon, *Wanderings,* 69; "Voyage to Liberia: Gallinas," ACS, 1857, 339; Johnston, *Liberia,* 166; Rankin, vol. 1, 146, 148, 209.

22. "Plan of the Slave Ship Brooks, ca. 1850," London: Day & Son, Lithograph, New-York
Historical Society Library, Department of Prints, Photographs, and Architectural Collections. Figure VII shows the area identified as "N" replete with what appear to be
children, and Figure IV, shows area "A" in between the "store room" similarly stacked
full with children. Drawing of a cross section of a slaver ship in Brazil, from Walsh,
Notices.

23. Forbes, *Six Months,* 87; British and Foreign Anti-Slavery Society, *Proceedings,* 239–40;
Walsh, *Notices,* vol. 2, 480, 485.

24. Leonard, *Records,* 104–5. Likely the *Voyages,* Voyage ID 2420, *Primeira* (1831), under
Gabriel Perez.

25. "Case of the Africans," in *Trial,* 27.

26. Cinquez's experience was similar. Before the district court he stated, "In vessel that
brought us to Havana we were chained—hand and feet together." "Testimony of
Cinque, January 8, 1840, U.S. District Court, Connecticut." During his testimony he
sat down on the floor of the court and held his hands together to show how they were
manacled. His description of shackling resembled Leonard's observations aboard the
Primeira in 1831 and Captain Fitzgerald's account of the *Empreendedor,* captured by
the *Buzzard* (and James Covey) in October 1838. NYCA, November 15, 1839: "All the
stout men were manacled, leg to leg, and hand to hand, with small bolts." "Case of the
Africans," in *Trial,* 27; September 8, 1841, Norton; in an interview with Dwight Janes
in New London in August 1838, "he said he was brot [*sic*] to Havanna when we was

a very small boy." Janes to Baldwin, August 31, 1839, AMA, #F1-4594. But in a larger group interview with Tappan, Cinquez, and others in New Haven, he stated in Spanish, that he was "born in Havana," *NYJC*, September 12, 1839.

27. September 8, 1841, Norton; Longo, *Isabel*, 86, citing a description from the Sierra Leone newspaper the *Watchman*. *Voyages*, Voyage ID 3598.

28. BNA, FO 315/77/68: "Papers of the Spanish Schooner Segunda Socorro," captained by José de Inza. Inza later "openly confessed" to having made fourteen slave voyages, the last four from Galinhas. British and Foreign Society for the Universal Abolition of Negro Slavery and Slave Trade, *Abolitionist* 1, no. 2 (June, 1834): 69. Leonard, *Records*, 104–5. *Segunda Socorro* had 104 boys, 107 men, 37 women, and 59 girls; Thompson to Campbell, July 12, 1833, SNLA, Liberated African Department Letterbook, 1831–34, 188.

29. *Voyages: The Trans-Atlantic Slave Trade Database*, Emory University, http://slave voyages.org/tast/database/search.faces?yearFrom=1833&yearTo=1839&mjbyptimp =60200; *Voyages: The Trans-Atlantic Slave Trade Database*, Emory University, http:// slavevoyages.org/tast/database/search.faces?yearFrom=1833&yearTo=1839&mjbyptim p=60208; Madden, "In Re, Slave Trade," in *Poems*, 133.

30. The adult males' Middle Passage from Africa to Havana was on a different ship, and the precise length of time at sea is unknown because reports vary—from "four weeks" and "one and a half moons" to "three months" or "three moons." "The Captured Slaves," *NYMH*, September 2, 1839; "To the Committee on Behalf of the African Prisoners," *NYJC*, September 10, 1839; "African Testimony," *NYJC*, January 10, 1840; "Plans to Educate the Amistad Africans in English," *NYJC*, October 9, 1839. Both Cinquez and Fuliwa described their voyage as spanning "three moons." Testimony of Cinquez; Testimony of Fuliwa; forty-five days (one and half months) would have been considered a relatively slower Atlantic passage, but three months was an exceptionally long journey and likely resulted in high mortality. Jones, *Mutiny*, 13–16, claims one-third died aboard the *Teçora*. *Voyages: The Trans-Atlantic Slave Trade Database*, Emory University, http://slavevoyages.org/tast/database/search.faces?yearFrom =1514&yearTo=1866&mjbyptimp=60200&mjslptimp=31300; *Voyages: The Trans-Atlantic Slave Trade Database*, Emory University, http://slavevoyages.org/tast/data base/search.faces?yearFrom=1819&yearTo=1866&mjbyptimp=60200&mjslptimp =31300; for Baltimore Clippers, see Chapelle, *Search*, and *Baltimore*; Madden, "In Re, Slave Trade," in *Poems*, 133.

31. Ricketts, *Narrative*, 218; Nelson, *Remarks*, 43–56; *Voyages: The Trans-Atlantic Slave Trade Database*, Emory University, http://slavevoyages.org/tast/database/search.faces ?yearFrom=1514&yearTo=1866&mjbyptimp=60200&mjslptimp=31300; *Voyages: The Trans-Atlantic Slave Trade Database*, Emory University, http://slavevoyages.org/tast/ database/search.faces?yearFrom=1819&yearTo=1866&mjbyptimp=60200&mjslptim p=31300; Miller, "Mortality"; Eltis, "Mortality"; Madden, "In Re, Slave Trade," 133.

32. Over fifty slave ships departed Havana and Matanzas ports in 1838. Saco, *Historia*, 4, 334, cited by Zeuske and García Martínez, "La Amistad," 218; Madden, "In Re, Slave Trade," in *Poems*, 132, mentions fifteen to twenty ships from Matanzas. Voyages lists fifty-three ships departing Cuban ports in 1838. *Voyages: The Trans-Atlantic Slave*

Trade Database, Emory University, http://slavevoyages.org/tast/database/search.faces?yearFrom=1838&yearTo=1838&ptdepimp=31300; of these, 26 ships were seized by anti-slavery patrols. *Voyages: The Trans-Atlantic Slave Trade Database*, Emory University, http://slavevoyages.org/tast/database/search.faces?yearFrom=1838&yearTo=1838&ptdepimp=31300&fate4=3; "Case of the Africans," in *Trial*, 8, 29; *Voyages*, Voyage IDs 1789, 2706, 1792.

33. Tappan to Leavitt, "Excursion with the Amistad Africans," in Sturge, *Visit*, xliv; *Voyages*, Voyage IDs 2678, 2623, 2670, 2596, 5083, 2614, 2666; *Voyages*, Voyage ID 2590 (*Circe*); Fitzgerald's version of the capture of the *Circe* (*Cirse*) appeared in the NYCA, November 15, 1839; Tappan may be referring to information elicited from the adults by interviews conducted by Booth in July–October 1841, a narrative correlated by a later interview by Hannah More in Sierra Leone. Personal communication with Joseph Yannielli. Or it may be, as Ellen Lawson asserted, a reference to one of the children, namely Mar'gru. Lawson, *Three Sarahs*. Although it remains impossible to verify this story, Tappan's letter indicates it was part of the chronicle that emerged after the Supreme Court victory. Because such a tale would have made the adults' narrative of illegal smuggling even more compelling, its omission adds to the sense that this story came from one of the children. But the adults were equally terrified in the early days of 1839, and by late 1841 several were still not talking about their experience. Booth to Tappan, July 27, 1841, AMA, #F1-5038.

34. "To the Committee on Behalf of the African Prisoners," *NYCA*, September 10, 1839; *Voyages: The Trans-Atlantic Slave Trade Database*, Emory University, http://slavevoyages.org/tast/database/search.faces?yearFrom=1831&yearTo=1840&mjbyptimp=60700&mjslptimp=31300; *Voyages*, Voyage IDs 1874 and 1782. See Arnalte, *Los últimos*.

35. http://www.pbenyon.plus.com/18–1900/B/00747.html. It was the last of its class, the most famous of which was Darwin's *Beagle*. The ship was under the West Africa commands of Frederick Warren (1834), Patrick Campbell (1835–37), George Elliot (1838–39), and William Tucker (1840). BNA, Royal Navy, ADM 51/3064; ADM 53/214-217; ADM 37/8796-8800. The *Buzzard* intercepted the Spanish *Formidable* commanded by Don Manuel Mateu in the Bight of Benin. After forty-five minutes, the *Formidable* surrendered with the loss of seven men. Two of the *Buzzard*'s crew were killed. The *Formidable* was taken to Freetown, but 307 of the 707 African slaves "perished from disease and misery." Clowes et al., *Royal Navy*, 275. In 1835 it had captured the Iberia with 313 slaves, the *Bien Venida*, with 430 slaves, the *Semiramis*, the *Norma* with 234 slaves, and the *Ligera* with 198 slaves. In 1836 it captured eight ships, carrying 2,102 slaves in total. In April 1837 it approached the Sierra Leone coast to rejoin the greater part of the West African Squadron under the leadership of Lieutenant Commander John Luke Richard Stoll.

36. Lord Aberdeen, Palmerston's successor, reined in this policy. *The Times*, April 30, 1842. Calvin Lane explains that "the American public did not make this nice semantic distinction," and the possibility of war escalated. Lane, "African Squadron." For an 1842 discussion of the legal basis for the "right of search" as it pertained to illegal slavers operating under the U.S. flag, see "The Right of Search," ACS, 1842, 247–53. *Voyages*, Voyage ID 2615, *Eagle* (1839), and Voyage ID 2682, *Clara* (1839). BNA, Royal

Navy, ADM 53/216, Log entry of Capt. Fitzgerald, March 12, and 19, 1839; Martínez, "Antislavery," 605. For Fitzgerald's deposition on the matter of the *Clara*, see Madden, *Letter*, 29–30. BNA, FO 84/338/104, February 12, 1840, and FO 84/338/106, December 14, 1839. Also, Adderley, "New Negroes," 129. In 1838–39, in the absence of U.S. support, the Royal Navy increased seizures, including American ships because American capital was being invested in Cuba, facilitating circumvention of the new treaty between Spain and Britain, and because Spanish and Portuguese vessels hoisted U.S. flags. Madden, *Letter*, 5–6. For American involvement in the 1840s, see Rickett, *Six Months*, 31, 37, 77, 101.

37. AHN, Madrid, leg. 21. Bozales, tráfico, leg. 22a.-1835; Sedgwick, "Case of the Africans," in *Trial*, 8; Zeuske and García Martínez, "La Amistad," 211; "Affidavit of Bahoo," in "Case of the Africans," in *Trial*, 27.

38. *Voyages: The Trans-Atlantic Slave Trade Database*, Emory University, http://slave voyages.org/tast/database/search.faces?yearFrom=1831&yearTo=1840&mjslptimp =31312; Domingo del Monte wrote José Antonio Saco: "From Havana there leave every year on average 36 ships, and from Matanzas various Catalans send another 15 or 20." Saco, *Historia*, 4, 334, cited by Zeuske and García Martínez, "La Amistad," 218, possibly drawing originally on Madden, "In Re, Slave Trade," 132.

39. Turnbull, *Travels*, 59–60.

40. Massé, *L'île de Cuba*, 97, 350–59.

41. Madden I; Madden II; "African Testimony," NYJC, January 10, 1840.

42. "The Amistad" translation from *Noticio de Ambos Mundos* in *New York Advertiser and Express*, October 5, 1839; Rediker, *Amistad*, 67; "African Testimony," NYJC, January 10, 1840.

43. At some point the surviving adults claimed not to be able to calculate the time since the revolt, but at other instances it was described as "3 moons and a half from Havana." "Testimony of Cinque, January 8, 1840, U.S. District Court, Connecticut," NARA; Celestino, the murdered cook aboard *La Amistad*, had told the Africans they were to be eaten upon arrival. He had also slapped Cinquez in the face with a plantain. The Africans had been whipped repeatedly by the late Captain Ferrer and his sailors and put on half-rations of food and water.

44. Rediker, *Amistad*, 166–67, 255–56, n.28: Cinquez likely clubbed him to death with a "billet of wood"; NYJC, September 12, 1839; interview of Antonio, "The Long, Low Black Schooner," NYS, August 31, 1839; Griswold to Tappan, April 25, 1840, AMA.

45. "Examination of the Persons taken in the Long, Low, Black Schooner," *Public Ledger*, September 2, 1839, p. 4; Madden to A. Blackwood, Esq., October 3, 1839, BNA, CO/318/146, correspondence from Dr. R. R. Madden et al.; "The Case of the Africans Decided for the Present," NYMH, September 25, 1839; Rediker, *Amistad*, 71.

46. Tappan to Leavitt, "Excursion," in Sturge, *Visit*, xlv.

47. Dougall to Leavitt, April 26, 1841, AMA, #F1-4983; Townsend to Tappan, May 10, 1841, AMA, #F1-4994.

48. *Hartford Daily Courant*, October 21, 1841; November 1, 1841; December 23, 1841.

49. Tappan to Frye, November 23, 1841, AMA, #F1-5223A; for the slave trade practice, see "James Jones to Lord Hawksbury" (1788) in Donnan, *Documents*, vol. 2, 592; Brown-

Kubisch, *Queen's Bush Settlement*, 185. Whereas Tappan proudly proclaimed the adult males were Christian and most of them "teetotalers," Iyunolu Osagie describes a struggle over alcohol. Tappan to Leavitt, "Excursion," in Sturge, *Visit*, xliv; Osagie, *Amistad*, 59; Jocelyn, Tappan, and Leavitt to Steele, Raymond, and Wilson, November 2, 1841, AMA, #F1-5238; Tappan to HM Commanding Officer, November 24, 1841, AMA, #F1-5240.

50. ACS, 1842, 158; Steele to Tappan, February 1, 1841, AMA, #F-5349; Raymond to Tappan, September 10, 1845, AMA; Thompson, *Letters*, vol. 1, vi.

51. Bergad et al., *Cuban Slave Market*, 72; Misevich, "Origins," 158–59; it is indisputable that, during the 1830s and 1840s, the majority of slaves arriving in Cuba and Brazil came from West Central Africa, not Sierra Leone or neighboring ports. *Voyages: The Trans-Atlantic Slave Trade Database*, Emory University, http://slavevoyages.org/tast/database/search .faces?yearFrom=1830&yearTo=1849&mjslptimp=31300.50000; *Voyages: The Trans-Atlantic Slave Trade Database*, Emory University, http://slavevoyages.org/tast/database/ search.faces?yearFrom=1807&yearTo=1829; *Voyages: The Trans-Atlantic Slave Trade Database*, Emory University, http://slavevoyages.org/tast/database/search.faces?yearFrom =1807&yearTo=1829&mjslptimp=31300; *Voyages: The Trans-Atlantic Slave Trade Database*, Emory University, http://slavevoyages.org/tast/database/search.faces?yearFrom=1830 &yearTo=1866; *Voyages: The Trans-Atlantic Slave Trade Database*, Emory University, http://slavevoyages.org/tast/database/search.faces?yearFrom=1830&yearTo=1866&mjslpt imp=31300; Misevich, "Origins," 161, describes the "highpoint" for Sierra Leone overall (not Sierra Leone and Cuba specifically) as 1816–20. *Voyages: The Trans-Atlantic Slave Trade Database*, Emory University, http://slavevoyages.org/tast/database/search.faces?year From=1820&yearTo=1829&mjslptimp=31300; *Voyages: The Trans-Atlantic Slave Trade Database*, Emory University, http://slavevoyages.org/tast/database/search.faces?yearFrom =1830&yearTo=1839&mjslptimp=31300; *Voyages: The Trans-Atlantic Slave Trade Database*, Emory University, http://slavevoyages.org/tast/database/search.faces?yearFrom=1840 &yearTo=1849&mjslptimp=31300.

52. Corry, *Observations*, 54; Viscount Palmerston to H. U. Addington, Esq., December 24, 1830, reprinted in *Colonies and Slaves*, Session 14 June–20 October 1831 (1831), 14; Walsh, *Notices*, vol. 2, 473–74; *Colonies and Slaves*, Session 14 June–20 October 1831 (1831), 70–74; Alexander, *Excursions*, vol. 1, 103. Letter of Captain Charles Bell, of the U.S. brig *Dolphin*, Monrovia, Liberia, April 3, 1840, ACS, 1840, 296. See also Thomas, *Cuba*, 162, who stated that if one of three or four were successful, it would be profitable; Alexander, *Excursions*, vol. 1, 139.

53. *Voyages: The Trans-Atlantic Slave Trade Database*, Emory University, http://slave voyages.org/tast/database/search.faces?yearFrom=1514&yearTo=1866&mjbyptimp= 60200; John Atkins to Guinea, 1735, in Donnan, *Documents*, vol. 4, 275; *Voyages*, Voyage ID 2599; Forbes, *Six Months*, 87.

54. *Voyages: The Trans-Atlantic Slave Trade Database*, Emory University, http://slave voyages.org/tast/database/search.faces?yearFrom=1807&yearTo=1830&mjbyptim p=60100.60200.60300; *Voyages: The Trans-Atlantic Slave Trade Database*, Emory University, http://slavevoyages.org/tast/database/search.faces?yearFrom=1807&yearT o=1866&mjbyptimp=60100.60200.60300

55. *Voyages: The Trans-Atlantic Slave Trade Database*, Emory University, http://slave voyages.org/tast/database/search.faces?yearFrom=1514&yearTo=1866&mjbyptimp= 60208; *Voyages: The Trans-Atlantic Slave Trade Database*, Emory University, http:// slavevoyages.org/tast/database/search.faces?yearFrom=1514&yearTo=1866.

56. *Voyages: The Trans-Atlantic Slave Trade Database*, Emory University, http://slave voyages.org/tast/database/search.faces?yearFrom=1808&yearTo=1839&mjbyptimp= 60200; *Voyages: The Trans-Atlantic Slave Trade Database*, Emory University, http:// slavevoyages.org/tast/database/search.faces?yearFrom=1808&yearTo=1839; *Voyages: The Trans-Atlantic Slave Trade Database*, Emory University, http://slavevoyages.org/tast/ database/search.faces?yearFrom=1808&yearTo=1839&mjbyptimp=60700; *Voyages: The Trans-Atlantic Slave Trade Database*, Emory University, http://slavevoyages.org/tast/ database/search.faces?yearFrom=1808&yearTo=1839&mjbyptimp=60500; age data is known for only six voyages. *Voyages: The Trans-Atlantic Slave Trade Database*, Emory University, http://slavevoyages.org/tast/database/search.faces?yearFrom=1808&yearTo =1839&mjbyptimp=60800; Misevich, "Origins," 161.

57. Grandío Moráguez, "African Origins," 188; *Voyages: The Trans-Atlantic Slave Trade Database*, Emory University, http://slavevoyages.org/tast/database/search.faces?year From=1514&yearTo=1866&mjslptimp=31300; *Voyages: The Trans-Atlantic Slave Trade Database*, Emory University, http://slavevoyages.org/tast/database/search.faces?year From=1514&yearTo=1866&mjslptimp=31300; *Voyages: The Trans-Atlantic Slave Trade Database*, Emory University, http://slavevoyages.org/tast/database/search.faces?year From=1514&yearTo=1866&mjbyptimp=60200; *Voyages: The Trans-Atlantic Slave Trade Database*, Emory University, http://slavevoyages.org/tast/database/search.faces ?yearFrom=1514&yearTo=1866&mjslptimp=31300.

58. *Voyages: The Trans-Atlantic Slave Trade Database*, Emory University, http://slave voyages.org/tast/database/search.faces?yearFrom=1820&yearTo=1866&mjslptimp=31 300&mjbyptimp=60200; *Voyages: The Trans-Atlantic Slave Trade Database*, Emory University, http://slavevoyages.org/tast/database/search.faces?yearFrom=1820&yearTo =1866&mjslptimp=31300; Grandío Moráguez, "African Origins," 186–87.

59. Turnbull, *Travels*, 61.

60. Leonard, *Record*, 253–54; Bolster, *Black Jacks*, 161.

61. Schwarz, "Extending," 137–63; Clarke, *Inhabitants*, 337. SLNA, Register of Liberated Africans, 1808–12, recaptives numbered 64, 67, 75–76, 419–22, 442, as cited by Schwarz, "Extending," 151–52; Narrative of Samuel Crowther's enslavement, February 22, 1837, CMS/ CA1/O 79.

62. For crew lists during the period, see BNA, Royal Navy, ADM 37/8799: Ship: BUZZARD Type: B, July 1838–December 1839. Wyatt-Brown, *Lewis Tappan*, 207, refers to Covey as a "cabin-boy"; Covey I; Covey II; complaints about impressment of American sailors into the British navy in 1842 turned on the fact that impressment of Africans was illegal, but Americans were not yet protected. See Benton, *Thirty*, 430–32. It became a subject of the Webster-Ashburton Treaty after the revolt aboard the ship *Creole* in 1841. See Baxter, *One and Inseparable*, 349–50; "Report of Bathurst for the Quarter Ending 25th December 1833." CMS/B/OMS/CA 1/O 219, Letters and journal extracts, 1825–53.

63. Graham, *Journey*, 151; Leonard, *Record*, 253–54; "Regulations," CMS/B/OMS/CA 1/O 11/4.

64. Leonard, *Record*, 255; BNA, Royal Navy, ADM 37/8799: Ship: BUZZARD Type: B, 1838 July–1839 Dec.; NYCA, November 15, 1839.

65. NYCA, November 15, 1839; Leonard, *Record*, 253–54; Document #417, Secretary Peyton to Colonial Secretary, March 8, 1852, CMS/B/OMS/CA 1 O 4; Colonial Secretary to Peyton, May 25, 1852, CMS/B/OMS/CA 1 O 4.

66. Alexander, *Excursions*, vol. 1, 109; MSS LUB 39/21, Record of Service, HM brig *Black Joke*, 1827–1832. Caird Library, National Maritime Museum, Greenwich, U.K. (thanks for Padraic X. Scanlan for Caird Library reference); Clarke, *Inhabitants*, 328.

67. Christopher, *Slave Ship Sailors*, 16; Candido, "Different Slave Journeys," 395–409; Law and Lovejoy, *Baquaqua*, 163–67; Rodrigues, *De costa*.

68. "First Enclosure. Report of the Case of the Brig 'Eliza Davidson,' Alexander B. Hanna, Master. Sierra Leone, April 24th, 1840," *Correspondence with the British Commissioners*, 1840, 73; Christopher, *Slave Ship Sailors*, 51–90; also McKnight, *Afro-Latino Voices*; Duffield, "Skilled Workers"; Matthews, *Voyage*, 173; Mann, "Shifting Paradigms"; Doherty, "Olaudah Equiano." For the Equiano/Vassa debate, see Carretta, "Introduction"; Carretta, *Equiano*; Carretta, "Olaudah Equiano or Gustavus"; Lovejoy, "Issues of Motivation"; Chambers, "Almost an Englishman"; Gates, *Black*, 6.

69. Richardson, "Shipboard Revolts"; Christopher, *Slave Ship Sailors*, 17; Candido, "Different Slave Journeys," 397; Doonan, *Documents*, vol. 3, 341, as cited by Christopher, *Slave Ship Sailors*, 60; Rowland, *History*, 186; Garcia Rodriguez, *Voices*, 103; Rawley and Behrendt, *Transatlantic*, 248; Woodard, *Republic*, 43; Jarvis, *Eye of All Trade*, 149; South Carolina, Court of Appeals [J. S. G. Richardson], *Reports of Cases*, 1859, 288.

70. Putney, *Black Sailors*, 38; Morgan, "Maritime Slavery," 317; Bolster, *Black Jacks*, 77–79.

71. "The Captured Slaves," *NYMH*, 2 September, 1839; Leonard, *Record*, 108; Sweet, "Mistaken Identities," 298; Hawthorne, "Being Now," 56; for ties between a slave and cabin boy, see Ginway, "Nation Building"; Miller, "Retention."

72. For maritime slavery, see Morgan, "Maritime Slavery," 311–26; *Voyages*, Voyage ID 1327. See Rankin, vol. 2, 96–99; and, Church, *Sierra Leone*.

73. Hawthorne, "Gorge," 412, 425: citing Arquivo Nacional da Torre do Tombo, Lisbon, Portugal, Negocios Estrangeiros, Commissaõ Mixta, cx. 228, and, BNA, FO 84/12; 'Lei de 7 de Novembro de 1831,' 182–84; Adams, April 3, 1841. Baldwin 252.

74. Swain and Hillel, *Child*; Kershaw and Sacks, *New Lives for Old*; King, *Stolen*; Schwarz, *Migrants*; Fischer and Kelly, *Bound Away*; Mitchell, *Raising*; Sherington and Jeffery, *Fairbridge*; Wilson, *Freedom*, 10–13.

75. NYCA, January 15, 1840; Forsyth to Holabird, January 17, 1840, 26th Congress, 36; Townsend to Tappan, March 27, 1841, AMA, #F1-4954; Townsend to Tappan, March 30, 1841, AMA, #F1-4961; Tappan to Baldwin, March 11, 1841, Baldwin; numerous advertisements and notices appear in Toronto's *Voice of the Fugitive*, published by Henry Walton Bibb, from January 1851 to October 1853; Winks, *Blacks*; Bertley, *Canada*; Landon, "Negro Migration," 22–36; *Toronto Patriot*, July 3, 1840: "Two persons, Irishmen we believe by birth, but Yankeefied by habit, were charged on Thursday last,

before Aldermen Gurnett and King, with an attempt to kidnap a coloured man whom they asserted to be their slave, and with drawing bowie knives on another person"; Calarco et al., *Places,* 184–86.

76. *AFASR* 2 (June 20, 1842): 70; Raymond, to Tappan, July 1, 1845, AMA, #F1-5569; also, *AM,* November 1848, 3; Raymond to Tappan, April 27, 1846, AMA, #F1-5628.

77. Johnson, "American Missionary Association," 305; Raymond to Tappan, July 1, 1845, AMA, #F1-5569; *AM,* vol. 1, no. 12, October 1847.

78. Raymond to Tappan, July 1, 1845, AMA, #F1-5569; September 10, 1845, AMA, #F1-5590; November 10, 1845, AMA, #F1-5606.

79. Raymond, September 10, 1846, AMA; letter from William Raymond, September 10, 1846, AMA; *AM,* January 1847; *AM,* June 1847, 62.

80. *AM,* April 1848, 42; *AM,* January 1848, 20; *AM,* February 1848, 28; Raymond to Tappan, April 27, 1846, AMA, #F1-5628.

81. See Lawrance, "Documenting," 163–82; Albert Bellows, superintendent of the First Baptist Church of St John, Charleston, [no state], May 25, 1841, to The Amistad Captives, AMA, #F1-5007; "Contributions of Children" *AM* December 1847, 13, and August 1848, 77; Thompson, *AM,* January 1850, 29; *AM,* May 1849, 59; Thompson, *Letters.*

5. THE LIBERATIONS OF AMISTAD'S ORPHANS

1. 40 U.S. 518 (1841), 551.
2. Rediker, *Amistad,* 191; Jones, "Impact"; Osagie, *Amistad,* 141 n.31; Christensen, *Rebellious,* 128, discussing DeSouza-George, *Broken Handcuff;* Gold, *United States,* 7; for example, Hale Woodruff's three-part mural in the Talladega College Library, or Powers, "Undertow," 69. See Schama's amusing discussion of Spielberg's film "What Hollywood."
3. See Huggins, *Black Odyssey,* xliv; also, Glickman, *Living Wage.*
4. 40 U.S. 518 (1841), 593.
5. "Answer of S. Staples, R. Baldwin, and T. Sedgwick . . . ," January 7, 1840, NARA; "Rough draft of Andrew Judson's ruling on the Africans," January 1840. Judson.
6. 40 U.S. 518 (1841), 558.
7. For a discussion of the court and the author of the Amistad decision, see Newmyer, *Supreme;* also, *John Marshall;* by contrast, Rediker, *Amistad,* 190–91, provides a very personal and cautious narrative of how the decision spread from Washington, D.C., to New Haven.
8. Brooks, *Western,* 85.
9. Covey II; *Voyages,* Voyage IDs 3014, *Hosse* (1829); 2862, *Laure* (1829) from Sherbro; 2414, *Nueva Isabelita* (a) Numero Un (1830); 2409, *Loreto* (a) Corunera (1830); 2406, *Maria de la Concepción* (1830) from Rio Pongo; 2425, *Maria* (1830); 2407, *Manzaneras* (1830) from Gallinas; 2427, *Ninfa* (1830) from Rio Pongo; 2871, *Virginie* (1831); 2418, *Maria* (1831) from Gallinas; 2420, *Primeira* (1831) from Gallinas; 2435, *Segunda Socorro* (1833) from Gallinas; BNA, FO 315/77/68: "Papers of the Spanish Schooner Segunda Socorro" captained by José de Inza; SNLA, Register of Liberated Africans.

10. PPHC, vol. 51 (1835), 13; Mbaeyi, "British Navy," 209, lists four ships; not all are in the database, see *Voyages*, Voyage IDs 1307, 2436, 2487, 1388, 2510, 2509, 2508; see also http://www.pbenyon.plus.com/18-1900/T/04884.html.

11. Lloyd, *Navy*, 82; Brooks, *Western*, 85–89.

12. Scanlan, "MacCarthy's Skull"; Lloyd, *Navy*, 80–81; Pearsall, "Sierra Leone"; Lloyd, *Navy*, 82.

13. BNA, FO 315/77/68. A second set of records (a copy of the Freetown register 37430-43537, housed in the BNA [BNA, FO 84/147]), lists a second boy with the spelling "Covee," Sierra Leone ID # 42694, eight years old. Notwithstanding the possibility that this second exemplar is a notation error or duplication, I can't envision any means of establishing unequivocally which of the two boys was James Covey. Deepest thanks to Phil Misevich and Richard Anderson for assistance with this matter. *Voyages: The Trans-Atlantic Slave Trade Database*, Emory University, http://slavevoyages.org/tast/database/search.faces?yearFrom=1514&yearTo=1866&shipname=socorro.

14. Personal communication, August 25, 2011. The possibility that "Bathurst" indicates Bathurst on the Gambia River is unlikely because recaptives marked for this region were usually listed as sent to "St. Mary's, Gambia River." For a discussion of the work of the Vice Admiralty Court and the legal framework within which it operated, see Helfman, "Court." Document 216: Private Secretary, Robert Dougan, Freetown, August 26, 1833, to Rev. Schön, CMS/B/OMS/CA 1/O 4 1828-42; "Special Meeting at Kissy," Wednesday, August 28, 1833, CMS/B/OMS/Q A 1/O 1-2: Minutes of Sub-Committees. For Crowther in Freetown, see Sanneh, *Abolitionists*.

15. Helfman, "Court"; PPHC, vol. 51 (1835), 13–14; Barber, 15: "and remained in this place five or six years, and was taught to read and write the English language, in the schools of the Church Missionary Society. . . . His Christian name, James, was given him by Rev. J. Weeks, a Church Missionary, at Sierra Leone." Covey I and II, respectively; Gibbs, "Mendi," 44.

16. Hanciles, *Euthanasia*, 9, 72–73 (my emphasis); Macaulay to Campbell, June 20, 1798, Campbell; indeed, Christian expansion and enslavement have a complicated relationship. One of the first CMS missionaries, Peter Hartwig, abandoned the mission in 1804 and became a slave trader. Nine years later a second also abandoned the station, "married an African girl," and "turned slave trader" (Hanciles, *Euthanasia*, 13, n.27); Fyfe, *History*, 74, 94–95. The Rio Pongo CMS station was destroyed by slaver John Ormond in 1816. Ormond was one of the most active slavers in the Rio Pongo region in the 1810s and 1820s. Great Britain, Foreign and Commonwealth Office, British and Foreign State Papers (HMSO, 1846), 61.

17. Fyfe, *History*, 213; Hanciles, *Euthanasia*, 51; Weeks, Bathurst, Sierra Leone, to Jowett, London, February 23, 1834, CMS/B/OMS/CA 1/O 219: Letters and journal extracts, 1825–53, of the Rev. John William Weeks; Weeks, September 4, 1835, CMS/B/OMS/CA 1/O 219; Special Meeting at Kissy," Wednesday, August 28, 1833, CMS/B/OMS/QA 1/O 1–2: Minutes of Sub-Committees; Hanciles, *Euthanasia*, 73.

18. "Regulations for the guidance and management for the Cossoo boy's school at Bathurst," CMS/B/OMS/CA 1/O 11/4; Rankin, vol. 2, 92; see Schwarz, "Extending," 151; Rankin, vol. 1, 258; Leonard, *Records*, 82–83.

19. Viscount Greenwich, October 4, 1832, concerning Portuguese vessel *Rosa*. SLNA, Colonial Correspondence, 1833. The letter observed, "formerly liberated and had been again made slaves by the connivance or with the knowledge of any British subjects." Ricketts, *Narrative*, 215; Leonard, *Records*, 79–82; Rankin, vol. 2, 92; Madden, "In Re, Slave Trade," in *Poems*, 131.

20. Rankin, vol. 2, 92.

21. Raymond to Tappan, July 10, 1844, *UM*, vol. 50 (January 1845), 3; Alexander, *Excursion*, vol. 1, 97; Hawthorne, *Africa to Brazil*; Brooks, *Western*.

22. Rankin, vol. 1, 233, 241–43.

23. Haensel, February 26, 1829, CMS/B/OMS/CA 1/O 108: Papers and reports, 1827–34; Leonard, *Records*, 78; Minute by Schön, CA 1/M 6 1831–34 [mission book], 411.

24. Weeks to Jowett, February 23, 1834, CMS/B/OMS/CA 1/O 219: Letters and journal extracts, 1825–1853.

25. Leonard, *Records*, 83; SLNA, Colonial Correspondence, 1835.

26. Leonard, *Records*, 86–88, 106.

27. Gibbs's account indicated that on Staten Island Covey was "found, amid some twenty Africans." Gibbs stated that it was through "the kindness of Captain Fitzgerald, his [Covey's] services as an interpreter were procured"; the captain was likely involved in the negotiation. Barber, 15. The temporary nature of the arrangement is underscored by Townsend to Leavitt, October 3, 1839, AMA, #F1-4638A. Also, *UMH*, vol. 1, no. 2 (February 1842): 71; Tappan, Abel, and Klingberg, *Association*, 61; Covey II; Mitchell, *History*, 37, 96–97. For his business relationship with Baldwin, see *Price & Lee*'s New Haven, 103, 105.

28. Townsend to Tappan, October 30, 1839, AMA, #F1-4655. Tappan instructed Staples to tell Baldwin to "detain" Covey on October 30 and explained that he would get Fitzgerald's "consent." He claimed "there will be no difficulty. It would be better to have a legal process however." Tappan to Townsend, October 31, 1839, AMA, #F1-4657.

29. http://www.pbenyon.plus.com/18-1900/B/00747.html; the precise early arrangements are unclear. Townsend wrote: "My present opinion tonight is, that if neither of them [James Covey and Charles the Cook] would voluntarily remain they had better go down in the morning and then the committee in New York might prevail, by the aid of Capt. Fitzgerald to persuade one of them to return. They might be willing to return after a visit to their shipmates as they came up with the expectation of staying but a few days." Townsend to Tappan, October 30, 1839, AMA, #F1-4655; Tappan to Townsend, November 12, 1839, AMA, #F1-4675.

30. Townsend to [Tappan?], November 19, 1839, AMA, #F1-4705; Tappan to Townsend, November 12, 1839, AMA, #F1-4675. "As to the employment of James—He has spent much time in the prison in assisting the teachers and in teaching them himself. He is now engaged a portion of his time in study himself by the kindness of some of the young men in college and is at this time manifesting some tender regard for his own spiritual good." Townsend to Tappan, [February 1840], AMA, #F1-4731.

31. "Case of the Africans," in *Trial*, 7.

32. Ibid., 9, 12, 28 (italics in original).

33. Judson to Wilcox, August 29, 1839, 26th Congress, 33; affidavit of Wilcox, August 29, 1839, 26th Congress, 33; 26th Congress, 3; Holabird to Forsyth, January 11, 1840; 26th Congress, 35.

34. New Haven County, Connecticut Federal Census Index, M704–27, M704–28. See Rediker, *Amistad*, 195 n.21. Thanks to Thomas Thurston for his assistance with this matter.

35. Tappan? to Adams, March 12, 1841, Baldwin 251; May 4, 1841, Norton; Jocelyn, Leavitt, and Tappan to Baldwin, March 11, 1841, Baldwin 251.

36. Townsend to Tappan, October 3, 1840, AMA, #F1-4747; Ka'le to Tappan, February 9, 1841, AMA, #F1-4901; a number of letters from Covey and others described Pendleton's brutality. Covey to Tappan, December 28, 1840, AMA. Letters from Cinque and others repeatedly complained about Pendleton. Another version of Ka'le's letter to Tappan, from Cinque to Baldwin, February 9, 1841, explained how "he do bad to Mendi people, and, when he came here with chains, he put on some hands and he whip them too hard, and we afraid"; Baldwin 250; Townsend to Tappan, March 11, 1841, AMA, #F1-4925; Tappan to Baldwin, [March 17?], and March 22, 1841, Baldwin.

37. Tappan to Baldwin, April 1, 1841, Baldwin 251; "Amos Townsend Junior vs. Stanton Pendleton," March Term 1841, New Haven County Court Records, Connecticut State Library, Hartford viewed on microfilm, courtesy of and thanks to Joseph Yannielli. The Connecticut State Library has misplaced the original documents.

38. Warren, *Women*, 117.

39. Yannielli, "Dark Continents."

40. "The Amistad Captives," *New York Evangelist*, March 27, 1841; for Connecticut law on guardian *ad litem*, see *Rhinelander et al. v. Sanford et al.* [1 Brunner, Col. Cas. 51; 1. 3 Day, 279], 1808.

41. Tappan to Jocelyn, March 18, 1841, AMA, #F1-4937; Yannielli, citing, Olmstead, diary, 1841–42, pp. 53–62, Olmstead Papers; Yannielli, citing Leonard Bacon, diary, March 17–19, 1841, box 2, series III, Bacon Family Papers; Yannielli, citing Aaron Barlow Olmstead, diary, 1841–42, pp. 53–62, esp. 58–59, Olmstead Papers, NYHS; "The Amistad Negro Girls," NHCR, March 20, 1841; "New Haven," NYH, March 23, 1841.

42. Yannielli, chap. 1, drawing on "Kidnapping in New Haven," NHCR, March 23, 1841; Leonard Bacon, diary, March 19, 1841, Bacon Family Papers.

43. "Testimony of Antonio, January 9, 1840, U.S. District Court, Connecticut"; "Narrative of the Africans," NYJC, October 10, 1839.

44. Madden to A. Blackwood, Esq., October 3, 1839, BNA, CO/318/146: Correspondence from Dr. R.R. Madden et al.; "The Case of the Africans Decided for the Present," NYMH, September 25, 1839; Rediker, *Amistad*, 71.

45. Rediker, *Amistad*, 255–56 n.28; interview of Antonio, "The Long, Low Black Schooner," NYS, August 31, 1839.

46. "The Captured Slaves," NYMH, September 2, 1839.

47. Ibid.; "The Case of the Captured Negroes," NYMH, September 9, 1839.

48. "To the Committee on Behalf of the African Prisoners," NYJC, September 10, 1839; 26th Congress, 29; Anderson et al., "Using Pre-Orthographic."

49. Charlotte to Samuel Cowles, March 24, 1841, ACCHC; September 26, 1841, Norton.
50. Charlotte to Samuel Cowles, March 30, 1841, and April 8, 1841, ACCHC; Te'me joined a temperance society; *UMH*, vol. 1, no. 4, 11. On two separate occasions, Kag'ne met both Henry Highland Garnett and James Pennington; August 25 and November 15, 1841, Norton.
51. Tappan to Baldwin, April 27, 1840, Baldwin 244; Calarco et al., *Places*, 184–86.
52. Tappan to Baldwin, April 1, 1841, and Judson to Baldwin, April 7, 1841, Baldwin 252; Tappan to Baldwin, April 24, 1840, Baldwin 244; Bigelow to Tappan, March 24, 1841, AMA, #F1-4950; Covey to Tappan, June 16, 1841, AMA. He complained that he was "not well" and "now I am sick." He may have received money in response to his earlier letter, but "you can not look doctor for the moneny [*sic*] what you brought from Mr. Thomas Van." Pease and Pease, *They Who Would Be Free*, 79–80, 100–101, 138, 178, 185; Freeman, "Free Negro," 71, 98, 100, 193–95, 197, 200, 284–85, 353, 365.
53. April 15, and August 29, 1841, Norton. Norton stayed with known Underground Railroad conductors in the strategically important Burlington Town, N.J., during this crucial period. Not to be confused with Courtland van Renssaeler, Thomas Van ("from New York") lodged with John Pitkin Norton and brought "strangers" with him in August 1841. Tappan to Baldwin, March 24, 1841, Baldwin 252; Townsend to Tappan, March 27, 1841, AMA, #F1-4954; Tappan to Baldwin, April 1, 1841, Baldwin 252.
54. Townsend to Tappan, March 30, 1841, AMA, #F1-4961; Tappan to Baldwin, April 1, 1841, Baldwin 252.
55. Tappan to Baldwin, April 1, 1841, Baldwin 252; March 18, October 28, December 9, 1837, CA.
56. Tappan to Baldwin, April 1, 1841, Baldwin 252.
57. Forsyth to Holabird, January 17, 1840, 26th Congress, 36; Jones, *From Slaves*, 126–27; "The Captured Slaves," NYMH, September 2, 1839.
58. Tappan to Baldwin, March 11, 1841, Baldwin 251; Baldwin to Jocelyn, Leavitt, and Tappan, March 12, 1841 (emphasis in original), Baldwin 252.
59. "Extract of a letter from the Hon. J. Q. Adams," April 3, 1841, Baldwin 252; Jones, *From Slaves*, 126; "The Captured Slaves," NYMH, September 2, 1839
60. Hawthorne, "Being Now"; NYCA, September 28, 1839. Sidney O. Francis was taken to Cartersville, Va., by Shearer and sold to Wilkinson; Adams to Baldwin, April 3, 1841, Baldwin.
61. Sherman to Simeon Eben Baldwin, February 16, 1888, Baldwin, series 6; Viau, *Ceux*; Yeoman, "Je Me Souviens." The "Rock" is located on what was once the property of Philip Luke, a Loyalist officer who settled in the area after the American Revolution and who, some suggest, arrived with slaves he inherited from his mother. For "Slavery in St. Armand," see http://townshipsheritage.com/news/slavery-saint-armand (last retrieved May 13, 2012).
62. Collison, *Shadrach*, 179, 197, 210; Dougall to Leavitt, April 26, 1841, AMA, #F1-4983; "Mendis Perform," NYH, May 15, 1841; LAC, John Dougall and family fonds, Correspondence, memoranda and poetry, 1837–51, R7457-0-9-E; Janes is listed with several others from Montreal in *Voice of the Fugitive*, vol. 1, no. 23, November 5, 1851.

63. Israel, "Montreal Negro," 65, cited by Williams, *Les noirs*, 38; Trudel, *L'esclavage*; Statistics Canada, LC Table VI—Occupations, Coloured Race, 1844—Lower Canada (table), 1844—Census of Lower Canada.

64. "Present State of the Amistad Case," *NYCA*, October 1, 1839; Covey to Tappan, December 14, 1840, AMA; Townsend to Tappan, July 23, 1840, AMA, #F1-4737; *UMH*, vol. 1, no. 2, 71.

65. Covey to Tappan, December 14, 1840, AMA; Foole [Woola] to Covey, October 19, 1841, AMA, #F1-5087; for naming and renaming practices among freed children in the South, see King, *Stolen*, 150.

66. Booth to Tappan, March 18, 1841, AMA; Townsend to Tappan, March 24, 1841, AMA, #F1-4949; Townsend to Tappan, March 31, 1841, AMA, #F1-4963; the passage to New York cost $2. "Amos Townsend's Jr's a/c with Committee for Mendians. Expenses incurred for James Covey," AMA, #F1-4659; Foolea to Tappan, April 15, 1841, reprinted in Blassingame, *Slave Testimony*, 41.

67. Townsend to Tappan, May 10, 1841, AMA, #F1-4994.

68. Covey to Tappan, June 9, 1841, June 29, [month unknown] 29, 1841, AMA. For further discussion, see Lawrance, "Your Poor Boy"; Lawrance, "La Amistad's 'Interpreter' Reinterpreted."

69. Covey to Tappan, June 16, 1841, AMA; Jeremiah 22:19: "He shall be buried with the burial of an ass, drawn and cast forth beyond the gates of Jerusalem." Covey to Tappan, June 29, 1841, AMA. Address listed as 101 Anthony Street, New York. I visited the Brooklyn site in May 2009, and there exist only derelict warehouses at the address.

70. "Minutes of Committee for the Mendians," August 24, 1841, AMA, #F1-5054A; Charlotte to Samuel Cowles, April 8, 1841, *ACCHS*; Norton to Tappan, August 27, 1841, AMA, #F1-5056; Foole to Covey, October 19, 1841, AMA, #F1-5087.

71. Carly to Covey, October 19, 1841, AMA, #F1-5086; *UMH*, vol. 1, no. 2 (February 1842), 71; Tappan to Frye, November 23, 1841, AMA, #F1-5223A.

6. THE RETURN OF AMISTAD'S ORPHANS

1. "Testimony of Grabeau, January 8, 1840, U.S. District Court, Connecticut," and "Testimony of Cinque, January 8, 1840, U.S. District Court, Connecticut," NARA; "Case of the Amistad, To the Right Honorable Lord Palmerston, Her Majesty's Principal Secretary for Foreign Affairs, &c &c." (November 9, 1839), FO 1, Memorials and Petitions of the British and Foreign Anti-Slavery Society, 1839–50, Rhodes House, Oxford, E2/19.

2. "Instructions to the Missionaries," *UMH*, vol. 1, No. 2 (February 1842), 74; *CO*, vol. 2, no. 9, January 1840; the literature on the slave family, and its de facto prohibition during the antebellum era, is extensive. For example, see Fede, *People*; Blassingame, *Slave*; Gutman, *Black*; Oakes, *Slavery*.

3. For uninitiated children, see Ferme, *Underneath*, 200.

4. For divisions between the AMA and other organizations with slavery sympathies, such as the American Home Missionary Society and the American Board of Commissioners for Foreign Missions, see DeBoer, "Role of Afro-Americans." *Signal of Liberty*,

October 21, 1841 (published by the Michigan Anti-Slavery Society); Burin, *Slavery*; Staudenraus, *African*; Wander, "Salvation."

5. 40 U.S. 518 (1841), 562; *CO*, vol. 4, no. 6 [October 1841], 4; Cinquez, Kinna, and Ka'le "for the Mendi people" to Adams, reprinted in "Mendis Depart," *NYJC*, November 27, 1841; *CO*, vol. 5, no. 1 [July 1842], 1.

6. Townsend to Tappan, March 11, 1841, AMA, #F1-4925; Leavitt to Adams, August 29, 1841, AMA, #F1-5060.

7. Owens, *Black Mutiny*; 302–6; Gold, *United States*, 114; Chambers and Lee, *Amistad Rising*.

8. Walker, *We Can't*; Howe, *Afrocentrism*.

9. Film by Alvaro Toepke and Angel Serrano, "The Language You Cry In" (California Newsreel, 1998); BBC News, "Priscilla: The Story of an African Slave," November 23, 2005, http://news.bbc.co.uk/2/hi/africa/4460964.stm (last retrieved May 30, 2012); Shaw, *Memories*, 250–51.

10. Williams to Tappan, September 23, 1841, AMA, #F1-5069, and August 18, 1841, AMA, #F1-5052. For funeral rituals, see the account of Griswold, in Barber, 27; Holloway, *Africanisms*, 172.

11. Charlotte to Samuel Cowles, April 12, 1841, ACCHS; August 7, 1841, Norton. Charlotte Cowles described him as "about fifteen or sixteen years of age." Charlotte to Samuel Cowles, April 8, 1841, ACCHS; Williams to Tappan, August 18, 1841, AMA, #F1-5052; Booth to Tappan, August 27, 1841, AMA, #F1-5057; Raymond to Tappan, October 12, 1841, AMA, #F1-5077A.

12. Tappan to Leavitt, "Excursion with the Amistad Africans," November 15, 1841, reprinted in Sturge, *Visit*, li.; Tappan to Jocelyn, March 18, 1841, AMA, #F1-4937; Williams to Tappan, March 13, 1841, AMA, #F1-no ref.; *UMH*, vol. 1, no. 2 (February 1842), 54; *AFASR* 2 (June 20, 1842): 70; Banna, for example, returned to the mission "destitute of clothing." *AFASR* 2 (June 20, 1842): 70. For discussion of this, see Yannielli, "Dark Continents"; *New York Tribune*, reprinted in ACS, 1842, 158.

13. Leonard, *Records*, 144; Leighton Wilson to Benjamin Griswold, December 20, 1840, AMA, #F1-5017; *UMH*, vol. 1, no. 6 (June 1842), 125; *UM*, vol. 1, no. 1 (May 1844), 10; Thompson, *Palm Land*, 233; *AFASR* 2 (June 20, 1842): 70; see Rediker, *Amistad*, 218–23, for details of family reunification.

14. "Mendis Perform," *NYH*, May 15, 1841; *AFASR* 2 (June 20, 1842): 70

15. Baldwin to Jocelyn, Leavitt, and Tappan, March 12, 1841, Baldwin 252.

16. Davidson, "Trade and Politics," 232–33; Migeod, *Mende*, vii.

17. White, *Sierra Leone's Settler*, 5, 49–52; Ferme, *Underneath*, 200.

18. "Instructions to Mr. and Mrs. Wilson," *UMH*, vol. 1, no. 2 (February 1842), 67

19. *AFASR* 2 (June 20, 1842): 70; for the letters from Mar'gru, see Lawson, *Three Sarahs*.

20. N.B. data exists for thirty-six individuals, though one (Foone) later died in Farmington, Connecticut.

21. *UM*, vol. 1, no. 1 (May 1844), 10; Jones, *Mutiny*, 52–54. Jones omits Vai. In September 1839 "Garrah" [Grabeau] described himself as "Manding-Fay." "The Captured Africans of the Amistad," *NYMH*, October 4, 1839; Day, *Gender*, 9, for bilateral descent

among Mende. For Bandi, see Babaev, "On the Origins"; for bride-price negotiation in Mende, see Alldridge, 212–18.

22. Jones, *From Slaves*, 63–80.

23. Ibid., 55–80; Davidson, "Trade and Politics," 232–43; Holsoe, "Cassava-Leaf People," 120–55; Day, *Gender*, 15–62.

24. Ellis, *Mask*, 34; Ferme, "Staging."

25. Barber, 10–14, 26; for Grabeau, also see "The Captured Africans of the Amistad," *NYMH*, October 4, 1839.

26. Lave, *Apprenticeship*, 30, citing Holsoe, "Slavery and Economic Response"; Day, *Gender*, 19–39; Ellis, *Mask*, 34; MacCormack, "Bundu," 157; "To the Committee on Behalf of the African Prisoners," *NYJC*, September 10, 1839; MacCormack, "Madam Yoko"; Day, *Gender*.

27. Jones, *From Slaves*, 73–76; Madden I; Barber, 10.

28. "To the Committee on Behalf of the African Prisoners," *NYJC*, September 10, 1839; Gibbs to Tappan, July 1841, AMA, #F1-5042; Barber, 10; Gibbs to Tappan, July 1841, AMA, #F1-5042.

29. Alldridge, *Sierra Leone*, 213.

30. Leach, *Rainforest*, 65–66; Afzelius, *Journal*, 126; Matthews, *Voyage*, 119; AFASR 2 (June 20, 1842): 70; see Rediker, *Amistad*, 158–59.

31. Winterbottom, *Account*, vol. 1, 81–82; houses in Mende today may comprise several rooms, and there exist big houses. In a big house scenario, each co-wife has her own bed in a single, large room, and it is the husband who has his own private bedroom, where the wives alternate in turn sleeping with him. See Leach, *Rainforest*, 65–67; Ferme, *Underneath*; Barber, 27; J. M. Brown, reprinted in Brandegee and Smith, *Farmington*, 171–72.

32. Njoku, "Labor Utilization," 6–11, 20; Matthews, *Voyage*, 144; Winterbottom, *Account*, vol. 1, 145, 171–72; Brooks, *Western*, 72–73; Karr, Njoku, and Kallon, "Economics"; Njoku, "Economics"; Carney, *Black Rice*, 15–16, 21–22; Hawthorne, *Planting Rice*; Hawthorne, "From 'Black Rice,'" 151–63; Larson, *History and Memory*; Sachs, *Gendered Fields*, 89; Rich, *A Workman*, 27; Fields-Black, *Deep Roots*.

33. Jones, *From Slaves*, 50; Harris and Sawyerr, *Springs*, 129; Barber, 10–25.

34. Ranso, *Sociological*; "Meetings of the Liberated Africans," *CA*, May 22, 1841. Child mortality in nineteenth-century Africa was very high, but there is limited research. Liberia provides some comparable context. See McDaniel, "Extreme Mortality."

35. Madden I; these circumstances may or may not point to abandonment of children as responses to drought and poverty in the late eighteenth century, particularly from western central Africa. See also, Diptee, "African Children," 187.

36. Barber, 27.

37. Afzelius, *Journal*, 33; Bledsoe, *Women*, 67; Harley, "Notes," 29, cited by Bledsoe, *Women*, 67.

38. Hawthorne, *Planting Rice*; Hawthorne, "From 'Black Rice'," 151–64; Fields-Black, *Deep Roots*; Jones, *From Slaves*, 73–77.

39. *UMH*, vol. 1, no. 2 (February 1842), 71–72.

40. Covey I and II, respectively; Dougar to [Rev. Schon?], August 26, 1833, CMS/B/OMS/G C1/13, Committee Minutes, April 12, 1833–November 8, 1834, p. 224; "Special Meeting at Kissy," August 28, 1833, CMS/B/OMS/Q A 1/O 1–2: Minutes of Sub-Committees.
41. "Regulations for the guidance and management for the Cossoo boys school at Bathurst," CMS/B/OMS/C A1/O11/4.
42. "Regulations for the guidance of the schools in the Liberated African Villages," CMS/B/OMS/CA 1/O 4: 1828–42, Doc. 112.
43. Haensel, February 26, 1829, CMS/B/OMS/CA 1/O 108: Papers and reports, 1827–34; Mary Church to her sister Bertha, in Church, *Sierra Leone*, 46; Fyfe, *History*, 213; "Regulations," CMS/B/OMS/CA 1/O 11/4.
44. Schön to Private Secretary, August 29, 1833, CMS/B/OMS/CA 1/O 4: 1828–42, Doc. 217. "Report of Bathurst for the Quarter Ending 25th September 1833," and "Report of Bathurst for the Quarter Ending 25th December 1833," CMS/B/OMS/CA 1/O 219: Letters and journal extracts, 1825–53; Weeks to ?, September 4, 1835, CMS/B/OMS/CA 1/O 219. For the lesson plan, see CMS/B/OMS/CA 1/O 4 1828–42.
45. "Extracts from the Regulations Respecting the Liberated Africans, Issued by His Excellency, Sir. Neil Campbell," December 18, 1826, CMS/B/OMS/CA 1/O 4: 1824–27, Doc. 27; "Regulations," CMS/B/OMS/CA 1/O 11/4.
46. "Report of 25 June 1834"; "Report of 25 September 1834," CMS/B/OMS/CA 1/O 219.
47. Minute of Schön [undated], CMS/B/OMS/CA 1/M 6 1831–34 [mission book], 411; "Report of 25 December 1834," CMS/B/OMS/CA 1/O 219.
48. Minute of October 6, 1835, CMS/B/OMS/QA 1/O 1–2: Minutes of Sub-Committees; April 25, 1838, CMS/B/OMS/QA 1/O 1–2: Minutes of Sub-Committees. "The Rev'd Weeks . . . expressed his desire of placing a number of Liberated Africans at Regent, to attend the Society's School there, . . . it was resolved that 25 youths be taken under the charge of the Society, and that they be placed at Regent, . . . the expense of their clothes and maintenance being defrayed by government."
49. "To the Committee on Behalf of the African Prisoners" and "To the Marshal of the District of Connecticut," *NYJC*, September 10, 1839, 2.
50. George Day, "Narrative of the Africans," *NYJC*, October 10, 1839; Barber, 28; Day to Tappan, October 19, 1839, AMA, #F1-4648; "The Captured Africans of the Amistad, Teaching Philosophy to Lewis Tappen [sic] & Co.," *NYMH*, October 4, 1839; "Extract of a letter dated, New Haven, Saturday evening, Oct. 5, 1839," "Plans to Educate the Amistad Africans in English," *NYJC*, October 9, 1839; Griswold to Gallaudet, October 5, 1839, LOC, Gallaudet Papers; Speech by Cinquez, "The Captured Africans of the Amistad," *NYMH*, October 4, 1839; see Silva, "Signs."
51. "Account of the Treatment of the Blacks Taken from the Amistad," by "B," *New York American*, November 16, 1839; Norton, "Cinques, the Black Prince," 175; Dougall to Leavitt, April 26, 1841, AMA, #F1-4983.
52. "'Mendi,'" 171; "Ka-le" to Adams, January 4, 1841, published in the *Emancipator*, March 25, 1841; Tappan to Baldwin, March 22, 1841, Baldwin; Tappan to Baldwin [March 17?], 1841, Baldwin.
53. "Meetings of the Liberated Africans," *CA*, May 22, 1841; Brandegee and Smith, *Farmington*, 171; Hinks, "Underground Railroad."

54. Charlotte Cowles to Samuel Cowles, March 24, April 8, and April 12, 1841, ACCHC; J. M. Brown, reprinted in Brandegee and Smith, *Farmington*, 171–72.

55. Charlotte to Samuel Cowles, April 8, 1841, ACCHS. Norton to Tappan, August 27, 1841, AMA, #F1-5056.

56. Booth to Tappan, May 7, 1841, AMA, #F1-4992, July 26, 1841, AMA, #F1-5037; Charlotte to Samuel Cowles, April 8, 1841, ACCHS; August 25, 1841, Norton.

57. On two separate occasions, Kag'ne met both Henry Highland Garnett and James Pennington. August 25, 1841, Norton; Sturge, *Visit*, 1, 50; "Meetings of the Liberated Africans," *CA*, May 22, 1841; "Mendis Perform," *NYH*, May 15, 1841.

58. Charlotte to Samuel Cowles, April 8, 1841, ACCHS; "Mendis Depart," *NYJC*, November 27, 1841; Raymond to Tappan, October 12, 1841, AMA, #F1-5077A.

59. *AFASR* 2 (June 20, 1842): 70; Ferguson to Tappan, October 23, 1841, *UMH*, vol. 1, no. 2 (February 1842), 74–75.

60. Afzelius, *Journal*, 141: "The girls are married without any right of contradicting to the match, though always under pretence of freedom."

61. White, *Sierra Leone's Settler*, 5, 49–52.

62. *AFASR* 2 (June 20, 1842): 70; a subsequent published account was more innocuous, and omits discussion of circumcision. *AM*, May 1847, 55.

63. Jones, *From Slaves*, 181–82.

64. Day, *Gender*, 9, 17; for secrecy and secret knowledge, see Ferme, *Underneath*, 2–30, 160–67.

65. MacCormack, "Madam Yoko," 172; Alldridge, *Transformed*, 220–22; Hoffer, "Sande," 42–50; MacCormack, "Control."

66. Knörr, "Female," 80–98; White, *Sierra Leone Settler*, 5, 49–52.

67. McCullock, *Western*, 20; Jones, *From Slaves*, 182; Matthews, *Voyage*, 72–73; Afzelius, *Journal*, 141; Alldridge, *Tranformed*, 220, 224.

68. Bledsoe, *Women*, 67; MacCormack, "Bundu," 157.

69. For an extensive discussion of secrecy in *bondo*, see Ferme, *Underneath*; Matthews, *Voyage*, 70–72; Alldridge, *Tranformed*, 223, 228; Matthews, *Voyage*, 73; *AFASR* 2 (June 20, 1842): 70.

70. *AFASR* 2 (June 20, 1842): 70; Ericksen codes Mende as requiring cutting, preferring chastity, and having active "menarcheal" ceremonies. Ericksen, "Female," 190; Matthews, *Voyage*, 70–73, emphasis in original; Afzelius, *Journal*, 109, 126–27, 141; Northcote Thomas (*Anthropological Report on Sierra Leone*, London, 1916, vol. 3, 13, 151–52) suggests there is no evidence to show how and under what circumstances the practice spread. Schlenker (*A Collection of Temne Traditions, Fables, and Proverbs*, London, 1861) asserted that it was spread from the Mende to the Temne. Winterbottom, *Account* (vol. 1, 107) considers it universal at one point, and then restricted to the Muslim north in another context (vol. 2, 235, 237). See Kup, *History*, 164; Ericksen, "Female."

71. Matthews, *Voyage*, 73; MacCormack, "Sande," 32; MacCormack, "Bundu," 157; Fanthorpe, "Sierra Leone," 20; Jedrej, "Cosmology," 497–515; Ferme, *Underneath*, 1–3.

72. MacCormack, "Bundu," 157.

73. Chevrier, "Note," 359–76; Caulker, "Problem," 30, cited by Kalous, "Human," 310; Banfield to Ritson, April 10, 1917, BFBS.

74. Gaby, *Relation*, 40–45; Banfield to Ritson, April 10, 1917, BFBS.

75. Wilberforce, *Sherbro*, 26; Dapper, *Naukeurige*, 413–15, as translated by Jones, *From Slaves*, 179; Jobson, *Golden Trade*, 139–41; Matthews, *Voyage*, 82; Jones, *From Slaves*, 179.

76. Gaby, *Relation*, 42; see Kalous, "Human," 305–29, for the most extensive discussion of ethnic variation; Testimony of J. C. E. Parkes, Secretary for Native Affairs, in Sierra Leone Protectorate, *Report*, 34.

77. Büttikofer, *Reisebilder*, vol. 2, 306; Matthews, *Voyage*, 83; personal communication, Emma Christopher, August 2012. See also documentary film, Emma Christopher, "They Are We" (2013).

78. Dapper, *Naukeurige*, 413–15 is ambiguous on this aspect; Kalous rejects the two primary theses—that it emerged endogenously in West Africa (A. E. Jensen, 1933) or that it spread from Egypt (M. D. W. Jeffreys, 1949). Kalous, "Human," 305–29; "To the Committee on Behalf of the African Prisoners," *NYJC*, September 10, 1839; Jones, *From Slaves*; Leonard, *Records*, 105; Koelle, "Narrative," 29; Büttikofer, *Reisebilder*, vol. 2, 306; Little, *Mende*, 119–20; Gorvie, *Old and New*, 15–16; for early sixteenth-century explanations, including a lack of capacity to procreate see Pereira, *Esmeraldo*, 81–83.

79. Kalous, "Human," 323; Jones, *From Slaves*, 181; Davidson, "Trade and Politics," 237–38; Matthews, *Voyage*, 83; d'Azevedo, "Gola Society," 70–76; Rediker, *Amistad*, 74–75, 81–82; Abraham, *Mende*, 1–30; Wilberforce, *Sherbro*, 26; BNA, CO 267/467/36: Despatches.

80. Rediker, *Amistad*, 219, citing the *Emancipator* April 28, 1842. Yannielli, "Dark Continents"; Davidson, "Trade and Politics," 239; d'Azevedo, "Gola Society," 70–76; Raymond to Tappan, February 9, 1846, AMA, #F1-5624; for details of the violence, see Chalmers's report, Great Britain, *Report*, 489; Yannielli, *Cinqué*, 17; *UM*, vol. 50 (Extra) (January 1845), 12; Abraham, *Mende*, 159–60; letters from William Raymond, "Terrible War in the Sherbro," *UM*, vol. 2, no.12 (May 1846), 105; Raymond, "Interesting Intelligence from Africa," *UM*, vol. 3, no.2 (July 1846), 9–10.

81. Dapper, *Naukeurige*, 413; Cole, *Revelation*, 50; Jones, *From Slaves*, 181.

82. Davidson, "Trade and Politics," 240–41; Brooks to Thompson, August 25, October 5, 1850, AMA; Banfield to Ritson, April 10, 1917, BFBS; Koelle, "Narrative," 29.

83. Leonard, 143–44.

84. Holsey, *Routes*, 67.

85. Ferme, *Underneath*, 200–201.

EPILOGUE

1. Raymond, July 7, 1844, and August 26, 1844, *UM*, vol. 50 (Extra) (January 1845), 1–2, 8; "Journal of Messrs. Raston and Raymond," *UM*, vol. 50 (Extra) (January 1845), 16.

2. "Journal of Messrs. Raston and Raymond," *UM*, vol. 50 (Extra) (January 1845), 16; Raymond to Tappan, October ?, 1844, *UM*, vol. 2, no. 5 (April 1, 1845), 51.

3. Raymond, April 21, 1845 and July 1, 1845, *UM*, vol. 2, no. 8 (October 1845), 76, 79; Raymond, November 10, 1845, *UM*, vol. 2, no. 12 (May 1846), 105; Raymond to Tap-

pan, February 9, 1846, *UM*, vol. 3, no. 2 (July 1846), 9–10; Davidson, "Trade and Politics," 234.

4. Brooks to Thompson, August 25, and October 5, 1850, AMA.

5. Brooks to Thompson, August 25, and October 5, 1850, AMA; Barber, 15; Raymond to Hannah Harnden, August 26, 1844, *UM*, vol. 50 (January 1845), 6; James Cutler Tefft to George Whipple. September 10, 1852, AMA, #F1-6398-99.

6. Tefft to Whipple. September 10, 1852, AMA, #F1-6398-99; Thompson, *Palm Land*, 233; Raymond to Tappan, July 10, 1844, *UM*, vol. 50 (January 1845), 3.

7. Raymond, July 1, 1845, *UM*, vol. 2, no. 8 (October 1845), 79; *UM*, vol. 50 (Extra) (January 1845), 11; Thompson, *Thompson in Africa*, 63; Alldridge, *Transformed*, 262.

8. Lawrance and Roberts, "Contextualizing Trafficking," 1–34; for examples of such accounts, see Greene, *West African*; Lawrance "Documenting Child Slavery," 163–82.

BIBLIOGRAPHY

PRIMARY SOURCES

ARCHIVAL REPOSITORIES

Amistad Research Center, Tulane University, New Orleans
    American Missionary Association Archives
Archivo Histórico Provincial de Camagüey, Camagüey, Cuba
    Fondo Protocolos
Archivo Histórico Provincial-Matanzas, Matanzas, Cuba
    Fondo: Gobierto Provincial Esclavos (Bozales), Leg. 21 and 183
Archivo National de Cuba, Havana, Cuba
    Tribunal de Comercio
Beinecke Rare Book and Manuscript Library, Yale University
Bodleian Library, Rhodes House, Oxford University
    FO 1, Memorials and Petitions of the British and Foreign Anti-Slavery Society
British National Archives, Kew, Surrey
    FO 84
    FO 315
    CO 267
    CO 318/146
    CO 1069/88
Cadbury Research Library, Special Collections, University of Birmingham, U.K.
    Archives of the Christian Missionary Society
Caird Library, National Maritime Museum, Greenwich
Cambridge University Library
    British and Foreign Bible Society Archives
Connecticut Historical Society, Hartford
    Charlotte and Samuel Cowles Correspondence, 1833–46
Connecticut State Library, Hartford
    New Haven County Court Records

Duke University Library Manuscript Collection
  John Campbell Papers, 1795–1814
Drew University, Madison, N.J.
  General Commission on Archives and History of the United Methodist Church
Library of Congress
  Papers of Lewis Tappan
  Papers of Thomas H. Gallaudet
Mystic Seaport Museum, Mystic, Conn.
  Andrew T. Judson Papers
National Archives, Washington, D.C.
  Despatches from United States Consuls in Havana, Cuba, 1783–1906
National Archives and Records Administration, Northeast Region, Waltham, Mass.
  Records of the District Courts of the United States
National Archives of Canada, Ottawa
  John Dougall and family fonds
New Haven County Archives, New Haven, Conn.
  Connecticut Federal Census Index
New-York Historical Society Library
  Department of Prints, Photographs, and Architectural Collections
Sierra Leone National Archives
  Colonial Correspondence, 1833
  Freetown Register of Liberated Africans
  Liberated African Department Letterbook, 1831–34
United Kingdom Hydrographic Office
Yale University Library and Manuscripts
  Baldwin Family Papers
  Norton Family Papers

GOVERNMENT REPORTS AND PUBLICATIONS

*Correspondence with the British Commissioners at Sierra Leone, The Havana, Rio de Ja-
  neiro, and Surinam Relating to the Slave Trade.* London, 1833–45.
Great Britain, Immigration Commission. *General Reports of the Immigration Commis-
  sioners,* 1839–45.
Great Britain, Foreign and Commonwealth Office. *British and Foreign State Papers*
  (HMSO), 1830–45.
Great Britain, Parliamentary Papers. *House of Commons Papers,* 1830–45.
Great Britain, Sierra Leone Protectorate, *Report by Her Majesty's Commissioner and Cor-
  respondence on the Subject of the Insurrection in the Sierra Leone Protectorate,* 1898.
  London: Darling and Son, 1899.
*Report from the Select Committee of the House of Lords, Appointed to Consider the Best
  Means Which Great Britain Can Adopt for the Final Extinction of the African Slave
  Trade, Session 1849.* London, 1849.

Reports of Cases at Law Argued and Determined in the Court of Appeals and Court of Errors of South Carolina, vol. 11, South Carolina, Court of Appeals, J. S. G. Richardson A. S. Johnston, 1859.

United States of America, Bureau of the Census. *Sixth Census of the United States, 1840*. Washington, D.C.: National Archives and Records Administration, 1840.

NEWSPAPERS AND PERIODICALS

Abolitionist
American and Foreign Anti-Slavery Reporter
American Missionary
Charter Oak
Colored American
Emancipator
Hartford Daily Courant
New Haven Columbian Register
New York American
New York Advertiser and Express
New York Commercial Advertiser
New York Evangelist
New York Herald
New York Journal of Commerce
New York Morning Herald
New York Sun
New York Tribune
Richmond Enquirer
Signal of Liberty
Times (London)
Toronto Patriot
Union Missionary
Union Missionary Herald
Voice of the Fugitive
Watchman

DISSERTATIONS AND UNPUBLISHED SOURCES

Anderson, Richard, Alex Borucki, Daniel Domingues da Silva, David Eltis, Paul Lachance, Philip Misevich, and Olatunji Ojo. 2012. "Using Pre-Orthographic African Names to Identify the Origins of Captives in the Transatlantic Slave Trade: The Registers of Liberated Africans, 1808–1862." Paper presented in Freetown, Sierra Leone, "Sierra Leone: Past and Present," April 22–27, 2012.

Babaev, Kirill. 2011 "On the Origins of Southwest Mande Ethnonyms." Unpub. paper. http://llacan.vjf.cnrs.fr/fichiers/mande2011/bublio/babaev.pdf.

Banfield, Alexander W. 1934. "A Short History of the Life and Work of A. W. Banfield." Bethel College Library Manuscripts, Bethel College, Mishawaka, Ind.

Caulker, Glenn Augustus. 1957. "The Problem of African Youth in Contact with Western Culture." Master's thesis, Fourah Bay College, University of Sierra Leone.

Davidson, John. 1969. "Trade and Politics in the Sherbro Hinterland, 1849–1890." Ph.D. diss., University of Wisconsin.

DeBoer, Clara M. 1973. "The Role of Afro-Americans in the Origin and Work of the American Missionary Association, 1839–1877." Ph.D. diss., Rutgers University.

Freeman, Rhoda G. 1966. "The Free Negro in New York City in the Era Before the Civil War." Ph.D. diss., Columbia University.

Hinks, Peter. 2000. "Underground Railroad Report." Unpub. research report, Connecticut Commission on Culture and Tourism, Hartford.

Hofstee, Erik J. W. 2001. "The Great Divide: The Social History of the Middle Passage in the Trans-Atlantic Slave Trade." Ph.D. diss., Michigan State University.

Holsoe, Svend. 1967. "The Cassava-Leaf People: An Ethnohistorical Study of the Vai People with a Particular Emphasis on the Tewo Chiefdom." Ph.D. diss., Boston University.

Israel, W. 1928. "The Montreal Negro Community." Mémoire de Maîtrise en Sociologie, Montreal, McGill University.

Johnson, Clifton H. 1958. "The American Missionary Association, 1846–1861: A Study of Christian Abolitionism." Ph.D. diss., University of North Carolina, Chapel Hill.

Lane, Calvin. n.d. "The African Squadron: The U.S. Navy and the Slave Trade, 1920–1862." http://amistad.mysticseaport.org/discovery/themes/lane.navy.html#text.17 (retrieved May 6, 2009).

Misevich, Philip R. 2009. "On the Frontier of 'Freedom': Abolition and the Transformation of Atlantic Commerce in Southern Sierra Leone, 1790s to 1860s." Ph.D. diss., Emory University.

Njoku, Athanasius O. 1971. "Labor Utilization in Traditional Agriculture: The Case of Sierra Leone Rice Farms." Ph.D. diss., University of Illinois at Urbana-Champaign.

Powers, Nicholas. 2008. "The Undertow of Reason: Redefining the Sublime Through the Middle Passage." Ph.D. diss., CUNY Graduate School.

Scanlan, Padraic X. 2013. "MacCarthy's Skull: Abolition in Sierra Leone, 1806–1823." Ph.D. diss., Princeton University.

Yannielli, Joseph. 2014. "Dark Continents: Africa and the American Abolition of Slavery." Ph.D. diss., Yale University.

BOOKS AND ARTICLES

Abraham, Arthur. 1978. *Mende Government and Politics Under Colonial Rule: A Historical Study of Political Change in Sierra Leone, 1890–1937.* Freetown: Sierra Leone University Press.

Ackerson, Wayne. 2005. *The African Institution (1807–1827) and the Antislavery Movement in Great Britain.* Lewiston, N.Y.: E. Mellen Press.

Adams, John. 1823. *Remarks on the Country Extending from Cape Palmas to the River Congo.* London: Whitaker.

Adams, John Quincy. 1841. *Argument of John Quincy Adams, Before the Supreme Court of the United States: In the Case of the United States, Appellants, vs. Cinque, and Others, Africans, Captured in the Schooner Amistad, by Lieut. Gedney, Delivered on the 24th of February and 1st of March, 1841.* Boston: S. W. Benedict.

Adderley, Rosanne Marion. 2006. *"New Negroes from Africa": Slave Trade Abolition and Free African Settlement in the Nineteenth-Century Caribbean.* Bloomington: Indiana University Press.

Adejunmobi, Moradewun. 2004. *Vernacular Palaver: Imaginations of the Local and Non-Native Languages in West Africa.* Tonawanda, N.Y.: Multilingual Matters.

Afzelius, Adam. 1967. *Sierra Leone Journal, 1795–1796,* ed. Alexander Peter Kup. *Studia Ethnographica Upsaliensia* 27. Uppsala.

Ahsan, Monira. 2009. "The Potential and Challenges of Rights-Based Research with Children and Young People: Experiences from Bangladesh." *Children's Geographies* 7, no. 4: 391–403.

Aimes, Hubert Hillary. 1907. *The History of Slavery in Cuba, 1511–1868.* New York: G. P. Putnam and Sons.

Alagoa, E. J., and A. M. Okorobia. 1994. "Pawnship in Nembe, Niger Delta." In Toyin Falola and Paul E. Lovejoy, eds., *Pawnship in Africa: Debt Bondage in Historical Perspective,* 72–85. Boulder: Westview Press.

Alexander, James Edward. 1840. *Excursions in Western Africa, and Narrative of the Campaign in Kaffir-Land.* 2 vols. London: Henry Colburn.

Alldridge, Thomas Joshua. 1901. *The Sherbro and its Hinterland.* London: Macmillan.

———. 1910. *A Transformed Colony: Sierra Leone as It Was, and as It Is: Its Progress, Peoples, Natives Customs and Undeveloped Wealth.* London: Seeley.

Anderson, Benjamin. 1971 [1887]. *Narrative of a Journey to Musardu, the Capital of the Western Mandingoes.* 2nd ed., with introduction by Humphrey Fisher. London: Taylor and Francis.

Anderson-Levitt, Kathryn M. 2005. "The Schoolyard Gate: Schooling and Childhood in Global Perspective." *Journal of Social History* 38, no. 4: 987–1006.

Arendt, Hannah. 1958. *The Human Condition.* Chicago: University of Chicago Press.

Ariès, Philippe. 1960. *L'enfant et la vie familiale: sous l'ancien régime.* Paris: Librairie Plon.

Arnalte, Arturo. 2007. *Los últimos esclavos de Cuba: los niños cautivos de la goleta Batans.* Madrid: Alianza Editorial Sa.

Austen, Ralph. 2010. *Trans-Saharan Africa in World History.* New York: Oxford University Press.

Bacon, David Francis. 1843. *Wanderings on the Seas and Shores of Africa.* New York: Joseph Harrison.

Baldwin, Roger Sherman. 1841. *Argument of Roger Baldwin, of New Haven, Before the Supreme Court of the United States.* New York: Benedict.

Baldwin, Simeon E. 1886. *The Captives of the Amistad.* Vol. 4 of the Papers of the New Haven Historical Society. New Haven.

Barcia, Manuel. 2012. *The Great African Slave Revolt of 1825: Cuba and the Fight for Freedom in Matanzas.* Baton Rouge: Louisiana State University Press.

Barcia, María del Carmen. 1987. *Burguesía esclavista y abolición*. Havana: Editorial de Ciencias Sociales.

Barclay, Oliver. 2001. *Thomas Fowell Buxton and the Liberation of Slaves*. York, U.K.: William Sessions.

Barry, Boubacar. 1997. *Senegambia and the Atlantic Slave Trade*. New York: Cambridge University Press.

Batibo, Herman. 2005. *Language Decline and Death in Africa: Causes, Consequences, and Challenges*. Tonawanda, N.Y.: Multilingual Matters.

Baxter, Maurice Glen. 1984. *One and Inseparable: Daniel Webster and the Union*. Cambridge: Harvard University Press.

Bell, James. 1832. *A System of Geography, Popular and Scientific*. Glasgow: Archibald Fullarton; Edinburgh: W. Tait; Dublin: W Curry, Jun; London: Simpkin and Marshall, and W. S. Orr.

Bendor-Samuel, John, and Rhonda L. Hartell, eds. 1989. *The Niger–Congo Languages: A Classification and Description of Africa's Largest Language Family*. Lanham, Md.: University Press of America.

Benton, Thomas Hart. 1873. *Thirty Years' View; or, A History of the Working of the American Government for Thirty Years, from 1820 to 1850*. New York: D. Appleton.

Bergad, Laird W. 1987. "Slave Prices in Cuba, 1840–1875." *Hispanic American Historical Review* 67, no. 4: 631–55.

———. 1990. *Cuban Rural Society in the Nineteenth Century: The Social and Economic History of Monoculture in Matanzas*. Princeton: Princeton University Press.

Bergad, Laird W., Fe Iglesias García, and María del Carmen Barcia. 1995. *The Cuban Slave Market, 1790–1880*. New York: Cambridge University Press.

Bernstein, Robin. 2011. *Racial Innocence: Performing American Childhood from Slavery to Civil Rights*. New York: New York University Press.

Bertley, Leo W. 1997. *Canada and Its People of African Descent*. Pierrefonds, Quebec: Bilongo Publishers.

Bethell, Leslie. 1966. "The Mixed Commissions for the Suppression of the Transatlantic Slave Trade in the Nineteenth Century." *Journal of African History* 7, no. 1: 70–93.

Bickford-Smith, Vivian, and Richard Mendelsohn. 2007 *Black and White in Colour: Africa's History on Screen*. Athens: Ohio University Press.

Blake, William O. 1861. *The History of Slavery and the Slave Trade, Ancient and Modern*. New York: H. Miller.

Blassingame, John W. 1977. *Slave Testimony: Two Centuries of Letters, Speeches, Interviews, and Autobiographies*. 2nd ed. Baton Rouge: Louisiana State University Press.

Bledsoe, Caroline. 1980. *Women and Marriage in Kpelle Society*. Stanford: Stanford University Press.

Bogen, Hyman. 1992. *The Luckiest Orphans: A History of the Hebrew Orphan Asylum of New York*. Champaign: University of Illinois Press.

Bolster, Jeffrey. 1997. *Black Jacks: African American Seamen in the Age of Sail*. Cambridge: Harvard University Press.

Bornstein, Erica. 2010. "The Value of Orphans." In Erica Bornstein and Peter Redfield, eds., *Forces of Compassion: Humanitarianism Between Ethics and Politics*, 123–48. Santa Fe: School of Advanced Research.

Bouët-Willaumez, Louis-Edouard. 1848. *Description nautique des côtes de l'Afrique occidentale*. Paris: Robiquet.

Boyle, James T. 1831. *A Practical Medico-Historical Account of the Western Coast of Africa: Embracing a Topographical Description of Its Shores, Rivers, and Settlements, with Their Seasons and Comparative Healthiness, Together with the Causes, Symptoms, and Treatment, of the Fevers of Western Africa*. London: S. Highley.

Brandegee, Arthur, and Eddy N. Smith. 1906. *Farmington, Connecticut: The Village of Beautiful Homes*. Farmington, Conn.

Brenzinger, Matthias, Bernd Heine, and Gabriele Sommer. 1991. "Language Death in Africa." *Diogenes* 39, no. 2: 19–44.

British and Foreign Anti-Slavery Society. 1841. *Proceedings of the General Anti-Slavery Convention*. London: British and Foreign Anti-Slavery Society.

Brooke, Henry K. 1841. *Book of Pirates: Containing Narratives of the Most Remarkable Piracies and Plunders Committed on the High Seas*. Philadelphia: J. B. Perry.

Brooks, George E. 2011. *Western Africa and Cabo Verde, 1790s–1830s*. AuthorHouse.

Brown, Christopher Leslie. 2006. *Moral Capital: Foundations of British Abolitionism*. Chapel Hill: University of North Carolina Press.

Brown, Vincent. 2008. *The Reaper's Garden: Death and Power in the World of Atlantic Slavery*. Cambridge: Harvard University Press.

———. 2009. "Social Death and Political Life in the Study of Slavery." *American Historical Review* 114 (December): 1231–49.

Brown-Kubisch, Linda. 2004. *The Queen's Bush Settlement: Black Pioneers, 1839–1865*. Toronto: Dundurn Press.

Brunton, Henry. 1802. *Grammar and Vocabulary of the Sosso Language*. Edinburgh: J. Ritchie.

Bruun, Malthe Conrad. 1823. *Universal Geography; or, A Description of All the Parts of the World*. Vol. 4. Edinburgh: Adam Black.

Burin, Eric. 2005. *Slavery and the Peculiar Solution: A History of the American Colonization Society*. Gainesville: University Press of Florida.

Burton, E. J. 1842. "Observations on the Climate, Topography, and Diseases of the British Colonies in Western Africa." *Provincial Medical and Surgical Journal* 3. London: Churchill.

Burton, Gera. 2007. "Liberty's Call: Richard Robert Madden's Voice in the Anti-Slavery Movement." *Irish Migration Studies in Latin America* 5, no. 3 (November): 199–206.

Büttikofer, Johann. 1890. *Reisebilder aus Liberia: Resultate geographischer, naturwissenschaftlicher und ethnographischer Untersuchungen während der Jahre 1879–1882 und 1886–1887*. Leiden: E. J. Brill.

Byrd, Alexander X. 2006. "Eboe, Country, Nation, and Gustavus Vassa's Interesting Narrative." *William and Mary Quarterly* 63, no. 1: 123–48.

———. 2006. "Olaudah Equiano, the South Carolinian? A Forum." *Historically Speaking* 7, no. 3: 2–16.

Cable, Mary. 1977. *Black Odyssey: The Case of the Slave Ship "Amistad."* New York: Penguin.

Caillié, Réné. 1830. *Travels Through Central Africa*. Vol. 1. London: Colburn and Bentley.

Calarco, Tom. 2010. *Places of the Underground Railroad: A Geographical Guide*. Santa Barbara: ABC-CLIO.

Campbell, Gwyn, Suzanne Miers, and Joseph C. Miller. 2009. *Children in Slavery Through the Ages*. Athens: Ohio University Press.

———. 2011. *Child Slaves in the Modern World*. Athens: Ohio University Press.

Candido, Mariana P. 2010. "Different Slave Journeys: Enslaved African Seamen on Board of Portuguese Ships, c. 1760–1820s." *Slavery and Abolition* 31, no. 3: 395–409

———. 2013. *An African Slaving Port and the Atlantic World: Benguela and Its Hinterland* Cambridge: Cambridge University Press.

Carey, Brycchan. 2005. *British Abolitionism and the Rhetoric of Sensibility: Writing, Sentiment, and Slavery, 1760–1807*. Basingstoke: Palgrave Macmillan.

Carney, Judith. 2002. *Black Rice: The African Origins of Rice Cultivation in the Americas*. Cambridge: Harvard University Press.

Carretta, Vincent. 1999. "Olaudah Equiano or Gustavus Vassa? New Light on an Eighteenth-Century Question of Identity." *Slavery and Abolition* 20, no. 3: 96–105.

———. 2003. "Introduction." In *The Interesting Narrative and Other Writings*, edited with an introduction and notes by Vincent Carretta. New York: Penguin.

———. 2005. *Equiano, the African: Biography of a Self-Made Man*. Athens: University of Georgia Press.

———. 2007. "Response to Paul Lovejoy's 'Autobiography and Memory: Gustavus Vassa, alias Olaudah Equiano, the African.'" *Slavery and Abolition* 28, no. 1: 115–19.

Chambers, Douglas B. 1997. "'My Own Nation': Igbo Exiles in the Diaspora." *Slavery and Abolition* 18, no. 1: 72–97.

———. 2007. "'Almost an Englishman': Carretta's Equiano—Review of Vincent Carretta, *Equiano the African: Biography of a Self-Made Man*." H-Net Reviews, November. http://www.h-net.org/reviews/showrev.cgi?path=53611200252153 (last retrieved March 15, 2013).

Chambers, Veronica, and Paul Lee. 1998. *Amistad Rising: A Story of Freedom*. New York: HMH Books for Young Readers.

Chatterjee, Indrani. 1999. "Colouring Subalternity: Slaves, Concubines and Social Orphans Under the East India Company." In Gautam Bhadra, Gyan Prakash, and Susie Tharu, eds., *Subaltern Studies*, vol. 10. Delhi: Oxford University Press.

———. 2000. "A Slave's Search for Selfhood in Eighteenth-Century Hindustan." *Indian Economic and Social History Review* 37, no. 1.

Chess, Stella, and Mahin Hassibi. 1986. *Principles and Practice of Child Psychiatry*. 2nd ed. New York: Springer.

Chevrier, Marc A. 1906. "Note relative aux coutumes des adeptes de la société secrète des Scymos: indigènes fétichistes du littoral de la Guinée." *L'Anthropologie* 27: 359–376

Childs, G. Tucker. 1995. *A Grammar of Kisi: A Southern Atlantic Language*. Berlin: Walter de Gruyter.

———. 2000. *A Dictionary of the Kisi Language: With an English-Kisi Index*. Cologne: Koppe.

———. 2009. "The Mande and Atlantic Groups of Niger-Congo: Prolonged Contact with Asymmetrical Linguistic Consequences." Special issue of the *Journal of Languages in Contact*, ed. F. Lüpke and M. Raymond.

———. 2010. "Language Contact in Africa: A Selected Review." In *The Handbook of Language Contact*, ed. Raymond Hickey, 695–713. New York: Wiley.

———. 2011. *A Grammar of Mani*. Berlin: Mouton de Gruyter.

Christensen, Matthew J. 2012. *Rebellious Histories: The Amistad Slave Revolt and the Cultures of Late Twentieth-Century Black Transnationalism*. Albany: SUNY Press.

Christopher, Emma. 2006. *Slave Ship Sailors and Their Captive Cargoes, 1730–1807*. Cambridge: Cambridge University Press.

Christopher, Emma, Cassandra Pybus, and Marcus Rediker. 2007. *Many Middle Passages: Forced Migration and the Making of the Modern World*. Berkeley: University of California Press.

Church, Mary. 1835. *Sierra Leone; or, The Liberated Africans in a Series of Letters from a Young Lady to Her Sister in 1833 and 34*. London: Longman.

Clacherty, Glynis, and Donald, David. 2007. "Child Participation in Research: Reflections on Ethical Challenges in the Southern African Context." *African Journal of AIDS Research* 6, no. 2: 147–156.

Clarence-Smith, William Gervase. 1984. "The Portuguese Contribution to the Cuba Slave and Coolie Trades in the Nineteenth Century." *Slavery and Abolition* 5, no. 1: 24–33.

Clarke, Robert B. 1843. *Sierra Leone: A Description of the Manners and Customs of the Liberated Africans, with Observations upon the Natural History of the Colony and a Notice of the Native Tribes*. London: James Ridgway.

———. n.d. *The Inhabitants of Sierra Leone: (with pictorial illustrations, from original drawings by Mrs. Clarke)* Freetown. (Originally published as *Sketches of the Colony of Sierra Leone and Its Inhabitants*. London: T. Richards, 1863.)

Clowes, W. L. 1997. *The Royal Navy; A History from the Earliest Times to 1900*. Vol. 6. London: Chatham Publishing.

Clowes, W. Laird et al. 1897. *The Royal Navy, a History from the Earliest Times to Present*. London: Low, Marston.

Cmiel, Kenneth. 1995. *A Home of Another Kind: One Chicago Orphanage and the Tangle of Child Welfare*. Chicago: University of Chicago Press.

Cohn, Raymond L., and Richard A. Jensen. 1982. "The Determinants of Slave Mortality Rates on the Middle Passage." *Explorations in Economic History* 19: 269–82.

Cole, J. August. 1886. *A Revelation of the Secret Orders of Western Africa: Including an Explanation of the Beliefs and Customs of African Heathenism*. Dayton: United Brethren Publishing House.

Collison, Gary. 1995. "'Loyal and Dutiful Subjects of Her Gracious Majesty, Queen Victoria': Fugitive Slaves in Montreal, 1850–1866." *Québec Studies* 19: 59–70.

———. 1997. *Shadrach Minkins: From Fugitive Slave to Citizen*. Cambridge: Harvard University Press.

Conder, Josiah. 1830. *The Modern Traveller*. Vol. 3. London: Duncan.

Conrad, Robert E. 2000. *Children of God's Fire: A Documentary History of Black Slavery in Brazil*. State College: Pennsylvania State University Press.

Corry, Joseph. 1807. *Observations upon the Windward Coast of Africa*. London: G. and W. Nicol.

Crooks, J. J. 1903. *A History of the Colony of Sierra Leone in West Africa*. Dublin: Browne and Nolan.

Cunningham, Hugh. 1991. *The Children of the Poor: Representations of Childhood Since the Seventeenth Century*. Oxford: Blackwell.

Curtin, Philip. 1955. *Two Jamaicas: The Role of Ideas in the Tropical Colony, 1830–1865*. Cambridge: Harvard University Press.

d'Azevedo, Warren L. 1959. "The Setting of Gola Society and Culture: Some Theoretical Implications of Variation in Time and Space." *Kroeber Anthropological Society Papers* 21: 43–125.

———. 1962. "Some Historical Problems in the Delineation of a Central West Atlantic Region." *Annals of the New York Academy of Sciences* 96: 512–38.

———. 1962. "Common Principles of Variant Kinship Structure Among the Gola of Western Liberia." *American Anthropologist* 64: 504–20.

———. 1971. "Tribe and Chiefdom on the Windward Coast." *Rural Africana* 15: 10–29.

Dalby, David. 1965. "The Mel Languages: A Reclassification of Southern 'West Atlantic.'" *African Language Studies* 6: 2–17.

———. 1965. "Mel Languages in the Polyglotta Africana. Part 1: Baga, Landuma and Temne." *African Language Studies* 6: 129–35.

———. 1966. "Mel Languages in the Polyglotta Africana. Part 2: Bullom, Kissi and Gola." *Sierra Leone Language Review* 5: 139–51.

Dalleo, Peter D. 1984. "Africans in the Caribbean: A Preliminary Reassessment of Recaptives in the Bahamas, 1811–1860." *Journal of the Bahamas Historical Society* 6: 15–24.

Dapper, Olfert. 1688. *Naukeurige Beschrijvingen der Afrikaensche gewesten*. Amsterdam.

Davis, David Brion. 2008. *Inhuman Bondage: The Rise and Fall of Slavery in the New World*. Oxford: Oxford University Press.

Davis, R. W. 1995. *Origins of Modern Freedom in the West*. Stanford: Stanford University Press.

Day, Lynda Rose. 2012. *Gender and Power in Sierra Leone: Women Chiefs of the Last Two Centuries*. New York: Palgrave Macmillan.

Despicht, Stanley M. 1939. "A Short History of the Gallinas Chiefdoms." *Sierra Leone Studies* 21: 5–11.

Diedrich, Maria, Henry Louis Gates, Carl Pedersen, eds. 1999. *Black Imagination and the Middle Passage*. New York: Oxford University Press.

Diptee, Audra A. 2006. "African Children in the British Slave Trade During the Late Eighteenth Century." *Slavery and Abolition* 27, no. 2: 183–96.

Diptee, Audra A., and Martin A. Klein. 2010. "African Childhoods and the Colonial Project." *Journal of Family History* 35, no. 1: 1–10.

Doherty, Thomas. 1997. "Olaudah Equiano's Journeys: The Geography of a Slave Narrative." *Partisan Review* 64, no. 4 (Fall): 572–81.

Donnan, E., ed. 1969. *Documents Illustrative of the History of the Slave Trade to America*, vol. 2: *Eighteenth Century*. New York: Octagon Books.

Dorjahn, Vernon R., and Barry L. Isaac, eds. 1979. *Essays on the Economic Anthropology of Liberia and Sierra Leone*. Philadelphia: Institute for Liberian Studies.

Dorsey, Joseph C. 2003. *Slave Trade in the Age of Abolition: Puerto Rico, West Africa and the Non-Hispanic Caribbean, 1815–1859*. Gainesville: University of Florida Press.

Drake, Richard. 1972. *Revelations of a Slave Smuggler*. Northbrook, Ill.: Metro Books.

Drescher, Seymour. 1977. *Econocide: British Slavery in the Age of Abolition.* Pittsburgh: University of Pittsburgh Press.

DuBois, Laurent. 2005. *Avengers of the New World: The Story of the Haitian Revolution.* Cambridge: Belknap Press of Harvard University Press.

———. 2006. *Colony of Citizens: Revolution and Slave Emancipation in the French Caribbean, 1787–1804.* Chapel Hill: University of North Carolina Press.

Duffield, Ian. 1993. "Skilled Workers or Marginalized Poor? The African Population of the United Kingdom, 1812–52." *Immigrants and Minorities* 12, no. 3: 49–87.

Dunaway, Wilma. 2003. *Slavery in the American Mountain South.* Cambridge: Cambridge University Press.

Durrant, Emily. 1883. *The Good News in Africa, Scenes from Missionary History.* London: Seeley Jackson.

Edwards, Judith. 2004. *Abolitionists and Slave Resistance: Breaking the Chains of Slavery.* Berkeley Heights, N.J.: Enslow Publishers.

Ekechi, Felix K. 1994. "Pawnship in Igbo Society." In Toyin Falola and Paul E. Lovejoy, eds., *Pawnship in Africa: Debt Bondage in Historical Perspective,* 83–104. Boulder: Westview Press.

Elkins, Stanley. 1959. *Slavery: A Problem in American Institutional and Intellectual Life.* Chicago: University of Chicago Press.

Ellis, Stephen. 2001. *Mask of Anarchy: The Destruction of Liberia and the Religious Dimension of an African Civil War.* New York: New York University Press.

Eltis, David. 1984. "Mortality and Voyage Length in the Middle Passage: New Evidence from the Nineteenth Century." *Journal of Economic History* 44, no. 2 (June): 301–8.

———. 1987. *Economic Growth and the Ending of the Transatlantic Slave Trade.* Oxford: Oxford University Press.

———. 2013. "Age Categories." http://www.slavevoyages.org/tast/database/agecategories .faces (accessed May 6, 2013).

Eltis, David, and Stanley L. Engerman. 1992. "Was the Slave Trade Dominated by Men?" *Journal of Interdisciplinary History* 23, no. 2 (Autumn): 237–57.

———. 1993. "Fluctuations in Sex and Age Ratios in the Transatlantic Slave Trade, 1663–1864." *Economic History Review* 46, no. 2: 308–23.

Eltis, David, S. Behrendt, D. Richardson, and Herbert S. Klein, eds. 1999. *The Trans-Atlantic Slave Trade: A Database on CD-ROM.* Cambridge: Cambridge University Press

Eltis, David, Stephen D. Behrendt, David Richardson, and Herbert Klein, eds. 2000. *The Trans-Atlantic Slave Trade: A Database on CD-ROM.* Cambridge: Cambridge University Press.

Ericksen, Karen Paige. 1989. "Female Genital Mutilations in Africa." *Cross-Cultural Research* 23: 182–204.

Fairhead, James, Tim Geysbeek, Svend E. Holsoe, and Melissa Leach, eds. 2003. *African-American Exploration in West Africa: Four Nineteenth-Century Diaries.* Bloomington: Indiana University Press.

Falconbridge, Anna Maria. 1794. *Two Voyages to Sierra Leone During the Years 1791–2–3, in a Series of Letters.* London. For the Author.

Falola, Toyin, and Paul E. Lovejoy, eds. 1994. *Pawnship in Africa: Debt Bondage in Historical Perspective*. Boulder: Westview Press.

———. 2002. "Pawnship in Historical Perspective." In P. E. Lovejoy and T. Falola, eds., *Slavery, Pawnship, and Colonialism in Africa*. Trenton, N.J.: Africa World Press.

Fanthorpe, Richard. 2007. "Sierra Leone: The Influence of the Secret Societies, with Special Reference to Female Genital Mutilation." WRITENET/UNHCR (August).

Fass, Paula. 2006. *Children of a New World: Society, Culture, and Globalization*. New York: New York University Press.

Fede, Andrew. 1992. *People Without Rights: An Interpretation of the Fundamentals of the Law of Slavery in the U. S. South*. New York: Garland.

Ferme, Mariane. 1999. "Staging Politisi: The Dialogics of Publicity and Secrecy in Sierra Leone." In John and Jean Comaroff, eds., *Civil Society and the Political Imagination in Africa*, 161–91. Chicago: Chicago University Press.

Ferme, Mariane. 2001. *Underneath of Things: Violence, History, and the Everyday in Sierra Leone*. Berkeley: University of California Press.

Ferreira, Roquinaldo. 2012. *Cross-Cultural Exchange in the Atlantic World: Angola and Brazil During the Era of the Slave Trade*. New York: Cambridge University Press.

Fields-Black, Edda L. 2008. *Deep Roots: Rice Farmers in West Africa and the African Diaspora*. Bloomington: University of Indiana Press.

Finkelman, Paul. 1985. *Slavery in the Courtroom: An Annotated Bibliography of American Cases*. Washington, D.C.: G.P.O.

———. 1988. *Slavery, Race, and the American Legal System, 1700–1872*. New York: Garland.

———. 1988. *The African Slave Trade and American Courts: The Pamphlet Literature*. New York: Garland.

Fischer, David Hackett, and James C. Kelly. 2000. *Bound Away: Virginia and the Westward Movement*. Charlottesville: University of Virginia Press.

Flickinger, D. D., and William McKee. 1885. *History of the Origins, Development and Condition of the Missions Among the Sherbro and Mendi Tribes in Western Africa*. Dayton: United Brethren Publishing House.

Forbes, Frederick Edwyn. 1849. *Six Months' Service in the African Blockade, from April to October, 1848, in Command of the H.M.S. Bonetta*. London: Bentley.

Fraginals, Manuel Moreno. 1964. *El Ingenio: el complejo económico social cubano del azúcar*. Havana: Comisión Nacional Cubana de la Unesco.

Freeman, Derek. 1983. *Margaret Mead and Samoa: The Making and Unmaking of an Anthropological Myth*. New York: Pelican.

Fuller, James Clare. 2001. *Banfield, Nupe, and the UMCA*. Ilorin, Nigeria: World Partners/United Missionary Church of Africa.

Fyfe, Christopher. 1962. *A History of Sierra Leone*. London: Oxford University Press.

Gaby, Jean-Baptiste. 1689. *Relation de la Nigritie: contenant une exacte description des ses Royaumes et de leurs Gouvernements, la Religion, les Moeurs, Coustumes et raretez de ce Païs*. Paris: Éditions Couterot, 1689.

García Martínez, Orlando, and Michael Zeuske. 2013. *La sublevación de los cautivos de la goleta Amistad: Ramón Ferrer y las redes de contrabando en el mundo Atlántico y en Cuba*. Havana: Editorial de Ciencias Sociales.

García Rodríguez, Gloria. 2011. *Voices of the Enslaved in Nineteenth-Century Cuba: A Documentary History.* Chapel Hill: University of North Carolina Press.

Gardiner, Daniel. 1844. *A Treatise on International Law, and a Short Explanation of the Jurisdiction and Duty of the Government of the Republic of United States* Troy: N. Tuttle.

Gates, Henry Louis, Jr. 2011. *Black in Latin America.* New York: New York University Press.

Getz, Trevor. 2004. *Slavery and Reform in West Africa: Toward Emancipation in Nineteenth-Century Senegal and the Gold Coast.* Athens: Ohio University Press.

Gibbs, Josiah W. 1840. "A Mendi Vocabulary." *American Journal of Science* 38: 44–48.

———. 1840. "A Vai Vocabulary." *American Journal of Science* 38: 49–52.

Ginway, M. Elizabeth. 1998. "Nation Building and Heroic Undoing: Myth and Ideology in 'Bom-Crioulo.'" *Modern Language Studies* 28, no. 3/4 (Autumn): 41–56.

Glickman, Lawrence B. 1999. *A Living Wage: American Workers and the Making of Consumer Society.* Ithaca: Cornell University Press.

Gold, Susan Dudley. 2007. *United States v. Amistad: Slave Ship Mutiny.* Tarrytown, N.Y.: Marshall Cavendish.

Gomez, Michael A. 1998. *Exchanging Our Country Marks: The Transformation of African Identities in the Colonial and Antebellum South.* Chapel Hill: University of North Carolina Press.

Gorvie, Max. 1945. *Old and New in Sierra Leone.* London: United Society for Christian Literature.

Gottlieb, Alma. 2004. *The Afterlife Is Where We Come From: The Culture of Infancy in West Africa.* Chicago: Chicago University Press.

Goveia, Elsa V. 1965. *Slave Society in the British Leeward Islands at the End of the Eighteenth Century.* New Haven: Yale University Press.

Grace, John J. 1975. *Domestic Slavery in West Africa.* New York: Harper and Row.

———. 1977. "Slavery and Emancipation Among the Mende in Sierra Leone, 1896–1928." In Suzanne Miers and Igor Kopytoff, eds., *Slavery in Africa: Historical and Anthropological Perspectives,* 415–35. Madison: University of Wisconsin Press.

Graham (Chalcotte), Maria. 1824. *Journey of a Voyage to Brazil, and Residence There.* London: Longman.

Grandío-Moráguez, Oscar. 2008. "The African Origins of Slaves Arriving in Cuba." In *Extending the Frontiers: Essays on the New Transatlantic Slave Trade Database,* ed. David Eltis and David Richardson. New Haven: Yale University Press.

Greene, Sandra. 2011. *West African Narratives of Slavery: Texts from Late Nineteenth- and Early Twentieth-Century Ghana.* Bloomington: Indiana University Press.

Grégoire, Claire, and Bernard de Halleux. 1994. "Etude lexicostatistique de quarante-trois langues et dialectes mande." Africana Linguistica XI, *Annales du Musée Royal de l'Afrique Centrale, Sciences Humaines* 142: 53–71.

Grier, Beverly C. 2006. *Invisible Hands: Child Labor and the State in Colonial Zimbabwe.* Portsmouth, N.H.: Heinemann.

Gronniosaw, James Albert Ukawsaw. 1770. *Narrative of the Most Remarkable Particulars in the Life of James Albert Ukawsaw Gronniosaw, African Prince, as Related by Himself.* Bath, U.K.: S. Hazzard.

Gutman, Herbert. 1976. *The Black Family in Slavery and Freedom, 1750–1925.* New York: Vintage Books.

Hacsi, Timothy A. 1997. *Second Home: Orphan Asylums and Poor Families in America.* Cambridge: Harvard University Press.

Hair, P. E. H. 1965. "The Enslavement of Koelle's Informants." *Journal of African History* 4: 193–203.

———. 1967. "Ethnolinguistic Continuity on the Guinea Coast." *Journal of African History* 8, no. 2: 247–68.

———. 1968. "An Ethnolinguistic Inventory of the Lower Guinea Coast Before 1700: Part 1." *African Language Review* 7: 47–73.

———. 1969. "An Ethnolinguistic Inventory of the Lower Guinea Coast Before 1700: Part 2." *African Language Review* 8: 225–55.

Hall, Gwendolyn Midlo. 2005. *Slavery and African Ethnicities in the Americas: Restoring the Links.* Chapel Hill: University of North Carolina Press.

Hall, H. U. 1938. *The Sherbro of Sierra Leone.* Philadelphia: University of Pennsylvania Press.

Hall, James. 1850. "Abolition of the Slave Trade of Gallinas." *Annual Report, The American Colonization Society* 33: 33–36.

Hanciles, Jehu. 2002. *Euthanasia of a Mission: African Church Autonomy in a Colonial Context* Westport, Conn.: Greenwood.

Handler, Jerome S. 2002. "Survivors of the Middle Passage: Life Histories of Enslaved Africans in British America." *Slavery and Abolition* 23, no. 1: 25–56.

Harley, G. W. 1941. "Notes on the Poro in Liberia." *Papers of the Peabody Museum* 19, no. 2.

Harms, Robert. 2007. "The Transatlantic Slave Trade in Cinema." In *Black and White in Colour: African History on Screen,* ed. Vivian Bickford-Smith and Richard Mendelsohn, 59–81. Athens: Ohio University Press.

Harris, William, and Harry Sawyerr, 1968. *The Springs of Mende Belief and Conduct: A Discussion of the Influence of the Belief in the Supernatural Among the Mende.* Freetown: Sierra Leone University Press.

Hartman, Saidiya. 2007. *Lose Your Mother: A Journey Along the Atlantic Slave Route.* New York: Farrar, Straus, and Giroux.

Hawthorne, Walter W. 2001. "Nourishing a Stateless Society During the Slave Trade: The Rise of Balanta Paddy-Rice Production in Guinea-Bissau." *Journal of African History* 42, no. 1: 1–24.

———. 2003. *Planting Rice and Harvesting Slaves: Transformations Along the Guinea-Bissau Coast, 1400–1900.* Portsmouth, N.H.: Heinemann.

———. 2008. "'Being Now, as It Were, One Family': Shipmate Bonding on the Slave Vessel Emilia, in Rio de Janeiro and Throughout the Atlantic World." *Luso-Brazilian Review* 45, no. 1: 53–77.

———. 2010. *Africa to Brazil: Culture, Identity, and an Atlantic Slave Trade, 1600–1830.* Cambridge: Cambridge University Press.

———. 2010. "From 'Black Rice' to 'Brown': Rethinking the History of Risiculture in the Seventeenth and Eighteenth Century Atlantic." *American Historical Review* 115 (February): 151–63.

——. 2010. "Gorge: An African Seaman and His Flights from 'Freedom' Back to 'Slavery' in the Early Nineteenth Century." *Slavery and Abolition* 31: 411–28.

Helfman, Tara. 2006. "The Court of Vice Admiralty at Sierra Leone and the Abolition of the West African Slave Trade." *Yale Law Journal* 115: 1122–56.

Henige, David. 1974. *The Chronology of Oral Tradition.* Oxford: Oxford University Press.

Hochschild, Adam. 2005. *Bury the Chains: The British Struggle to Abolish Slavery.* London: Macmillan.

Hoffer, Carol P. 1975. "Sande Women and Political Power in Sierra Leone." *West African Journal of Sociology and Political Science* 1: 42–50.

Hogerzeil, Simon, and David Richardson. 2007. "Slave Purchasing Strategies and Shipboard Mortality: Day-to-Day Evidence from the Dutch African Trade." *Journal of Economic History* 67, no. 1: 160–90.

Holloway, Joseph E. 2005. *Africanisms in American Culture.* Bloomington: Indiana University Press.

Holsey, Bayo. 2008. *Routes of Remembrance: Refashioning the Slave Trade in Ghana.* Chicago: University of Chicago Press.

Holsoe, Svend E. 1977. "Slavery and Economic Response Among the Vai (Liberia and Sierra Leone)." In Suzanne Miers and Igor Kopytoff, eds., *Slavery in Africa: Historical and Anthropological Perspectives,* 287–305. Madison: University of Wisconsin Press.

Hopgood, C. R. 1948. "Language, Literature, and Culture." *Africa: Journal of the International African Institute* 18, no. 2: 112–19

Howard, Allen M. 1994. "Pawning in Coastal Northwest Sierra Leone, 1870–1910." In Toyin Falola and Paul E. Lovejoy, eds., *Pawnship in Africa: Debt Bondage in Historical Perspective,* 267–83. Boulder: Westview Press.

——. 2006. "Nineteenth-Century Coastal Slave Trading and the British Abolition Campaign in Sierra Leone." *Slavery and Abolition* 27, no. 1: 23–49.

Howe, Stephen. 1998. *Afrocentrism: Mythical Pasts and Imagined Homes.* London: Verso.

Hubble, Andrew. 2001. "A View of the Slave Trade from the Margin: Souroudougou in the Late Nineteenth-Century Slave Trade of the Niger Bend." *Journal of African History* 42, no. 1: 25–47.

Huggins, Nathan Irvin. 1990. *Black Odyssey: The African-American Ordeal in Slavery.* New York: Random House.

Huzzey, Richard. 2012. *Freedom Burning: Anti-Slavery and Empire in Victorian Britain.* Ithaca: Cornell University Press.

Ingham, E. G. 1894. *Sierra Leone After a Hundred Years.* London: Seeley.

Jackson, Michael. 1977. *The Kuranko: Dimensions of Social Reality in a West African Society.* London: C. Hurst.

James, Allison, and Adrian L. James. 2004. *Constructing Childhood: Theory, Policy, and Social Practice.* New York: Palgrave Macmillan.

Jarvis, Michael J. 2010. *In the Eye of All Trade: Bermuda, Bermudians, and the Maritime Atlantic World, 1680–1783.* Chapel Hill: University of North Carolina Press.

Jedrej, Charles. 1986. "Cosmology and Symbolism on the Central Guinea Coast." *Anthropos* 81: 497–515.

Jobson, Richard. 1623. *The Golden Trade; or, A Discovery of the River Gambra, and the Golden Trade of the Aethiopians.* London: Speight and Walpole.

Johnson, Clifton. 1990. "The Amistad Case and Its Consequences in U.S. History." *Journal of the New Haven Colony Historical Society* 36, no. 2: 3–22.

Johnson, Keith. 1881. *A Physical, Historical, Political, and Descriptive Geography.* London: Stanford.

Jones, Adam. 1981. "Theophile Conneau at Galinhas and New Sestos, 1836–1841: A Comparison of the Sources." *History in Africa* 8: 89–106.

——. 1981. "Who Were the Vai?" *Journal of African History* 22, no. 2: 159–78.

——. 1983. *From Slaves to Palm Kernels: A History of the Galinhas Country (West Africa), 1730–1890.* Wiesbaden: Steiner Verlag.

——. 1985. "Some Reflections on the Oral Traditions of the Galinhas Country, Sierra Leone." *History in Africa* 12: 151–65.

——. 1990. "Recaptive Nations: Evidence Concerning the Demographic Impact of the Atlantic Slave Trade in the Early Nineteenth Century." *Slavery and Abolition* 11, no. 1: 42–57.

Jones, Howard. 1988. *Mutiny on the Amistad: The Saga of a Slave Revolt and Its Impact on American Abolition, Law, and Diplomacy.* Oxford: Oxford University Press.

——. 2002. "The Impact of the Amistad Case on Race and Law in America (1841)." In Annette Gordon-Reed, ed., *Race on Trial: Law and Justice in American History: Law and Justice in American History,* 14–25. New York: Oxford University Press.

Kalous, Milas. 1995. "The Human Archetype of Male Circumcision and the Poro-Type Secret Society on the Upper Guinea Coast of West Africa." *Archiv orientální* 63, no. 3: 305–29.

Karr, G. L., A. O. Njoku, and M. F. Kallon. 1972. "Economics of the Upland and Inland Valley Swamp Rice Production Systems of Sierra Leone." *Illinois Agricultural Economics* 12, no. 1: 12–17.

Kastenholz, Raimund. 1997. *Sprachgeschichte im West-Mande: Methoden und Rekonstruktionen.* Cologne: Rüdiger Köppe Verlag.

Kaufmann, Chaim D., and Robert A. Pape. 1999. "Explaining Costly International Moral Action: Britain's Sixty-Year Campaign Against the Atlantic Slave Trade." *International Organization* 53, no. 4: 631–68.

Kea, Ray. 1982. *Settlements, Trade, and Polities in the Seventeenth-Century Gold Coast.* Baltimore: Johns Hopkins University Press.

——. 1986. "'I Am Here to Plunder on the General Road': Bandits and Banditry in the Pre-Nineteenth Century Gold Coast." In Donald Crummey, ed., *Banditry, Rebellion, and Social Protest in Africa,* 109–32. London: James Currey.

Kershaw, Roger, and Janet Sacks. 2008. *New Lives for Old: The Story of Britain's Child Migrants.* London: National Archives.

King, Wilma. 2011. *Stolen Childhood: Slave Youth in Nineteenth-Century America.* 2nd ed. Bloomington: Indiana University Press.

Klein, Herbert S., and Francisco Vidal Luna. 2010. *Slavery in Brazil.* Cambridge: Cambridge University Press.

Klein, Martin A. 1983. "Women and Slavery in the Western Sudan." In Claire C. Robertson and Martin A. Klein, eds., *Women and Slavery*, 67–78. Madison: University of Wisconsin Press.

———. 1998. *Slavery and Colonial Rule in French West Africa*. Cambridge: Cambridge University Press.

———. 2011. "Children and Slavery in the Western Sudan." In Gwyn Campbell, Suzanne Miers, and Joseph C. Miller, eds., *Child Slaves in the Modern World*, 124–40. Athens: Ohio University Press.

Kopytoff, Igor, and Suzanne Miers. 1979. "African 'Slavery' as an Institution of Marginality." In Suzanne Miers and Igor Kopytoff, eds., *Slavery in Africa: Historical and Anthropological Perspectives*, 3–84. Madison: University of Wisconsin Press, 1979.

Knight, Charles. 1866. *The English Cyclopaedia: Geography*. London: Bradbury/Evans.

Knight, Franklin. 1970. *Slave Society in Cuba During the Nineteenth Century*. Madison: University of Wisconsin Press.

Knörr, Jacqueline. 2000. "Female Secret Societies and Their Impact on Ethnic and Transethnic Identities Among Migrant Women in Freetown, Sierra Leone." In Jacqueline Knörr and Barbara Meier, eds., *Women and Migration: Anthropological Perspectives*, 80–98. New York: Campus Verlag/St. Martin's.

Koelle, Sigismund W. 1849. "Narrative of an Expedition in the Vy Country of West Africa." London: Seeleys.

———. 1854. *Polyglotta Africana, or a Comparative Vocabulary of Nearly Three Hundred Words and Phrases, in More Than One Hundred Distinct African Languages*. London: Church Missionary House.

———. 1854. *Outlines of a Grammar of the Vei Language: Together with a Vei-English Vocabulary, and an Account of the Discovery and Nature of the Vei Mode of Syllabic Writing*. London: Church Missionary House.

Kup, P. 1961. *History of Sierra Leone, 1400–1787*. Cambridge: Cambridge University Press.

Laing, Alexander Gordon. 1825. *Travels in the Timanee, Kooranko, and Soolima Countries*. London: John Murray.

Lambert, David. 2005. *White Creole Culture, Politics, and Identity During the Age of Abolition*. Cambridge: Cambridge University Press, 2005.

Landon, Fred. 1920. "The Negro Migration to Canada After the Passing of the Fugitive Slave Act." *Journal of Negro History* 5: 22–36.

Larson, Pier. 2000. *History and Memory in the Age of Enslavement: Becoming Merina in Highland Madagascar, 1770–1822*. Portsmouth, N.H.: Heinemann.

Lave, Jean. 2011. *Apprenticeship in Critical Ethnographic Practice*. Chicago: Chicago University Press.

Law, Robin. 1995. *From Slave Trade to "Legitimate" Commerce: The Commercial Transition in Nineteenth-Century West Africa*. Cambridge: Cambridge University Press.

———. 1997. *The English in West Africa, 1681–1683*. Oxford: Oxford University Press.

———. 2004. *Ouidah: The Social History of a West Africa Slaving "Port," 1727–1892*. Athens: Ohio University Press.

Law, Robin, and Paul Lovejoy. 2009. *The Biography of Mahommah Gardo Baquaqua.* Princeton, N.J.: Marcus Wiener.

Lawrance, Benjamin N. 2011. "'All We Want Is Make Us Free': The Voyage of La Amistad's Children Through the Worlds of the Illegal Slave Trade." In Gwyn Campbell, Suzanne Miers, and Joseph C. Miller, eds., *Child Slaves in the Modern World*, 13–36. Athens: Ohio University Press.

———. 2012. "Documenting Child Slavery with Personal Testimony: The Origins of Anti-Trafficking NGOs and Contemporary Neo-Abolitionism." In Benjamin N. Lawrance and Richard L. Roberts, eds., *Trafficking in Slavery's Wake: Law and the Experience of Women and Children in Africa*, 163–82. Athens: Ohio University Press.

———. 2013. "'Your Poor Boy No Father No Mother': 'Orphans,' Alienation, and the Perils of Atlantic Child Slave Biography," *Biography: An Interdisciplinary Quarterly* 36, no. 4 (Fall): 672–703.

———. 2014. "La Amistad's 'Interpreter' Reinterpreted: James Kaweli Covey's Distressed Atlantic Childhood and the Production of Knowledge About Nineteenth-Century Sierra Leone." In Suzanne Schwarz and Paul Lovejoy, eds., *Slavery, Abolition and the Transition to Colonialism in Sierra Leone*, 215–56. Trenton: Africa World Press.

Lawrance, Benjamin N., and Ruby P. Andrew. 2011. "A 'Neo-Abolitionist Trend' in Sub-Saharan Africa? Regional Anti-Trafficking Patterns and a Preliminary Legislative Taxonomy." *Seattle Journal for Social Justice* 9, no. 2: 599–678.

Lawrance, Benjamin N., and Richard L. Roberts. 2012. *Trafficking in Slavery's Wake: Law and the Experience of Women and Children in Africa.* Athens: Ohio University Press.

———. 2012. "Contextualizing Trafficking in Women and Children in Africa." In B. N. Lawrance and R. L. Roberts, eds., *Trafficking in Slavery's Wake: Law and the Experiences of Women and Children in Africa*, 1–33. Athens: Ohio University Press.

Lawson, Ellen NicKenzie, and Marlene Merrill. 1984. *The Three Sarahs: Documents of Antebellum Black College Women.* Lewiston: E. Mellen Press.

Leach, Melissa. 1994. *Rainforest Relations: Gender and Resource Use Among the Mende of Gola, Sierra Leone.* Edinburgh: Edinburgh University Press.

Leinaweaver, Jessaca B. 2007. "Choosing to Move: Child Agency on Peru's Margins." *Childhood* 14, no. 3: 375–92.

Lemisch, Jessie. 1999. "Black Agency in the Amistad Uprising: or, You've Taken our Cinque and Gone." *Souls* 1 (Winter): 57–70.

Leonard, Peter. 1832. *Records of a Voyage to the Western Coast.* Edinburgh: William Tate.

Levine, Robert Steven. 2003. *Martin R. Delany: A Documentary Reader.* Chapel Hill: University of North Carolina Press.

Lewis, A. 1963. "Symposium: Training for Child Psychiatry." *Journal of Child Psychology and Psychiatry* 4: 75–84.

Lewis, Maureen Warner. 2002. *Central Africa in the Caribbean: Transcending Space, Transforming Culture.* Kingston, Jamaica: University of the West Indies Press.

Little, Kenneth L. 1948. "The Mende Farming Household." *Sociological Review* 40: 2–56.

———. 1951. *The Mende of Sierra Leone* London: Routledge.

Lloyd, Christopher. 1968. *The Navy and the Slave Trade: The Suppression of the African Slave Trade in the Nineteenth Century.* Cass Library of African Studies, No. 4. London: Cass.

Lofkrantz, Jennifer, and Olatunji Ojo. 2012. "Slavery, Freedom, and Failed Ransom Negotiations in West Africa, 1730–1900." *Journal of African History* 53, no. 1: 25–44.

Longo, James McMurtry. 2008. *Isabel Orleans-Braganca: The Brazilian Princess Who Freed the Slaves.* Jefferson: McFarland.

Lovejoy, Paul E. 1980. "Kola in the History of West Africa." *Cahiers d'Etudes Africaines,* 20, no. 1/2: 97–134.

———. 1994. "Background to Rebellion: The Origins of Muslim Slaves in Bahia." *Slavery and Abolition* 15, no. 2: 151–80.

———. 2006. "Autobiography and Memory: Gustavus Vassa, alias Olaudah Equiano, the African." *Slavery and Abolition* 27, no. 3: 317–47.

———. 2006. "The Children of Slavery: The Transatlantic Phase." *Slavery and Abolition* 22, no. 2: 197–217.

———. 2007. "Issues of Motivation: Vassa/Equiano and Carretta's Critique of the Evidence." *Slavery and Abolition* 28, no. 1: 121–25.

———. 2011. *Transformations in Slavery: A History of Slavery in Africa.* 2nd ed. Cambridge: Cambridge University Press.

———. 2014. "Pawnship, Debt, and 'Freedom' in Atlantic Africa During the Era of the Slave Trade: A Re-Assessment." *Journal of African History* 55, no. 1: 1–24.

Lovejoy, Paul E., and David Richardson. 1999. "Trust, Pawnship, and Atlantic History: The Institutional Foundations of the Old Calabar Slave Trade." *American Historical Review* 104, no. 2: 333–55.

———. 2001. "The Business of Slaving: Pawnship in West Africa, c. 1600–1810." *Journal of African History* 42, no. 1: 67–89.

———. 2007. "African Agency and the Liverpool Trade." In D. Richardson, S. Schwarz, and A. Tibbles, eds., *Liverpool and Atlantic Slavery,* 43–65. Liverpool: Liverpool University Press.

Lovejoy, Paul E., and Toyin Falola, eds. *Pawnship, Slavery, and Colonialism in Africa.* Trenton, N.J.: Africa World Press, 2003.

Lydon, Ghislaine. 2012. *On Trans-Saharan Trails: Islamic Law, Trade Networks, and Cross-Cultural Exchange in Nineteenth-Century Western Africa.* Cambridge: Cambridge University Press.

MacCormack, Carol Hoffer. 1974. "Madam Yoko: Ruler of the Kpa Mende Confederacy." In Michele Z. Rosaldo and Louise Lamphere, eds., *Woman, Culture and Society,* 171–187. Stanford: Stanford University Press.

———. 1975. "Bundu: Political Implications of Female Solidarity in a Secret Society." In Dana Raphael, ed., *Being Female: Reproduction, Power, and Change,* 155–65. The Hague: Mouton.

———. 1977. "Wono: Institutionalized Dependency in Sherbro Descent Groups (Sierra Leone)." In Suzanne Miers and Igor Kopytoff, eds., *Slavery in Africa: Historical and Anthropological Perspectives,* 181–204. Madison: University of Wisconsin Press.

——. 1979. "Sande: The Public Face of a Secret Society." In B. Jules-Rosette, ed., *The New Religions of Africa.* Norwood, N.J.: Ablex Publishing.

——. 1982. "Control of Land, Labor and Capital in Rural Southern Sierra Leone." In Edna G. Bay, ed., *Women and Work in Africa.* Boulder: Westview Press.

Madden, Richard Robert. 1835. *A Twelvemonth's Residence in the West Indies: During the Transition from Slavery to Apprenticeship; with Incidental Notice of the State of Society, Prospects, and Natural Resources of Jamaica and Other Islands.* London: Carey, Lea and Blanchard.

——. 1839. *A Letter to W. E. Channing.* London: Ticknor.

——. 1840. *Poems by a Slave in the Island of Cuba, Recently Liberated; Translated from the Spanish, by R. R. Madden, M.D., with the History of the Early Life of the Negro Poet, Written by Himself; to Which Are Prefixed Two Pieces Descriptive of Cuban Slavery and the Slave-Traffic, by R.R.M.* London: Thomas Ward.

——. 1853. *The Island of Cuba: Its Resources, Progress, and Prospects.* London: Partridge and Oakey.

——. 1891. *The Memoires (Chiefly Autobiographical) from 1798 to 1886.* London: Ward and Downey.

Mann, Kristin. 2001. "Shifting Paradigms in the Study of the African Diaspora and of Atlantic History and Culture." *Slavery and Abolition* 22, no. 1: 1–2.

Manning, Patrick. 1990. *Slavery and African Life: Occidental, Oriental, and African Slave Trades.* Cambridge: Cambridge University Press.

——. 2009. *The African Diaspora: A History Through Culture.* New York: Columbia University Press.

Manzano, Juan Francisco. 1981. *The Life and Poems of a Cuban Slave: Juan Francisco Manzano, 1797–1854.* Trans. Edward Mullen. Hamden, Conn: Archon.

Martin, Christopher. 1970. *The Amistad Affair.* New York: Abelard-Schuman.

Martinez, Jenny S. 2008. "Antislavery Courts and the Dawn of International Human Rights Law." *Yale Law Journal* 117 (January): 550.

Massé, Étienne-Marcel. 1825. *L'île de Cuba et la Havane, ou, histoire, topographie, statistique, mœurs, usages, commerce et situation politique de cette colonie: d'après un journal écrit sur les lieux.* Paris: Lebégue, Audin.

Massing, Andreas. 1980. "A Segmentary Lineage Society Between Colonial Frontiers: The Kissi of Liberia, Sierra Leone, and Guinea, 1892–1913." *Liberian Studies Journal* 9: 1–12.

——. 1985. "The Mane, the Decline of Mali, and Mandinka Expansion Towards the South Windward Coast." *Cahiers d'Études Africaines*, ser. 25, no. 97: 21–55.

Matson, Henry James. 1848. *Remarks on the Slave Trade and African Squadron.* London: James Ridgway.

Matthews, John. 1791. *A Voyage to the River Sierra-Leone, on the Coast of Africa: Containing an Account of the Trade and Productions of the Country, and of the Civil and Religious Customs and Manners of the People; in a Series of Letters to a Friend in England.* London: White and Son.

Mbaeyi, Paul M. 1982. "The British Navy and 'Southern Nigeria' in the Nineteenth Century." In Boniface I. Obichere, ed., *Studies in Southern Nigerian History*, 201–18. London: Frank Cass.

McCullock, M. 1950. *Western Africa, Part II: The Peoples of Sierra Leone.* London: International African Institute.

McDaniel, Antonio. 1992. "Extreme Mortality in Nineteenth-Century Africa: The Case of Liberian Immigrants." *Demography* 29, no. 4 (November): 581–94.

McKee, William. 1874. *History of the Sherbro Mission in West Africa.* Dayton: United Brethren Publishing House.

McKnight, Kathryn Joy. 2009. *Afro-Latino Voices: Narratives from the Early Modern Ibero-Atlantic World, 1550–1812.* Indianapolis: Hackett.

McMahon, Elisabeth. 2012. "Trafficking and Reenslavement: The Social Vulnerability of Women and Children in Nineteenth-Century East Africa." In B. N. Lawrance and R. L. Roberts, *Trafficking in Slavery's Wake.* Athens: Ohio University Press.

———. 2013. *Slavery and Emancipation in Islamic East Africa: From Honor to Respectability.* Cambridge: Cambridge University Press.

Mead, Margaret. 1928. *Coming of Age in Samoa: A Psychological Study of Primitive Youth for Western Civilisation.* New York: William Morrow.

Meier, Helmut. 2007. *Thomas Clarkson: "Moral Steam Engine" or False Prophet? A Critical Approach to Three of His Antislavery Essays.* Stuttgart: Ibidem.

Meillassoux, Claude. 1991. *The Anthropology of Slavery: The Womb of Iron and Gold.* Trans. Adlide Dasnois. Chicago: University of Chicago Press.

"'Mendi' or 'Amistad' Negros." 1906. In Arthur Brandegee and Eddy N. Smith, eds., *Farmington Connecticut, the Village of Beautiful Homes.* Farmington, Conn.

Menschel, David. 2001. "Abolition Without Deliverance: The Law of Connecticut Slavery, 1784–1848." *Yale Law Journal* 111: 183–222.

Metaxas, Eric. 2007. *Amazing Grace: William Wilberforce and the Heroic Campaign to End Slavery.* New York: Harper.

Miers, Suzanne, and Igor Kopytoff, eds. 1977. *Slavery in Africa: Historical and Anthropological Perspectives.* Madison: University of Wisconsin Press.

Migeod, Frederick W. H. 1913. *The Mende Language Containing Useful Phrases Elementary Grammer Short Vocabularies.* London: Kegan Paul, Trench, Trübner.

Miller, Joseph C. 1981. "Mortality in the Atlantic Slave Trade: Statistical Evidence on Causality." *Journal of Interdisciplinary History* 11, no. 3 (Winter): 385–423.

———. 1982. "The Significance of Drought, Disease, and Famine in the Agriculturally Marginal Zones of West-Central Africa." *Journal of African History* 23, no. 1: 17–61.

———. 1988. *Way of Death: Merchant Capitalism and the Angolan Slave Trade, 1730–1830.* Madison: University of Wisconsin Press.

———. 2004. "Retention, Reinvention, and Remembering: Restoring Identities Through Enslavement in Africa and Under Slavery in Brazil." In José C. Curto and Paul E. Lovejoy, eds., *Enslaving Connections: Changing Cultures of African and Brazil During the Era of Slavery,* 81–124. Amherst, N.Y.: Humanity Books.

Miller, Joseph C., ed. 1980. *The African Past Speaks: Essays on Oral Tradition and History.* New York: Dawson and Archon.

Mills, Job Smith. 1898. *Mission Work in Sierra Leone, West Africa.* Dayton: United Brethren Publishing House.

Mintz, Steven. 2004. *Huck's Raft: A History of American Childhood*. Cambridge: Belknap Press of Harvard University Press.

Mintz, Sidney, and Richard Price. 1992. *The Birth of African-American Culture: An Anthropological Perspective*. Boston: Beacon Press.

Misevich, Philip. 2008. "The Origins of Slaves Leaving the Upper Guinea Coast in the Nineteen Century." In David Eltis and David Richardson, eds. *Extending the Frontiers: Essays on the New Transatlantic Slave Trade Database*, 155–75. New Haven: Yale University Press.

Mitchell, Mary Hewitt. 1942. *History of the United Church of New Haven*. New Haven: United Church.

Mitchell, Mary Niall. 2008. *Raising Freedom's Child: Black Children and Visions of the Future After Slavery*. New York: New York University Press.

Mitchell, Samuel Augustus. 1839. *An Accompaniment to Mitchell's Map of the World* Philadelphia: Barnes.

——. 1842. *A General View of the World*. New York: David Jewitt.

Morgan, Philip D. 2010. "Maritime Slavery." *Slavery and Abolition* 31, no. 3: 311–26.

Morris, Thomas D. 1999. *Southern Slavery and the Law, 1619–1860*. Chapel Hill: University of North Carolina.

Mouser, Bruce L. [and Samuel Gamble]. 2002. *A Slaving Voyage to Africa and Jamaica: The Log of the Sandown, 1793–1794*. Bloomington: Indiana University Press.

Mundy, John Hine. 1995. "Medieval Urban Liberty." In R. W. Davis, *Origins of Modern Freedom in the West*, 101–34. Stanford: Stanford University Press.

Mundy-Castle, Talent Chioma. 2012. *A Mother's Debt: The True Story of an African Orphan*. London: AuthorHouse.

Murdoch, Lydia. 2006. *Imagined Orphans: Poor Families, Child Welfare, and Contested Citizenship in London*. New Brunswick: Rutgers University Press.

Murphy, William H. 2010. "Patrimonial Logic of Centrifugal Forces in the Political History of the Upper Guinea Coast." In Jacqueline Knörr and Wilson Trajano Filho, eds., *Powerful Presence of the Past: Integration and Conflict Along the Upper Guinea Coast*, 24–52. African Social Studies Series, vol. 24. Leiden: E. J. Brill.

Murray, David R. 1980. *Odious Commerce: Britain, Spain, and the Abolition of the Cuban Slave Trade*. Cambridge: Cambridge University Press.

Murray, Hugh. 1834. *An Encyclopædia of Geography*. London: Longman.

Nelson, Thomas. 1846. *Remarks on the Slavery and Slave Trade of the Brazils*. London: Halchard.

Newmyer, R. Kent. 1985. *Supreme Court Justice Joseph Story: Statesman of the Old Republic*. Chapel Hill: University of North Carolina Press.

——. 2001. *John Marshall and the Heroic Age of the Supreme Court*. Baton Rouge: Louisiana State University Press.

Njoku, Athanasius. 1979. "The Economies of Mende Upland Rice Farming." In Vernon R. Dorjahn and Barry L. Isaac, eds., *Essays on the Economic Anthropology of Liberia and Sierra Leone*, 103–20. Liberian Studies Monograph Series, No. 6. Philadelphia: Institute for Liberian Studies.

Nwokeji, G. Ugo. 2010. *The Slave Trade and Culture in the Bight of Biafra: An African Society in the Atlantic World*. Cambridge: Cambridge University Press.

Nwokeji, G. Ugo, and David Eltis. 2002. "Characteristics of Captives Leaving the Cameroons for the Americas, 1822–37." *Journal of African History* 43, no. 1: 191–210.

Nyambedha, Erick Otieno. 2008. "Ethical Dilemmas of Social Science Research on AIDS and Orphanhood in Western Kenya." *Social Science and Medicine* 67, no. 5: 771–79.

Norton, Charles Ledyard. 1906. "Cinques, the Black Prince." *Farmington Magazine* (February 1901). Reprinted in Arthur Brandegee and Eddy N. Smith, eds., *Farmington Connecticut, the Village of Beautiful Homes*. Farmington, Conn.

Nyländer, Gustavus Reinhold. 1814. *Grammar and Vocabulary of the Bullom Language*. London: Church Missionary Society, Ellerton and Henderson.

Oakes, James. 1998. *Slavery and Freedom: An Interpretation of the Old South*. New York: W. W. Norton.

Ojo, Olatunji. 2007. "Èmú" (Àmúyá): The Yoruba Institution of Panyarring or Seizure for Debt." *African Economic History* 35: 31–58.

Ortiz, Fernando. 1996. *Los Negros Esclavos*. Havana: Editorial de Ciencias Sociales.

Osagie, Iyunolu Folayan. 2000. *The Amistad Revolt: Memory, Slavery, and the Politics of Identity in the United States and Sierra Leone*. Athens: University of Georgia Press.

Paquette, Robert L. 1998. "From History to Hollywood: The Voyage of 'La Amistad,'" *New Criterion* 16 (March): 74.

Parsons, Robert T. 1964. *Religion in an African Society: A Study of the Religion of the Kono People of Sierra Leone in its Social Environment with Special Reference to the Function of Religion in That Society*. Leiden: E. J. Brill.

Patterson, Orlando. 1985. *Slavery and Social Death: A Comparative Study*. Cambridge: Harvard University Press.

———. 1991. *Freedom*, vol. 1: *Freedom in the Making of Western Culture*. New York: Basic Books.

———. 2006. *Freedom*, vol. 2: *Freedom in Modern World*. New York: Basic Books.

Pearsall, A. W. H. 1959. "Sierra Leone and the Suppression of the Slave Trade." *Sierra Leone Studies* 12: 211–29.

Pease, Jane H., and William H. Pease. 1974. *They Who Would Be Free: Blacks' Search for Freedom, 1830–1861*. New York: Atheneum.

Pereira, Duarte Pacheco. 1903. *Esmeraldo de Situ Orbis*, ed. Augusto Epiphanio da Silva Dias. Lisbon: Imprensa Nacional.

Person, Yves. 1961. "Les Kissi et leurs statuettes de pierre dans le cadre de l'histoire ouest africaine." *Bulletin de l'IFAN* (Dakar) 23, ser. B, nos. 1–2: 1–57.

———. 1971. "Ethnic Movements and Acculturation in Upper Guinea Since the Fifteenth Century." *African Historical Studies* 4, no. 3: 669–90.

Philadelphia Yearly Meeting of the Religious Society of Friends. 1851. *An Exposition of the African Slave Trade*. Philadelphia: Rakestraw.

Phillips, Ulrich Bonnell. 1918. *American Negro Slavery; a Survey of the Supply, Employment, and Control of Negro Labor, as Determined by the Plantation Regime*. New York: D. Appleton.

Piot, Charles. 1996. "Of Slaves and the Gift: Kabre Sale of Kin During the Era of the Slave Trade." *Journal of African History* 37, no. 1: 31–49.

Pollock, Linda. 1983. *Forgotten Children: Parent-Child Relations from 1500 to 1900.* Cambridge: Cambridge University Press.

Price and Lee. 1840. *Price & Lee's New Haven City Directory, Including West Haven, East Haven, and Woodbridge.* New Haven: Price & Lee.

Price, Neil. 1996. "The Changing Value of Children Among the Kikuyu of Central Province, Kenya." *Africa* 66, no. 3: 411–36.

Prichard, James Cowels. 1837. *Researches into the Physical History of Mankind.* 3rd ed. Vol. 2. London: Sherwood, Gilbert and Piper.

Prince, Mary. 2008. *The History of Mary Prince, a West Indian Slave.* Radford, Va.: Wilder Publications.

Purdy, John. 1822. *Memoir, Descriptive and Explanatory, to Accompany the New Chart of the Ethiopic or Southern Atlantic Ocean, with the Western Coasts of South-America, from Cape Horn to Panama.* London: Laurie.

Putney, Martha. 1987. *Black Sailors: Afro-American Merchant Seamen and Whalemen Prior to the Civil War.* New York: Greenwood.

Ragsdale, Bruce A. 2002. "Amistad: The Federal Courts and the Challenge to Slavery." Washington, D.C.: Federal Judicial Center Publication.

Rankin, F. Harrison. 1836. *White Man's Grave: A Visit to Sierra Leone in 1834.* London: Bentley.

Ranso, Brian H. A. 1968. *A Sociological Study of Moyamba Town, Sierra Leone.* Zaria, Nigeria: Ahmadu Bello University.

Rawley, James A., and Stephen D. Behrendt. 2005. *The Transatlantic Slave Trade: A History.* Lincoln: University of Nebraska Press.

Rediker, Marcus. 2007. *The Slave Ship: A Human History.* New York: Penguin.

———. 2012. *The Amistad Rebellion: An Atlantic Odyssey of Slavery and Freedom.* New York: Viking.

Reynolds, Pamela. 1990. *Dance Civet Cat: Child Labor in the Zambezi Valley.* London: Zed Books; Athens: Ohio University Press.

Rich, Jeremy. 2007. *A Workman Is Worthy of His Meat: Food and Colonialism in the Gabon Estuary.* Lincoln: University of Nebraska Press.

Richards, Paul. 1985. *Indigenous Agricultural Revolution: Ecology and Food Production in West Africa.* Boulder: Westview Press.

———. 1996. *Fighting for the Rain Forest: War, Youth, and Resources in Sierra Leone.* Portsmouth, N.H.: Heinemann.

———. 1996. "Forest Indigenous Peoples: Concept, Critique and Cases." *Proceedings of the Royal Society of Edinburgh: Section B, Biological Sciences* 104: 349–65.

———. 2005. "To Fight or to Farm? Agrarian Dimensions of the Mano River Conflicts (Liberia and Sierra Leone)." *African Affairs* 104, no. 417: 571–90.

Richardson, David. 2001. "Shipboard Revolts, African Authority, and the Atlantic Slave Trade." *William and Mary Quarterly* 58, no. 1: 69–92.

Ricketts, H. I. 1831. *Narrative of the Ashantee War: With a View of the Present State of the Colony of Sierra Leone.* London: Simpkin and Marshall.

Roberts, Richard L. 1987. *Warriors, Merchants, and Slaves: The State and the Economy in the Middle Niger Valley, 1700–1914.* Stanford: Stanford University Press.

——. 2012. "The End of Slavery, 'Crises' over Trafficking, and the Colonial State in the French Soudan." In B. N. Lawrance and R. L. Roberts, eds., *Trafficking in Slavery's Wake,* Athens: Ohio University Press.

Rodney, Walter. 1967. "A Reconsideration of the Mane Invasions of Sierra Leone." *Journal of African History* 8, no. 2: 219–46.

Rodney, Walter. 1970. *History of the Upper Guinea Coast, 1545–1800* New York: Monthly Review Press.

Rodrigues, Jaime. 2005. *De costa a costa.* Rio de Janeiro: Companhia das Letras.

Rowland, Lawrence Sanders. 1996. *The History of Beaufort County, South Carolina, 1514–1861.* Columbia: University of South Carolina Press.

Sachs, Carolyn E. 1996. *Gendered Fields: Rural Women, Agriculture, and Environment.* Boulder: Westview Press.

Saco, José Antonio. 1974 [1938]. *Historia de la esclavitud de la raza africana en el Nuevo Mundo y en especial en los países américo-hispanos por José Antonio Saco con documentos y juicios de F. Arango y Parreño, Félix Varela, Domingo del Monte, Felipe Poey, José de la Luz y Caballero, José Silverio Jorrin, Enrique José Varona y otros.* Havana: Ediciones Júcar.

Sale, Maggie Montesinos. 1997. *The Slumbering Volcano: American Slave Ship Revolts and the Production of Rebellious Masculinity.* Durham: Duke University Press.

Sanneh, Lamin. 2001. *Abolitionists Abroad: American Blacks and the Making of Modern West Africa.* Cambridge: Harvard University Press.

Schama, Simon. 1998. "What Hollywood and Herodotus Have in Common." *New Yorker* 73 (January 19).

Schwartz, Marie Jenkins. 2000. *Born in Bondage: Growing Up Enslaved in the Antebellum South.* Cambridge: Harvard University Press.

Schwarz, Philip J. 2001. *Migrants Against Slavery: Virginians and the Nation.* Charlottesville: University of Virginia Press.

Schwarz, Suzanne. 2010. "Extending the African Names Database: New Evidence from Sierra Leone." *African Economic History* 28: 137–63.

Scott, Rebecca. 1985. *Slave Emancipation in Cuba: The Transition to Free Labor, 1860–1899.* Princeton: Princeton University Press.

Scott, Rebecca J., and Jean M. Hébrard. 2012. *Freedom Papers: An Atlantic Odyssey in the Age of Emancipation.* Cambridge: Harvard University Press.

Searing, James. 1993. *West African Slavery and Atlantic Commerce: The Senegal River Valley, 1700–1860.* Cambridge: Cambridge University Press.

Shadle, Brett L. 2006. *"Girl Cases": Marriage and Colonialism in Gusiiland.* Portsmouth, N.H.: Heinemann.

Shankman, Paul. 2009. *The Trashing of Margaret Mead: Anatomy of an Anthropological Controversy.* Madison: University of Wisconsin Press.

Shaw, Rosalind. 2002. *Memories of the Slave Trade: Ritual and Historical Imagination in Sierra Leone.* Chicago: University of Chicago Press.

Shennan, Stephen. 1994. *Archaeological Approaches to Cultural Identity.* London: Routledge.

Sherington, Geoffrey, and Chris Jeffery. 1998. *Fairbridge: Empire and Child Migration.* Abingdon, U.K.: Woburn Press.

Sherwood, Mary Martha. 1822. *Dazee; or, The Recaptured Negro.* Newburyport, Mass.: Gilman.

Shumway, Rebecca. 2011. *The Fante and the Transatlantic Slave Trade.* Rochester: University of Rochester Press.

Silva, Kim A. 2014. "Signs of Freedom: Deaf Connections in the Amistad Story." In Kristin Snoddon, ed., *Telling Deaf Lives: Agents of Change*, 136–47. Washington, D.C.: Gallaudet University Press.

Smallwood, Stephanie. 2007. *Saltwater Slavery: A Middle Passage from Africa to the American Diaspora.* Cambridge: Harvard University Press.

Smith, Robert. 1973. "Peace and Palaver: International Relations in Pre-colonial West Africa." *Journal of African History* 14, no. 4: 599–621.

Smith, Venture. 1798. *A Narrative of the Life and Adventures of Venture, a Native of Africa: But Resident Above Sixty Years in the United States of America.* New London, Conn.: Holt.

Smith, William Henry. 1903. *A Political History of Slavery.* Vol. 1. New York: G. P. Putnam and Sons.

Spicksley, Judith. 2013. "Pawns on the Gold Coast: The Rise of Asante and Shifts in Security for Debt, 1680–1750." *Journal of African History* 54, no. 2: 147–75.

Spilsbury, Francis B. 1807. *Account of a Voyage to the Western Coast of Africa.* London: Richard Phillips.

Stampp, Kenneth. 1956. *The Peculiar Institution: Slavery in the Ante-Bellum South.* New York: Knopf.

Staudenraus, P. J. 1961. *The African Colonization Movement, 1815–1865.* New York: Columbia University Press.

Stearns, Peter N. 2005. *Growing Up: The History of Childhood in a Global Context.* Waco, Tex.: Baylor University Press.

Stephens, Sharon. 1995. "Introduction: Children and the Politics of Culture in 'Late Capitalism.'" In Sharon Stephens, ed., *Children and the Politics of Culture*, 3–48. Princeton: Princeton University Press.

Stevenson, Brenda. 1997. *Life in Black and White: Family and Community in the Slave South.* New York: Oxford University Press.

Sturge, Joseph. *A Visit to the United States in 1841.* London: Hamilton Adams.

Sundstrom, Lars. 1965. *The Trade of Guinea.* Studia ethnographica Upsaliensia, no. 24. Upsala.

Swain, Shurlee. 2009. "Sweet Childhood Lost: Idealized Images of Childhood in the British Child Rescue Literature." *Journal of the History of Childhood and Youth* 2, no. 2: 198–214.

Swain, Shurlee, and Margot Hillel. 2010. *Child, Nation, Race and Empire: Child Rescue Discourse, England, Canada and Australia, 1850–1915.* Manchester: Manchester University Press.

Sweet, James. 2006. *Recreating Africa: Culture, Kinship, and Religion in the African-Portuguese World, 1441–1770.* Chapel Hill: University of North Carolina Press.

———. 2009. "Mistaken Identities? Olaudah Equiano, Domingos Álvares, and the Methodological Challenges of Studying the African Diaspora." *American Historical Review* 114, no. 2 (April): 279–306.

Tappan, Lewis, Annie Heloise Abel, Frank Joseph Klingberg, and Association for the Study of Negro Life and History. 1927. *A Side Light on Anglo-American Relations, 1839–1858: Furnished by the Correspondence of Lewis Tappan and Others with the British and Foreign Anti-Slavery Society.* New York: Association for the Study of Negro Life and History.

Temperley, Howard. 1972. *British Antislavery, 1833–1870.* Columbia: University of South Carolina Press.

Thomas, Hugh. 1971. *Cuba, or the Pursuit of Freedom.* New York: Harper and Row.

———. 1997. *The Slave Trade: The Story of the Trans-Atlantic Slave Trade.* New York: Simon and Schuster.

Thomas, Northcote W. 1919–20. "Who Were the Manes?" *Journal of the African Society* 19: 176–88, 20: 33–42.

Thompson, George. 1852. *Thompson in Africa; or, An Account of the Missionary Labors, Sufferings, Travels, and Observations, of George Thompson in Western Africa, at the Mendi Mission.* New York.

———. 1855. *Letters to Sabbath School Children on Africa: Written While on a Mission to Africa, and During a Visit Home.* Cincinnati.

———. 1859. *The Palm Land; or, West Africa, Illustrated. Being a History of Missionary Labors and Travels, with Descriptions of Men and Things in Western Africa. Also, a Synopsis of All the Missionary Work on That Continent.* Cincinnati: Moore, Wilstach, Keys.

Thornton, John. 1983. "Slave Trade and Family Structure." In Claire C. Robertson and Martin A. Klein, eds., *Women and Slavery in Africa.* Madison: University of Wisconsin Press.

Tinnie, Dinizulu Gene. 2008. "The Slaving Brig Henriqueta and Her Evil Sisters: A Case Study in the Nineteenth-Century Slave Trade to Brazil." *Journal of African American History* 93, no. 4: 509–31.

Tonkin, Elizabeth. 1992. *Narrating Our Pasts: the Social Construction of Oral History.* Cambridge: Cambridge University Press.

Trist, Nicholas P. 1913. "Case of the Crew of the Ship 'William Engs,' Embracing the Inquiry Who Is Richard Robert Madden? The Friend, Confederate, and Witness of Ferdinand Clark." Extract of document printed by order of House of Representatives, May 1913, Washington, D.C.

Trotman, David V., and Paul E. Lovejoy. 2003. *Transatlantic Dimensions of Ethnicity in the African Diaspora.* London: Continuum.

Trudel, Marcel. 1960. *L'esclavage au Canada français.* Quebec: Presses Universitaires Laval.

Turay, A. K. 1978. "Language Contact: Mende and Temne — a Case Study." *Africana Marburgensia* 11, no. 1: 55–73.

Turnbull, David. 1840. *Travels in the West: Cuba with Notices of Porto Rico and the Slave Trade.* London: Longman.

Twum-Danso, Afua. 2009. "Situating Participatory Methodologies in Context: The Impact of Culture on Adult-Child Interactions in Research and Other Projects." *Children's Geographies* 7, no. 4: 379–89.

Van Cleve, George William. 2010. *A Slaveholders' Union: Slavery, Politics, and the Constitution in the Early American Republic.* Chicago: University of Chicago Press.

Vansina, Jan. 1967. "The Use of Oral Tradition in African Culture History." In Creighton Gabel and Normal Bennett, eds., *Reconstructing African Culture History*, 55–82. Boston: Boston University Press.

Vaughan, David J. 2002. *Statesman and Saint: The Principled Politics of William Wilberforce.* Nashville, Tenn.: Cumberland House.

Vaughan, Megan. 2007. "Scarification in Africa: Re-reading the Colonial Evidence." *Cultural and Social History* 3, no. 4, 385–400.

Viau, Roland. 2002. *Ceux de Nigger Rock.* Montreal: Libre Expression.

Vos, Jelmer. 2012. "'Without the Slave Trade, No Recruitment': From Slave Trading and 'Migrant Recruitment' in the Lower Congo, 1830–1890." In B. N. Lawrance and R. L. Roberts, eds., *Trafficking in Slavery's Wake.* Athens: Ohio University Press.

Walker, Clarence E. 2001. *We Can't Go Home Again: An Argument About Afrocentrism.* New York: Oxford University Press.

Walsh, Robert. 1830. *Notices from Brazil in 1828 and 1829.* London: Westley.

Wander, Philip C. 1971. "Salvation Through Separation: The Image of the Negro in the American Colonization Society." *Quarterly Journal of Speech* 57: 57–67.

Warren, Joyce. 2009. *Women, Money, and the Law: Nineteenth-Century Fiction, Gender, and the Courts.* Iowa City: University of Iowa Press.

Weigold, Isabel. 2007. *Hannah Moore: A Biography of a Nineteenth Century Missionary and Teacher.* iUniverse.

Weiner, Mark. 2006. *Black Trials: Citizenship from the Beginnings of Slavery to the End of Caste.* New York: Vintage.

Wells, Karen. 2009. *Childhood in Global Perspective.* Cambridge: Polity Press.

White, Luise, Stephan Miescher, and David William Cohen, eds. 2001. *African Words, African Voices: Critical Practices in Oral History.* Bloomington: Indiana University Press.

Wilberforce, Daniel. 1886. *Sherbro and the Sherbros.* Dayton: United Brethren Publishing House.

Williams, Dorothy. 1998. *Les noirs à Montréal: essai de demographie urbaine.* Montreal: LVB Éditeur.

Williamson, Kay, and Roger Blench. 2000. "Niger–Congo." In Bernd Heine and Derek Nurse, eds., *African Languages: An Introduction*, 11–42. Cambridge: Cambridge University Press.

Wilson, Carol. 1994. *Freedom at Risk: The Kidnapping of Free Blacks in America, 1780–1865.* Louisville: University Press of Kentucky.

Winks, R. 1971. *The Blacks in Canada: A History.* Montreal: McGill–Queen's University Press.

Winterbottom, Thomas. 1803. *An Account of the Native Africans in the Neighbourhood of Sierra Leone.* London: Wittingham.

Wood, Peter. 1974. *Black Majority: Negroes in Colonial South Carolina from 1670 Through the Stono Rebellion.* New York: Knopf.

Woodard, Colin. 2008. *The Republic of Pirates: Being the True and Surprising Story of the Caribbean Pirates and the Man Who Brought Them Down.* New York: Houghton Mifflin Harcourt.

Wright, Marcia. 2008. *Strategies of Slaves and Women: Life-Stories from East/Central Africa.* London: James Currey.

Wright, Richard. 1984. *African Philosophy: An Introduction.* 3rd ed. Lanham, Md.: University Press of America.

Wyatt-Brown, Bertram. 1971. *Lewis Tappan and the Evangelical War Against Slavery.* New York: Atheneum.

Yannielli, Joseph L. 2010. *Cinqué the Slave Trader: Some New Evidence on an Old Controversy.* New Haven: Amistad Committee.

Yeoman, Elizabeth. 2004. "Je Me Souviens: About the St. Armand Slave Cemetery, Memory, Counter-Memory, and Historic Trauma." *Topia* 12 (Fall): 9–24.

Zelizer, Viviana A. 1994. *Pricing the Priceless Child: The Changing Social Value of Children.* Princeton: Princeton University Press.

Zeuske, Michael. 2011. "The Names of Slavery and Beyond: The Atlantic, the Americas, and Cuba." In Ulrike Schmieder, Michael Zeuske, Katja Füllberg-Stolberg, eds., *The End of Slavery in Africa and the Americas: A Comparative Approach,* 51–80. Berlin: LIT Verlag.

———. 2012. *Die Geschichte der Amistad: Sklavenhandel und Menschenschmuggel auf dem Atlantik im 19. Jahrhundert.* Stuttgart: Reclam.

———. 2013. "Rethinking the Case of the Schooner *Amistad:* Contraband and Complicity After 1808/1820." *Slavery and Abolition* 34, no. 3: 156–64.

Zeuske, Michael, and Orlando García Martínez. 2009. "La Amistad de Cuba: Ramón Ferrer, contrabando des esclavos, captividad y modernidad Atlantíca." *Caribbean Studies* 37, no. 1: 97–170.

Zmora, Nurith. 1995. *Orphanages Reconsidered: Child Care Institutions in Progressive Era Baltimore.* Philadelphia: Temple University Press.

Zulueta, Pedro de, William Brodie Gurney, Great Britain. Central Criminal Court, Great Britain. 1844. *Trial of Pedro de Zulueta, Jr.: on a Charge of Slave Trading, Under the 5 Geo. IV, cap. 113, on Friday the 27th, Saturday the 28th, and Monday the 30th of October, 1843, at the Central Criminal Court, Old Bailey, London. A Full Report from the Shorthand Notes of W. B. Gurney.* London: C. Wood.

But the mingled, mingling threads of life are woven by warp and woof: calms crossed by storms, a storm for every calm. There is no steady unretracing progress in this life; we do not advance through fixed gradations, and at the last one pause. . . . Our souls are like those orphans whose unwedded mothers die in bearing them: the secret of our paternity lies in their grave, and we must there to learn it.
—Herman Melville, *Moby-Dick*, chapter 114

INDEX

Page numbers in italics refer to illustrations